*Interesting, well developed, and chal[lenging.] The basic theme is that as organizatic[nal] behavior is governed by their personali*ty, changing organizational cul*ture requires that we recognize how personality can be our greatest ally or worst enemy. Knowing who you are as a leader, and knowing the people you lead, is essential to the success of the change-journey. Every leader in both the public and private sectors will find the lessons in Island of Excellence essential to harnessing the creative power of their greatest asset—their employees.*

— Paul J. Seligman, M.D., MPH, Director
Office of Pharmacoepidemiology and Statistical Science
U.S. Food and Drug Administration

Bodnarczuk takes us on the exciting journey of learning the principles of creative thinking and the creative process itself. He gives leaders, managers, and workers a road map for building high-performing teams and organizations—for becoming an Island of Excellence in a sea of mediocrity. Your organization will benefit enormously from this book.

— Rick Brodie, President, TCD Corporation

Island of Excellence is a gripping and sensitive "real fiction" novel that applies a new understanding of creativity to the critical problem of organizations in society. Mark Bodnarczuk molds the personal and organizational experiences of his nine characters into a must-read book for anyone who strives for excellence and fulfillment at work in a post-911 world.

— Lillian Hoddeson, Ph.D., author
True Genius: The Life and Science of John Bardeen

Also by Mark Bodnarczuk
Diving In:
Discovering Who You Are in the Second Half of Life

ISLAND of EXCELLENCE

3 *Powerful* Strategies for Building Creative Organizations

MARK BODNARCZUK

ELTON-WOLF PUBLISHING

ISLAND OF EXCELLENCE
3 Powerful Strategies for
Building Creative Organizations

© 2004 Mark Bodnarczuk
All rights reserved.

Text edited by Cliff Carle
Cover design by Jamie O'Neill
Text layout by Paulette Eickman
Front and back cover photographs © Mark Bodnarczuk

Published by Elton-Wolf Publishing
Seattle, Washington

Myers-Briggs Type Indicator® and MBTI® are registered trademarks of CPP, Inc.
(Consulting Psychologists Press, Inc.)

The author would like to thank the following for permission to reprint from copyrighted works: From *The Wisdom of the Enneagram* by Don Riso and Russ Hudson, copyright © 1999 by Don Riso and Russ Hudson, p. 32. Used by permission of Bantam Books, a division of Random House, Inc. From Chris Argyris, *Knowledge for Action*, San Francisco, CA: Copyright© 1993 by Jossey-Bass Publishers, p. 52. This material is used by permission of John Wiley & Sons, Inc. From W. Edwards Deming, *Out of Crisis*, Cambridge, MA: Copyright © 2000 by The MIT Press, p. 60-61. Reprinted by permission. From Anne Wilson Schaef and Diane Fassel, *The Addictive Organization*, San Francisco, CA: Copyright © 1990 by Harper Collins Publishers, p. 1 and 4. Reprinted by permission.

This account is based on real events. The names, descriptions, and characteristics have been changed to protect the privacy of the individuals involved. Any resemblance to real people is purely coincidental.

No part of this book may be reproduced or utilized in any form or by any means, electronic or mechanical, including photocopying and recording, or by any information storage and retrieval system, without permission in writing from the author.

ISBN: 0-9755115-1-3
Library of Congress Catalog Number: 2004109122
08 07 06 05 04   1 2 3 4 5

First Edition August 2004
Printed in Canada

ELTON-WOLF PUBLISHING

2505 Second Avenue Seattle Washington 98121
1.800.281.5965
www.elton-wolf.com

DEDICATION

For Gorab, who overcame the world by viewing it through the eyes of a little boy—a free and creative spirit who was and will always be my friend though he sleeps…

ACKNOWLEDGMENTS

It was Anne Avery, Jungian analyst and friend, who taught me to probe and respect the unfathomable depths of the unconscious. In my mind, her greatest contribution will always be the trail of changed lives that she left behind her.

Don Richard Riso and Russ Hudson trained me in the Enneagram, and they remain mentors and professional associates. The value of Don's contribution to the Enneagram body of knowledge is unquestionable. He and his teaching have made a profound difference in my life, and I feel honored to call him my teacher and my friend.

Margaret Hartzler taught me to administer the Myers-Briggs Type Indicator® assessment tool—and much more. Her depth of knowledge about type theory and Jungian psychology, and her commitment to psychological truth provided a powerful model for me to try to emulate.

Most of the diving stories in this book came from my trip aboard the Peter Hughes boat, Star Dancer. I would like to thank Peter Hughes for giving me permission to use my picture of the Star Dancer on the back cover. I would also like to thank the Star Dancer crew, including Captain Jock McKinney, Patrick Pon, Valia Togis, and Reginia Chare. Annie Crawley, Jana Viktorova, and Jonah Billy were my underwater guides and diving companions during the trip. Annie showed me how to see the underwater world in new ways and taught me a deeper respect for the ocean and the life it contains. I would especially like to thank Andrew Robertson who was a wealth of information about Papua New Guinea. Andrew spent hours recounting his experiences growing up in the Highlands and helping me connect my own life and worldview to the rich and exotic culture of this faraway land.

In terms of the writing and production of the book, I would like to thank Lynn Kaemmerer, Carmen Johnson, and Larry Lunceford who read earlier drafts and gave me valuable feedback. Anthony Malensek, one of my closest friends and a business associate, helped me in more ways than I can explain, especially on the Island of Excellence™ Organizational Assessment. Probably the most substantial contribution to the production of the book came from my editor, Cliff Carle whose critical eye and encouragement mentored me through the difficult process of bringing the book to completion.

Most of all, I would like to thank my dear wife, Elin, who supported me in the writing of this book even when times were hard. My stepdaughter Juliana, a newly certified diver, has a passion for animals and underwater sea life that always inspired me. Finally, my two-year-old son, Thomas, continues to provide leadership for my life by teaching me the meaning of love and innocence, and helping me see the world through the eyes of a little boy.

CONTENTS

LIST OF FIGURES ... xiii

INTRODUCTION ... 1

TRAVELLING TO ANOTHER WORLD

    A Reunion in the High Country ... 6

    Into the Depths ... 31

    Converging on Walindi ... 54

    Foundational Principles and Housekeeping Stuff ... 77

DAY 1: DIVING THE REEFS OF KIMBE BAY

    Strategy 1: Learn to Find Meaning and Significance in Work ... 130
    The Day Begins

    Session 1: Experience the Creative Process ... 132

    Session 2: Learn How Fear Inhibits Creativity ... 169

    Session 3: Build Inner Collaboration and Alignment ... 190

DAY 2: DUGOUT CANOES AT THE REAR OF THE SHIP

    Strategy 2: Use Alignment to Gain Competitive Advantage ... 232
    The Day Begins

    Session 1: Align the Organization to Speak with One Voice ... 233

    Session 2: Follow the Red Flags to Squandered Energy ... 275

    Session 3: Build a Portfolio of Creative Employees ... 301

DAY 3: LIFE IN THE WITU ISLANDS

Strategy 3: Allow a Culture of Creativity to Emerge
The Day Begins ... 329

Session 1: The Emergence of Organizational Culture ... 336

Session 2: Counting the Cost ... 360

The Journey Back to the Real World ... 386

EPILOGUE (ONE YEAR LATER) ... 393

A BRIEF SUMMARY OF THE CHARACTERS' PERSONALITY TYPES ... 397

SYNTHESIZING THE ENNEAGRAM, MBTI® TOOL, AND POST-JUNGIAN PSYCHOLOGY ... 406

ENDNOTES ... 413

ABOUT THE AUTHOR ... 435

CONTACT INFORMATION ... 436

LIST OF FIGURES

Figure 1
The ODPT for a One-Person Company — 101

Figure 2
The ODPT for a One Hundred-Person Company — 105

Figure 3
The First Strategy: Learn to Find Meaning and Significance in Work — 133, 170, 191, 215

Figure 4
The Creative Process as a Volcano — 141

Figure 5
Edison's Team as a Volcano — 144

Figure 6
The Creative Process — 148, 209

Figure 7
The Three Kinds of Authority — 151

Figure 8
Dive Slate Session 1 Review — 161

Figure 9
The Four Dimensions of Fear — 171

Figure 10
Dive Slate Session 2 Review — 182

Figure 11
The Cultural Chasm and Symbolic Connection — 188, 323

Figure 12
Teasing Apart Training from Personality   197

Figure 13
The Disruption of Dan's Intentions   198

Figure 14
Dive Slate Session 3 Review   217

Figure 15
The Problem of Enneagram Connecting Points   222

Figure 16
The Second Strategy: Use Alignment to
Gain Competitive Advantage   234, 278, 302

Figure 17
Island of Excellence™ Self-Assessment Level 1 Analysis   250

Figure 18
Island of Excellence™ Self-Assessment Level 2 Analysis   252

Figure 19
Island of Excellence™ Self-Assessment Level 3 Analysis   254

Figure 20
Island of Excellence™ Self-Assessment Level 4 Analysis   256

Figure 21
Dive Slate Session 4 Review   265

Figure 22
MBTI® Communication Gradients   273

Figure 23
Four Levels of Organizational Consciousness   276

Figure 24
Disruption of Organizational Intentions   280

Figure 25
Dive Slate Session 5 Review   293

Figure 26
The Creativity Distribution   304

Figure 27
The Six-Step Decision Making Model   309

Figure 28
Dive Slate Session 6 Review   313

Figure 29
The Third Strategy:
Allow a Culture of Creativity to Emerge   337

Figure 30
The Emergence of Organizational Culture   344, 364, 366

Figure 31
Dive Slate Session 7 Review   355

Figure 32
A Cycle of Continuous Growth   373

Figure 33
Dive Slate Session 8 Review   374

Figure 34
Island of Excellence™ Enneagram and MBTI® Types   398

Introduction

It's hard to fully grasp the impact that creativity has had on our world. Imagine if you could snap your fingers and make the products of human creativity disappear—everything that is man-made. How would your world change? Our ability to obtain shelter from the natural elements, control our food and water supply, harness and use energy sources, create and sustain currency-based economies, and invent social structures, science, technology, and culture are all the result of human creativity. *Reality is a product of the creative process.* Reality is a social construct. Reality is man-made.[1]

Creativity is the natural problem-solving mechanism of the human brain.[2] It provides survival advantage through innovation, improvement, and the ability to adapt to an ever-changing world. Creativity occurs naturally in all people, in all times, in all cultures, unless frustrated and opposed by psychological, organizational, or cultural obstructions. So igniting and fueling our creativity are more about not opposing this natural process than they are about learning how to be "more creative." Plato taught that gaining knowledge about reality was a process of regaining contact with, and recalling, innate and tacit knowledge that we already possess.[3] In the same way, people don't have to "learn" to be creative any more than they have to "learn" to be human. Understanding how the creative process gets "stopped up" and learning how to free its power and energy are two of the most fundamental issues in life.

In the wake of an economic downturn, companies are focused on nagging questions like, How do I maximize shareholder value? How do I please customers, increase profits, and gain competitive advantage in the current business environment? Post September 11, 2001, employees in these same organizations have been brutally confronted with questions like, How do I make a living that supports my lifestyle and find a sense of meaning and significance in my work? Will pouring my heart and soul into this job prevent me from discovering my unique calling in life? In this book, *I claim that the answer to all these questions is to build creative organizations—one person at a time*. When allowed, creativity funds innovation, improvement, and complex problem solving in organizations. Likewise, employees who learn to connect their creative abilities to their work *will* find meaning and significance in that work.

Island of Excellence™ is a teaching novel that takes readers on a two-fold diving expedition that simultaneously explores the depths of the ocean and the barriers to corporate and personal creativity. Why write a business book that teaches through the genre of an adventure story? Robert Quinn, a professor in the graduate school of business at Michigan State, was asked to design a new MBA course on leadership, vision, and change. He devoted half the class sessions to case studies presented by business leaders and the other half to movies that exemplified leadership and organizational change. Students would watch the movies at home and come to class prepared to discuss insights gained about leadership, vision, and change.

In reflection, Quinn observed, "While the business leaders were often inspiring, their sessions turned out not to be the most important part of the class. The movies proved more instructive. The business cases were usually washed clean of conflict, failure, and error. They were stories told by companies for public consumption."[4] Movies and biographies that accurately depict the realities of organizational life carry the projection of the most intimate and troubling situations that people face in the workplace. That's why they resonate with us so deeply. *Island of Excellence*™ is both a story and a series of teaching sessions that present three powerful strategies for building creative organizations. Because it teaches through a story, likewise, there is no need to sanitize it of conflict, failure, error, or the irrational elements of creativity in organizations.

As a series of teaching sessions, *Island of Excellence*™ is like a modern Socratic symposium that explores the nature of creativity in individuals and organizations. With their experiences as owners, managers, and workers as background and a wealth of empirical research from the *Harvard Business Review* and important business books, the nine characters in the story are used as mouthpieces to articulate and debate three strategies for building creative organizations.

As a story, *Island of Excellence*™ was created from my actual experiences in Papua New Guinea—scuba diving some of the finest coral reefs in the world, adventure trekking through remote villages in the Highlands with a local guide, interviewing locals, and further researching the people and culture.[5] In the story, a cast of nine characters attends a dive workshop aboard the one hundred twenty-foot ship *Origin* in Papua New Guinea that totally removes them from the context of their everyday lives. Each of them has run the race to construct a life and a self, and each one runs smack into a brick wall of either outer crisis and pressure in their professional lives, or the inner crisis and pressure to find a sense of meaning and significance in their work.

The nine characters are composites of real people whose personal and organizational identities have been changed, so, to coin a phrase, the book is *real fiction*. I chose these nine people because the course of their lives powerfully exemplifies and synthesizes the characteristics of the nine personality types of the Enneagram, the Myers-Briggs Type Indicator® assessment tool (MBTI®), and Jungian psychology.[6] Parts of their story will be your story, or the story of people you know. So, while some familiarity with these bodies of knowledge is helpful, it is not necessary. For those who are interested in these details, I've included them at the back of the book.

Each day, as the story unfolds, the attendees at the dive workshop learn about and debate the three strategies in one-hour sessions held around an enormous wooden teaching table on the main deck of a ship that is floating seemingly in the middle of nowhere. Each teaching session is followed by a one-hour reflective time of diving where the characters view the spectacular coral reefs and undersea life of Papua New Guinea, and hear nothing underwater but the sound of air bubbles. During these times of reflection, powerful elements of human creativity are unleashed as each person is forced to engage with the transforming power of their own creative process. Their experiences at the dive workshop inwardly motivate them to return to the organization they own, manage, or work in and to transform it into a creative organization—an *Island of Excellence*™ in a sea of mediocrity.

Whether you are a scuba diver who enjoys diving in exotic places; a top, middle, or first-line manager in a company who wants to stimulate innovation and improvement; a professional coach or career counselor who helps people navigate life changes and find new directions in their career path; an owner, manager, or worker in a small business who is struggling to survive in a competitive world; a student or teacher of the Enneagram, MBTI® assessment tool, or Jungian psychology; or an organizational consultant looking for new models to break through resistance to change in client organizations—come along on the dive ship *Origin* and discover how to transform your creative abilities into a valuable corporate and individual resource.

Travelling to Another World

A REUNION IN THE HIGH COUNTRY

The light from the perfectly rounded moon reflected so brightly off the snow-packed road and the eight-foot–high walls of snow that bordered it that they drove over the continental divide at Hoosier Pass with the headlights of the car turned off. James and Dan were exhausted from skiing deep powder all day long on Peak 10 in Breckenridge, Colorado, but it was a satisfying feeling. It's one thing to talk about skiing thigh-deep champagne powder, it's quite another to actually do it.

"Oh! That feels good!" Dan said, as the two of them eased their way into the hot tub back at James's house high above Placer Valley in Alma. James's wife, Victoria, and the kids were in Colorado Springs, so they had the place to themselves. This quaint log home built at nearly eleven thousand feet above sea level was a remnant of the life James and his wife had before they moved to the flat lands of Colorado's front-range.

It was only six degrees, and the air was dry, crisp, with the sweet smell of pine—and when the jets from the hot tub timed out and they weren't speaking, there was utter silence. James and Dan tried not to disturb this peace with the roaring sound of their breath. Given the frenetic world they both lived in, there was something healing about hearing nothing—absolutely nothing.

Dan Wright was a tall, lanky redhead with a thin, freckled nose that came to a sharp point. He carried himself with the confident tone of a man who knew he was right about everything, and he enjoyed wagging his long bony index finger in people's faces when he was trying to set them straight. As a hard-driving, perfectionist, workaholic, Dan wore a serious look on his face, almost a frown—he rarely laughed and never told jokes. He had a traditional, shiny, clean, well-scrubbed Ivy League look about him—with every hair in place. People rarely saw him without a shirt and tie on, but this night was an exception to that rule. James and Dan had remained friends since they met at a dive workshop a couple of years ago. Dan had decided to attend a different workshop about building creative organizations and was trying to talk James into going with him.

A requirement for enrolling in the workshop was that each attendee had to complete two self-scoring personality profiles: the Riso-Hudson Enneagram Type Indicator (RHETI) and the Myers-Briggs Type Indicator assessment tool (MBTI).[7] Dan had previously completed both and knew his MBTI preference scores were ISTJ and that he was an Enneagram Type One, meaning he was principled, orderly, self-controlled, perfectionist, and self-righteous.[8]

Workshop attendees also received a list of select business books and article reprints from the last ten years of the *Harvard Business Review*. They were to examine the list, read articles that were relevant to issues they were facing in their work environment, then come to the workshop prepared to discuss those problems.

Dan was the founder and CEO of the SciTech Corporation—a company in Westchester County, New York, that produced sophisticated, high-resolution airport X-ray equipment that was computer automated, and removed much of the human error in scanning baggage that was checked by airlines. Now, with thick steaks on the grill and a glass of wine in his hand, Dan, an engineer turned businessman, poured his heart out to his friend James, a lawyer turned Episcopal priest, about the crisis he was having in his business.

"SciTech had meager beginnings you know," Dan said proudly. "We started in a garage behind my house and now the company is housed in a forty thousand square foot facility that we could expand to a hundred thousand square feet if we needed it. We grew largely because there was almost no competition for the sophisticated products we produced and the demand was extremely high, especially following 9/11.

"In the early years, revenues followed a typical pattern of rising then leveling off, but after twelve years we had over one hundred employees and were generating gross revenues of over one hundred twenty-five million dollars per year." Dan's voice had an edge of excitement in it as he recalled the *good old days*.

"Wow—that's phenomenal growth," James interjected.

"You bet!" Dan snorted. "From a business perspective, we were damned lucky." Then he looked down onto the snow-covered deck next to the barbecue grill, took a large sip of wine, as his demeanor quickly shifted to a tone of self-reproach. "But within the last year, our market demand has leveled off and new competitors started producing devices with equal or greater technological sophistication to ours. They've made their engineering function Web-based, outsourced it to engineers in India, and relocated their manufacturing plants to Canada or Mexico where labor is cheaper. I couldn't believe it, James, but they're able to market and sell products that are superior to ours for thirty percent less than we can. We've lost some of our long–established customers to these competitors and our revenue has begun a slow, but perceptible, decline."

"Man—how do you begin to solve *that* kind of problem?" James commented, trying to be supportive.

"Yeah—I'm afraid that the company may not be able to recover its market strength because these competitors are smaller, more adaptable, with much less overhead," Dan carped in somber agreement. "In addition, I've got a hot button about 'red ink' on the balance sheet, and for the first time in years that's what I'm beginning to see."

Dan gazed out into the night as James locked his eyes on Dan's. Even in the partial light of the moon, he could see Dan's eyes moving quickly from side-to-side as he thought through the deeper implications and ramifications of his problems. After what seemed like an eternity of silence, the right words finally came.

"I'm convinced that the company has to take immediate, concrete action and go into survival mode," Dan said in exasperation. "I've tried to explain this to Cindy, SciTech's president, but for reasons beyond my comprehension she doesn't think things are so bad yet!"

Dan practically yelled into the night. "She claims we need a 'long-term' vision for solving the company's problems and repositioning it in the frenetically changing business environment. Honestly James, I don't think we have the time to fool with a long-term solution—we need to do something right now. I have tried and tried to communicate my sense of urgency to her, but it's like I talk till I'm blue in the face and she stubbornly maintains the view that a short-term solution won't solve our long-term problems."

Cindy Reeder was SciTech's first employee as Director of R&D, and her scientific and technical acumen was a major reason why the company had achieved such incredible success. But even though Cindy had only been SciTech's president for less than two years, Dan blamed her for the problems they were having. Dan's style was to force his internal ideas and standards on his managers and employees as if issues always had black-and-white solutions defined by his objective truth. Cindy was a moderating force with the company's employees, which made Dan appear to be a much better executive than he actually was. Cindy was the primary reason that more of his managers and staff didn't hate him and his browbeating.

"She's too soft on them, James—even poor performers," Dan complained bitterly. "Just last week I said to her, 'Why don't you lean harder on these people when they don't perform up to the company's high standards?' She just looked at me in disbelief, and in a recalcitrant tone that made my blood boil she snipped back, 'That's not how you motivate people, Dan.' Then she just turned and walked away."

I'd fire her in a minute, James thought to himself as the flames of his own rage were stoked by the scenes Dan was recounting.

As president, Cindy categorically disagreed with Dan's leadership and management style and refused to adopt his way of doing business, and her ongoing refusal infuriated him. Dan was rigid and inflexible about holding to schedules. He hammered on managers and employees when they deviated even slightly from their procedures, and was critical and judgmental of everyone even if it ruptured important relationships. He never trusted anyone to do a job right, so he refused to fully delegate responsibility and authority and micro-managed employees to the point where they wished he would just do the work himself—and many times he did. He was so focused on immediate problems and coming to closure on a solution that he rarely considered the broader implications of his decisions. For Dan, any decision was better than no decision at all. Cindy always felt pressured into coming to closure on issues but normally felt she needed more time and information to make up her mind before moving on.

But the root causes of SciTech problems went back much further than the brief stint on Cindy's watch. Two years ago when she was still

Director of R&D she told Dan he needed to invest in the latest technology that could fabricate electronic components more cost effectively, with higher levels of quality, and virtually no scrap or rework. Cindy argued that automating SciTech's fabrication functions might decrease their production costs by as much as ten to fifteen percent, all of which would go right to the bottom line. She also advised Dan that they needed to bring new blood into the organization by hiring some summer students from their alma mater, MIT. Using Cindy's approach, SciTech's managers could observe how well these potential employees worked first-hand, then hire the brightest and the best right out of school. Dan just wanted to fire long-time employees, and hire new ones.

"She wants me to lighten up," Dan bellowed in a mocking tone as he watched James open the top of the sizzling grill and turn the steaks a final time. "She tells me that my personality is fixated—that I only focus on the details and concrete reality of SciTech's present situation, and that in my mind the possibility of turning the company around in the future hardly exists. Part of me knows she's right, but that kind of feedback really doesn't help. Besides, I can't see how her 'long-term' solution holds any more promise of real change than mine does. I tell you James, I'm convinced that failure to take immediate and decisive action is downright irresponsible of me as the CEO."

James could no longer resist saying what he'd been thinking. "Why don't you just *fire* her," he blurted out, "or move her back to R&D and take the company over till you pull out of this nosedive?" He lifted the steaks off the grill with his tongs and motioned for them to go inside.

"I may have to do that in the end, but I'll tell you, buddy—I'm tired from the long years of building this company. I feel like I've already got the weight of the world on my shoulders, and taking SciTech over again would have to be the last possible solution." As James reached the dinner table and set the steaks down, Dan looked at him and said with sincerity, "Besides, I can't fire Cindy. We go way back. Despite what I'm telling you about her, she's a loyal friend. Cindy's probably one of the few people in life who really knows me, understands me, and will put up with me."

Two or three years ago, when there were no competitors on the horizon, Dan was equally bogged down in a short-term, present focus that led him to resist Cindy's suggestions about improving technological capability and human resources because implementing her proposal would have driven up overhead costs. Dan always based his assessment of current and future situations on his past experience and even the small risk that her proposal required moved him way out of his comfort zone. In his rush to blame her for the company's problems, Dan conveniently forgot the numerous e-mails and memos she'd sent him warning him about what the competition were doing. Had he listened to her then and chartered a different course, they could have avoided the crisis they were headed toward today. Now that revenues had started falling and competitors were backing them into a performance and pricing corner by taking away their best clients, SciTech had no alternative but to spend money on the infrastructure that Cindy recommended back then—just to stay in the game.

"But she's being insubordinate *and* irresponsible if she refuses to take immediate action to save the company," James counseled. "Friend or no friend, she sounds like some futuristic university-type who doesn't understand the realities of the dog-eat-dog world of business."

Softening his tone, Dan tried to clarify his position. "Well, she did agree that we needed to take some immediate action to slow the flow of revenue from the company's assets, but she keeps trying to convince me that we need to develop a three- to five-year strategic plan that defines SciTech's purpose, core values, business objectives, and strategies.

I've fought her every step of the way on this. I insisted that all we needed to do was to continue our quarterly budget reviews where I publicly grill line managers for missing their numbers—I call it the 'public embarrassment' method. My view is that if we bear down even harder on these guys, we can drive them and the company back on course. Cindy won't take part in any of this. She told me I'm being punitive and that using this method to date hasn't kept the company from getting into the trouble we're in. Then she and I go round and round again and I just get more disgusted with her because she's so stubborn, and with myself for not taking more decisive action."

"What's the first thing *you* think should be done to get the company turned around?" James asked, hoping to move him toward corrective action.

"Bottom line," Dan said confidently. "I believe we need to get our overhead down quickly with a reengineering initiative that will reduce head count by at least twenty percent." Dan let the gravity of his words resonate with a sense of finality and certitude.

"Cindy wants no part of this solution regardless of how logical and bottom line oriented my argument is. Instead, over my objections, she initiated a long-term strategic planning process, a thorough analysis of the internal strengths and weaknesses of the company's human resource and technology base, and began critically exploring the opportunities and threats in the business environment. She spent thousands of dollars on a Harvard-based consulting firm. They performed a detailed study of market realities and demands, customer expectations and requirements, the cost of the knowledge and skill base to staff-up the company, and the technological forces and trends that competitors were using to take over SciTech's market share. Don't get me wrong, James—these are all good things and I support them in their proper place. But my point is that when the boat is sinking you've got to focus your time and energy on bailing water to stay afloat, not studying *why* the boat is sinking."

James was shaking his head in full agreement as he poured them both another glass of wine.

"The other day Cindy told me that her ultimate plan was to change SciTech's culture—something she views as the root cause of the company's problems. My intuition tells me that there's some substance to her view, but I rarely take my intuitions at face value without running them through the hard rigors of analysis and examination. This drives her absolutely crazy because she wants me to just adopt her approach. I just can't do that, James—I've been fooled by that kind of touchy-feely stuff before."

Unfortunately for Cindy and the company, Dan was only comfortable using the "facts" to correct, improve, and align the very insights and intuitions that could help him and his business situation. In more reflective moments, Dan sensed he was stiff-arming Cindy because the dysfunctional characteristics of SciTech's culture that she wanted to change were a collective reflection of dysfunctional characteristics in his own personality—things that have plagued him throughout his life. Consequently, changing SciTech's culture would require Dan to pursue deep personal change first. That was a price he might not be willing to pay.

"Look, I work really hard at trying to understand Cindy's way of leading and managing the company, but my rational approach to problem solving rebels against her 'strategies' when they don't make sense to me. I told her we needed to get rid of some of our long-time employees who have no idea where technology is going and who are too comfortable in their jobs—they're dead wood. I told her we needed to fire these technological dinosaurs and replace them with smart young people who were more motivated to move up the ladder."

Unbeknown to Cindy, Dan has begun to lobby the members of the Board of Directors—all of whom are his hand-picked cronies—to put pressure on her to proceed with the reengineering effort. As each board member contacted her privately by phone or cornered her after a meeting, Cindy tried to explain that laying people off would create fear and panic throughout the company as employees started to worry about whether they'd be the next to go. She knew that once you violated an employee's trust it was almost impossible to win it back. A wholesale layoff might also drive away SciTech's best talent because this caliber of employee knew they'd be able to find another job. Cindy feared that star performers would make the decision to leave on their own terms, just to maintain some level of control.

"After the last board meeting, Cindy button-holed me and told me that she didn't want the responsibility of being president without the authority that went with it." Dan shook his head in disbelief. "She said that my side-discussions with the board and even with some of her staff were undermining her authority as president. She told me that if I didn't stop this inappropriate behavior immediately she was going to resign."

At this point, James was shaking his head too, as Dan continued. "She almost demanded that I attend the dive workshop on building creative organizations with her as a way of getting through the impasse we've come to. She thinks it may be the only way of saving what's left of our faltering relationship."

After listening to about all he could stand about Cindy's actions, James blurted out, "You're the boss, make her do what you want! I'd never put up with that kind of behavior from anyone. If she can't get people to do their jobs and turn the company around, you should *fire* her and find someone who *can*."

Although he'd never met her, it was hard for James not to get a negative opinion of Cindy based on what Dan had told him. His experience taught him that dealing with people who caused these kinds of problems might be necessary with your family and those closest to you, but it had little or no place in running a business.

James Tuffs carried himself with the unmistakable authority of a powerful stealth tiger that could turn on you in the blink of an eye. A six foot six, olive skinned body builder with an enormously developed chest, arms like tree trunks, and meaty hands, James's brown eyes were almost always hidden behind dark sunglasses so that his face communicated no emotion. He was kind and loving to his family and inner circle of friends, but he loved to provoke those outside this small and protected fold. James pushed people's boundaries, then gave them the message to stay away. When they were foolish enough to push back, he either exploded in rage or withdrew and became as cold, unforgiving, and intolerable as a January night in North Dakota. James had previously completed the RHETI and MBTI tools and knew that he was an INTJ, Type Eight who was powerful, aggressive, self-confident, strong, and assertive.[9]

James had been chosen to be the rector of St. Peter's Episcopal Church in Colorado Springs because his energy, drive, determination, and leadership skills held the promise that the parish could change their track record as a revolving door for priests and parishioners—especially conservative families with young children. St. Peter's had recently experienced a serious exodus of members and a drop in financial support because of the denomination's decision to consecrate an openly gay bishop and the practice of some dioceses to solemnize same-sex marriages. The parishioners who were left at St. Peter's were long-time liberal members who supported the decision—the so-called "frozen chosen." James liked new challenges that tested his imagination and complex problem-solving skills and viewed "practical" problems as a waste of his time.

Shawna, a tall, slender woman of unusual beauty, was the top elected layleader of the vestry committee that ran the parish. She was committed to St. Peter's—the church of her childhood—and she spearheaded the process to find a new priest after the last rector was driven out. Of all the candidates they interviewed, Shawna was convinced that James was what St. Peter's needed, so she pressed the search committee to increase the salary offer, agree to remodel the rectory, and throw in a few other perks to lure him into accepting the job. Given the church's history of running off priests who actually dared to initiate change rather than just talk about it, the Bishop of Colorado, Rod Sands, believed James was the right person for the job and gladly installed him as rector when he accepted the call to the parish. Bishop Sands knew that James was self-confident, domineering, would not back down, and wanted to give orders not take them.

The Bishop was eager to meet with James within his first month at St. Peter's to learn how he planned on handling his new assignment. "My philosophy is that while the purpose, objectives, strategies, and revenue-base of St. Peter's are different than for-profit businesses like the law firm I came from, there are no fundamental reasons why the church cannot be operated in a more efficient, effective way like a business," James insisted passionately as Bishop Sands nodded in agreement.

"I've been there less than a month and I see the vacuum of leadership and strategic direction that this parish is suffering from. All of my predecessor priests have tried to initiate change and failed. There's a pattern here, Bishop, and even my cursory analysis has shown that one of the constants over time is the ongoing financial support and hidden agendas of a small group of key church members, including three generations from Shawna's family. I've got an inner vision about the future of this church, and I'm going to begin communicating it to the vestry and parish members with the passion of an Old Testament prophet." The Bishop's eyes widened and he smiled approvingly.

In the first two weeks of James's tenure at St. Peter's, he had invited the powerful group of layleaders who ran the church to meet with him one-on-one to share what their hopes and visions were for the parish. James also interviewed parishioners who were not part of this power structure and did an anonymous written survey that gathered extensive input about where the parish had been, was currently, and needed to go. More importantly, James began to contact people who no longer attended the church to determine why they had left. As he digested this confused and sometimes contradictory array of information, a picture began to emerge.

"What these interviews revealed, Bishop, was a self-defeating pattern where powerful church members would *say* they wanted change and would support a new priest's approach. But when change took them out of their comfort zone they would covertly undermine the priest's efforts until he became so frustrated that he eventually left in defeat." James paused and looked the Bishop directly in the eye. "I can tell you right now, I'm determined that I'm not going to be the next casualty of this dysfunctional cycle of events. That's why I'm trying to lay the groundwork for change with *you* first to make sure we're on the same page. I can't have you backing out on me when the going gets rough—and it's going to get rough real soon." Once again the Bishop shook his head in concurrence and acknowledged James's concern about his own commitment to change.

"I want to use a strategic planning process and the information that I collected in my interviews to begin challenging some of the deep assumptions that people in the St. Peter's power structure have about the purpose, strategies, and objectives of the church." As James continued laying out the details of his plan, the Bishop got increasingly excited, sat straight up in his chair, and nodded affirmatively with each point James made.

"This is exactly what this diocese needs!" the Bishop exclaimed when James had finished. "I promise you, James, not only will I stand behind you and your vision, but I want to use your approach in other problematic parishes throughout this diocese."

As James walked down the steps of the Diocesan Center, he whispered to himself, *I'm going to set this whole thing up without any input from Shawna or the vestry.*

When James knew there would be conflict and resistance, he just ignored what didn't fit into his plans and strategies. When people resisted his approach, James would publicly and privately engage them in intellectual mind games and argue over abstract ideas and issues. He wasn't very good at weighing the impact that his style, behavior, and decisions had on others, and many times he just didn't care what effect it had—he was determined to get his way, regardless of the consequences.

At his second monthly vestry meeting, James announced, "I want to have a vestry retreat to begin a strategic planning process. I've already contacted a professional facilitator who will help us develop the information I've been gathering through interviews and documents into a SWOT analysis. The S and W will indicate the internal *strengths* and *weaknesses* of the parish. I've also hired an outside consulting firm to begin gathering demographic data, studies performed on church growth in modern culture, and feedback from people who have left the parish. This will give us the O and T of the SWOT—*opportunities* and *threats* that our parish is facing from the environment outside the church."

The vestry members were speechless. Shawna was enraged as people hesitantly looked at each other, then at James, and shook their heads in confusion, but no one dared confront him about what he'd done.

James had secretly arranged to have the Bishop conduct worship services that Sunday and voice strong support for his approach to strategic planning as a model he would use throughout the diocese. "St. Peter's will be charting new territory," Bishop Sands exclaimed during his sermon, "and providing new leadership for the entire diocese."

While she congratulated James in the Bishop's presence after the Sunday service, inwardly Shawna was torn about what he had done. On the one hand, she was pleased that he was moving so quickly and decisively to exert his leadership and authority, especially by getting positive visibility with the diocese. But on the other hand, he had not consulted her about any of this and she didn't like surprises where she was left out of the loop and suddenly had the Bishop show up at a Sunday service. Her initial ambivalence to his approach became strong opposition when James began talking to her and others about doing "lay" ministry based on a human resource development and management model that he'd read about.

"Shawna?" James said over the phone. "I want to develop a plan that helps parishioners explore their natural strengths, interests, and creative abilities and then educate and train teams of people to do the work of the church's ministry. I'm talking about things like visiting the sick, going to nursing homes, teaching classes, and helping people inside and outside the parish who are having financial, social, or family problems." Shawna just held the receiver of the phone to her ear while James gave her no opportunity to speak.

"I've already contacted someone I met in seminary to help us develop a parish-wide human resource plan that will define all the jobs that need to be done in the church and assign people to do them based on their competencies and availability. I expect everyone in the church to participate, and fleshing out the details of the plan will be part of the strategic planning process that begins with the vestry retreat. I'll make sure I leave the paperwork in your in-box at the church, okay?"

Shawna muttered, "Sure, no problem." But James could tell that it *was* a problem.

Although Shawna didn't confront James directly, she was furious. She believed these tasks were *his job*—things he should be doing personally. In private conversations with other vestry members where she tried to stir them up to support her position, she argued that James's job was to minister *to them*, not to train lay people to do the work of the ministry. Many of the others agreed. James had hardly gotten himself and his family unpacked during the first two months of his pastorate, and Shawna was already building a coalition against him. From her perspective, the problem that St. Peter's faced wasn't getting parish members involved in doing the work of the ministry. The problem was James not doing the job they were paying him to do.

Finally, Shawna showed up at the church one morning, marched into James's office unannounced, and nearly exploded. "Look—ministry is *your* job. You shouldn't be pawning your work off on parish members under the guise of training them for lay ministry. I don't know if you're misguided in your vision for the church or just plain lazy."

"I'm annoyed by your bitchy attitude," James snapped back. "If *you* had run the search committee more like a business you would have had a written set of roles and responsibilities for my job. If my duties had been well-defined, you wouldn't be standing here making a fool out of yourself by arguing about what *you* think my job is."

Then, James growled sardonically, "Maybe hammering out my roles and responsibilities is another issue to take on at the vestry retreat." He sat back in his chair and spitefully wrote it on the meeting agenda. "I know that you, your family, and your tight-knit circle of friends have run this church and chased priests off when they didn't do your bidding. But let me remind you that as an ordained priest in the Episcopal Church I report directly to the Bishop and ultimately to God, *not* to you or your vestry!"

Shawna stormed out of the church, devastated by the destructive confrontation. Over the next couple of weeks, James continued to ignore the feelings and opinions of Shawna and others who opposed him. He was extremely independent, iconoclastic, and was not swayed by barriers that people like Shawna threw up at him—instead he battered them down. James was determined to carry out his vision of the future possibilities for St. Peter's, regardless of the devastating effects his hostile attitude had on his relationships. Not surprisingly, from that time on, he saw the resistance that had defeated many other priests aimed squarely at him, but James was equal to the task. He was not like the others. He would never leave. He would never back down.

Shawna's vestry coalition and James started butting heads over every little thing from how he conducted the service and decorated the sanctuary to why *he* wasn't bringing more members into the church. Shawna tried to micro-manage him by dictating how much time he spent in the office—admonitions that he simply ignored. James knew the church secretary was stirring things up by calling Shawna and other vestry members and asking, "Where is he? He's never here. What's he doing all day long?" The secretary was not only a real-time conduit of information to Shawna and the vestry about James's coming and going, she began documenting his activities in preparation for a final showdown between James, Shawna, and the Bishop.

Until he could get others trained to assume these tasks, James was out trying to build relationships in the community and win back people who had stopped coming to the church, visiting parishioners in hospitals and nursing homes, and ministering to the sick. One Sunday, a family who had stopped coming to St. Peter's showed up because James had convinced them that things would change under his leadership. One of the vestry members cornered James in the parking lot and demanded to know, "What are those people doing back! I thought we got rid of them." Rather than explode in a rage like he wanted to, James just walked away, said nothing, but was determined that he would teach that person a lesson. Vengeance was something he had struggled with his entire life.

Shawna and other vestry members were threatening to boycott the retreat, but given the Bishop's support for James and his vision, she had no alternative but to appear as if she was going along with his plan. James continued to meet this resistance head-on and scheduled the retreat, informed the vestry of the time and date, and demanded that they all be present. To ensure that they came, he asked the Bishop give a kick-off speech about the need for change at St. Peter's and throughout the diocese. James felt he should give Shawna one last chance to understand his perspective and get behind his plan before slugging it out with her and the vestry all weekend long, so he asked her to meet him one-on-one the night before the retreat to do some planning.

Reluctantly, she agreed to meet him in the restaurant of the hotel where the retreat would be held. James wasted no time driving the conversation to his agenda. "Look, Shawna—currently I'm doing most or all of the ministry jobs in the church myself. I can only be in one place at a time, so making all of these tasks only my responsibility will continue to be the limiting factor of this parish's growth. If I could train other people to do these jobs, then the number of prospective members could double or triple and I could spend my time providing leadership and long-term direction for the congregation. I thought this was what you wanted me to do when you called me to be your rector."

Shawna took a sip of her wine, listened intently, and her face seemed to soften as James explained his perspective on the situation. "When I was a lawyer in a firm," he continued, "my experience was that most people were desperate to find a sense of meaning and significance in their work. Many organizations did nothing but stifle their creativity and innovation. Over the course of my ministry, I've come to believe that many of these people can fill this void in their lives through service to the church. That's why I am pushing lay ministry here at St. Peter's."

For the first time, Shawna actually heard what James was saying and her heart felt strangely warmed by his words and the softness and empathy in his presence. Her eyes teared up as she moaned painfully, "I'm one of those people you're talking about—I serve the church because I find so little fulfillment in my professional life. I guess I didn't realize how deeply and sincerely you were committed to your vision and the direction you're trying to take the church. Now I feel ashamed about having spearheaded the opposition against you and your plan." Shawna began confessing the ways in which she'd been covertly opposing him and undermining his work. "I promise you, James, that tomorrow at the opening meeting of the retreat I will make a public statement of apology in the presence of the Bishop and the entire vestry about how I've been wrong. From this moment on, I'll support you in any way that I can. Maybe my public confession will sway others to support you, too."

With the hard part of their disagreement behind them, they ordered another glass of wine and Shawna began to open up to James about her family, the church, and her personal struggles in life, including her failing marriage. This level of intimacy always made James feel uncomfortable but it was one of things he needed to work on as a priest—allowing people to get close to him without fearing they would try to control him. But as he listened to her story, James began to sense something desperately needy and longing in the way Shawna looked at him. His instincts told him that underneath the battle and conflict that had characterized their relationship to date, she was sexually attracted to him.

The role of sex in professional situations is often right below the surface of consciousness. In the business world, increasing prohibitions about ever talking about sexual feelings have buried them alive—driven them deep inside—where they live, fester, then resurface in neurotic and disguised ways. There is even less tolerance for an open and honest dialogue about sexual feelings in the church because to even contemplate these feelings is to open Pandora's box. People fear that there's no solution that resolves the problem. If James or Shawna were to openly discuss their attraction to determine if it was mutual, that would be like throwing gasoline on a blazing fire. Yet when such feelings are not discussed openly, inner psychological and sexual pressure builds that can erupt when people act out these feelings when least expected.

James was no stranger to sexual conquest, especially when women came on to him. Although that's why he was forced out of the Dallas law firm he'd worked at years ago, he denied this, blamed the senior partners, and saw the problem as being outside of himself. He believed he was treated unfairly, that his colleagues were out to get him, and that he was an innocent victim who was punished for standing his ground. He'd managed to keep his lust under control since he'd married Victoria because he loved her deeply, but he now realized he was really attracted to Shawna.

As they continued talking, their sexual feelings hovered just below the surface of consciousness and slowly intensified. Shawna felt her body tingling with excitement as she became like a giddy schoolgirl who couldn't take her eyes off James's massive, muscular torso.

I wonder what it would be like to hold him and touch him, she thought, becoming more turned on by the prospect with every passing minute.

James felt the passion of his lust consuming him, lowering the defenses he maintained as a married man and a priest. "Well, it's getting late and we have a big day ahead of us tomorrow," James finally said, yawning for effect.

"Yeah—I better head back to my room," Shawna reluctantly concurred as she sat back in her seat and James paid the tab. They continued chatting as they walked to the elevator, then went their separate ways, tacitly agreeing to keep their experience undiscussible, at least for now.

∽∽∽∽

Once again Dan implored, "James, why don't you come to the dive workshop?"

James hesitated before answering, "I guess I could focus on learning more about how nonprofit organizations like my parish can operate more effectively. I've also been thinking about the possibility of starting a church school or radio ministry somewhere in the world." Secretly James was hoping the trip might give him some time and distance away from the experience with Shawna and help him get a grip on how to confront this ongoing problem of handling sexual attraction in his professional life.

"I'll think about it, Dan," James said, seriously considering the offer. "You know I'd love to go diving with you again."

After loading the dishes into the dishwasher, they sat silently in front of a roaring fire. Then James mentioned in passing, "Don't forget we're meeting Maggie and her daughter tomorrow for dinner after we get off the hill. I made reservations at one of the finest restaurants in Breckenridge, the Briar Rose. It's named after that powder run we've been skiing."

∽∽∽∽

The next day, with twemty-five thousand feet of vertical drop under their belts, James and Dan locked their skis on the roof rack of James's car and walked to the restaurant. The air in the high-country where Breckenridge sits is clean and clear and punctuated by the smell of wood-burning fireplaces and finely prepared food. Breckenridge is a real Victorian mining town that sits at nine thousand six hundred feet above sea level in the shadow of thirteen thousand foot, snow-covered peaks. Breckenridge is a genuine Colorado ski town that's like no other place on earth.

They walked into the bar at the Briar Rose and saw Maggie waving at them furiously. Maggie Spinner was a short, muscular, blue-eyed blonde with designer sunglasses propped stylishly on her thick, curly, immaculately cut hair. Her soft perfectly-formed facial features, accentuated by sky-blue eyeshadow, large eyelashes, and ruby red lipstick made her strikingly beautiful and always the center of attention, especially with men. Maggie's voice was sweet but hard. The image of this articulate, savvy business woman in cosmopolitan-style power suits and spiked high-heels that made her appear taller and more powerful radiated a presence of authority and self–confidence that announced she was not to be taken lightly. Maggie was just over forty, but could pass for twenty-five. Recently married for the second time, she loved it when people thought her daughter Rena and her were newlywed friends or even sisters. Maggie had previously completed the RHETI and MBTI tools and knew that she was an ENTJ, Enneagram Type Three who was adaptable, success-oriented, self-assured, attractive, and charming.[10] Dan always had a thing for Maggie and she knew it—but then most men had a thing for Maggie.

"Hey! How are you guys doing?" she called out as the two men approached. "This is my daughter Rena." Maggie quickly turned and motioned to the bartender to bring a couple of cold, frosty mugs of beer for her friends. Dan threw his arms around her and gave Maggie a hug that was tighter and longer than she expected, then kissed her on the corner of her mouth. James was introducing himself and chatting with Rena, but the extended physical contact with Dan made Rena wonder if something else had gone on between them.

Rena Unitus was mid-twenties, with a healthy, outdoor, sensual beauty that came from a lifestyle of backpacking, skiing, and mountain biking. She had become a vegetarian in college largely for health reasons, although her growing social consciousness about environmental issues also supported her choice. From a partly Hispanic background on her father's side, her long, straight brown hair, streaked from the sun, reached down to her small waist, then fanned out across broad curved hips and muscular thighs—Rena was in incredible physical shape. The pearly white teeth that filled her mouth were visible through parted pink lips that curved up the sides of her face, forming an inviting, easygoing, and receptive smile. She almost always dressed casually and wore a plain, thin gold wedding band as a symbol of her commitment to her new husband and a small, silver and gold cross necklace as a quiet witness to her faith in God. She had previously completed the RHETI and the MBTI tools in a teambuilding exercise at work that showed her to be an ISFP, Enneagram Type Nine who was easygoing, self-effacing, accepting, trusting, and stable.[11] There was no doubt that she looked just like Maggie, yet Rena's Hispanic features made James curious—but he didn't ask.

Over dinner, Dan opened up about the problems he was having at SciTech and James discussed a sanitized version of what he was experiencing in his new parish. Rena always intentionally stayed in the background of discussions yet listened carefully to what James and Dan had to say. But she totally checked out whenever Maggie was speaking and especially when Maggie talked about the problems she was having with her new company.

The effect of alcohol is doubled at nine thousand six hundred feet above sea level, and although James had warned him, Dan drank a little too much wine during the meal. Dan shifted the conversation to skiing and then to Maggie's new husband, Troy, who was a ski instructor at the Winter Park ski area about an hour's drive from Breckenridge. Maggie gave some of the highlights from their wedding that Rena attended, and then Dan brazenly asked, "Soooo…are you guys going to have kids?"

Then slurring his words like a town drunk he chuckled, "I'd hate to see you ruin that great body of yours!"

Rena stared at Dan in disbelief of his rudeness, but said nothing. Maggie was also taken aback by his comment, but she decided to chalk it up to the wine, the altitude, and the fact that they were old friends.

"Troy wants to have kids and I kinda do, but I've got a new business to run and I don't know where children and motherhood fit into that picture," Maggie said uncomfortably, as Rena shook her head in muted annoyance to her mom's answer.

James kicked Dan under the table, and his stern, rebuking stare told Dan how inappropriate his comment was. James tried to steer the conversation onto a more constructive and serious plane by talking about the powerful effect that having children later in life had on him.

Maggie decided that she'd had enough of this "personal" stuff and changed the subject back to professional matters by following up on Dan's earlier comments. "So Dan, what else has been going on at SciTech?"

"Well, we had Thomas come out and do some work with us soon after the last dive workshop when Cindy took over as president, and we got some good results." Dan paused and took another sip of wine. "He's holding another dive workshop, you know—in Papua New Guinea. The topic's on how to build creative organizations. I'm going and I'm trying to talk Father James here into going with me."

Maggie looked confused. "Why in the world would anyone go to Papua New Guinea to do a workshop on creativity?"

"Well, you know Thomas," Dan chorted admiringly. "He looks at the world through a different set of lenses than most of us do. I've already seen the format and teaching objectives of the workshop, and it may help to get me past the brick wall I'm facing in my business and with Cindy."

"Why don't you go too?" Dan looked intently at Maggie, hoping to spark her interest in another adventure.

Rena just shook her head from side to side, convinced that Dan's invitation was just another come-on to her mom.

Maggie smiled, turned to Rena, and clasped her hand. "Why don't we *all* go as a kind of reunion?"

Although nothing was said, Dan sensed the passive, silent tension between Rena and her mom, but he spoke up anyway. "Yeah—why don't you come too, Rena?"

The young woman winced as she sat up in her chair and moved away from the table, clearly uncomfortable at his suggestion. "I probably couldn't get away. I've got too much work to do at the office. Besides, I'm still a newlywed and I don't think my husband would let me go. Plus, I haven't been diving for a while and I'd probably have trouble getting up to speed."

Despite the wine, Dan could feel the enormous resistance to his suggestion and *for once* he backed off. But Maggie said, "I'll send an e-mail to Bethany, Nikki, and Lindsey and see if I can get them to go too." Then looking squarely at her daughter she said, "Rena and I will talk about it some more. I think I can solve her work and husband problems, and we'll sign her up for a scuba refresher course to get her confidence back. What do you think Rena, dear?" Maggie looked at her daughter imploringly.

"Whatever you say mother." Rena just rolled her eyes in disgust and withdrew deep inside of herself.

INTO THE DEPTHS

Cindy Reeder was staring at a woman with enormous black breasts who was nursing an infant on one, and a tiny piglet on the other. Cindy wasn't really thinking, she was directly experiencing this moment through her five senses, but at the same time it seemed like a dream—a haunting place she'd been before. The bright shafts of sunlight that were penetrating through the rain forest canopy, the multitude of birds singing, and the clean mountain air of this remote village in the Highlands of Papua New Guinea seemed mysteriously familiar to her—like coming home after a long journey.

The village woman turned to face her and made direct eye contact, almost like she sensed Cindy was staring at her. The woman's eyes looked serious, distant, withdrawn, and very far away. The intensity of the woman's gaze disrupted Cindy's experience and she became self-conscious about looking at her, but she refused to breakoff the visual communication that was happening. Both women looked intently into each other's eyes with deep inquiry, curiosity, and a silent interrogation that was searching for answers to life's fundamental questions.

Without breaking eye contact, Cindy found herself in deep reflection on the psychological and cultural distance between the two of them. The reality was that the village woman's existence was unrelentingly cruel, demeaning, and short. Yet Cindy was grieving with an aching pain that hungered and thirsted for this woman's simple life—a desire that went to the depths of her soul and made no rational sense.

Like the woman, Cindy's eyes were dark, sunken portals that told a melancholy and tortured story of a lifetime of pain, suffering, and longing for what she didn't have—her calling in life and a long-term relationship. When Cindy spoke, her deep, masculine sounding voice and polished Harvard-style Boston accent gave her a captivating presence and authority over those who listened. She always wore jasmine and, in a Pavlovian way, when people smelled the sweet fragrance of the flower they knew she was present. Cindy and the village woman could have passed for sisters. Cindy was five foot two inches tall, with ebony skin, a wide flat nose, corn rows banded at the ends with golden rings, and large firm breasts. But nothing else about the two women was similar.

∿∿∿∿

Cindy liked the sense of entitlement that came with being in academia, and a Ph.D. from MIT in electrical engineering and computer science and an adjunct faculty position at Harvard only reinforced this. She made an excellent researcher and scientist because her intuition motivated her to map out the behavior of nature and search for truth in the physical world. The university was a rarified atmosphere that had sheltered her from the harsh realities of the business world—a social structure based on tenure that went back to the Middle Ages. When she left her full-time position at Harvard to become the Director of R&D at SciTech, she had the best of both worlds. Her department was charged with keeping SciTech at the cutting edge of technology, and Cindy's technological vision and genius were a crucial part of the company's competitive advantage. In addition, her boss, Dan, made sure that her salary and benefits were more than enough to keep her happy, and he sheltered her from the harsh, bottom line, day-to-day realities of running a start-up company. As an INFP, Enneagram Type Four who was introspective, romantic, self-aware, sensitive, and reserved, this setup was exactly what she wanted and a condition she set for coming to work for Dan in the first place.[12]

Over the last few years, Dan had begged her to take over as the company president. Cindy hated the mundane, pedestrian realities of business and much preferred to bring the cutting edge of science and technology to bear on SciTech's problems as Director of R&D, but about two years ago she finally capitulated to Dan's pleading and whining.

Only a few weeks ago, Cindy and Dan got into it after a board meeting. "Look, Dan, I took over as SciTech's president with the understanding that as CEO you'd back away from day-to-day operations and empower me to hire a COO of my choosing to run the day-to-day business of the company. I told you I wanted to focus on developing a technological vision and the long-term direction for the company—something I believed we lacked. But you never let that happen and I'm starting to feel like I want out."

Dan was pacing the empty boardroom furiously, his face red with anger, and his presence almost threatening. He was trying to give her the message that he really didn't want to hear what she had to say—he just wanted things done his way.

"You know how much I hate the minutia of managing this company," Cindy pleaded, trying to engage him in a discussion. "I feel demeaned by the day-to-day, ordinary tasks that need to be done. I glaze over when I see financial spreadsheets or P&L statements. I dislike the endless detail of the problems the fabrication facility is up against. I have little or no interest in the extraverted skills needed to run the marketing department. Yet I'm supposed to *manage* and *lead* all these organizational functions? I'll tell you, Dan—this puts an enormous pressure on me, one that's harder and harder to bear."

Dan had stopped pacing, grabbed a chair, and looked at Cindy with confusion and regret because he knew she was telling the truth.

"You've known this about me for years," Cindy insisted with increased intensity in her voice. "The only reason I agreed to take the job as president was because you promised me that I could hire someone to run this place. But then you reneged on your deal, claiming that another senior manager would drive the company's overhead costs up too high. Instead, you said you would 'help' me with day-to-day operations. But you know what, Dan? Your 'help' is my biggest problem. My managers and staff are entirely confused when the CEO and founding owner shows up in their workspace, sees something he doesn't like, then reverses decisions that I made only an hour earlier. They don't know who to listen to and they're sick and tired of you and I disagreeing over everything publicly."

Now Cindy started pacing the floor of the boardroom as Dan's head turned from side to side trying to follow her long, deliberate steps.

Most people were loyal to Cindy and would tell her when Dan changed a decision she had made, then she would reverse it again behind his back. This just infuriated him. A few employees stuck by Dan and would stir the pot by tattling to him about Cindy, and Dan would subsequently take issue and embarrass her in staff meetings. Her feelings and emotions ran like a deep underground river and she had a highly developed set of values that inwardly affected her. But most times her emotions remained unexpressed to Dan and others as she faded into the background even at meetings she was supposed to be leading. Yet she had a subtle, but important effect on Dan and others by silently setting aesthetic and moral standards that they felt obliged to meet without her having to preach or lecture about them.

Cindy wasn't a good manager—and she didn't want to become one. She knew she had a tendency to reject decisions based solely on logic and reason even when they would lead to more effective and value-added solutions for the company. Often she would continue to argue in support of her view, long after others had already made up their minds and mentally moved on. Cindy also knew that she could be impractical and had a difficult time estimating goals, timelines, budgets, and a critical path for projects, things Dan did quite well. But she felt that the way Dan reneged on his promise to let her hire a COO and the way he continued to undermine her authority with the staff were inexcusable.

Cindy stopped pacing, plopped into one of the high-back, cushy, black leather chairs directly across the table from Dan, and poured herself a glass of water. She sat back, sipped the water and let the silence between them quell her anger and bring perspective.

"Look, Dan, I know you believe that your intervention in the day-to-day operation of the company is necessary to keep the company on track. But what I'm hearing through the grapevine is that it's lowering morale and making managers and front-line workers wonder who's running the company. That really makes problems for me."

Cindy looked deeply into Dan's eyes. "We go way back, right, Dan?" she almost whispered.

"Yeah," he replied as his mood softened and he began to connect with her on an emotional level.

"I told you I've been seeing a Jungian analyst named Miranda right? Miranda is trying to help me understand the twists and turns of my life, my growing sense of desperation with this job, and the bizarre dreams I've been having."

Dan nodded slowly, almost afraid to go on listening, but Cindy began sharing from a still deeper place in her soul.

"I've been troubled about what to do with my life ever since I became president of SciTech, Dan. I find myself envying people who know what they want out of life and know where they're going. Truthfully, the pressure and constant battling with you has eroded my psychological energy to the point where I'm in a crisis. It's as if my identity is collapsing into an inner black hole. You know how moody I can be. I've always lived out my life on an emotional stage that is dark, melancholy, and sad—almost like I'm in mourning about life itself. But in these last days it's getting more difficult to tolerate, Dan."

Cindy's eyes welled up with tears, her face became contorted by waves of excruciating psychological pain and suffering that rose from within. Dan, taken by surprise, leaned toward her out of compassion as she sobbed like a frightened child.

She felt desperately alone, abandoned in some collective existential way that she didn't understand and couldn't move beyond. She was unable to reach out to family, friends, and colleagues, and at the same time Cindy felt profoundly unreachable by them. Over the course of her lifetime, she tried to challenge and question the power and authority of these destructive waves of emotion. But intellectual models were powerless against the intensity and force of the feelings that gripped her spirit like a vice and shook her in a visceral, to-the-bone way that she never knew how to escape.

She experienced herself as being born alone, living alone, and probably dying alone—a discrete psychological-biological organism who was without origin and roots, unanchored, and drifting through life. Brief, stormy, intense sexual relationships were a distraction from the isolation and loneliness of her inner landscape. A couple of months ago on a dive trip to Bonaire, she hooked up with a nineteen year old local boy for a week of round-the-clock emotional and sexual catharsis that allowed her to reconnect to the lost depths of her emotions. These brief romantic encounters had become a way of life, they energized her with overwhelming emotional intensity—they were how she got that quick emotional high that breathed new life into her otherwise mundane and arid experience of life.

"Cindy, you claim that what you really want is a long-term relationship, or even to get married," her analyst Miranda said to her during a recent session. "But it's important that you learn to see how you unconsciously frustrate, undermine, and reject that kind of relationship when you're actually in one."

Cindy allowed the heuristic power of Miranda's words to penetrate deeply. She shuffled in her chair then quietly spoke. "I know. I talk about how I long for the simple pleasures of life and the ongoing stability and true companionship that a long-term relationship brings. But somehow my insatiable longing to be connected in a relationship has become an end in itself. In a very bizarre and self-defeating way, I long for the experience of longing for a relationship more than actually having one."

Miranda smiled warmly and approvingly in the presence of Cindy's utter honesty with herself and her analyst. When she first started seeing Miranda, Cindy had a difficult time expressing herself verbally and withdrew from people and situations. Witnessing these powerful moments of insight and integrity were what Miranda lived for because she knew they were the signatures of personal transformation.

Despite her increasing insight into the fundamental nature of her inner life, two years of heated conflict with Dan and the pressure of running SciTech had produced a deep sense of inner grief and hopelessness about ever really finding herself and being content with her life. At the office and with friends, she tried to appear to be happy, keeping her powerful feelings to herself and expressing them indirectly in her journal or through the ingenious technological designs she developed for SciTech. But this was a façade that masked a deep and abiding sense of despair—an inner concentration camp—that went to the depths of her soul and left her feeling as if she was somehow sentenced to an eternity of being on the outside of a "normal" life looking in.

She was longing for a new perspective and decided to attend the dive workshop on building creative organizations to purposely stir up the unconscious in the hope of finding new direction. At some level, she missed the work of academia and teaching, but she didn't really want to go back to the publish-or-perish culture at Harvard. She was perplexed about what would scratch her inner itch and give her a sense of meaning and significance in her professional life.

Cindy regained her composure, took another sip of water, rose, and started pacing around the empty boardroom again, as her mood became more direct and confrontational. "I'm really trying to resist my natural tendency to change outer things like jobs and relationships just to take the pressure off. That's why I need to go to this dive workshop and that's why you *must* come with me, Dan," she demanded, pounding her fist on the table.

"Cindy—you've got to get a grip. We're writing red ink for the first time in years! Revenues are down, competitors are eating our lunch and stealing our best clients, and you want me to go to a dive workshop? I don't get it," Dan yelled as he pounded his fist on the table.

"I'm not sure our relationship will survive if we don't," she said with finality.

"Okay, you win. I'll go, but *not* because I want to! Leaving the helm of this company at a desperate time like this is the most irrational and irresponsible thing I've ever done in my life," Dan exclaimed incredulously. "I'll do it for you. But it's against my better judgment and if it fails to really help the situation, it'll be the last time I ever listen to you."

Dan stormed toward the door, opened it, and without looking back at her said, "I'm tired of your psychodramas, Cindy. I've got a company to run." He turned and locked his eyes on hers. "If this turns out to be just another one of your vacation junkets, you won't ever have to threaten to quit again. I'll fire you!" With that he slammed the door and stormed off.

The sound of a man's voice disrupted the eye contact between the two women. "In the Highlands, pigs are a symbol of wealth and prestige."

Startled, Cindy turned and saw their tour guide, Norman, speaking. Norman had picked her, Dan, and James up at the Highlander Hotel in Mt. Hagen that morning at 6:30 A.M. for a full day of touring in remote villages of Papua New Guinea (PNG).

Cindy looked back at the woman and smiled at her. They had both been caught in a reverie that had touched something deep inside.

"Okay, let's keep moving," Norman said as he walked on and picked up his commentary on village life and the culture in this remarkable country.

Cindy made one last silent gesture toward the woman, then turned and followed the others as Norman rattled on: "Women are responsible for the day-to-day work of gardening, caring for animals, children, and running the household. Traditionally, men have been responsible for hunting, trading, religious rituals and ceremonies, negotiating compensation settlements, and waging tribal warfare."

Cindy was in a daze as her mind was consumed by the direct experience of the cultural distance between her and the woman who was simultaneously nursing the child and the piglet. She had been talking to Dan about changing the organization's culture, which by definition was invisible to her managers and staff because it was taken for granted as the way things were done. How could she get Dan to view himself and the organizational culture at SciTech from a perspective outside of the one he was used to—like she was doing today with the woman? Maybe this village experience could provide a common foundation for her to discuss changing the company, because, in her mind, creating and changing SciTech's culture was fundamentally no different than creating and changing *any* culture.

Cindy had devoted her life to research, science, technology, and progress and had made significant contributions in these areas through creative innovations, with many patents to her credit. But staring across the great cultural divide she was experiencing today, she understood how deeply she'd set science, technology, and progress up as an objective standard of cultural truth by which cultures like this one were judged and found wanting. If the way of science, technology, and progress was really *the way*, then why did her heart long to live the village woman's life? What had Cindy sacrificed to become a modern person and how was that lost dimension of her life embodied in the woman? Must she literally take on the woman's life to feed this inner hunger? If she did, wouldn't she miss the life she had now just as badly?

They reached the end of the central compound of the village of Korobul, and Dan, James, and Cindy sat down on some logs that doubled as benches. Cindy twisted the cap off her bottled water and drank deeply in the heat of the midday sun, as she gazed over the fertile expanse of the Waghi Valley.

Norman, a graduate of the University of Goroka with a major in cultural anthropology, continued the tour. "I want to give you a more detailed overview of the history of PNG, our culture, and the role this valley played in that history before we move on to the next village."

Norman picked up a stick and drew an outline of PNG in the dirt. "Papua New Guinea is a country of over six hundred islands, six degrees south of the equator. Stone axes found in archeological digs suggest that people have been living here in the Highlands for thirty thousand years." Norman raised his arm and pointed across the valley. "In fact, people have been cultivating crops in garden plots like those over there for nine thousand years, making them the first farmers in the world. The lives of village people are still governed by their belief in spirits, ritual, and magic. In fact, PNG is the only country in the world that has a Parliamentary law about the use of magic."

"What does the law say?" Cindy interjected, her curiosity aroused by the anachronistic oddity of Norman's statement.

"The use of black magic is forbidden, and white magic is allowed when used for the common good of supporting village life." Norman smiled, pleased by Cindy's interest in the cultural realities of his country. "Hereditary knowledge about magic has been passed down from father to son for generations, and it applies to almost every aspect of village life—things like growing taro and sweet potatoes, fishing the reef, finding spirits that cause sickness, or laying out the geometry of villages."

"Do they teach this magic in your schools?" Cindy inquired, now more puzzled than before.

"No," Norman replied flatly, "and this is a big cultural clash between the power and authority that chiefs and village elders derive from hereditary knowledge and the knowledge our young people learn in school. For example, if the taro crop fails, the village elder who possesses the hereditary knowledge of taro magic calls a meeting of the village and goes to the spirits of our ancestors to solve the problem. When young village members who have graduated from the University of Goroka challenge this elder with their knowledge of crop rotation, irrigation, and the use of fertilizer, the entire fabric of authority and power in the village is challenged."

"That sounds familiar." Cindy glanced at Dan then back to Norman. "When we hire young people from top technical schools and they question our long-time employees about better ways to do things using the latest technology, or when a new manager suggests we change a business process, these innovations and improvements challenge the power structure and culture in our company too. Looks like there's nothing new under the sun."

Dan glared at Cindy and said cynically, "I don't get the connection; do you, James?"

James said nothing and continued to take in Cindy from behind the anonymity of his dark sunglasses.

Norman sat down on a log to rest his tired feet, then turned his gaze to the broad, lush, heavily forested expanse of the Wahgi Valley. "Up until 1933, people believed that the Highlands was uninhabited. Imagine their surprise when Mick and Dan Leahy found this heavily populated valley nested here between these fourteen thousand foot mountains. Our families were even more surprised because they had no idea that there was a world outside the Highlands—they had no exposure to European culture and had never seen white people.

"Many areas in the Highlands remained unaffected by any change until the mid-1970s, but as you can see today, this fertile valley is covered with tea and coffee plantations, interspersed with villages that are surrounded by traditional food gardens tended by women, much like they were nine thousand years ago.

"PNG has over seven hundred distinct languages, not dialects, distinct languages as defined by linguists and anthropologists—that is one-third of all the languages in the world. They are regional, so that if you are from a village that is a small distance away you will probably be partially understood when you speak. Although most people speak Pidgin as a common language of trade and commerce, it is the language of our village that binds us together as a people. We call this *wantok*, meaning that 'one talks' your language, but it means more than this. Someone who is a *wantok* is your family member, countryman, friend, and a person from your village, tribe, and clan.

"We don't have a system of individual ownership as you do in western societies. Every person who is born into a clan and village is a *wantok* and has the right to be housed, fed, and to share in any assets owned by the community. This is the equivalent of your social security system. *Wantoks* also have an obligation and family responsibility to give back to those in the village when they are in need.

"Our highly organized society of clans, villages, tribes, and families has a hierarchical social structure where different kinds of power are vested in chiefs, village elders, and what we call *bigmen*. In the former days, the title *bigman* was only passed on to sons from their fathers and this was done through gift exchanges called '*mogas*', where countless numbers of villagers were given gifts as a way of obligating them to reciprocate at some future time. Today being a *bigman* is more about how much money a person has, their ability to broker deals and bring consensus through the network of relationships and friends who are obligated to them."

"Sounds just like the power structure inside corporate America where people cut deals and wield enormous power," Cindy chuckled. "We don't call them bigmen, but we have a saying, 'It's not what you know, it's *who* you know.' Isn't that right, Dan?"

Dan simply ignored her but was thinking, *I wish she'd just stop trying to fabricate these forced cultural connections.*

Norman paused for a moment to let the silence and natural wonder of the valley close in around them before continuing. "Things move slowly here because villagers have a different understanding of time and punctuality than most Americans. Each family and village produces all the food they need to live from their own land, so we don't have *jobs* like you do in your culture although there is plenty of *work* to be done to maintain village life. The whole concept of a cash economy where people sell their labor and their time for money is very foreign to us. We don't connect work to jobs that a boss hires us to do, and we don't view time as being worth money. Ours is an ancient understanding that is reflected in our language that has only two words for time. One word means the present and the other word means yesterday, tomorrow, and all future time. People know the difference between the multiple meanings of the second one by the context in which it's used."

Cindy looked at Dan and once again tried to engage him in a

discussion about culture that linked what they were hearing in the village to cultural change at SciTech. "You know, Dan, this is a fundamental concept that even effects our employees. They sell their time and labor to us and we give them money in exchange, but that lacks the kind of meaning and significance these villagers get from working the same land that their families have for generations. Like American farmers who move to cities and get jobs, the work done by our employees is separated from the means of production in a company that is owned exclusively by you. This has to produce a sense of distance and alienation from nature and the land—a distance we don't see here in this village."

Dan was visibly angered by Cindy's insinuation that his employees were being harmed by their jobs, but before he could counter her claim, Norman excitedly interjected, saying, "You are correct, Cindy. It's the land that links us to our ancestors and the ancient ways of the spirit world and tribal law. We come from the land, we live from the land, and we die and go back to the same land as our ancestors have since the beginning of time. The land connects us to our dead ancestors in the spirit world who still live and help us in life."

Dan bit his tongue and looked away as Norman stood and gestured with his hand. "Let's begin walking back to the van and I'll tell you about another aspect of our culture and social structure that is just as important as *wantok*.

"Our ancient system of law and order is called 'compensation and payback' and is not unlike the notion of an eye for an eye, and a tooth for a tooth in the Bible." Norman walked over to the edge of the village, looked down into a deep ravine with a river at the bottom and pointed to the lush vegetable gardens on both sides. He raised his finger to indicate the land on the other side of the river. "This river is the boundary between two tribes. If people from that tribe cross the river and take crops from this garden, the village we are in will demand compensation for the wrong done in the form of food and other goods. If the other tribe meets the demand, there is peace and harmony. If they refuse, this tribe will go to war with them as payback for the wrong done. This is tribal law."

In the spirit of connecting what they were seeing in the village to life back in America, James scoffed, "Yeah, we call the police, hire lawyers, and go to court and fight it out."

"Yes…" Norman smiled, pleased that James was also showing interest, "but violence and anger play a very different role here in the Highlands than in your country and they happen for very different reasons. Violence and anger have been woven into the fabric of our culture to intentionally accomplish various goals and purposes."

"Really?" James asked, his interest now fully engaged in the dialogue Norman had been having only with Cindy.

"Yes, when people from outside PNG see tribal warfare and payback they view it as a breakdown of law and order, but for us this is our ancient way of keeping and restoring law and order. There are known consequences for those who do wrong. What to you looks like a violent assault on a person or family is often payback that is sanctioned and agreed to by an entire community of chiefs, elders, and *bigmen* as a way of carrying out our sense of justice and maintaining our tribal law."

That really is a different spin on law and order, James thought. *It actually makes more gut-level sense than our way of doing things back in the States.*

When they reached the van, Cindy looked back at the village for a moment, then hopped into the front seat. The long day of touring was over and the four of them were silent as the truck moved past unforgettable scenes of mountain splendor. Cindy finally broke the silence with another probing question. "Norman, from your perspective, what is the biggest difference between what your culture teaches about work and organizations, and ours in America?"

Norman took a minute to formulate a thoughtful answer. "I have only been to America once, but my observation was that it was not a 'natural' culture. Your culture uses creativity to dominate and oppose nature and the natural flow of life with science, technology, and the power of money. While many of your people view us as primitive, ours is a natural culture where we use our creativity to *integrate* the way we live with nature and the natural flow of life. So the organizational structure and authority of our tribal system and our view of work and time do not alienate us from nature or from ourselves like your companies and organizations do."

Cindy asked a follow-up question, then a second and third question as Dan just rolled his eyes, glancing over at James who continued listening, watching, and taking it all in from the anonymous position behind his dark sunglasses. Displeased at getting no reaction from James, Dan turned his gaze toward the mountains around them and mentally disappeared.

James had not met Cindy before this trip, but he was already tired of her intensity and constant introspection. Based on his discussion with Dan back in Colorado, James's intuition about Cindy was confirmed.

Dan needs to straighten this woman out or just get rid of her, James thought.

Cindy was still hoping that their experiences during the village trip and the enormous differences in culture they were seeing would provide a common foundation for her and Dan to discuss cultural change back at SciTech. After all, the entire purpose of this trip was for the two of them to try to define a common view of the problems they faced with the company, and begin to define a path forward.

Since he wasn't joining in on the conversation she was having with

Norman, Cindy tried to draw Dan into the discussion by looking right at him and softly commenting, "You know, Dan, there's something intriguing and inviting about this place—far away from our fast-paced world of technology and science."

Dan snapped back loud enough for everyone to hear. "I wouldn't want to live in this kind of primitive squalor—no electricity, no indoor plumbing, no air conditioning, with pigs and dogs running in and out of huts, breeding disease, and that awful, filthy stink of people who don't bathe! Quite frankly, I find nothing intriguing or inviting about this whole experience. I can't wait to get back to the hotel."

Cindy scowled at Dan, then glanced at Norman who was smarting from the sting and insensitivity of the comments. Devastated by his rudeness, she barked back at Dan, "The humans in our Western culture are like a virus: they come to a place like this and dominate everything; they consume the resources of the land like gluttons. They don't live in harmony with nature like these people do. We forget that it was only a hundred and twenty-five years ago that native Americans lived side by side on the land with nature and the animals, then Europeans came with their culture and devoured the land. There are many valuable things we can learn from people in PNG, especially ways to get closer to nature without *destroying* it! That's why so many Americans like backpacking and tent-camping—it gets you back to basics without all the complications of life. I guess that's something you just don't get!"

James felt the power of Dan's rage in response to Cindy's rebuke and realized the depth of their mutual disrespect for each other's worldview. He remained silent, but for the first time, he began to really hear what Cindy had been saying. He saw how she kept trying to bring the conversation back to SciTech in an attempt to constructively engage Dan in solving their problems. On reflection, he realized that her intuitions and curiosity about this strange and exotic land were giving *him* new insights about himself and how his attempts to change the culture at St. Peter's have been met with such heated debate and opposition. Most of all, he resonated deeply with her insights about nature and being connected to the land—that's why he loved going to his house in Alma so much.

Dan was suddenly embarrassed about showing his rage in front of James, even though he believed she'd provoked him with her incessant questions. He regained his composure and said in a consciously controlled tone of voice, "Look, Cindy, I hear what you're saying about getting back to nature. Camping for a weekend is fine—I enjoy that. But these people camp for a lifetime. They have been camping for nine thousand years without any significant technological progress or development. No thanks—that's not for me. I think the connections you're trying to make between SciTech's organizational culture and this culture might make for interesting discussion over drinks later on, but they have little or no value in solving the bottom line financial and business problems we're having back in New York."

Cindy wanted to respond, but bit her tongue.

As they reached Mt. Hagen, the streets were filled with young restless boys and men who seemed to be looking for trouble. As the truck pulled up to the gate of the Highlander Hotel and honked the horn, they waited for five or six guards with automatic weapons to open the gate into the hotel compound. The hostile-looking youths moved closer to the locked doors of their vehicle.

They waited anxiously for the gate to open. Keeping an eye on the slowly approaching men, Dan tipped Norman, and then said in the most conciliatory tone of voice he could muster, "Hey, you two, let's meet in the bar at seven thirty for drinks and then have dinner."

"Sounds good to me," James seconded, looking forward to a hot shower before meeting his friends. Cindy said nothing and grew more anxious by the second about the group of men who were closing in on their car.

Mt. Hagen felt like an old west town that had run the sheriff off and was ruled by how fast you could draw your six-shooter. The nature and meaning of violence and anger was different in Mt. Hagen than in the remote villages. It was patterned after an American Rambo, urban ghetto kind of lawlessness where wandering gangs of youths called *rascals* held people up on the Highlands road, broke into houses, and frequently murdered innocent folks for their wallets or the clothes they were wearing. Rascals moved to Mt. Hagen from the more isolated Southern or Enga provinces looking for work and lived in squatter's villages. Others arrived on daily flights from the capital city of Port Moresby, committed crimes, then skipped town on the next flight.

Rascals fell outside of the traditional clan and tribal social system of *wantok* because they came from families who lived somewhere else. So rascals had no recourses because there were no government programs to replace *wantok*. The opportunities for uneducated people were few and far between. Western-style TV shows had brought them the images of wealth, material possessions, and violence, so they become rascals—outlaws in the truest sense of the word.

Gee—where are these guys? Dan whispered under his breath, still waiting for the guards.

When the hotel gates thankfully swung closed behind them and the armed guards dispersed the young men, Dan, Cindy, and James found themselves in yet another world of a self-contained, Western-style five star hotel—the kind you'd find in any large city around the world. As Cindy walked across the beautifully manicured ten-acre grounds with flowers, singing birds, rare trees, walking paths, and a swimming pool, she was struck by the harsh reality of more armed guards walking the perimeter of the eight-foot–high wall topped with concertina wire that made all this opulence possible. When she got back to her room, she was exhausted and tired of trying to work things out with Dan.

A couple of hours later, the three of them were sipping a glass of vintage wine in front of a blazing fire in the hotel bar when they were approached by a PNG local.

∿∿∿∿

"May I join you?" he asked politely.

"Sure." Cindy nodded, eager to bring other perspectives into their conversation. After the three of them introduced themselves, Nelson Bamu told them he was the Dean of the Faculty of Science at the University of Goroka, the capital of the Eastern Highlands Province—only a twenty-minute flight from Mt. Hagen.

"What brings you to PNG?" Nelson inquired with sincere interest.

"We're attending a dive workshop on building creative organizations," Cindy answered, eager to see his reaction. It's being held on a ship that leaves from the Walindi Plantation Resort, and we're flying down there early tomorrow."

"Really—a workshop on creativity?" Nelson took a sip of wine and sat back in his chair. "The motto of the University of Goroka is 'Creating the Future,' and our core values and philosophy are all built around discovering and learning to use our creativity. The university is built on the premise that all people have creative intellectual ability, and that finding solutions to the challenges PNG faces as a society requires our students and the university to develop and use their creativity. We encourage students to use their intellectual abilities to *create* their future and the future of our country, rather than just be followers.

Intrigued by the coincidence of the encounter, Cindy leaned forward. "What brings you to Mt. Hagen, Nelson?"

"I have a meeting tomorrow about making Goroka a center of

excellence for the whole country and part of this is a new Associate of Arts degree we're starting in electronics and computer science. The university currently offers courses that apply mathematics to solving problems in social science, agriculture, business, and economics, and the few classes that we currently offer in computer science are only designed to develop basic computer literacy. My vision is to build the new electronic and computer science program into a fully accredited BS degree in the next three to five years."

"That's my background—computing and electrical engineering!" Cindy gushed with the enthusiasm and serendipity of discovering a long-lost friend. She gave him a brief overview of her academic credentials, excited to be talking about her education and experience with a knowledgeable person from such a different cultural background.

"Are you interested in spending a year in Goroka to help us get started?" Nelson asked, showing his own excitement at the prospect. "We would *love* to have someone of your caliber here in PNG."

Dan was squirming in his seat as Cindy quickly inquired, "What kind of resources do you have to get started?"

"Our new seventy-five thousand square foot library building has over one hundred twenty-five thousand volumes automated on a computer system plus two high-speed satellite modems for doing Web-based research in university libraries around the world." Nelson sat up in his chair as he spoke proudly. "In addition, we have two fully-equipped computer laboratories, and several well-equipped science labs. I want the program to focus on information technology system design, building linked networks, and applying low-cost, high-power computing solutions to applications in the oil and gas industry, mining, and computerizing PNG's fastest growing industry—private security firms. I also envision graduates of the new program playing a role in the design, acquisition, and statistical analysis of data from sociological, medical, community, agricultural, and economic research conducted in Goroka."

Dan was getting noticeably nervous as Cindy's interest continued to grow.

She's really yanking Dan's chain, James thought. *It's fun to watch him squirm for a change.*

"Wow!" Cindy gasped. "Do you really have that much research going on currently in Goroka?"

"Absolutely." Nelson nodded vigorously. "In addition to the university, Goroka is home to the Institute of Melanesian Research, the Medical Research Institute and Hospital, and the Aiyura Agriculture Research Institute. We've just developed a strategic plan for getting other research entities to co-locate in Goroka, and for participating in research projects using high-speed internet connections with faculty members who are doing research here but are based at places like Harvard and the University of Chicago."

Nelson's eyes were suddenly drawn to the door as he reached into his jacket for a business card and handed it to Cindy. "I'm sorry, I have to leave–my colleagues are here. Call me if you're at all interested and we'll talk before you leave the country."

Nelson was hardly out of ear shot when Dan barked, "What are you doing? You're not actually thinking of coming here are you?"

Cindy, tired of dealing with Dan's inconsiderate barbs all day, rolled her eyes and sighed. "I'm just having a conversation about some interesting possibilities, that's all."

Dan snapped back, "Just remember we came here to find solutions to problems we have to fix back in New York."

"Dan!" Cindy moaned in exasperation. "I've been trying to engage you in a discussion about what's going on back at SciTech all day long to no avail—*now* you're interested? Well I'm not."

She stood abruptly and grabbed her glass of wine. "You always have to spoil a good time by hammering on people when they don't do exactly what you want."

She touched James on the shoulder and spoke politely to him, "I'm sorry, James," then turned to Dan and said, "I think I'm going to head back and order room service—I'll see you both tomorrow."

Too bad she's leaving, James thought, surprised that he was actually starting to enjoy her company. *She's got an interesting perspective on life and she really knows how to put Dan in his place.*

∽∽∽∽

James awoke in the night and lay there confused about where he was. As he realized he was in his hotel room in the Highlands, powerful images of a dream flooded into his consciousness. He reached for the light, sat up on the edge of the bed, and grabbed his journal and a pen from the nightstand. He allowed himself to sink fully back into the inner images of the dream and used his pen to force them into the concrete world of paper in his journal.

I was in the rain-forested mountains of Papua New Guinea with a young, beautiful black Melanesian woman and we were both naked and sexually attracted to each other. We climbed up to a high place in the mountain. We came to a round flat part on top of a pinnacle that had about a two-foot high stone wall around it and this is where we would consummate our attraction. I sat down on the rock wall and the young woman embraced me. Our passionate lovemaking was a sacred fertility ritual—a celebration of the power of creativity. Afterwards we walked to a thatched spirit hut near the top of the mountain where her mother and father were chanting a sacred mantra. I stood face to face with her mother. Then, in the next part of the ceremony, the mother began crying, except tears didn't come from her eyes, instead they fell from the sky. Then it was my turn and I began to cry, and tears fell from heaven. I had a deep sense of completion and release at the deepest and most vulnerable place in my soul, but I wasn't terrified by being in this place. The ceremony was over and we all had a sense of "completion"—of being made whole.

Father James Tuffs, Episcopal priest, closed his journal, turned out the light, and lay back in his bed as the night sounds of the rain forest closed in around him. He felt a deep and profound sense of quiet within—a holy silence—the wholeness he felt in the dream. The thing that disturbed him most profoundly was that somehow he knew that the young Melanesian woman was Cindy.

James had learned that his dreams were complex communications that combined feelings, intuitions, bodily sensations, and thoughts in ways that ignored the constraints of space and time and combined the past, present, and future. His dreams often deconstructed the personal, organizational, social, and cultural distinctions he used to make sense of life, and confronted him with psychological truth clothed in the visual language of metaphors, riddles, and parables. But as James lay there in a quasi dream state—sexually tensed up—he wondered what this communication might mean at this particular point in his life's journey.

CONVERGING ON WALINDI

Frank Brighton arrived at the Walindi Plantation Resort at about 8:00 A.M. Friday morning. Walindi is a fifteen–minute van ride from Kimbe, the capital of the West New Britain Province—a portion of PNG that is relatively untouched and undeveloped. The resort is surrounded by thick, impenetrable rain forests that are virtually unexplored and inaccessible except by foot. You could get lost in this jungle forever—and unfortunately, some people have. The few dirt roads that do exist were carved out of the rain forest by the brute force of local employees of the palm oil and timber industry.

Frank was just five feet tall, slight of build, with jet-black hair and almond brown eyes that confirmed his Asian background. His laid-back appearance was a remnant of growing up on "island time" in Honolulu, but underneath this easy going exterior was a stern, formal, hard-driving, distant man with the sensitivity of a Samurai warrior. Frank always fulfilled his obligations to his wife and daughter out of honor and duty, but rarely was it done with demonstrable love and affection. He even tolerated his lazy, irresponsible son-in-law Rick who had caused him untold problems in his business—again, out of the Asian obligation of honor and duty. Frank used his intellectual power and presence to create the impression that he was larger than he was, and he was just bright enough to actually pull this off. He read voraciously, on myriad topics, but always non fiction. While most people used novels to relax and forget about life for a while, Frank read to increase his intellectual prowess. So he imbibed on tomes about experimental and theoretical particle physics, cosmology, and the biological and social sciences. He completed the RHETI and MBTI tools in preparation for the workshop and knew that he was an INTP, Enneagram Type Five who was perceptive, intellectually alert, insightful, and curious.[13]

Frank walked up onto the deck of Walindi's main area and saw that the resort was on a marvelous black sand beach. This main area had an inviting pool surrounded by a well-appointed dining room, a new bar area with hand carved wooden beams, a library, shop, and an enormous deck with chairs and picnic tables to sit on and gaze over Kimbe Bay and beyond to the Bismarck Sea.

His driver accompanied Frank to the front desk as the boys followed with his luggage and dive gear. Martha, the receptionist, said cheerfully from behind the counter, "Good morning, Frank," like they were old friends. "Come, sit, relax and have something cold to drink while the boys take your luggage to your room. You're only a stranger once here at Walindi."

After a short check-in procedure, Frank and Martha strolled leisurely to a couple of chairs near the beach. Frank sipped from a bottle of cold water and looked out over the sea, as Martha volunteered, "Walindi is a privately owned palm-oil plantation and a world-class resort with twelve thatched huts and four bungalows that are only fifty feet from the black volcanic sands of Kimbe Bay." She raised her arm and pointed toward the semicircle shaped bay. "The resort is framed by sixteen volcanoes, five of which are still active with streams of smoke rising from their central craters—like that one over there. Kimbe Bay is the bottom curvature of the Ring of Fire, the great fiery circle of volcanoes and seismic activity that traces the Pacific Ocean north from PNG along the Chilean, California, and Oregon coasts to Alaska, then circles South through Japan, the Pacific Rim, Indonesia, and back to PNG." Frank's eyes were wide and his mind receptive as Martha commented on this natural wonder that he'd always heard about.

A few minutes later, as Martha walked him to his bungalow, Frank was surrounded by Eucalyptus and Rain Trees that were one hundred twenty-five feet tall with deep red, royal purple, orange, and yellow flowers on vines wrapped seventy-five feet up tree trunks that were three feet in diameter. As he passed the tennis courts, the well-manicured grounds revealed numerous fruit tress that bore pineapples, bananas, breadfruit, mangos, coconuts, and papaya. Walindi was like an outdoor hothouse where trees grew to this height in only twenty-five years. The fruit used for palm-oil was harvested once every ten weeks—year round—and some of the same plants that were small enough to fit in the terrarium on Frank's desk grew to be ten feet tall here in PNG.

Frank walked up three stairs, past the soft, inviting chairs on a front porch that faced the ocean, and into the thatched hut that was to be his room for the night. It was palatial with a living room, bedroom, full kitchen and bath—a stark contrast from the small shanties he saw on the way from the airport in Hoskins where a family of eight or ten people lived in a space smaller than his room. The splendor of Walindi and his living space was a powerful reminder of the cultural and social distance between him and the people he was among.

"Will there be anything else?" Martha asked politely, eager to be of service.

"No, thank you. I just need some time to relax." Frank bowed in the traditional Japanese manner as Martha smiled at him, turned, and left the cottage. Cooled from the mid-morning heat by the overhead fans in his hut, Frank laid down on a king-sized bed and fell asleep—exhausted from his twelve thousand mile, two day journey.

Lindsey, Nikki, and Bethany had arrived in PNG on separate flights and met up at the airport in Port Moresby where they ran to catch the hot, noisy, one-hour puddle-jumper flight to this remote part of the country. They arrived at Walindi just in time for lunch and were shown to the table reserved for people attending the dive workshop on building creative organizations. They had some time to chat in the van about the last dive workshop they had attended together, but Nikki, a tall, skinny red head, was anxious to hear more about what had been going on with the two of them. She was glad they had the table all to themselves.

"So what's going on with you, Bethany?" Nikki asked enthusiastically. "You look great!"

Bethany Wringer was a strikingly beautiful and gentle Southern woman with smooth, cinnamon skin, penetrating auburn eyes, and shoulder-length black hair that she pulled back into a ponytail. The daughter of an ultra-fundamentalist preacher, Bethany broke free from this bondage with the help of her therapist and the last dive workshop. Her white pearl earrings, touch of make-up, and elegant-but-conservative dress revealed just enough of her shapely hips and thighs to let you know she had them, but without drawing attention to herself. The dark, sunken bags under her eyes and her furrowed brow were the daily remnant of long, sleepless anxiety-filled nights where inner voices and fears taunted her, causing Bethany to second-guess her decisions and ultimately doubt everything she said, knew, and believed. She and her husband, Matt, were trying to get pregnant, to no avail, and her doctor warned that pregnancy was unlikely until she significantly reduced her level of stress. Bethany had previously completed the RHETI and MBTI tools and knew that she was an ESTP, Enneagram Type Six who was committed, security oriented, reliable, hard working, responsible, and trustworthy.[14]

Bethany was action–oriented, loved the simple things in life, and was very accepting of other people. She had been a caseworker for the Social Services Department of the city and county of Myrtle Beach, South Carolina, for many years. She had a passion for helping children who came from dysfunctional families and her job allowed her to make a difference in some of their lives. Bethany had become increasingly cynical about the seriousness of the problems she encountered in the families she and her fellow caseworkers confronted every day. But in the last year or two she became aware that her cynicism was partly rooted in her own personality.

Being a manager in a government organization is normally a bureaucratic and thankless job, so Bethany avoided applying for promotions for years. She preferred doing, acting, and being out in the field, working with clients to sitting around in meetings, talking with other managers, and dealing with the complexities of politics, spin control, and posturing in the bureaucracy. Her client's problems, while challenging and requiring patience and understanding, were concrete and practical—they needed shelter, safety, and a way to make a living.

One day the director of the entire social services agency, Dana, invited Bethany to go to lunch, but asked her not to mention it to anyone in the office. After some pleasant chit chat, Dana cut right to the chase.

"I've been watching you for a long time, Bethany, and I'm impressed by your performance and your commitment to your clients. My guess is that you've purposely stayed out of management." Bethany nodded suspiciously, wondering where the conversation was going, as Dana moved on to the other items on her agenda.

Dana spent fifteen or twenty minutes explaining her vision for refocusing the entire agency on serving clients. Bethany listened and heard many of the things that she saw needed improvement but formerly had no hope of changing. When Dana was done talking, she asked Bethany what she thought about her plan.

"I've had the same vision as you just described for years," Bethany gushed with renewed hope. "But what can *I* do to help?"

"That's why we're having lunch." Dana smiled. "I'm going to be moving your department head, Jane, to another position and I want to know if you'd consider taking over as the new department head?"

While Bethany gave the impression of being friendly and warm, she was extremely perceptive about other people and was looking for Dana's hidden agenda—her "real" motivation—and any missing pieces of information that might reveal the underlying truth of what she was asking her to do. Bethany's suspicions created constant anxiety in her, anxiety that she projected onto people and situations in the world. She doubted her perceptions and intuitions and found it difficult to act independently of other people's opinions, especially people in authority over her.

Bethany lacked a sense of inner guidance, and had a difficult time recognizing this in herself. But Dana seemed sincere, and Bethany could not detect any underlying intentions or ulterior motives in her plan.

Partly out of a sense of obligation and partly because she felt the time was right, Bethany accepted the job offer and two weeks later she was the department head. As she sat in an office that was three times the size of any work space she had ever had, Bethany was waiting for the other shoe to drop. She wondered if Dana's promises of change would turn out to be empty like all the other unimplemented change initiatives she had lived through during her tenure at the agency. About a month into the job, Dana called a meeting with Bethany and a consultant named Toni.

"I want Toni to perform an organizational assessment of your department as a pilot program for refocusing the entire agency on serving clients rather than the endless series of forms and paperwork that typifies the operation now," Dana said, gazing intently at Bethany, then alternatively at Toni. "I know this is unfamiliar territory for you Bethany, but you can rely on my authority and guidance to support you through this complex and unfamiliar process. I want you to feel secure in the fact that your views and mine are aligned and that we're going in the same direction."

It took about four weeks for Toni to conduct the client satisfaction assessment, and when she presented the findings from her report in a close-out meeting to Bethany and Dana, it became clear that Bethany's department had some very unhappy clients. Many felt they were not getting the attention that they needed, especially in serious situations like spousal abuse and being victimized or sexually harassed by their employers. A two-year-old child had been murdered the previous year by her parents, partly because members of Bethany's staff had ignored fairly clear warning signs. These problems and more were manifested in the survey results. Bethany understood the factuality of the findings as well as anyone because she had seen it first hand, was deeply grieved, but formerly felt helpless to change it. She was very conscious of her experience in the outer world, so the images of poverty and squalor that she encountered day in and day out were indelibly impressed on her.

While Bethany gave the impression of living on the surface of life, without depth, soul, intuition, or feelings, her emotional connection to what she experienced in clients' homes and in the lives of the women and children she worked with went deep. Now, with Toni's report, her own experiences, and the client situations known to her fellow social workers, Bethany knew that what had troubled her for so long was finally documented by a third party outside consultant, hired by the Agency Director. Bethany asked Toni to make a presentation to her staff, and Dana attended to show her support for a change initiative.

Toni stood in the darkened room and talked her way through the presentation slides. "Studies have shown that seventy percent of all improvements to business processes come from the suggestions of customers and the end users of products and services." Toni gestured toward the data on the screen with her hand, confident about the factuality of the information. "My proposal is that Bethany head up an employee focus group made up of people from this department to study the client survey results and to look for both strengths and areas for improvement. Then the focus group should formulate an action plan for correcting the problems we've identified."

"I agree completely," Dana echoed immediately, giving Toni then Bethany a thumbs-up. "I'm putting Bethany in charge of this task and expect all of you to give her your full support in this new assignment." Dana scanned the roomful of staff members who were listening intently.

It didn't take long for the focus group to find that a large part of the tasks and responsibilities of social workers were filling out forms and paperwork to document what was going on out in the field. The front line social worker's attention was on office work, not serving clients. Bethany's focus group made three recommendations. First, they suggested the agency hire more staff to help with the office paperwork. Second, they recommended that the organization purchase an electronic record system with handheld electronic devices so data could be entered at a client's location in the field. Third, they wanted to shift the performance weighing factors in the social workers' performance appraisals to focus on measured client satisfaction, not completing paperwork. The focus group subsequently came up with a new set of performance criteria and presented their recommendations to the entire department. There was some slight concern on the part of a few staff members that the change was radical and could have ramifications they didn't yet understand, but by and large the rank and file of the department accepted the changes. Dana approved all three recommendations and the new performance criteria immediately.

Bethany's problems began six months later when she did her first performance review using the new criteria and people saw the consequences of shifting the weighing factors. Many employees who were formerly ranked as high performers because of how efficiently they did their paperwork became moderate performers using the new criteria. Not surprisingly, those who were formerly viewed as being moderate performers because they spent so much time in the field rather than doing paperwork became the star performers as the input of their clients counted much more heavily in the new measurement system. When these rankings were translated into the number of dollars that people received for their annual and merit raises, those who ranked lower were livid. Bethany told them that she would provide training to help them improve their performance, but many didn't want more training—that would require them to change the way they'd been doing their jobs for years.

This opposition to change from her staff only solidified Bethany's paranoid belief that life was a matter of survival and endurance and that her staff was trying to pull her down so they didn't look bad in front of Dana. Bethany's life had always been dominated by fear and she viewed herself as weak and helpless in a hostile, dog-eat-dog world of self-interest and Darwinian survival. Bethany feared that she was cowardly and weak and didn't have what it took to make it in the day-to-day struggle of life. The mounting conflict in the office was another reason why she had stayed out of management all these years. It was better to be a worker and make some difference in people's lives than to become a cynical manager who was powerless to change the system. She began to seriously doubt whether she had made the right decision by taking the job.

One of her direct reports named Joan spearheaded a character assassination of Bethany, saying that when she was a social worker Bethany was a poor performer and never did her paperwork on time or correctly. "That's why she's picking on us now," Joan snipped as three or four of Bethany's staff stood around the coffeepot waiting for it to finish brewing. "I can tell you story after story about all the problems *she* had accepting structure, taking orders, meeting deadlines. I have personal knowledge about how her 'dedication' to clients and the amount of time that she spent away from the office was really a cover-up for her to conduct personal business and run errands on company time." The others wagged their heads in agreement. "She doesn't see the implications that her decisions have on us and she doesn't care. You can't even discuss it with her without her getting in your face."

"Yeah..." the gossip group acknowledged in unison.

To Bethany's surprise, other managers at the agency began putting pressure on her to stop the initiative on client focus. They told her she was making too many changes too soon, but the reality was that she was making *them* look bad. They were maintaining the status quo—she was using innovative methods to improve the performance of her organization.

To top it off, Bethany's client-centered initiative was written up in the local papers as an example of how local government really cared about its constituents. The article infuriated her fellow managers. Joan clipped it out and taped it to the wall in the ladies room, then people began defacing it with pejorative graffiti.

"I'm sick and tired of how I'm being treated," Bethany complained bitterly to Dana.

"Trust me," Dana reassured her, "you have my full support. You are doing exactly what I want you to do. These people will not win in the end."

Dana sat forward in her chair, lowered her voice, and spoke seriously, "You know how dysfunctional and deeply entrenched the organizational culture is in this agency."

"Yes, I know you're right," Bethany replied in an exasperated tone. "I'm just shocked at how hard my staff and fellow managers are pushing back, knowing this is your initiative."

With the mid-year performance reviews behind her, Bethany decided to attend the dive workshop on building creative organizations in the hope of getting new insights and the courage to stay the course.

∽∽∽∽

After lunch, Bethany, Lindsey, and Nikki grabbed an ice cold drink, strolled out onto the deck over looking the magnificent ocean, grabbed some comfortable chairs, and sat like three kittens warming themselves in the sun as the pressure of their long trip began to fade away.

After a few minutes of welcomed silence, Nikki jumped out of her chair and pointed toward the ocean. "That must be the boat we're going on." Bethany and Lindsey peered out to sea between the hand-carved railings of the deck and said, "Wow!"—almost in unison.

"Man," Nikki said as the boat got closer to the dock, "that looks like a luxury yacht!"

Bethany chuckled, "Well that's because it is."

Lindsey was tired from all the action of the trip and she thought about going back to her room after lunch to get some time alone, but she hadn't seen her friends for so long that she decided to get her private space later. Her thoughts were interrupted when Nikki turned to her and asked, "So what's up with you, Lindsey? What have you been working on? Why did you come to the dive workshop?"

～～～～

Lindsey Barker had a chubby face framed by wire-rimmed glasses, short brown hair, a warm friendly smile, and the unmistakable twang of a thick New York accent. Lindsey's stocky frame, thick thighs, and meaty calves were normally clothed beneath loosely-fitting, conservative outfits in an attempt to hide her struggles with her weight and the endless string of diets she'd been on. Lindsey found much of her personal identity in her relationships, yet she didn't have a significant other and freely admitted that her Siamese cat, Oscar, was a vicarious stand-in for the husband she'd never found. Lindsey could work effectively with men in a professional capacity, but once the relationship crossed the threshold of romantic entanglements, things often became dysfunctional, emotionally disappointing, and ugly—that's why she preferred Oscar. Lindsey had previously completed the RHETI and MBTI tools and knew that she was an ISFJ, Enneagram Type Two who was caring, interpersonal, empathic, sincere, and warm-hearted."[15]

Lindsey had been the director of Human Resources for ten years before she was promoted to Vice President of Operations at the Brookhaven Corporation on Long Island, a company that performed engineering services and fabricated parts for the defense industry. People who knew her best argued that the personal changes she made outside of the office were largely responsible for her promotion to senior management. About eighty percent of the company's clients were either government contracts for the military or companies in Europe, and both market segments were increasingly demanding that Brookhaven become ISO 9000 certified just to do business with them.

Early in the twentieth century, standards were developed that placed systematic and statistical controls on manufacturing and production processes where scrap, rework, and the rejection of products through final inspection were costing companies enormous amounts of money. This body of knowledge became known as quality control.[16] While these techniques improved product quality and brought cost efficiencies, companies realized that organizational systems like procurement practices, training of workers, incoming inspection, and the documentation and reliability of these systems could also cause quality problems further downstream in the value chain. The body of knowledge and set standards that were developed to address these problems became known as quality assurance.

ISO 9000 is an international quality assurance standard that helps standardize work and business practices in countries that have very different cultures and performance standards. ISO 9000 establishes basic business practices that ensure quality products and services are provided to customers around the world. The ISO 9000 approach was simple: companies had to document what they did for work practices in policies and procedures; then they had to perform their work as described in the documentation. The company's motto became, document what you do, then do what you say. Brookhaven's president and CEO, Mario Migliore, made Lindsey responsible for developing and implementing the ISO 9000 program and for ensuring that the company passed the external audits that led to being certified. Over eighty percent of the company's revenue depended on her succeeding.

Mario had the utmost trust in Lindsey. She identified with him and supported him as his right-hand person and preferred to be the power behind the scene. Formerly, Lindsey had an unrecognized conflict about wanting to be in power and at the same time wanting to please people. Her colleagues interpreted this correctly as manipulative and duplicitous. She had in-groups and out-groups where decisions were weighted toward favorites, and no one dared cross her. But over the last couple of years, even those who hated and feared her admitted that she had honestly changed. Lindsey not only talked about helping her employees and how much she cared for them, but her deeds more closely matched her words—she treated people well regardless of where they appeared on Brookhaven's organizational chart.

Lindsey was "proud" about being such a loving, giving, and caring person, but she only focused on her positive feelings for others and was unaware of her repressed motives and needs. In the past, she would try to make herself indispensable to others and would purposely build dependencies through hidden strings that were attached to what she did for people. When they didn't respond to these tactics, she would flatter and manipulate them to get what she wanted. In other words, she gave in order to get. But more recently she had become a more honest and truly caring person who managers and workers trusted and wanted to be around.

Lindsey hired some consultants to help Brookhaven navigate the rigors of being certified. Early on in the ISO 9000 development process, Lindsey asked the two most senior consultants, "What's the relationship between the ISO 9000 program and the business objectives, goals, and performance measures in Brookhaven's strategic plan?" The two consultants looked at each other in confusion, then back at her, and the team leader said, "They're two separate programs and should remain so."

Their answer was a red flag. Lindsey found it odd that the systems used to define how work was performed would be disconnected from the strategic direction, objectives, and performance measures of the company. She began calling around to see how other organizations were approaching their ISO 9000 programs. To a person, other companies, top consultants, and even the ISO certifying body argued that they should remain separate programs. As implementation moved along, things did not improve and Lindsey began to realize that the strategic planning process and business objectives that gave overall direction to the company and the ISO 9000 program were destined to be two separate and almost unrelated systems in the company, like two organizational silos. This bothered her.

One day at a status meeting when the entire team was present, Lindsey began pushing on the consultants, pressuring them to help her solve the problem. "Look—there must be ways to integrate the ISO 9000 program and our strategic plan. I absolutely refuse to believe that there's no way to align the two systems and get them moving in the same direction. It's just good business sense—it has to be possible." Lindsey slapped her palm down on the table in utter frustration. She was surprised at the push back that she got from the consultants.

"Look—you hired us to help you get through the certification process, right?" The team leader asked rhetorically. "Well, I'm telling you—if you persist in trying to integrate the two systems in some 'innovative' way, I can't guarantee that Brookhaven will pass the external audits and get certified. Like it or not, our method has been proven to work." The team leader sat back in his chair, knowing how badly they needed certification and feeling confident that Lindsey didn't have enough time to switch consultants mid-stream.

"You've got me over a barrel," Lindsey snapped impatiently, shocked by the consultant's impertinence. "I'll back off publicly in meetings. But I am more convinced than ever that this is an ineffective add-on to our mushrooming overhead costs."

I'm going to find a way to solve this problem, Lindsey thought to herself. *I don't care what these morons tell me.*

As implementation progressed, Lindsey got lots of negative feedback from the managers and staff who had to write the ISO 9000 documentation. She honestly cared about how the extra workload caused people to put in extended hours and weekends, sometimes without pay. More importantly, she hated face to face hostility, confrontation, and rejection and took it very much to heart as a statement about *her* and how well she was doing her job. She was so concerned with getting approval from the staff that she became dependent on getting positive strokes. Now she missed the days where people appreciated her and what she did for them and the company. Lindsey was crushed by the disapproval and frustration employees were venting on her, despite the approval and encouragement that Mario heaped upon her privately and in the all-hands meetings.

Lindsey saw that ISO 9000 was just a big paper-generating exercise that did little to actually improve quality or organizational performance. Companies had spent hundreds of thousands of dollars and man-years of time and effort documenting their processes and procedures just to pass the certification audit. But when astute observers watched what actually happened on the shop floor, what was written in volume after volume of documented procedures was not the way people actually did their work.

One day she stormed into Mario's office and unloaded on him. "I'm telling you Mario, this 9000 thing has no return on investment other than to satisfy the requirement for bidding on contracts. It's one more thing to pile onto an already heavy workload for our managers and workers, and I can't see what it's going to do for us."

"I don't care if it doesn't do one blessed thing to improve the quality of our products or services," Mario yelled back. "The customer wants it. We're doing it. That settles it! Is there anything else I can do for you, Ms. Barker? If not, excuse me—I have work to do." He picked up a report, spun around in his chair so that his back was to her and began reading, signaling the conversation was over.

The whole situation infuriated Lindsey. She was becoming rigid, constantly complaining, overly focusing on the immediate impact of the ISO 9000 program and not seeing the broader implications of what it would do for the company.

She couldn't envision how the troublesome certification process would have a truly significant payoff because Lindsey viewed the present reality of implementation problems and the future possibilities for increased market share through the lens of her past experience. This told her that the company would probably do just fine without ISO 9000—despite what Mario said.

Riding together down the Long Island Expressway into Manhattan one day for a meeting, Lindsey tried to apologize and smooth things over with Mario.

"Look, Lindsey, I know how you get when you're stressed. Most times I dismiss it as an artifact of your personality." Mario quickly glanced at her, then back to the crowded freeway. "As sure as I'm sitting here, Lindsey, I never have, nor will I ever, loose sight of the urgency and importance of getting ISO certified as *required* to get future contracts. We need this just to stay in business. It's that crucial—that's why I put you in charge of it."

He's right, Lindsey said to herself, feeling ashamed at what a whiner she'd become. *I need to press on until the job's done and stop giving him grief.*

"There's enormous money to be made down the road, and the

increased revenue will easily pay the additional overhead costs of hiring more staff to get the work done and keep up with the paper," Mario reminded her, trying to broaden her perspective. "In fact, on some government funded projects we can actually tack the extra implementation costs back onto the contract as additional overhead, which raises our indirect cost recovery rate. So as counter intuitive as it sounds, the inefficiencies caused by the new quality program that you're so worried about will actually *make* the company money in the long run."

"I know that," she admitted softly, "but it flies in the face of everything I know about good business principles."

Mario gave her a sizable bonus when Brookhaven passed the final audit and became fully ISO 9000 certified. But in the days and weeks that followed, Lindsey found herself maintaining an enormous bureaucracy of notebooks filled with forms and procedures that did nothing to improve the quality of work, products, or services. At the same time she struggled to achieve the business objectives, goals, and targets she was responsible for in Brookhaven's strategic plan.

Over lunch with Mario one day, Lindsey laughed and shook her head. "You won't believe it. Me and five of my staff have been trained as ISO 9000 certified lead auditors, but it's nothing but a game of learning the rules and how to out smart the auditors who show up to assess the edifice of paper we've produced."

Mario shook his head too. "You've got it—all this quality stuff has nothing to do with being a high-performing organization." Mario smiled like the cat that swallowed the canary. "For us it's just the road to more contracts and more money."

On the surface, Lindsey came to the workshop to gain some insight on a path forward that would help her eliminate some of the non-value-added elements of the ISO 9000 program and more closely integrate its requirements with the day-to-day operation of the company. But down deep, she wanted to explore an abiding wound that prevented her from having satisfying relationships with men—something she was only marginally aware of.

※　※　※

Dan, James, and Cindy's plane arrived at the airport in Hoskins by 5:30 P.M. that evening, and as the resort's van sped toward Walindi they tried to take in as much of the scenery as they could with the last bit of daylight.

James could not take his eyes off Cindy's body as he drifted in and out of the powerful images of the erotic dream he'd had the night before. It was as if she was unconsciously hypnotizing him. The light of day had softened to the point where James had to abandon his usual position of anonymous safety behind his dark sun glasses, so there was no way to hide the fact that he was looking at her with longing. Out of the corner of her eye, Cindy began to sense him staring. She finally turned and shot him a disapproving look, hoping he would stop.

I feel like he's undressing me right here in the van, Cindy thought, surprised by his radical change of attitude toward her.

To break the mounting tension, Cindy finally said to no one in particular, "Look—the houses here are up on stilts rather than on the ground like up in the Highlands."

The driver immediately picked up on the cue. "Yes, in the Highlands the houses are built on the ground with a fire pit in the center of the floor because the high elevation makes it so cold. Here in the coastal regions we build our houses on stilts because the air flows under the house and relieves the pounding heat during the day."

The driver motioned off to the left of the van. "As you can see over there some people actually cook under their house in the evening so the heavy rains don't drown their fire. Other families have a separate cooking house like that one over there." He indicated another hut on the other side of the road.

They pulled into the Walindi Plantation Resort at about 6:15 P.M., just as the sun was setting, and went to the front desk to check in as their luggage and dive gear were taken to their respective thatched huts. Martha checked the list of dive workshop guests scheduled on the 5:30 P.M. van, then greeted each of them by name and welcomed them to the resort.

As she handed Dan an ice cold drink, he asked, "How many of the other people from the dive workshop are here already?"

"Everyone except Thomas, Maggie, and Rena is already here," Martha replied, fully informed about the whereabouts of the group's members. "They will arrive from Port Moresby tomorrow morning just before you board the ship. As for those who have already arrived, you'll see them here on the deck for drinks at seven o'clock tonight; then dinner will be served around that table at seven thirty." Martha pointed to where the group would be sitting.

Within an hour, James, Dan, Cindy, Lindsey, Nikki, and Bethany were laughing and talking over old times, reminiscing dive stories from the last dive workshop in Indonesia. It was just like they were at a class reunion. Martha approached them and introduced Frank as another member of the dive workshop that they hadn't met yet. The group welcomed him heartily as Lindsey said, "Come and join us, Frank."

James was hanging on Cindy's every word as she expounded on the insights she'd gained from their experience in the Highlands. Dan decided to abandon James in order to escape Cindy's intensity and introspection.

God—I can't take another minute of her philosophical mumbo jumbo, Dan lamented silently. *She's even got a spell over my buddy, James, now.*

Dan excused himself, moved over and started talking with others in the group who were exchanging diving stories and various lighter topics.

I wish Maggie were here already, Dan thought as he sipped wine, floated in and out of multiple discussions, and checked out the bodies of the women around him.

∿∿∿

That night, Cindy turned off the three circular fans in her thatched hut in order to hear the night sounds of the rain forest, the waves of the ocean crashing fifty feet away, and the sound of locals in the distance who talked and sang songs into the night. As the mechanical sound of the fan blades slowed then finally stopped, she laid in her bed thinking about the prospect of moving to Goroka for a year. She tuned in to the night sounds all around her, and felt like her thatched hut was an island in the midst of the rain forest where a collective, orchestrated symphony of frogs and crickets was punctuated by the lonely, melodic, occasional refrain of a single bird. She was listening to the night sounds of PNG—the same sounds that had been there for thousands of years, but soon she found herself pondering the meaning of James's long and penetrating stares in the van and then during dinner. She was both flattered and troubled by this change in his demeanor.

∿∿∿

One hut over, James was restless all night long, hovering on the edge of consciousness like the surf that met the black sand on Walindi's beach. He was unable to keep the dream image of Cindy and the ceremony out of his mind. By 5:00 A.M. Saturday morning, James was still half-awake, and the cool ocean air, aroma of sweet flowers, and lush jungle foliage were mingled with the smell of a fire from the hut of a local family who was already making breakfast. James dozed in and out of sleep, and by 6:30 A.M. he was startled by a deafening sound. It was raining—hard—as drops pounded on his roof like a hammer and smashed into the moss-covered rain forest floor with a fury. All he could think about was Cindy and the images in his dream, wondering what psychological truth they would reveal to him.

༄༄༄༄

At breakfast, James, Cindy, Lindsey, and Frank sat quietly, speaking only an occasional word as Bethany and Nikki chattered away at the other end of the table. The breakfast room at Walindi was magnificent, with hand-carved wooden beams containing storyboards, paintings, and pictures of fish and sea life. The table was covered with a fine linen cloth. Guests passed around hot coffee, tea, fruit, and requested their preferred style of eggs, bacon, or ham.

Cindy was quietly looking beyond the dining room to the ocean when she felt something stinging her legs. She looked across the table at James who pointed to a line of ants from the floor to the part of the table they were sitting at. "Are they biting you?" James asked, his face registering concern.

"Yeah," Cindy replied, suddenly tuning in to the fact that she was in PNG. She smiled at James and said, "This place is so pleasant that it's easy to forget where we are—it's like an island in the midst of a dream that's somewhere back in time."

Before James could respond, their conversation was interrupted by the sound of more guests arriving and the boys wrestling baggage and dive gear up onto the veranda outside the dining room. James heard heavy footsteps and recognized a voice as Thomas's as he poked his head into the dining room and said, "Good morning everyone! The crew said we could board the ship in about an hour, so get your dive gear and luggage together, check out of your hut, and I'll meet you on the boat for lunch. I've got some prep work to do, so I'll catch up with everyone later." Thomas left Maggie and Rena to greet the others, then went directly to the ship to begin preparing for the dive workshop.

∿∿∿∿

One by one the workshop attendees made the short walk from Walindi to the dock where the one hundred twenty foot ship *Origin* was tied up. Thomas Rose, the workshop leader, greeted each person as they boarded the boat. With light brown curly hair around the sides of his balding head, Thomas had deep blue searching eyes and was about twenty-five pounds overweight. An Enneagram Type Four with INFJ preference scores on the MBTI tool, Thomas had been a professional business consultant for over twenty years.

After some handshakes, hugs, and chitchat about people's trips and initial impressions of the ship, Thomas gathered the group together on the dive deck and announced, "I want to set sail as soon as possible. Lunch is at one o'clock in the dining room, and the opening session of the dive workshop will begin at three o'clock sharp around the wooden teaching table up on the Lido deck."

Various crewmembers showed people to their cabins and helped them get their dive gear set up. One level up from the dive deck was a dining room decorated in various shades of aqua and soft salmon. It was as well-appointed as the finest restaurants in PNG. The dining room could easily seat twenty-five guests although there were only nine workshop attendees, plus Thomas, on the boat. The large tinted windows that lined the dining room were designed for viewing the surrounding region in air-conditioned comfort like a high-end cruise ship. There were large racks full of books on the subjects of fish, coral reef, and underwater sea life. Cultural artifacts like handmade baskets, bows and arrows, stone clubs, spears, and feathered headdresses were mounted on the walls.

Outside the dining room on the Lido deck was an enormous wooden teaching table around which the dive workshop would be conducted. By the time the group arrived, Thomas had already turned the Lido deck into a seminar room with two flip charts and a white board at the front of the table. There were three clusters of chairs spread around the deck that would be used for small-group discussions. At 2:30 P.M., immediately after lunch, the ship began to pull away from the dock to make room for another dive boat. *Origin* would move to a mooring ball about one thousand feet offshore where Thomas and the group would spend the night, then sail to the first dive site in the wee hours of the next morning.

FOUNDATIONAL PRINCIPLES AND HOUSEKEEPING STUFF

At exactly 3:00 P.M., Thomas rang the mounted ship's bell that signaled an assembly. One by one people began coming from different parts of the ship to take their places at the wooden teaching table. In front of each chair there were handouts, name tents, booklets, pens, colored pencils and chalk for artistic drawing, a logbook, and a small, smooth stone. Thomas stood at the head of the table reviewing his notes as the last few people took their seats.

He introduced Anita and Janice as the scuba instructors who would be leading the diving part of the workshop. "I'll be doing all the dives with the group, bringing up the rear, so I can better observe. I'll turn the floor over to these fine instructors after this session so they can give us the opening briefing on the boat and our dive procedure."

Anita was about five foot three, mid-thirties, with light hair streaked from the sun, brown eyes, and a few freckles on her nose. With tanned skin, a blue and white baseball cap with the letters PADI embroidered across the front, and a bright red Speedo bathing suit that she was practically poured into, Anita *looked* like a dive instructor. It didn't take too long to tell that she'd been around the dive industry and knew what she was talking about. Intense, controlled, competent, and sometimes pushy when it came to what she thought about diving, Anita was the kind of dive professional that you'd trust with your life. She was a wizard behind the shutter of a camera or the button of an underwater video unit and had just accepted a new job shooting underwater documentaries that would start next month. Anita was obsessed with diving and felt called to teach everyone she dove with how to respect the sanctity of life in the underwater world. Hidden behind the image of a competent, all-knowing, former fourth grade teacher was a deeply reflective person with a child-like playfulness and sensitivity, but she didn't show this side of herself to many people.

Standing at the flip chart on the main deck of the ship, Thomas began. "Each of you has some three-by-five cards in your packet. I'd like you to take one and jot down a few lines about what you hope to get out of the workshop. Put your name on the card and when you're done writing, pass it up to me so I can read them over and learn what your expectations are for me and the workshop." A hush fell over the group as they began thinking and jotting things down on their cards.

∾∾∾∾

Frank Brighton didn't know what to write. He was a CPA who owned an accounting firm in the suburbs west of Chicago. A few years earlier, Frank had observed a trend. Clients who lived up to thirty minutes north of his location in Naperville, Illinois, were traveling to use his services because there were no established accounting firms in that immediate area. After writing a business plan, he opened another location up north and asked his son-in-law Rick to run the operation. The northern branch would focus on bookkeeping, accounting, and taxes, and Frank would still do CPA work and the more complicated business assessments that he had become noted for.

Frank rented the office space up north, made Rick the manager, and transferred three of his best staff and one hundred seventy-five thousand dollars in existing client revenues to the new location. The business grew to about a quarter of a million dollars in a little over eighteen months. The growth was due primarily to the word-of-mouth marketing that happened because of Joanne, an aggressive, competent, go-getter who had worked for Frank for over ten years and handled some of the firm's larger accounts.

Frank needed customer-focused people like Joanne to grow and maintain the business because he wanted to concentrate on projects like complicated analysis of the feasibility of high-tech start-ups, business assumptions, and developing financial strategies for sustained financial growth. Frank's approach to business consulting was to always start by getting his research, assumptions, and strategies right, not by getting the day-to-day facts of running the business right. When he consulted with clients, he was always more interested in analyzing the problems and discovering solutions than in implementing those solutions—for Frank, that was the client's responsibility, not his.

Joanne dropped by Frank's office one day to deliver some client information that he'd asked for and decided she'd take this opportunity to try to get some things straight with him. "You know that I want to please you, Frank, and do a good job," she said, obviously disturbed, "but I've still got real problems with how Rick is managing the northern location." Frank looked up from the paperwork she'd given him, "Why? What's going on?"

"Can I be honest with you?" Joanne said nervously, waiting a moment for a positive nod from Frank. "He's lazy—he blames others for his mistakes, and he's constantly trying to push his work off on me and the other staff."

"Have you talked to him about it?" Frank responded, looking only mildly concerned.

"I've tried," Joanne pleaded, "but he gets passive-aggressive and plays dumb, as if he doesn't know what I'm talking about. The other two people in the office see what's going on too, and I spend a major portion of my time doing damage control with them so they don't quit."

This was not the first time Joanne had talked to Frank about Rick, and to date he'd done nothing to address her concerns. "These are all good points," Frank conceded "Let me think about how to handle it. It's a touchy situation for me because, while I know you're right, I've got family obligations—he's my son-in-law, if you know what I mean."

"I know," Joanne said apologetically, "that's why I hate to bring it up–but it's getting worse, Frank. Much worse."

"Let me think about it, and I promise I'll get back to you," Frank said walking Joanne out of his office.

He'll never get back to me, Joanne thought as she broke away from Frank and headed for her car, *he never does—he wants me to deal with it so he doesn't have to.*

~~~~

Frank was productive as a leader and decision-maker when he was insulated from front-line interactions and conflicts between employees. He made decisions based on unemotional facts, not on how people felt. Because the northern location was doing okay financially, at least on paper, he saw no need to shine the light on the personal problems that Joanne was having. On the occasions she brought the conflict with Rick up, Frank would appear to go along with what she wanted, but in the end he took no specific action. Joanne had some legitimate complaints and Frank knew it, but facing the situation directly would cost him plenty, especially with his wife and daughter. The family dynamics were just too complicated to try and explain to Joanne.

One day after Rick had just infuriated Joanne by blaming her for losing a client that *he* had driven away with his incompetence, she unloaded on Sally, one of the others in the office, about Frank's failure to act on her concerns.

"After ten years of working with him, I can tell you—Frank thinks everything to death. It's almost like he has to understand every possible outcome before he acts," Joanne complained, utterly frustrated. "He's one of the smartest guys I know. He reads constantly and stores up enormous amounts of knowledge like a squirrel gathering food for the winter, but he rarely acts on his knowledge."

Sally shook her head in full agreement. "I know, it's almost like he *substitutes* thinking for doing."

"Precisely," Joanne snapped her fingers and pointed at Sally. "Thinking about solving the Rick problem and running through scenarios of how to deal with it is far less threatening than actually *doing* something about it! I think he's overwhelmed by the practical problems of life, so he lives in some inner intellectual world that he's made for himself. He watches life go by like a spectator at a parade."

"Bingo," Sally concurred, shaking her head sadly, "you hit the nail on the head."

As the conflict with Joanne got worse, Rick ignored it hoping it would just go away and painted nothing but rosy pictures in his weekly reports to Frank. But Frank knew better because of his private conversations with Joanne. The real depth and magnitude of the problem was almost completely masked by the increase in clients and revenues secured by Joanne, and the only question was when she would quit out of utter frustration.

Joanne's non-compete agreement with the firm expired and the task of renewing it fell through the cracks. Things had gone from bad to worse between her and Rick, and despite her continued discussions with Frank, there was no change in sight. Joanne knew she was the backbone of the business because the clients she serviced were about sixty percent of the total revenues of the northern location, plus her reputation had brought in most of the new accounts. She decided it was time for a showdown. She began confronting the situation with Rick and Frank by documenting the mismanagement of the business in weekly memos. Rick would meet with her, admit that he needed to do better, but then almost nothing would change.

When she finally reached her last straw, Joanne walked in and dropped her resignation on Frank's desk. "I told you it was either him or me," she said simply, then turned around and marched out of his office. Frank was speechless.

The following day, he tried to smooth things over by taking her out for a farewell lunch to "wish her well." Rather than rehash the problems yet one more time, they both decided to just chat about the good old days and things that were happening outside of the office. "So what are you going to do now, Joanne?" Frank asked after an uncomfortable lull in the conversation.

"Oh, I'll probably just try to do a little accounting work from home and take more time to do things I've been wanting to do for a long time."

Frank wished her well, having no idea what her leaving would mean for him.

Within two weeks, the majority of the big clients that she'd serviced had called to tell Frank that they were changing accountants. Although they didn't say why, it didn't take Frank long to figure out where the clients were going.

"Joanne!" Frank's voice threatened over the phone. "What are you doing stealing my customers? I'll take legal action against you. You've got a signed 'non-compete' that forbids you from doing this."

"We wouldn't be having this conversation now if you had been this upset about how Rick was mismanaging your company and making my life miserable," Joanne snarled back. "Other than that, all I have to say is, you'll be hearing from my lawyer," and she hung up.

The letter that Joanne's lawyer sent in response to Frank's threats over the phone included a copy of the expired non-compete agreement, proving it had been out of force for almost a year. Frank realized he had no legal recourse.

Frank grabbed the phone and called Rick.

"He's in a meeting with a client, Frank," Sally said timidly, sensing how angry he was.

"I don't care," Frank insisted. "I want to talk with him right now."

After a few seconds, Rick picked up the phone and Frank demanded an explanation for the expired non-compete agreement.

"It was one of the things that fell through the cracks. I've been slammed," Rick said defensively, hoping to deflect his responsibility for the problem. "You've seen the increase in the number of clients and revenue. How do you think that happens?" Now Rick was trying to take credit for Joanne's business success.

"You've got a lot of nerve calling up here and interrupting me when I'm with a client," Rick snapped, strategically turning Frank's anger around. "Where's your customer focus? I'm overworked and understaffed and I'm trying to keep my finger in the dike so this Joanne thing doesn't ruin us."

Frank was incredulous about these lame excuses. They only revealed the depth of Rick's blind spots and how unaware he was of his total lack of initiative, his weak management style, and his practice of pushing his own work off on others.

In frustration, Frank called Mike, an old friend in Honolulu, trying to get some perspective on how he should proceed. "Joanne's departure really puts me in a bind. If I fire Rick for incompetence like I should, I will seriously alienate my wife and daughter, and then they'll be on my back. I know Rick won't be able to find another job anywhere close to his current salary, so if he's unemployed for long enough, they'll lose their house and have to move in with Connie and me, again. But if I keep Rick on, I'm not sure I can salvage the northern location."

Frank was sounding deeply demoralized over what seemed like a hopeless situation, so Mike interjected, trying to relate Frank's situation to his experiences in Hawaii. "It's the same kind of problem I have with the culture here in the Islands. It's almost impossible to find good help. I always say, 'A warm body is better than nobody.' So we continue to pay poor performing employees a salary, take really important work away from them so they can't hurt the company, then do damage control with the few good staff—who are seriously overworked."

"Yeah," Frank sighed in shocked disbelief that he was contemplating doing the very same thing rather than deal with the family fall-out of making the right business decision.

Over the next few weeks, as Frank began picking up the pieces of his business, Rick still failed to sense how close to the line he was with his father-in-law. Frank now knew for a fact that his son-in-law was a loser he was saddled with for life. He never expressed his feelings about the situation directly, but Frank had powerful emotions and revealed little of this inner world. Instead, he concealed his true feelings and thoughts behind the mask of an unemotional, cognitive fortress and was convinced that others couldn't see behind the wall. With people other than Rick, Frank distanced himself from his feelings about what happened with Joanne and recounted the details with a detached objectivity that made people think he was talking about someone else.

These problems had only reinforced the fact that Frank had always felt restless in his profession. He had enormous intellectual capability and probably should have been a theoretical physicist or a philosophy professor. His intellectual curiosity, ingenuity, and myriad ideas and insights made the routine of running an accounting company difficult, so he fed this undernourished part of his personality by attending lectures and talks at the world-class particle physics laboratory, Fermilab, that was only a twenty-minute drive from his home. He got to know some of the physicists socially and felt a strange kinship with some of them. Like Frank, they had some difficulty communicating with people about the mundane, pedestrian realities of life. When a client asked Frank a simple question, he felt compelled to establish the conceptual and theoretical foundation upon which the question rested, qualifying all the exceptions he knew about. To do anything less made him feel like he wasn't truthfully answering the question to a level of precision he felt comfortable with.

※※※※

Within a few months of Joanne's departure, Frank brought Rick back to the main office as his special assistant and hired Mary Beth, an experienced accountant from an East Coast firm. She was as competent as Joanne was, so he asked her to run the northern location. Not only did Mary Beth begin to bring in new clients, she also contacted former clients who had left with Joanne and won some of them back by telling them that the operation was now under new management, sans Rick.

Back at the main office, Frank tried to find useful things for Rick to do, like reviewing the firm's payroll, writing up procedures, installing software, or helping with the HR function, but when he was honest with himself, Frank knew this was just busy work. The truth was that Rick was warehoused at a high salary, just like Joanne had predicted, and Frank's focus on the bottom line made carrying this dead weight very difficult.

But Frank couldn't write all *that* on the three-by-five.

After a few minutes had passed, Thomas circled the group and gathered up the cards. "I see James and some of the others have brought their journals, but for those of you who didn't, there's a logbook in front of you that can function as a journal for the trip. I'd like you to log your significant experiences, insights, and any dreams you may have.

"I'd like the workshop to be an adult learning environment, so if you want to stand and stretch your legs or walk over to the railing of the ship and listen from there for a while, feel free to do so. You should use the colored pencils and pens to draw, diagram, or visually express your thoughts and insights in your journal. If you want to diagram the relationships between some of the concepts I'll talk about, feel free to do that too, whether or not you share your work with the class."

"What are these stones for?" Nikki asked, picking up the one in front of her and rolling it around in her hand.

"Those are thinking stones," Thomas smiled as he pulled his out of his pocket. "A thinking stone is a tangible expression of the process of turning a thought or concept over and over in your mind." Thomas demonstrated the maneuver. "I use mine when I'm mulling over some problematic issue that I can't seem to break through on. Use yours however you want." He placed his stone back in his pants pocket.

"During some of the sessions, we'll break up into small groups so you can discuss and apply the workshop material to situations you're dealing with back in your organization. If you have a personal issue or question that you want to discuss with me, but you don't want to discuss in your small group or with the large group, write it on a three-by-five and put it in the center of the table face down. I'll collect them at the end of each session, then meet with you one-on-one between sessions.

"My goal is to make this workshop as participatory as possible.

That's why I had you read select articles from the *Harvard Business Review* prior to coming. I hope you've come prepared to discuss what you've read and to contribute and learn from each other's experiences. At the end of this first session you're going to do an exercise. I'm going to ask you to write a case study of your company that describes the most important problems you're currently facing. In no more than five hand-written pages, I want you to describe the problems and their root causes in as objective and honest a way as possible. When you're done, you'll give them to Anita who will make copies for everyone with the ship's Xerox machine. I'll hand a set of the nine case studies out to each of you at dinner tonight, so remember that what you write will not be confidential.

"The goal is for each attendee to read over all nine case studies and then use them to apply and better understand the material I'm presenting. Research has shown that people forget about seventy percent of what they learn in workshops within seventy-two hours. The percentage of material that is retained goes up enormously when we learn how to apply it to problems we're facing in our lives."

Thomas stood in silence for a few seconds to let his course preamble sink in. He then said seriously, "Look, I don't want to just stand up here and lecture for three days—*but I will if I have to*. I'd like you to participate as much as possible and I've set the workshop up so you can if you want to. I will be presenting and discussing timeless principles that apply to all organizations, regardless of context. *You* will have to apply them to the situation in your organization and share those insights with the group in order to get the most out of the workshop. My goal is to turn our time together into a graduate-level seminar on business excellence where you participate with your questions, comments, and insights—and in doing so you help teach the class."

Thomas waved the stack of three-by-five cards he had collected. "I have your expectations for the workshop here on these cards, but are you clear on what *my* expectations are for the workshop?" The group nodded in concert.

"Okay, then let's get started." Thomas walked to the railing of the ship, turned toward the group and asked rhetorically, "Why hold a workshop on building creative organizations in Papua New Guinea?"

He sauntered back to the head of the teaching table and continued. "There are two reasons. First, this setting completely removes you from your everyday life. While the ship has a two-way radio and satellite phone for emergencies, your cell phones, e-mail, and other electronic devices that you use to connect yourself to your everyday life won't work. Floating here in the midst of hundreds of islands is like being dropped in the middle of a wilderness, but with all the amenities of home. The location is designed to give you *perspective* on your life. My goal is to help you view your life back home from a distance. Being isolated and removed will coerce you into becoming a spectator of how you live, and becoming a spectator is one of the essential elements of all creative change.

"The second reason I chose PNG is that Papua New Guinea helps us to understand the impact that creativity has had on our world. Imagine if you could snap your fingers and make the products of human creativity disappear—everything that is man-made. How would your world change? How different would the result be here in Papua New Guinea as opposed to New York City?"

Thomas pointed to the shore. "The effect of human creativity is powerfully embodied in the differences between the amenities that we have on this boat and how the local people live there on shore. The world you live in back home, and on this boat, is made possible by our knowledge of how to obtain shelter from the natural elements, control our food and water supply, harness and use energy sources, create and sustain currency-based economies, and invent social structures, science, technology, and culture. This knowledge is all the result of human creativity, and that's why I claim that reality is a product of the creative process. Reality is a social construct. Reality is man-made."

Thomas grabbed a marker from the table, walked to the flip chart, and wrote the words REALITY IS MAN-MADE on the blank first page in large block letters. "Because the results of the creative process form so much of our everyday life, it's easy to forget that we are the *creators* and *builders* of this reality. When we forget that reality is our own creation, we *reify* it and defend it as if it were objective truth. The daily commute back and forth to work, office politics, a lack of meaning and significance in our work, our choices and the consequences of those choices become reified 'truths.' We find ourselves saying, 'that's just the way the world is.'

"Because it's so different from our lives back home, PNG is one of the few places left in the world that shows us the extent to which our Western reality results from human creativity. The creative process and its effect on our everyday life are easier to see when we juxtapose handmade dugout canoes like the ones that will pull up to the boat to trade with us, with the opulence of the ship we're on.

"So the ship," Thomas gestured stem to stern, "while it has all the comforts of home, except for your electronic devices, will create well-defined boundaries within which we will learn. Every workshop group is different because the people and the life experiences they bring to the table are so varied. You will bring who you are and where you've been to create the overall mix of the dive workshop experience."

Thomas rested both of his hands on the edge of the teaching table and his tone became more serious and intense. "Over the next several days, as we move into the routine of learning, then diving, and spending all of our time within the confines of the ship, the veneer of initial politeness will begin to fray. The ship will become a microcosm, a hothouse that will stimulate insights about you, other participants, and the organizations you own, manage, or work for. It may also create some tension between some of you as you spend lots and lots of time together and most probably get on each other's nerves, like the old phrase, 'familiarity breeds contempt.'

"The creative process is the engine that drives personal and organizational change," Thomas smiled and lightened up, "and you'll find that the routine of the dive workshop is built around that process. How many of you have had the experience where you've tried to remember someone's name and you just couldn't?"

Several people raised their hands.

"It's normally, when you stop thinking about it, that the name just pops into your head," Thomas chuckled. "That's how the creative process works—we apply sustained effort to learn something or solve a problem; then we stop thinking about it, do something totally unrelated like scuba diving, and that's when the creative insights usually come. That's how I've designed the dive workshop. There will be three intensive teaching sessions each day where we will learn about and debate the principles of business excellence and three powerful strategies for building creative organizations.

"Each session will be followed by a dive where you will see some of the most magnificent coral reefs in the world. As Anita and Janice will explain in more detail later, we will limit our bottom-time to sixty minutes because surfacing around the same time and getting everyone back on the boat will enable us to limit our nitrogen intake and keep to our schedule.

"My goal is to use the workshop material and the dive experiences to purposely *deconstruct* your views about how the creative process works in you, other people, and your organization." Thomas's eyes took on a deep intensity as he surveyed each member of the group. "I want to *stir up* the creative process in each of you and illustrate the three strategies by linking them to your personal experience and to the actual business problems that you face in your organization. I'll use the case studies you write to challenge you to think creatively.

"As I will describe in a few minutes, it's the unconscious dimension of the creative process that will produce deep change within you, with or without your conscious effort, and sometimes even against your desires. Likewise, implementing the three powerful strategies in your organization will produce deep cultural change below the surface of organizational consciousness, with or without the conscious consent of owners, managers, and workers, and sometimes even against their intentions."

Thomas gestured toward the ocean. "The underwater world is a great place to reflect on the material presented in the teaching sessions—it's quiet and all you'll hear is the sound of your bubbles. At the end of each session, you'll receive a dive slate with summary points of that session written on it. Clip it to your Buoyancy Control Device (BCD) so you can review the material underwater. But even if you don't consciously think about the workshop material and you just enjoy the dive, the creative process will continue working deep below the surface of your consciousness.

"As a practical note," Thomas said, waving a cautious forefinger, "some of you may start to have ear problems because you're not used to diving three tanks a day. If this happens, you'll have to take your one hour of reflective time by snorkeling, rather than diving. We'll try to arrange the dive sites so that, if people are forced to snorkel, there will be reef structure at about thirty to forty feet and you'll still get a good view of the underwater world here in PNG. But I can assure you, snorkeling will not have the same effect as the underwater experience of scuba diving."

∽∽∽∽

Maggie Spinner was staring off the port side of the boat at a fourteen thousand foot volcano with a tower of smoke protruding from its top as if she was being drawn into the inner world of feelings and ideas. Maggie had been Vice President of Public Relations for a large chemical company named Enton near Rocky Flats, Colorado, which put her center-stage in an enormous legal battle with environmental groups that accused the company of dumping toxic waste that was leaching into the aquifer of the city of Broomfield. After accidentally discovering that Enton *was* dumping toxic waste, she confronted the company president and demanded that they stop or she would turn them over to the authorities. She quit her job, ventured out on her own, and opened a marketing company called the Spinner Group.

Maggie was driven to succeed and valued success more than anything, even if it meant manipulating and deceiving people. She put her feelings aside, pressed on to attain her goals, and hid and repressed those parts of herself that were inconsistent with the image of success. It was difficult to know what Maggie really believed and who she really was because she was like a chameleon who took on whatever appearance was required to impress people and to get them to buy her ideas. But even Maggie underestimated how much time and energy it would take to make the new company go. She worked night and day, seven days a week and this still was not enough. Her personal life was almost non-existent. She had been doing graduate level studies in spirituality and world religions at CU Boulder but had to put that on hold. More importantly, Maggie had been going with Troy for three years and really wanted to marry him.

"Maggie, you know I love you more than life itself, but having at least one child is an important part of my one trip though life," Troy had whispered gently as they cuddled in front of the fireplace one night. "Dr. Bloom said you're healthy and can have children, but we can't wait too long. I want to be as honest with you as I can sweetheart…I love you and I really want to marry you, but I need to know that you'll have my baby. I realize how important your business is to you and I'll understand if you don't want to have another child. But I want to be straight with you—if it's something you're not up for, then I'll have to move on."

Secretly, Maggie felt that because she already had a child from her first marriage—her daughter Rena—to have another one was not what she wanted for her life at the age of forty-three. Changing diapers and caring for a baby just didn't fit into Maggie's image of being a successful professional. She knew this was her own ego and vanity, and she didn't know how to approach this issue with Troy without derailing the relationship—so she found ways to agree with Troy, yet postpone getting pregnant.

Maggie had put a lot of energy into learning how to come across well, where form was equally important as substance, and projecting the image of being pragmatic, goal-oriented, and efficient was paramount. She used these same skills to make money for her marketing clients, that's why she was so good at what she did. After two years of this grueling pace, she had managed to build a stable client portfolio. But her biological clock was ticking and Troy was starting to put more and more pressure on her to keep her promise about starting a family. Maggie increasingly had to lie about her true feelings. "Just give me a few more months to get over the hump on this new business," Maggie would plead, "I'm still on track to get pregnant—I just need a little more time."

Her daughter Rena graduated from Colorado College with a degree in business and marketing and joined the Spinner Group. From the start, Maggie wanted Rena to move to Boulder, learn the business, then move back to Colorado Springs and open a branch office as a way of growing the company even faster. In fact, Maggie wanted Rena to take over the company someday so she could reap the rewards of her hard work, retire, or move on to doing other things. Rena went along with Maggie, but she was under enormous pressure from her husband not to.

"Mom wants me to go back to Colorado Springs and start up a new office," she said to her husband Joel, with a desperate tone in her voice. "We've got lots of friends back in Colorado Springs…"

Joel cut her off bluntly. "But I've already found a job here in Denver because *this* is where you said you wanted to live. The last thing I want to do is to uproot ourselves again and to move back to Colorado Springs, just because your *mother* wants us to!"

Rena lowered her head as Joel continued to hammer on her with an ongoing criticism of Maggie's values and lifestyle. "You see how hard she works just to keep her business afloat. I won't allow you to even think about opening a new office in the Springs. You tell her to come talk to me—I'll set her straight about what's important in life."

"I agree," Rena pleaded, "but how do I approach this with Mom without causing waves?"

It angered Joel how easily she capitulated to Maggie, and Rena felt stuck in the middle. So she went to work day after day, and choked down her feelings, saying nothing.

Maggie attended a luncheon talk at the Boulder Rotary Club where John Brown discussed his book, *How to Run Your Business So You Can Leave It in Style*.[17] Even though she had only started the Spinner Group a few years ago, Brown's talk planted the seed in her mind that if she wanted to retire in about fifteen years she had to begin thinking seriously about two things in order to make that happen. First, she needed to build the kind of organizational structures, systems, and performance measurement system that would allow her to back away from the day-to-day operations of the business and either let someone else in the company take over, or to sell the company outright.

As Mr. Brown explained to the highly-attentive assembly, "When you're running a 'mom-and-pop' operation, a small number of people can operate with informal structures and systems where the knowledge of what the company does and how it does it is in people's heads—largely oral tradition. With small companies, informality can actually be a competitive advantage because informal business processes are very adaptable to the forces and pressures of customers and the business environment. But as the company grows, informality becomes a liability because communication, decision making, and the ways in which work is organized become increasingly complex.

"Knowing when to begin building more formal structures and systems is the key. This requires small businesses to 'boot strap' themselves into a new way of working. They have to document business knowledge and the business processes they use to produce products and services, and at the same time continue doing the work of serving customers. For most businesses, this is like driving a car and trying to change a tire at the same time."

The luncheon talk raised the question for Maggie of exactly *who* would take the company over when she retired. One option would be to develop a succession plan that earmarked a current or future employee to help Maggie build the company, then transition that person into the leadership role as she progressively backed away. Because Troy had spent so many years as a ski instructor and had no retirement or health care benefits, Maggie's company would have to provide their health insurance for the rest of their lives. Picking her successor would allow Maggie to maintain some level of control over the benefits the company offered even after she was disengaged from day-to-day operations.

Maggie's future would be secure if Rena would agree to step up to the plate in a leadership role. This had become a source of irritation between them because Rena didn't want to work as hard as a growing small business required—she wanted to settle down with her new husband, have a family, and enjoy the simple things in life. They had endless conversations where Maggie tried to force Rena to be more realistic about her expectations. One day they sat down and made a list of the things that Rena wanted to have, and possessions she wanted to own, then estimated the amount of money she would need to earn to support that lifestyle. The salary required was a shock to the idealistic Rena. Then they brainstormed which professions would allow her to earn that much money and not surprisingly the highest paying jobs were in areas that she was not trained in or was not interested in working in.

"Joel, you don't understand," Rena pleaded. "Taking over the Spinner Group is an option that would allow me to earn what we need to live well and would guarantee that I have a career that will give you, me, and our family the things we want in life."

Joel exploded, enraged by her conciliatory attitude toward Maggie's way of life, "I can't live with the constant stress, long hours, and financial pressure that running the Spinner Group requires. If you'd have told me *that* was what you wanted out of life, I might not have married you. I want you to get a nine-to-five job so you can leave your worries at the office when you go home and enjoy doing things and going places with me and the kids in the evenings and on weekends."

The alternating discussions with Maggie then with Joel only put Rena under more pressure.

Maggie surrounded herself with employees who thought like her—people who were bright, aggressive, competitive, and wanted to move up the career ladder as quickly as possible. The atmosphere and sense employees got when they worked for Maggie was that they needed to be hard driving and successful. But in more reflective moments, Maggie had some doubts about her own future. She feared spending what was left of her life solving problems, making her clients successful, building her company—and then, in the end, falling into the deep, dark emotional abyss where she questioned the meaning of her life and whether she had accomplished anything that was truly important. Despite how hard she was on Rena, Maggie secretly knew that her daughter's focus on enjoying life provided a desperately needed balance in her life, but she wasn't going to admit it.

The tension between Maggie and Rena over this issue had gotten to the point where it was difficult to hide during company meetings and even in casual conversation at the office. To make matters worse, Maggie had a high-performing employee named Shane who wanted a part of the action. He had followed Maggie to the new company from Enton and immediately sensed the conflict between the two women over the company's future. Shane was hardworking, made a valuable contribution, and tried to demonstrate all the leadership and management skills that would signal Maggie that *he* was the person to take over the Spinner Group.

One night over dinner, Maggie confided in Troy, "It's become increasingly difficult for Shane to hide his aggressive attitude toward building the business and his covert strategy for pushing Rena out of the way. You know, Troy, it puts me in a very tough spot. If I just look at it from the business perspective and the bottom line, Shane would probably do a much better job than Rena of running the business, and that would ensure a better future for us financially. But somehow, letting Shane take over and push Rena aside makes me feel like I'm selling my own daughter down the river."

Troy looked at her and nodded in silent agreement.

Maggie had this other, almost totally hidden, side to her. On the surface, she was so occupied with the outer world that she appeared cold and unemotional, and the power and depth of her feelings and emotions for Rena were rarely expressed directly in their relationship. When you would ask Maggie what she felt about something, she'd often reply, "I don't know what I feel"—and the truth was, she really didn't. She was at a loss to experience and articulate her feelings and motives because they were submerged like a sunken ship in the unconscious part of her personality. Maggie's emotions were undeveloped, infantile, and stunted, yet she vesseled them in her journal, writing long love letters to Rena—evidence of the deepest and most vulnerable part of her emotional life. Paradoxically, Maggie guarded these journal entries like her most valuable possession, yet in her everyday life she disowned this part of who she was. The secret depths of her love for her daughter were in stark contrast with how disgusted Maggie appeared to be with her about her future in the business. Maggie hated open-ended situations and demanded closure.

"You know, Troy, more and more I find myself thinking about just building the company and readying it for sale to the highest bidder. If I get enough money for the Spinner Group, it would provide the retirement income and health benefits you and I need, but that means giving up control of the company that I've worked so hard to build." Maggie locked eyes with Troy. "What really bothers me about that scenario is that I won't be able to ensure that Rena can earn the kind of salary she needs to get what she wants out of life."

Troy saw the tough spot Maggie was in but didn't know what to say to help her move beyond the dilemma.

Maggie attended the workshop to learn about building organizational structures and systems and to work through the succession plan issue with Rena. A secret reason for attending was to figure out how to tell Troy that she didn't really want more children. This was a pressing issue because backing out of her promise to Troy could harm their relationship—he would feel like he'd been lied to, and truthfully, Maggie had deceived him.

~~~~

A change in the cadence of Thomas's voice brought Maggie's attention back to the dive workshop. "There are as many approaches to organizational development, or OD, as there are people willing to buy them and they are constantly being repackaged and sold as something new—the 'real' answer to what ails your company. Some employees cynically refer to this repackaging process as the 'flavor of the month.' Others like Eileen Shapiro call it 'fad surfing in the boardroom'—riding the crest of the latest management wave, then paddling out just in time to catch the next one.[18] New OD methods rarely produce the results they promise and often fatigue the rank and file in organizations, as owners and managers quickly move on to the next 'flavor of the month.'"

Some workshop attendees wrote in their journal, while others nodded in first-hand agreement with what Thomas was saying.

"Organizations who are constantly switching from one management fad to another or continually reorganizing eventually lose hope that real change can ever happen. My own view is that the cure for the 'flavor of the month' is to find the timeless principles of OD, then stay with them for much longer than about thirty days.

"In fact," Thomas said, quickly glancing down at his notes, "one study evaluated more than two hundred well-established management practices over a ten-year period in one hundred sixty high-performing companies. The data showed that successful companies understood and implemented business basics like strategy, execution, organizational culture, and structure.[19] What mattered most wasn't *which* approach to organizational excellence was used, the key to success was developing and deploying it in a *consistent and thorough manner*.

"So how do you sort through the business literature and find the repository of organizational knowledge that actually produces business excellence?" Thomas asked, raising a rhetorical forefinger. "I use a three-step approach. First, I look for *timeless principles* of organizational development. Not only do they actually exist, one study of visionary companies showed that some of these methods date back to the 1800s.[20] I'm talking about timeless principles that have been articulated by people like Jim Collins, John Kotter, Peter Drucker, Edgar Schein, Daniel Goleman, Robert Kaplan and David Norton, Chris Argyris, Stephen Covey, Peter Senge, and others like them.[21]

"The second step is to follow the advice of Michael Dell."

Nikki's hand shot into the air as she blurted out, "Do you mean Michael Dell of Dell Computers?"

"Yes," Thomas said, picking up a three-by-five card. "I'd like to quote Dell's corporate strategy. 'Now if you're in a race with twenty players that are all vying to produce the fastest graphics chip in the world, do you want to be the twenty-first horse, or do you want to evaluate the field of twenty and pick the best one?'[22] Dell's business strategy is to choose the best computer components, build the device exactly the way the customer wants it, then provide outstanding customer service long after the sale.

"In much the same way, when you're looking for an approach to organizational excellence, how do you compete with the quality and diversity of research and ideas presented in publications like the *Harvard Business Review*, or the authors I just mentioned? The answer is, *you can't*, so why try?" To the group's surprise, Thomas's face took on a hopeful look. "Rather than jump into that race, I've taken the timeless principles they've developed and woven them into the fabric of this dive workshop. That's why I sent you the reading list from *HBR* and the other business writers."

Various people shook their heads, indicating they had read the material, while Frank shuffled through a massive pile of notes that he'd made from the reading list.

"The third step is to understand the cause and effect relationships between the generic functions found in any organization, how the complexity of those functions increases with organizational size, and how the timeless principles should be used to facilitate organizational effectiveness. I've developed something called the Organizational Diagnostic and Planning Tool, or the ODPT for short, that explains these interrelationships. It's shown up here in Figure 1." Thomas paused to turn a page on his flip chart, revealing a full-page image of Figure 1.

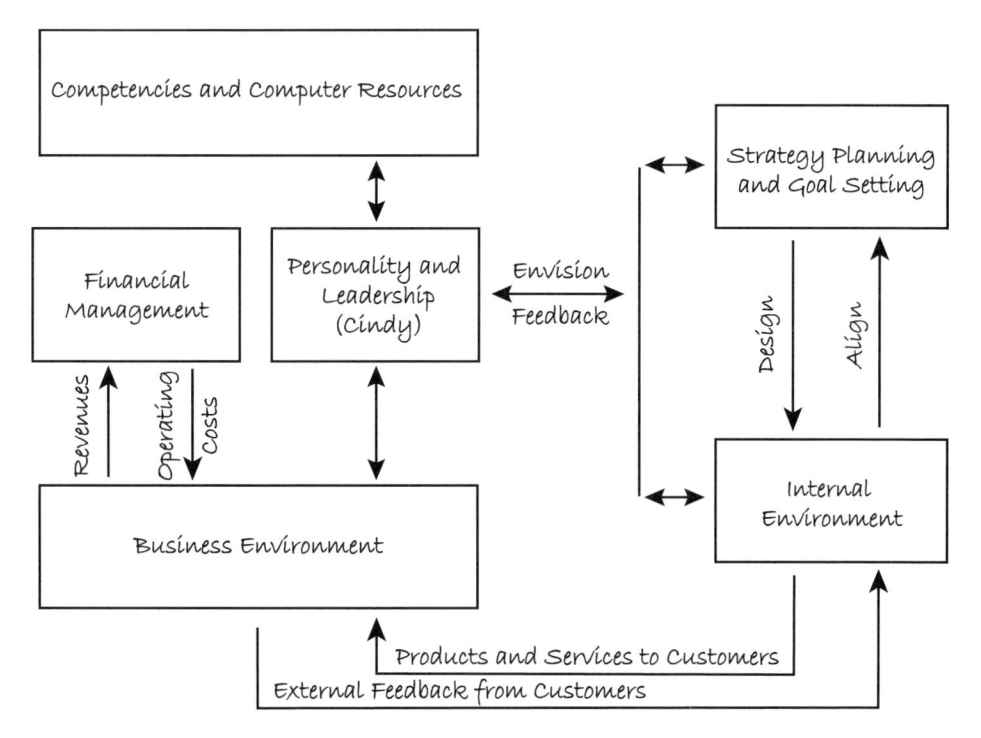

Figure 1

THE ODPT FOR A ONE-PERSON COMPANY

"In a one person company, the central perspective of the ODPT is Personality and Leadership, so for the sake of discussion let's put Cindy's name in that space and imagine she owns a company that makes shoes, and that she runs it out of her home." Thomas took a marker out of his chest pocket and wrote "Cindy" in the central perspective.

"As a one person company, Cindy has to perform all the functions shown in the six perspectives. She has to deal with customers and suppliers in the business environment and perform all the financial management functions that control the two kinds of dollars—those that go out of the company as operating costs and those that come in as revenues. She has to have the knowledge and competencies for designing and fabricating shoes and the computer resources and skills to automate and track the company's operation. In the strategy, planning, and goal-setting perspective of the ODPT, Cindy should concretize her corporate vision into a strategic plan that has quantitative business objectives, strategies, and goals. Finally, in the internal environment perspective, Cindy has to make the shoes, then sell them to customers in the business environment. If external feedback about the shoes is favorable, she sells more shoes and her business grows."

"I'm tired just looking at all those tasks," Maggie groaned. "In fact, I saw a billboard in the airport in Sydney that reminded me of how out of control my life is. It said, 'I'm an expert on stress, I run a small business.'"

Several people chuckled or nodded in agreement, most of all, Cindy.

Thomas could not suppress a grin. "Of course, when Cindy's business grows she can hire other people to do these jobs for her. In other words, she can either outsource the jobs or hire employees to do them, but she's got to have enough cash flow to do this.

"In the central perspective of the ODPT," Thomas continued, still pointing to the flip chart, "we have the characteristics of Cindy's personality that define how effectively she works with and communicates to customers, suppliers, and other business associates. Think of Cindy's personality as being like a psychological force field that people must interact with when they deal with her—sometimes the interactions go well, and other times they don't. The scope of Cindy's leadership abilities only extends to the vision she articulates in her business plan, and the way she leads her own life. It's crucial to notice that there's *no organizational culture* in a one-person company—there's only Cindy's personality. Her personality and the way she thinks about and organizes her work are the only drivers of organizational performance because she does every single job that gets done."

The group laughed as Cindy pretended to wipe the sweat off her brow from all the hard work that Thomas was describing.

"Using the six perspectives of the ODPT as a guide, let's say Cindy is really good at making and selling shoes, and her one-person company grows to be a ten-person company. What changes?"

"Her accounting and financial management workload will increase as the number of her business transactions increases," Frank said confidently, calling upon his vast knowledge and business experience. "She might also get more formal in the way she develops her business plan—things like including key employees in the planning process, or at least getting their input on the company's direction, its strengths, and areas for improvement. But the biggest difference will be selecting, training, and managing the human resources she hires to take over the work of making and selling shoes—what she did all by herself when she was a one-person company."

"That's correct," Thomas nodded, pleased at the thoroughness of Frank's analysis. "Now, Cindy's job is to be a *manager* and a *leader* of other people. She probably won't spend much time making and selling shoes anymore because she'll be training her employees to do those tasks and she'll focus on managing and leading the company. When employees deviate from how they were trained, Cindy will probably reinforce the lessons and mentor them until they 'get it right,' and getting it right will probably mean doing it Cindy's way. When the force-field of Cindy's personality and her preferences for how work should be performed are adopted by employees and are successful in generating revenue for the company and solving internal and external business problems, Cindy's personality preferences begin to create organizational culture. Yes, even companies with just a few employees can have very robust and well-defined cultures. In fact, organizational culture is easiest to observe and understand in small businesses."

"Are you saying that personality *is* organizational culture?" Cindy queried cautiously, thinking she had misunderstood what Thomas was getting at.

"That's precisely what I'm saying," Thomas shot back enthusiastically. "I'll discuss this in much more detail over the course of the workshop, but for now, suffice to say that organizational culture *is* personality type externalized and codified into organizational structures and systems."

Cindy's eyes were wide with insight as she sketched the words "Culture IS Personality Type Externalized and Codified" into her journal, then used the color pens and pencils to tastefully decorate each letter with a multi-colored pattern of pink, aqua, and violet.

"How complex would the ODPT model be for a company with one hundred employees?" Thomas asked, hoping to spark the group's imagination. "Take a look at Figure 2." Thomas grabbed the flip chart paper and turned to the next page.

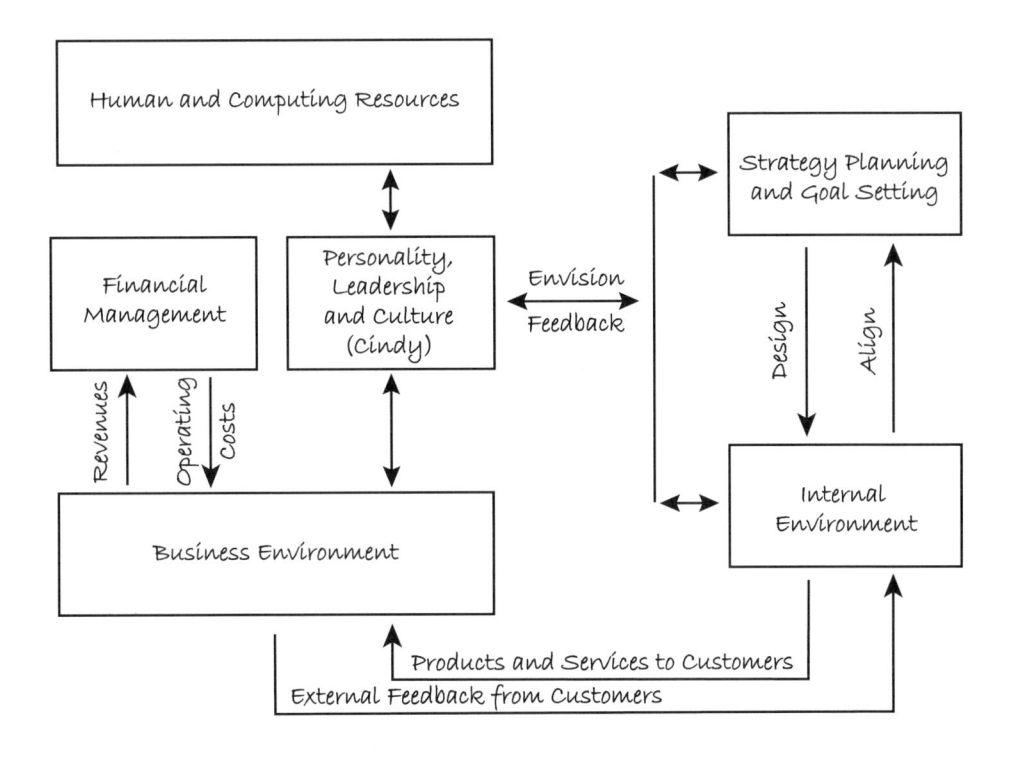

Figure 2

THE ODPT FOR A ONE HUNDRED-PERSON COMPANY

"How would you distribute one hundred employees across the six perspectives in Figure 2? How many people would you put in each perspective and why? How would you divide up their work and organize them to do it? How would you get them to communicate with each other and work together? When feedback from the business environment indicated that organizational change was needed, how would that be accomplished across the six perspectives? Now try to imagine how difficult it would be to distribute five hundred or one thousand employees across the six perspectives. How leaders and managers answer these and other OD questions is what distinguishes a high-performing creative organization from all other companies."

Thomas glanced down at his notes to refresh his memory. "Hammer and Champy liken the problem of dividing up work and organizing and distributing multiple levels of employees across the six perspectives to Humpty Dumpty who fell off a wall and all the King's horses and men had to glue him back together again.[23] When Cindy's one-person company grows to be one hundred employees, the processes for fabricating and selling shoes that were all once in her head are now broken into myriad jobs and organizational structures that are more and more specialized. Then, like Humpty Dumpty, they have to be glued back together with meetings, forms, organizational interfaces, e-mails, communication plans, and multiple layers of managers. Ironically, the organizational glue costs more money, time, and psychological energy than the process of making and selling shoes. So, how does Cindy figure all this out?"

"Beats me." Cindy shrugged her shoulders and feigned confusion, playing along.

"In a one hundred-person company, Cindy heads a group of senior, middle, and first-line managers and her job has almost nothing to do with making shoes. Cindy's job becomes almost exclusively one of providing leadership to her management team."

"What's becoming clear to me," Bethany offered reflectively, "is that Cindy is doing a different job at each level of complexity, and this requires a different set of skills and competencies."

"Absolutely right." Thomas smiled to encourage Bethany's and others' participation. "As a one-person company, Cindy had to perform the functions of a leader, a manager, and a worker who made and sold shoes. In the ten-person company, she delegated the work of making and selling shoes and assumed the roles of leader and manager. In the one hundred-person company, she no longer makes and sells shoes. Instead, levels of managers assume the role of overseeing the workers, so Cindy's primary job is providing leadership to her management team.

"Let's define some distinctions between what managers and leaders actually do." Thomas turned the page on his flip chart. "Here's how Kotter teases apart the distinction between leadership and management." He pointed to the two lists and began reading them aloud.

MANAGEMENT	LEADERSHIP
Planning and Budgeting	*Establishing Direction*
Organizing and Staffing	*Aligning People*
Controlling and Problem Solving	*Motivating and Inspiring*
Produce Predictability and Order	*Produce Change*[24]

Thomas had barely finished reading through the lists when Bethany jumped in again. "I never realized it before, but Kotter's distinction really shows me why I've never wanted to be a manager. It's a much different job than I used to have as a practicing social worker. But becoming a manager is one of the only ways to move up the ladder and make more money in most organizations."

"True," Thomas said, giving Bethany a thumbs-up. "There aren't a lot of non-managerial career paths, so workers often get promoted to management positions and wind up doing jobs they don't like and don't have the personality or core competencies to do. But like you said, Bethany, it's the only road to advancement presented to them, so they take it despite the fact that they're often not cut out to be managers or leaders."

"You know, Thomas," Frank chimed in, "I found the CEO of Johnson & Johnson's observation in *HBR* very interesting. He said that the skills needed to be an effective middle manager are heavy in quantitative analysis and decision making, while the enormously complex problems that senior managers normally face require a more developed sense of intuition."[25]

"Good point, Frank," Thomas replied, thrilled with how much the group was participating in the discussion. "My own view is that everyone has the seeds of being an effective leader, manager, or worker and can develop all of these skills when the situation requires it. In fact, the best senior managers are the ones who have a well-developed sense of intuition that is informed by managerial analysis, decision making, and a first-hand knowledge of how work is performed in the company."

Maggie raised her hand, "Why did you put human and computing resources together in the same perspective of the ODPT?"

Thomas walked to the flip chart and pointed to that perspective. "Knowledge is knowledge whether it is stored and manipulated in a silicon-based system like a computer, or a carbon-based system like your brain. In fact, when human and computing resources work together they become like a cross-functional work team. For example, one *HBR* study explored how Ernst & Young uses a *codification strategy* where vast amounts of business-related knowledge and best practices were stored in a sophisticated relational database that employees could access from anywhere in the world.[26] The computing side of the cross-functional work team was the primary repository of knowledge, and the human side tailored and applied that knowledge to a client's needs. The Boston Consulting Group used a *personalization strategy* where the primary repository of knowledge was in the person who developed it and who shared their knowledge through direct person-to-person interactions. As such, computing resources played a secondary support role in that cross-functional work team."

"It's an interesting perspective," Cindy mused aloud. "I'm a computing professional, but I've never thought about human and computing knowledge as a cross-functional team before, but I guess it's no different than a person operating a machine on the shop floor or someone driving a back hoe. Humans and non-human machines have to work together to get a job done."

"Precisely!" Thomas beamed as some of the group recorded Cindy's insight in their journals. "In fact, John Kao pushes the collaboration of human and computing resources even further by connecting it to four historical eras of economic activity. The first, second, and third eras were agricultural, industrial, and informational. The fourth is the era of creativity.[27] His claim is that the information age is driving our culture into the era of creativity because of the enormous amount of computing-based knowledge that is available and how that knowledge can be used and manipulated to stimulate human creativity, innovation, and improvement.

"Does that answer your question, Maggie?"

She nodded, then continued writing in her journal as Thomas scanned the group searching for unarticulated questions that showed only in facial expressions.

"Anything else…? Okay." He stepped to the head of the teaching table, "Let's begin to focus directly on the topic of creativity.

"A popular misconception is that only artists or poets have creative ability. I claim that creativity is the natural problem-solving mechanism of the human brain—our inner computer. Creativity, innovation, and improvement occur naturally in all people, in all times, in all cultures, unless frustrated and opposed by psychological, organizational or cultural obstructions. So igniting and fueling the creative process is more about removing the barriers that oppose this natural human process than it is about people learning to be more 'creative.'

"Plato taught that gaining knowledge about reality was really a process of regaining contact with and recalling innate and tacit knowledge that we already possess. In much the same way, people don't have to 'learn' to be creative or innovative any more than they have to 'learn' to be human. Understanding how to prevent creativity, innovation, and improvement from being frustrated and opposed is one of the most fundamental questions in life."

"You keep using the words 'creativity' and 'innovation' as if they're the same thing," Dan interrupted in an annoyed tone, as if to challenge what Thomas was saying. "Are they the same thing or are they different? If they're different, exactly how are they different?"

"No." Thomas shook his head, realizing he may have caused some confusion. "They're not the same thing, so I need to be careful how I use them. Innovation and improvement are the products or outcome of the creative process. Throughout the rest of the dive workshop when I use the word *improvement* I mean concrete actions that increase the productivity, performance, value, quality, uses, appearance, or customer desire of an existing product or service.

"My definition of the word *innovation* closely follows Peter Drucker's as being actions that take ideas or material things and turn them into new products and services—resources that customers will buy and that generate revenue for a company.

"Here's one of Drucker's examples." Thomas quickly found the note card and began reading. "'The penicillin mold was a pest, not a resource. Bacteriologists went to great lengths to protect their bacterial cultures against contamination by it. Then in the late 1920s, a London doctor, Alexander Fleming, realized that this 'pest' was exactly the bacterial killer bacteriologists had been looking for—and the penicillin mold became a valuable resource.'"[28]

He set the note card on the teaching table and continued—energized by the concepts and the ideas he was presenting. "An innovation is the creation of an entirely new resource, not the improvement of a product or service that already exists. Other examples of innovations that Drucker has identified are the seventeenth century development of textbooks that made wide spread education possible, and the nineteenth century emergence of installment credit that gave people the resource of 'purchasing power.'

"So to reiterate, both innovation and improvement are the *result* or *outcome* of the creative process. Innovation and improvement are the products of the natural problem-solving mechanism of the human brain."

Dan shook his head vigorously, satisfied with the clarity of the response Thomas had given.

"There's been some research on creativity in the workplace. For example, Robinson and Stern studied hundreds of creative acts of individuals in organizations, and they concluded that the true nature of corporate creativity is totally unpredictable in that it's impossible to know what creative acts will occur and who creative individuals are.[29] They identify some techniques for promoting creativity in organizations, one of which is for managers to allow what they call 'unofficial activity.'

"To illustrate their view, they recount the story of a Japanese researcher named Tomoshige Hori who accidentally stumbled onto a process for making cheese. Hori reported his discovery to his supervisor who quickly demanded that he 'get back to work' and forget this 'creative' diversion from his assignments. His colleagues gave him a similar response. Hori continued working on the cheese-making process for three years against the direct orders of his boss, then finally forced his company's management into considering the value of his work by publishing the process in the highly esteemed *Journal of Food and Science*.

"What's wrong with this picture?" Thomas implored, shaking his head sadly. "Robinson and Stern compare the Hori story to 3M's corporate policy of allowing employees up to fifteen percent of their time to work on creative projects that interest them without having to answer to their managers for this time. But the fifteen percent rule at

3M is a corporate policy that facilitates, supports, and enables the creative process. In other words, the fifteen percent rule is an *official activity* at 3M—sanctioned and encouraged as a competitive strategy from the highest corporate levels down through the line organization.

"Unlike the 3M policy, Hori's work was really *unofficial activity* and was opposed by his supervisor. In other words, the Robinson and Stern 'fix' is to encourage employees to work around the people, structures, systems, and strategies that oppose creativity in organizations. We hear echoes of the work-around approach in Rosabeth Moss Kanter's advice to erect 'protective shielding' around highly innovative projects because people in the organization will frustrate and oppose these projects.[30]

"Edgar Schein mouths the sad truth that in most companies innovative people have to lie, cheat, hide out, make themselves invisible, and even go underground to pursue creative work.[31]

"The scuttling of creative endeavors like Hori's is the result of *psychological and cultural barriers* that exist below the surface of organizational consciousness, barriers that frustrate and oppose innovation, improvement, and the creative process." Thomas began pounding one of his fists into the other palm. "The most important lesson that we can learn from Hori's story *is not* that we should work around these barriers to protect creativity. The most important lesson is that these psychological and cultural barriers *have names*—the names of the owners, managers, and workers who embody and act out the forces that oppose creativity in the day-to-day activities of organizational life."

Thomas walked resolutely to the railing of the ship and pointed down into the water. "Like coral reef that lurks below the surface of organizational consciousness, owners and managers who embody and act out these psychological and cultural barriers prevent any organization from becoming a creative organization.

"As I will discuss in more detail tomorrow, the *psychological barriers* are built on tacit assumptions and decision-making bias of employees' personality in combination with fear that is used to establish and maintain organizational control. When employees at any organizational level oppose the creative process, they are normally elevating their own self-interests and needs above what's in the long-term best interest of the company. Not surprisingly, employees who oppose the creative process out of self-interest are not open to feedback about their blind spots, are defensive, and don't act on feedback that they do receive.

"The *cultural barriers* are collective tacit assumptions from these same people about the 'way things are done around here.' These owners and managers are the guardians and transmitters of organizational cultures that oppose the creative process.

"Remember—organizational culture *is* personality type externalized and codified into organizational structures and systems, so these cultural guardians defend the status quo as if they were defending their own psychological orientation in life—and in a sense they are.

"These cultural guardians *are* the psychological and cultural barriers that oppose the creative process, stifle creativity, and mirror the message back to creative employees to forget all that talk about 'creativity'—just get back to work!" Thomas shouted playfully, trying to drive his point home.

"Creative organizations learn to *find* and *eliminate* these obstructions to the creative process, they don't allow employees at any organizational level to force creativity underground as 'unofficial activity' as if it were something to be ashamed of. Top managers who are committed to building a creative organization identify then systematically remove such barriers. They know that one of the most crucial roles of leadership is to *raise organizational consciousness* about who or what these obstructions are and how they operate.

"Like sailing through a barrier reef," Thomas said pointing up to the ship's bridge, "top managers up in the wheelhouse of corporate ships must learn to look off in the distance and detect the whitecaps that indicate below-the-surface reef structure that threatens the passage to a culture of creativity.

"Middle and first-line managers at the bow and along the railings of corporate ships, learn to peer down below the surface waters of organizational conscious and help top managers navigate the barriers to creativity.

"Rather than figuring out ways that creativity, innovation, and improvement can survive employees who oppose it, or shielding creative people from policies and operating goals that oppose their innovative contributions, why not show these barriers to the door?

"*Why not get a vision to build a creative organization?*" Thomas passionately implored. "Why not consciously design a culture that facilitates, supports, and enables the creative process? Why make creativity, innovation, improvement, and the development of intellectual property an option? Why not follow the CEO of British Petroleum's advice and insist that every employee who's not directly responsible for generating revenue be held accountable to create and distribute knowledge that can be used to generate revenue?[32] This captures the essence of the often used, but little understood descriptor—knowledge workers.

"We see how radical this view of knowledge management is when we reflect on Tom Peters' comment about the critical need for innovation in corporate America." Thomas flipped through his three-by-five cards until he found the Peters quotation he was looking for. "'Does anyone know what it means to *manage* the human imagination?...I don't know what it means to manage the human imagination either, but I do know that imagination is the main source of value in the new economy. And I know we better figure out the answer to my question—quick.'[33]

"I believe that Peters is asking the wrong question," Thomas countered in a wry tone. "Asking how you 'manage' the human imagination is like asking how you 'manage' and 'control' your deep emotions, desires, and the powerful pushes and pulls of your psychological life. The real question is how can we *stop* trying to manage the creative process and allow *our imagination* to lead, teach, and guide us to deep and previously unknown sources of knowledge, problem-solving abilities, and wisdom?

"Instead, we should be asking questions like, How do I stop talking and start listening to my creative abilities? How do I put my ego aside and start following the inner guidance of the creative process? How do I let the creative process provide leadership for my personal and professional life?" Thomas paused to let the power of his words sink in, then recapped. "So the key to building a creative organization is removing the barriers and opposition to creativity so that this naturally occurring process can become a part of the way companies do business.

"In what will follow, I present three powerful strategies that owners, managers, and workers can use to build creative organizations. Tomorrow we'll discuss the *first* strategy. We'll learn how to find meaning and significance in work by experiencing the creative process, learning how fear inhibits creativity, and by building the kind of inner collaboration and alignment that frees up squandered psychological energy and redirects it toward things that really matter in life.

"The first strategy helps us learn to see ourselves as creative people, to respect and encourage the creative process in others, and to view our organization's purpose and business objectives as a set of operational problems that creativity can help to solve."

Thomas held up two fingers. "The next day of the dive workshop we'll cover the *second* strategy, which is to use alignment to gain competitive advantage. This means ensuring that owners, managers, workers, organizational structures, and systems all speak with one voice, that they use the 'red flags' to identify activities that squander organizational energy through misalignments, and that they build a portfolio of employees that facilitates, supports, and enables the creative process.

"On the third day," Thomas smiled, now waving three fingers, "we cover the *third* strategy—to continue implementing strategies one and two and allow a culture of creativity to emerge. The sessions for the third strategy describe why organizational culture cannot be created *directly* any more than deep personal change can; rather culture emerges as the *indirect* product of thoroughly and consistently implementing the first two strategies.

"One day we come to work and find that the organization's culture has changed and the new cultural elements that foster the creative process come as easily as the ones that frustrated and opposed it. A culture of creativity makes formerly fixated psychological and organizational energy available and channels it toward fulfilling the organization's purpose and business objectives. Freed-up energy becomes a powerful engine to drive a company's performance to higher and higher levels.

"Higher performance levels can be measured quantitatively with financial indicators, the organization's ability to adapt to change quickly, the productivity of employees, and measured levels of customer satisfaction. As available levels of psychological and organizational energy increase, employees put their shoulders to the corporate wheel of fulfilling the organization's purpose, core values, and business objectives—and the cycle goes on."

"Suppose you're in an organization where the top manager won't support creativity—what do you do then?" Nikki queried, thinking about her own situation back at the office.

"A business unit within a larger organization can become a creative organization," Thomas explained, "but this must be done carefully so as not to optimize the business unit and sub-optimize the performance of the overall organization. The waves of the prevailing corporate culture will pound against this business unit and resist changes and initiatives, even when its goal is to produce superior performance that is measurable. When a business unit uses the three strategies and stays the course of becoming a creative organization, it becomes an *Island of Excellence* in a sea of mediocrity.

Several members of the group found themselves smiling at Thomas's description.

"Are there any other questions?"

Nikki raised her hand again with a sense of urgency. "What about if you're in a business unit or a small business and no one else wants to become a creative organization?"

Thomas leaned forward, rested both hands on the teaching table and looked directly at Nikki, wondering what was motivating her questions. "I'll be honest with you…being in that kind of organization takes an enormous amount of energy because you're set against the pounding surf and prevailing winds that frustrate and oppose your creative process. People who are in the situation you're describing should carefully examine their motivation for subjecting themselves to that kind of cultural pressure. But in the final analysis, each of us is ultimately responsible for the choices we make in life, so as an individual, Nikki, you can decide to become an *Island of Excellence* regardless of what anyone else does."

The atmosphere around the teaching table was contemplative as the group considered the seriousness of the challenge Thomas had set before them.

"Okay," Thomas clapped his hands together loudly to refocus the group on him, "let's review the schedule for the rest of the day. I'd like each of you to find a quiet place somewhere on the ship and take about an hour to write up your business case study. To reiterate, I want you to describe the most important problems you're currently facing in your organization and what you believe the root causes to be. Try to limit your case study to five hand-written pages so we don't overwork the ship's Xerox machine then give your write-up to Anita when you're done. I'll hand out the set of all nine at dinner. Read them over and be prepared to discuss salient issues you uncover during our sessions.

"Are there any questions on the assignment?" Thomas looked down at his watch, then back at the group. "It's 4:30 P.M. now. Anita and Janice will give the dive brief at 5:45 P.M. down on the dive deck, and dinner will be served at 8:00 P.M. right here around the teaching table. The first session tomorrow will begin after breakfast, at 8:00 A.M. sharp, right here."

The members of the group migrated to different parts of the ship and began writing. Thomas grabbed a cold bottle of water and a soft chair on the upper deck and tried to relax after the session. He gazed over the water and out onto the volcanic wonder that surrounded him in silence as his mind wandered from person to person in the group, recalling their questions, comments, and facial expressions during the session. He read through the expectations they wrote on the three-by-five cards, but wondered what their unspoken and even unconscious expectations were and how he could identify and speak to those as well.

What are my deepest expectations for this dive workshop, Thomas thought as he sipped his ice water, *and why do I feel so deeply troubled about my own life and where I'm going?*

Anita rang the bell that signaled the start of the dive brief 5:45 P.M.

"I would suggest that you get your dive gear set up today if you haven't already done so," Anita began. "That way you'll be ready for the first dive tomorrow morning. For assistance with underwater cameras or video units, see me. I'm in charge of the ship's E-6 film processing lab. If you have any problems with your dive gear see Janice. Weights and weight belts are right here. Janice will help you figure out how much weight you'll need and show you how to enter your nitrox numbers into the log, and how to use the gas analyzer."

Janice was mid-twenties with blonde hair, bright blue eyes, and a perfectly shaped body that filled out a bathing suit in a way that was exciting to look at. Originally from Hungary, she had lived in Australia for a few years, so when she spoke English she had an unmistakable Aussie accent. Janice was a kind-hearted person who had a warm smile and took great pride in helping and assisting people with anything they needed on the ship. She would see someone struggling to get their wetsuit off and would automatically help them. And she loved putting a hot towel on a diver's back when they got out of the water and giving them a back rub. But there was a remote, well-guarded, dark side to Janice, hidden beneath her smile, and it only became visible when she was sitting alone with a faraway look in her eyes, or when people pushed across some unspecified psychological boundary and tried to get her to "lighten up" when she wanted to be serious.

The dinner bell rang at 8:00 P.M. sharp. When the group assembled at what had formerly been the teaching table, it was now covered with a deep aqua tablecloth, accented with salmon colored dinner candles suitably protected from the wind in glass encasings, and a setting of fine china, silverware, and sparkling crystal glasses. The steward asked each guest for their wine preference, then poured whatever kind of red, white, or blush wine they preferred. This "fine-dining" atmosphere was punctuated by the stereo-sound of smooth Brazilian jazz that played softly in the background. Nikki was the last person to be seated, as the others talked and enjoyed each other's company. With a powerful display of stars overhead that resembled a planetarium, the steward carried on his ritual of serving a sumptuous four-course dinner.

Most of the discussion around the table focused on the dives that the group would do tomorrow. People asked Janice various questions about how deep the dives would be, whether there would be a strong current, what the visibility would be like, and who would be diving with nitrox.

Frank asked enthusiastically, "What kinds of marine life are we going to see?"

"Like Anita always says," Janice arched an eyebrow, "fish only do four things: they eat, sleep, fornicate, and get cleaned by other sea critters."

"It's true," Anita said confidently. "Try it on the first dive tomorrow—look closely at what the fish are doing and you'll see that they're either eating, sleeping, mating, or getting cleaned by a shrimp, wrasse, or some other kind of sea animal."

"I want to see the big stuff," James declared, unconsciously puffing himself up as he spoke, "I'm talking about manta rays, spotted eagle rays, bottle-nosed dolphins…"

"And the enviable list of hammerhead, gray reef, silver tip, and bull sharks," Dan added, his face beaming with excitement and anticipation.

"I just spent more money than I should have on camera equipment so I could take pictures of the small stuff," Bethany interjected, wanting to make her preference known.

"Because I've been diving these waters for a while, I've learned where all these critters hang out," Anita said proudly, then looked at Janice with a leer. "Unless you know exactly where these subtle creatures eat, sleep, fornicate, and get cleaned, only the most observant divers will ever detect them underwater."

"What kinds of small sea animals are we likely to see on this trip?" Bethany asked with a growing sense of anticipation in her voice.

"We'll see pigmy sea horses, various types of cleaner shrimp, dozens of kinds of sea worms, and magnificently colored nudibranchs that look a lot like sea worms, but aren't." Anita smiled from ear-to-ear, proud of the underwater world she was about to reveal to these eager divers.

"I love to watch the drama of survival on the reef," Cindy said, raising her wineglass as if to toast Darwin's theory of evolution. "It's amazing how the brightly colored hard and soft coral fight for precious space so they can gather plankton and sunlight—they try to crowd each other out and even grow on top of each other. And the reef fish are so interesting to watch—the anthias, butterfly, angel, damsel, and anemone fish all of whom struggle to avoid being eaten by predators."

Other people around the table discussed the material Thomas presented today, as Anita turned her attention to them. This was the first dive charter she'd ever worked where people were engaged in such serious conversations. Typically, divers wanted to explore the ocean world as a way of forgetting about the problems of life for a while. The usual conversations on dive boats focused almost exclusively on diving-related topics. That was all Anita ever talked about. People discussed other places they'd been diving, how they liked them, what kinds of new equipment they were using and how it performed, what they saw on the first dive, or how that last roll of pictures turned out. It was almost an unspoken rule that other than an occasional side conversation with someone, serious topics were off-limits on live-aboard dive boats. But given the purpose of the dive workshop and Thomas's opening remarks, Anita knew that serious topics would be a focal point of this dive trip, because deep discussion actually enriched the entire dive experience.

Maggie began talking to Thomas and some of the others about a few of the issues she was facing in her company. Rena, who sat across from her, had checked-out.

Maggie repeatedly tried to engage Rena in the discussion and finally said, "What I always tell Rena is that we need complete thinking and unflawed delegation in order to get things done. Communication is everything. Isn't that right, Rena?"

The young woman rejoined the conversation only long enough to shake her head and mutter her obligatory, "Yes, Mother," then disappeared back into her inner world of autonomy.

∿∿∿∿

Rena and Joel were not married until the week after she graduated from college because her mother, Maggie Spinner, demanded that she finish school first. After their honeymoon, the young couple moved from Colorado Springs, where they both had graduated from Colorado College, to the Denver area. Rena took a job at her mom's Boulder-based marketing company, the Spinner Group, and Joel accepted a position as a software engineer at the Coors Brewing Company in Golden—a suburb west of Denver.

Rena's values were quite different from Maggie's. She was laid-back and wanted to take time to enjoy life, have a family, and find a way to give her time and talents in service to volunteer charities. She and Joel were already talking about having children and decided that the Denver area would be their home. They wanted to make new friends, get plugged into their neighborhood, start attending a local church, set down roots, and move into the comfortable routine that comes from turning the place you live into a home.

Rena tended to withdraw from people and situations, especially when it involved conflict. She was extremely self critical, and at work she felt unappreciated and undervalued, especially by her mom. But outwardly, Rena made people in the office feel at ease and inspired a sense of teamwork and harmony. Rena's problem-solving skills and her ability to listen to people from the heart were focused on meeting the needs of the present. She had hardly been at the Spinner Group for two weeks when some people began using her as a sounding board for work-related problems and others began asking her to help reconcile and mediate differences between employees so that all parties felt heard. Her fellow employees found it difficult to believe that she was Maggie's daughter. In stark contrast to Rena, Maggie was extremely impersonal, critical, and intrusive, barked orders and directives, never really listened, and became abrasive and verbally aggressive.

Rena was empathic, could see others' points of view, was shy, and often had a difficult time knowing what she really felt about situations and expressing her opinions because her emotions ran like a deep underground river. When Maggie got in her face about something, it was hours later before Rena thought of a good response. Rena was so easygoing that she went along with others too much, she wanted peace at any price, and was too submissive and agreeable. She would even ignore negative things about people that she didn't want to see. She had a highly developed set of values that inwardly affected her, but she rarely expressed these to others and tended to fade into the background of activities. However, she had a subtle but important effect on people in the office almost as if she was setting standards and core values for fellow employees without ever talking about them.

Rena was never satisfied with her performance at work, and Maggie just couldn't understand why. "Rena," Maggie would utter in disbelief, "you have lots of competencies and strong points that you can use to improve your performance on the job. Why do you always underestimate your abilities, downplay your achievements, and view yourself as nobody special? Your presence matters to this company—we would be a much poorer place without you here."

Rena acknowledged the words of praise with an embarrassed grin, but was uneasy about being put center stage, so she said nothing.

Maggie began pressuring her to move back to Colorado Springs and open a branch office of the Spinner Group. It didn't take Rena long to figure out that running a small business would require her to work much harder than she wanted to work. She was bright and wanted to learn about the business, but viewed work as a means to an end—a way of providing for her family—not as a way of establishing her personal identity like her mom did.

But Maggie didn't get this and was mistakenly under the impression that Rena wanted to get more and more involved in the business. Her daughter did nothing to disabuse Maggie of that notion because she knew it would create enormous conflict if she told her mom how she really felt. Rena just sucked it in and expressed her hidden anger toward her mom's attitude and pressure by being passive aggressive, dragging her feet about things she was asked to do, and by saying yes to tasks when she had no intention of doing them.

Maggie put Rena in charge of the highest-pressure area of the company, business development and new accounts, and asked Shane to mentor her because he had a wealth of experience that he'd gained working with Maggie when she was back at Enton in Rocky Flats. She believed Rena needed to develop these skills in order to open the new office. This business function was the one that Maggie was most interested in because she believed it would determine the entire future of the company.

Rena hated this. She preferred doing routine tasks with definite procedures and wasn't attracted to jobs that required lots of energy, initiative, and frequent changes in direction like business development did. While Maggie and Shane helped Rena as much as they could, she was way out of her comfort zone—she preferred known strategies to the risk and uncertainty of charting new business territory. She didn't know where to begin.

One night when they were food shopping together, Rena tried to reason with Maggie. "Look, Mom, my goals and aspirations are to have a family and live life—I don't care about achieving high levels of professional success like you have."

"Why do you keep saying that?" Maggie roared as if more volume could change Rena's mind. "When you talk like that you sound lazy—like you've got no initiative. I don't understand why you set such low standards for yourself, young lady—you use such a small fraction of your ability.

"It just infuriates me that you don't want to be a leader and that you take every opportunity you can to avoid being in the spotlight." Maggie angrily pushed the shopping cart down the isle as Rena trudged behind, regretting that she'd brought the topic up and vowing not to do it again.

Rena had difficulty setting priorities for her own work and those who reported to her, but she was stubborn about taking direction from Maggie or Shane. Maggie constantly pushed Rena in meetings, demanding that she excel and step up to the plate if she wanted to take over the company some day. But on the rare occasion that Rena did try to assert her opinion about something, Maggie would become competitive and argue that she really didn't understand the full implications of the problem. When Shane jumped into the discussion in support of Maggie's view, Rena would simply withdraw and shut down, which was exactly what Shane wanted.

"She's just not ready to open the Colorado Springs office—she needs more time," Shane had said with concern, after cornering Maggie privately in her office after a company meeting.

"I know that," Maggie agreed, although reluctantly.

But that's not your real motivation, is it, Shane? Maggie thought to herself.

"If you want to open that new location now, we need someone more qualified, and more driven to do it," Shane announced with escalating apprehension in his voice.

"Who?" Maggie demanded.

"Well, it's something I'd consider doing if I had your confidence and full support."

Why is Shane's willingness to take on this assignment no surprise to me? Maggie frowned inwardly, well aware he wanted to push Rena aside.

"Why don't you give me a chance to prove myself?" Shane pressured. "In fact, although this is probably not the right time, I've been wanting to talk with you about my long-term future with the company. I want a stake in taking the company over someday when you decide to get out. I don't want anything for free—I'm willing to work hard for it. I'll even put my own money at risk if you let me buy into the company.

Shane paused for a second, then confidently made his do-or-die pitch. "How about if you give me a thirty percent reduction in pay, then base my compensation package on commission and performance? The harder I work, the more I'll make, and the more you'll make."

Wow! He's talking my language. Maggie couldn't help but appreciate his brash enthusiasm *But,* she also couldn't help thinking, *what would happen to my daughter?*

Things came to a head after a Monday morning status meeting in which Rena was exceptionally disengaged from what was going on. Maggie called Rena into her office, slammed the door, then exploded in rage. "Look, you need to decide whether you want to take over this business!"

Rena gathered the courage and finally told Maggie her true feelings about the matter. "I want no part of running this company! I never have, and I never will! I just want a nine-to-five job to help support my family. I don't want to be like you, Mom—I want to enjoy life." For probably the first time, Rena was as furious as Maggie was. "Fine," Maggie bellowed back, her face red and twisted with anger, "I'll turn the company over to Shane. He's already told me that he's unimpressed by your work performance. He thinks that your level of competency in business is mediocre at best. Once I'm out of the picture and Shane's running the company, I'll bet he fires you—then what'll you do?"

"I'll find another job where people want to pay me for a fair day's work, then let me go home to my family. I don't need you or your company. In fact, maybe I should just quit now and let you get on with building your 'precious' business!" Rena screamed at the top of her lungs as she yanked the office door open to escape Maggie's judgement and condemnation. The entire office staff was stressed and sitting on the edge of their seats listening to the altercation through the closed door. They jolted in speechless shock as "meek and mild" Rena threw the front door open and stormed away in a huff.

After the incident, the two interacted with a stilted-but-polite regard. Although Maggie said she'd given up on Rena taking over the company, she continued to push her harder and harder. In response, Rena just became more and more passive aggressive and increasingly stubborn—the harder Maggie pushed, the more Rena dug in her heels.

Rena was so sick of the stress that one day after meeting with a potential client, she stopped at the National Renewable Energy Laboratory in Golden to see if they had any job openings she could apply for. Unbeknownst to Maggie, a week later Rena had an interview for a position in the laboratory's Public Relations Department that seemed very promising, although the hiring manager said they wouldn't be filling the position immediately. Her responsibilities would be to maintain the laboratory's Web site, and produce the brochures and other printed material used to promote the renewable energy mission lab. Rena would have a bank of experts that she could refer people to when they had questions she couldn't answer, and this reassured her that she could actually do the job. Compared to doing business development at the Spinner Group, this job would take a lot of pressure off her. Most of all, it was steady employment with well-defined roles and responsibilities, and as a government contractor she would get great benefits and an excellent retirement plan.

Still secretly hopeful that she could pressure Rena into taking over the business, Maggie insisted that they go to the dive workshop together.

Maybe if she gets some new ideas about how to work smarter not harder, she'll reconsider her position, Maggie speculated prayerfully.

Rena didn't really want to go, and she decided that even if she didn't get the job she'd applied for, she was going to keep on looking until she found something else. Rena went to the dive workshop over the strong objections of her husband because she was sick of Joel ordering her around and she didn't want to make any more waves with Maggie.

~~~~~

By 9:00 P.M. most of the people were finished eating and had wandered away from the dinner table to other parts of the ship. James, Cindy, and Dan were still sitting at the table talking about their cultural experience in the Highlands even after the steward had removed the tablecloth.

Dan couldn't help but notice that something was different between James and Cindy after the Highlands trip, but he couldn't quite put his finger on exactly what had changed. This he knew: James looked at her differently. He listened carefully when she spoke and tried to make connections between SciTech's culture and what they'd experienced in the remote villages. James actually seemed to *get* what she was trying to say and had even begun to see applications of their cultural discussions for the strategic planning and change initiative he was leading in his parish.

Subconsciously, Cindy had begun to realize that James's interest in her cultural insights and his penetrating, visual exploration of her body were starting to excite her both intellectually *and* sexually. The intense gaze that had made her so uncomfortable earlier today in the van had become something she liked and even longed for.

Without looking at Dan, Cindy poured James and herself another glass of wine, shot James a suggestive glance, and said, "I think I'm going to go up on the top deck and look at the stars for a while."

James smiled in anticipation of where they might wind up that night. "Sounds nice. I think I'll join you."

My married priest friend is putting the move on my business partner right in front of me, Dan was now certain as his blood started to boil. *Has he no shame?*

"I think I'll just turn in," Dan muttered with purposeful disgust in his voice. But the two of them had already walked away.

Day 1
DIVING THE REEFS OFF KIMBE BAY

Strategy 1:

Learn to Find Meaning and Significance in Work

THE DAY BEGINS

They were tied up to the mooring ball off Walindi all night, and just before dawn Frank heard the sound of the engines start and felt the ship begin to sail to where they would do their first dive. He fell back into a deep sleep. By 6:00 A.M. Sunday morning they were tied up to the mooring ball at Restorf Island, and the smell of freshly brewed coffee, eggs, bacon, ham, and French toast permeated the entire ship.

Most people don't sleep well the first night on a live-aboard even when the ship is tied up to a mooring for most of the night. The motion of the boat and the sound of waves slapping against the hull less than a foot from your head make it difficult to sleep restfully. But after diving three tanks the first day, even the motion and sound of the ship sailing in open water become a non-problem as divers fall asleep from the deeply satisfying experience of physical exhaustion.

People began to make their way up the stairs to the dining room for breakfast, as Pachelbel played softly in the background. Thomas was the first one to the dining room. He always found it interesting to watch how people self-select and either gravitated toward or away from each other in the morning. Bethany, Nikki, and Maggie came a few minutes later, and in true extraverted style they sat at the table closest to the ship's galley and chattered away with Artie, the chef. They laughed and begged him to tell them other jokes and stories about growing up in the Highlands near Goroka.

Artie was a tall, rotund, gregarious Aussie with a long ponytail, light freckled skin, and bright, sparkling blue eyes. He had an enormous warm smile and the tender heart of an inquisitive little boy. Artie had moved to PNG with his parents in 1978 when he was only four years old, so he spoke perfect Pidgin and was deeply steeped in the fine points and intricacies of the history, people, and culture of this exotic land.

Artie scraped the hash browns off the sizzling grill and shouted to Nikki over the roar of the kitchen fans, "Yeah—last year when we were here, we got up one morning and saw an empty dugout canoe floating between the ship and the island. The next thing we knew a boat full of PNG police drove up and asked if we'd seen anyone in the dugout. They said there'd been an armed robbery of another boat. I guess they thought the dugout canoe was the *getaway car!*"

The four of them just roared with laughter at the idea of a dugout canoe being used for a quick "get away."

As more of the group arrived, Thomas noticed that the introverts hadn't quite shaken off the last remnants of sleep and were scattered around the other tables either talking quietly or keeping to themselves. Some read books about the underwater topography and sea life, some tried to get the settings on their camera just right, while others gazed out the window and tried to ponder the experience of where they were and what they were doing. Frank was staring through a pair of binoculars at the nests of five or six enormous sea eagles that were one hundred fifty feet up in the trees that towered over the ship. Cindy was watching two of the eagles off the starboard side as they circled about seventy-five feet in the air, then dove full throttle into the water, trying to catch fish. Over and over again the two eagles flew head-first into the ocean as a school of thousands of shiny, silver fish jumped completely out of the water, trying to escape their fate.

Thomas knew from experience that understanding and respecting peoples' preferences for quiet reflection or social interaction in the morning was one of the most important principles of having a good dive experience on a live-aboard.

Thomas was the first to finish breakfast, so he excused himself and went out on the deck to write notes, review his flip charts, and prepare for the opening session. At precisely 8:00 A.M., he wandered over to the dining room door and stuck his head inside. "We're going to get started." Then he rang the bell so that people in other parts of the ship would know that the first session was about to begin.

SESSION 1: EXPERIENCE THE CREATIVE PROCESS

Thomas waited patiently for people to find their places; then he began. "In today's economy, owners of companies are focused on nagging questions like, 'How do I maximize shareholder value? How do I please customers, increase profits, and gain competitive advantage in the current business environment?' Employees in these same organizations are confronted with other questions like, 'How do I make a living that supports my lifestyle and find a sense of meaning and significance in my work? How do I discover my calling in life?'

"My claim is that the answer to both sets of questions is to build creative organizations—one person at a time. When allowed, *creativity* funds the innovation, improvement, and complex problem solving of employees in an organization. Likewise, managers and workers who learn to *connect their creative abilities to their job* tend to find meaning and significance in that work.

"The first of three powerful strategies for building creative organizations is to learn to find meaning and significance in work." Thomas turned to the next page of his flip chart, then faced the group. "Figure 3 shows that we accomplish this by gaining competency in three practices that are joined by counter clockwise arrows."

```
        Practice 2
       Learn How Fear              BEGIN HERE
     Inhibits Creativity
                                    Practice 1
                                   Experience the
                                  Creative Process

      Practice 3
  Build Inner Collaboration
      and Alignment                             Finding Meaning and
                          Freed-up                Significance in Work
                       Psychological
                          Energy
```

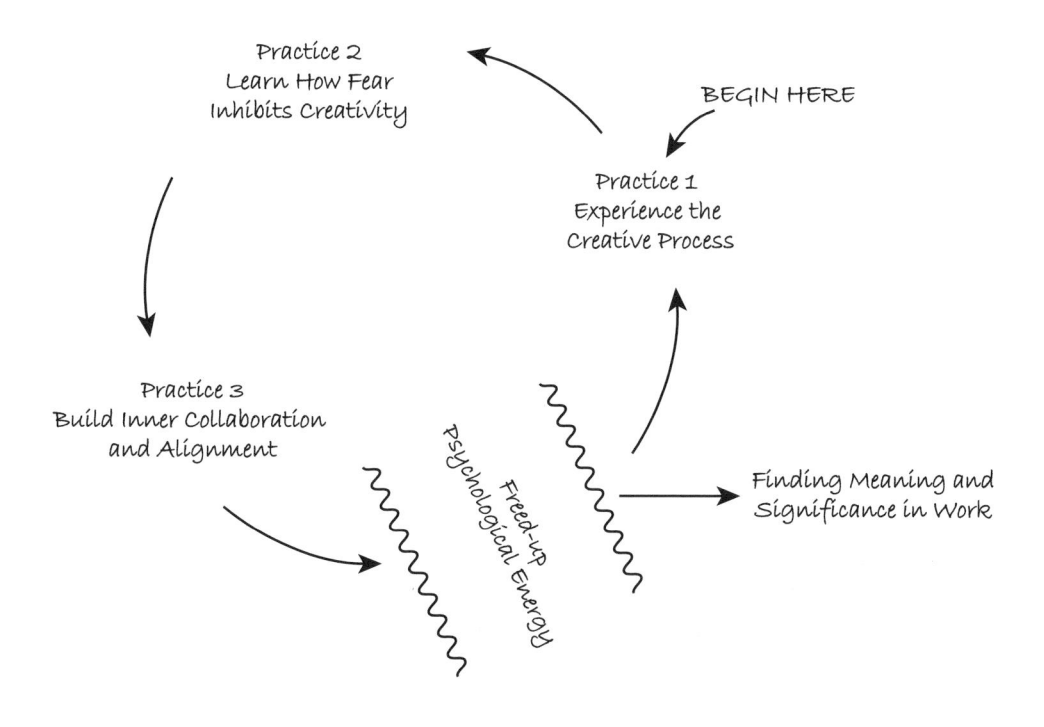

Figure 3

THE FIRST STRATEGY: LEARN TO FIND MEANING AND SIGNIFICANCE IN WORK

"In this session I'll discuss Practice 1—to experience the creative process. In the next session, I'll cover Practice 2, which is learning how fear inhibits creativity, and in today's final session, we'll present Practice 3 —how to build inner collaboration and alignment."

Thomas pointed to Figure 3. "Notice how building competency in Practices 1, 2, and 3 results in freeing up formerly squandered psychological energy that is redirected toward things that really matter in life—like finding meaning and significance in work.

"Creative organizations are possible because *everyone* has creative abilities."[34] He opened his arms wide to encompass the entire group. "The creative process is not something mystical, it's the natural problem-solving mechanism of the human brain. So, opposing the creative process is like fighting the natural order of things. This is consistent with Collins and Lazier's view that we don't have to stimulate creativity. Rather, our task is to nurture the creativity that's all around us and to transform it into the innovation needed to bring competitive advantage.[35]

"Owners, managers, and workers must learn to experience the creative process with concrete personal evidence in their lives. It's not enough to have an intellectual understanding of creativity, or even to acknowledge the value it might bring to your organization. People must *personally experience* their own creative abilities and see for themselves how it improves their problem-solving skills. Only then does creativity become a resource to them and their organization.

"There are three models that describe the creative process," Thomas said, wiping the sweat from his brow, as the morning heat intensified. "The first model is typified by writers like De Bono and Michalko who view creativity as an *intellectual process* consisting of a set of methodological tools. De Bono turns creativity into a rational method called 'the six thinking hats' based on a metaphor where people view problems from six different perspectives. He likens viewing the problem from each perspective as wearing a different colored hat.[36]

"Michalko takes a more substantive approach by presenting case studies of the work of recognized geniuses like Leonardo da Vinci and Thomas Edison and distilling their creative strategies into a method of thinking and working that anyone can learn.[37]

"The second model views creativity experientially as an inside out *psychological process*," Thomas said, shifting his weight from one foot to the other. "I'm talking about the views of Rollo May, Graham Wallas, Anthony Storr, and Arthur Koestler.[38] These writers focus on the conscious and unconscious psychological experience of the creative process—how it happened in creative people throughout history and how each of us can have similar experiences.

"The third model views creativity outside-in as a collective, social, *cultural process*." Thomas took a marker out of his shirt pocket and wrote the words, OUTSIDE-IN on the flip chart in large block letters. "According to this view, the creative process is a sociological phenomenon that always manifests itself within the social and cultural context of some domain of knowledge. In other words, creativity never occurs in an intellectual vacuum.[39]

"For example, the scientists who comprise the high-energy physics community are the gatekeepers for that domain of knowledge, and they control which novelties and innovations get included in that domain. On this view, creativity is the social process by which knowledge is developed and incorporated into an existing body of knowledge."

"So which model is correct?" Bethany shook her head and asked in consternation.

"Well," Thomas smiled, "they're all correct in their own way. That's why I've synthesized all three into a single model—all three describe the creative process from different perspectives."

He pointed off the side of the ship to an enormous, mushrooming cumulus cloud. "Do you see the beauty and shape of that cloud? If we were flying *through* that same cloud in a plane, we would see nothing but a kind of fog. Which is the 'true' view of the cloud? The fact is, a cloud looks differently depending on whether we view it from the outside-in or the inside-out."

To illustrate this, Thomas picked up a marker and drew a picture of a fluffy cloud on the flip chart, then sketched one stick figure outside and another inside the cloud and pointed to them alternately. "There's no one true view because we see differently when we change perspectives.

"I always try to piece together an increasingly robust definition of things like the creative process by viewing it from multiple perspectives simultaneously. So, Bethany," he said looking intently at her, "that's why I say that all three models are correct in their own way—creativity *is* an intellectual process, a psychological process, and a cultural process depending on how you look at it."

Bethany's eyes went wide. She reached for her thinking stone and pondered this new insight as she turned the small, smooth stone over and over in her hand.

"Let's move on and discuss how the creative process actually works." Thomas widened his focus to include the rest of the group. "To begin with, a prerequisite for creativity is that the person has some level of competency in a body of knowledge or discipline. It's unlikely that an individual will find a creative solution to an advanced problem in mathematics, physics, marketing, or product design if they have little or no knowledge in these bodies of knowledge."

"But I've seen people without any formal education in a discipline ask what they call really 'dumb' questions," Frank countered, "but their line of inquiry is often more insightful and penetrating than questions posed by professionals who've been formally training in that field."

"I've seen that too, Frank," Thomas nodded in acknowledgment. "But these individuals are often highly trained in some other unrelated body of knowledge. Viewing a physics problem through the lens of an unrelated discipline like philosophy can reveal deep connections between the two fields of knowledge. But without intellectual competency in *some* discipline, people usually develop uninformed, mediocre imitations of what others have already done. So it should come as no surprise that people are normally creative in areas in which they have been highly trained, have lots of experience, and have worked diligently and consciously for extended periods of time."

Frank nodded in hearty agreement.

"In fact," Thomas continued, "we often see the creative process in action when competent people spend extended periods of time trying to solve a problem, then reach an immovable brick wall with no path forward. Creative people know that if they occupy themselves with some unrelated activities, or just get a good night's sleep, the answer to the problem often emerges into consciousness *intact*. It's almost as if the solution resulted from unconscious problem-solving processes that continued to work long after *they* stopped consciously thinking about the problem."

"Are you saying that the emergence of creative solutions is not under the direct control of consciousness?" Dan asked in a skeptical tone.

"Yes," Thomas countered quickly, "but that doesn't mean these solutions just appear by accident or serendipity, nor is it as unpredictable as some authors suggest.

"Listen to what Rollo May has to say about this issue," he glanced down at a note card and read. "'Creativity goes on in varying degrees of intensity on levels not directly under the control of conscious willing. But let it be said immediately that unconscious insights or answers to problems that come in reverie do not come hit or miss....But what is entirely clear is that they pertain to those areas in which the person consciously has worked laboriously and with dedication.'[40]

"It's the *unconscious* aspect of mental life that comes closest to characterizing how we inwardly experience the creative process." Thomas paused to let the profundity of the concept sink in. "Once the unconscious elements of the creative process are more thoroughly understood, creativity becomes less 'mysterious' and our creative abilities become a more predictable and valued resource in our lives.

"A less tangible aspect of creativity is understanding how the creative process *links* invisible archetypal symbols from mythology to publicly observable forms of expression so that the invisible nature of the symbol is made partly visible in something we observe with one of the five senses."

Thomas positioned his hands as if he were playing a guitar. "In music, it might be Jimi Hendrix's ability to aurally represent the traumatic collective ethos of the Viet Nam War in his Woodstock rendition of the *Star Spangled Banner*.

"In science, it could be Stephen Hawking's ability to link mathematical equations to a model of cosmic space; or the combined efforts of the high-energy physics community's development of the Standard Model of the universe.

"In the business arena, it might be the link that Daniel Goleman made between the inner experience of emotions and our brain, Kaplan and Norton's development of a cause and effect Balanced Scorecard of measurement for organizational performance, or Collins and Porras' identifying and articulating what makes organizations truly visionary. Regardless of the field of endeavor, invisible symbols are concretized into tangible expressions that we can see, taste, touch, feel, and hear."

"But creativity can ultimately be reduced to creative ideas—right?" Frank insisted, though not altogether confidently.

"Not really," Thomas replied, sensing the emotional force in Frank's words. "While having creative ideas and being sensitized to and connected with underlying archetypal symbols is necessary, it's not sufficient to make a person *truly* creative. The truly creative person moves beyond ideas and concretizes their insights into something that is *publicly observable* by one of the five senses.

"If a creative insight doesn't get cashed-out into something physical, then nothing new has been 'created' and there has been no real creativity.

To be truly creative means, by definition, to give birth to something that previously did not exist.

"When creativity is real, it makes a physical difference. If a creative insight makes no physical difference, then it's not real. Like it or not, *true* creativity can only be seen in the *creative act*, and these acts must be capable of being known by others."

"Something deep within me rebels against what you're saying," Frank muttered in a troubled voice, "but I can't think of a single counter-example to your position."

Sensing how disturbed he was by the concept, Thomas nodded and said gently, "I believe there's a perfectly plausible explanation for your reaction based on your Enneagram and MBTI type. Write this issue down on a three-by-five card and put it in the middle of the table, and we'll talk about it between sessions."

Frank nodded, satisfied with Thomas's suggestion, then picked up a card and began to write.

"The greatest difference between a person who *seems* to have creative talent and the *truly* creative person is their ability to incarnate creative insights into something physical, be it equations, technological innovations, or a painting that captures the mood of an entire generation."

Rena suddenly had a mental image of Shane at last week's staff meeting. She looked directly at Maggie to get her attention, then raised her hand and said to Thomas, "The distinction between talking about creative ideas and the creative act reminds me of the *HBR* article on The Smart-Talk Trap. It describes people who focus on the negative aspects of issues in meetings and make things unnecessarily complicated and abstract just to impress others with how much they know.[41] I work with a guy who's a master at that kind of smart talk, but he can't produce most of what he brags about."

What's she trying to do with this Shane comment? Maggie wondered. *Is she taking a cheap shot at me in front of all these people?*

"Yes, Rena, that's sometimes the case." Thomas noticed the tension between her and Maggie as he quickly gave Rena a reassuring smile. "When creative ideas are cashed-out into innovations and improvements, not only is the world changed because something new comes into existence, but the person who is the channel, or conduit, of the creative act is also transformed in the process. When the creative person has the psychological strength to tolerate this inner essential tension, it often results in a truly creative expression. When they can't tolerate it, they cross the line into neurosis or psychosis. As Ludwig suggests, this is why creativity and genius have long been associated with insanity."[42]

"But," Cindy almost shouted, clenching both fists, "understanding *how* to give concrete physical expression to those inner pressures so they truly satisfy my deepest longing is not easy because the creative power within sometimes threatens to take me over and explode like a volcanic eruption."

"Precisely," Thomas nodded. "That's why it's crucial for each of you to experience the power of the creative process personally. It's impossible to know how deeply creativity is embedded in the human personality until you experience its transforming power firsthand." He paused to let the impact of his admonition sink in.

"Do you see that island over there?" Thomas pointed off the port side of the ship. "That's an enormous, active volcano. Can you see the smoke rising out of the central crater like a chimney?"

The group gazed at the mountain, and Nikki and Lindsey went to the railing to get a better view.

"What you see on the surface is an island that's become a magnet for terrestrial and marine life. It has incredible levels of biodiversity in the form of complex coral reef and a biological infrastructure that's developed around the sandy shoreline at the island's base.

"But the center of the volcanic cone has a channel that goes down to the core of the Earth's center—an inferno of liquid, molten lava. As Cindy's comment suggests, this volcano is a metaphor and image of the creative process in each of us."

Thomas turned a flip chart page to reveal Figure 4, then gestured to those at the railing to return to their seats so he would have their full attention.

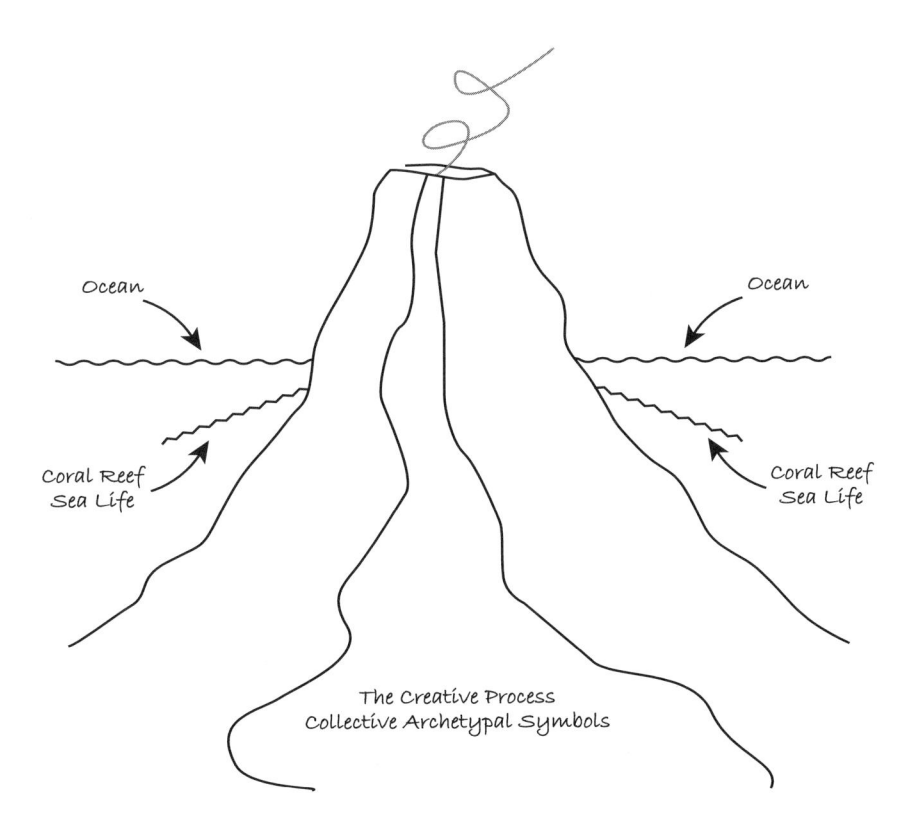

Figure 4
THE CREATIVE PROCESS AS A VOLCANO

"Figure 4 shows how each of us is like that volcano with a conduit that goes down to the archetypal symbols at the core of our being. The creative person becomes a channel for transmitting ideas that come from the deep symbolic core of our collective humanity up to the surface of everyday life. That volcano is an image and metaphor for how the creative process works in all of us, and I believe that was what Cindy was trying to get at with her comment."

"That's right," she whispered just loud enough for the group to hear.

"Studying the life and work of Thomas Edison gives us our first glimpse of what a creative organization looks like. Unlike the image of a *lone* inventor, Edison was an *independent* inventor who built a powerful team of highly skilled people around himself. He employed glassmakers, machinists, draftsmen, clockmakers, technicians, engineers, and people with other skills that he didn't have. Edison created the notion that 'inventing' was a cross-functional team activity. In fact, one of Edison's long-time assistants once said, 'Edison is in reality a collective noun and means the work of many men.'"[43]

"Can you give us an example of how that kind of team-innovation worked?" Lindsey implored.

"Absolutely," Thomas smiled, hoping to encourage more of her interaction in the group. "Edison took his ideas about the first phonograph and turned them into a diagram in one of the hundreds of notebooks that he kept over the course of his lifetime. He gave a copy of the diagram to one of his assistants, John Kruesi, and told him to build what he, Edison, had drawn.[44] Kruesi had no idea what the device was until Edison told him that it was going to be a machine that talked. Kruesi and the others on Edison's team just shook their heads in disbelief. But when they finished making the device, and they heard it parrot back their own voices just like Edison predicted, they were truly amazed.[45]

"Edison's team approach to creativity and innovation is precisely the issue that Frank and I were discussing a few minutes ago." Thomas pointed at Frank to draw him back into the conversation. "Edison generated ideas, and Kruesi knew how to build devices, so working together created a powerful synergy. Had the drawing of the phonograph stayed in Edison's notebook, it might not have been invented. Yet without Edison's creative vision and ideas, Kruesi would not have known what to build. True innovation requires both sides of the creativity equation—the creative idea and the creative act."

Frank looked somewhat relieved as he pondered the symbiotic relationship, then scribbled in his journal, "creative ideas + the creative act = true creativity."

"Edison's laboratory was a two-storied building that was like a big barn—twenty-five feet wide and one hundred feet long, it had worktables spread throughout." Thomas gestured with both hands to indicate the layout. "Each table had a different, often unrelated, project that he was working on.[46] Edison would work on a project on one table, then move to another one across the room as if his mind was working on *all* the projects at once. The set up of the tables allowed him to take insights that emerged from one project and apply them to others on tables one hundred feet away."

Thomas walked to the flip chart and drew a rough diagram of the way the tables were set up. "After reading about his life and work, my own sense is that the arrangement of the tables in the laboratory was an externalizing of how the creative process worked in his mind. He frequently got creative insights about connections between seemingly unrelated projects, and the layout of the tables allowed him to transform those insights into creative acts on other projects he was working on." Thomas paused to flip a page, revealing Figure 5.

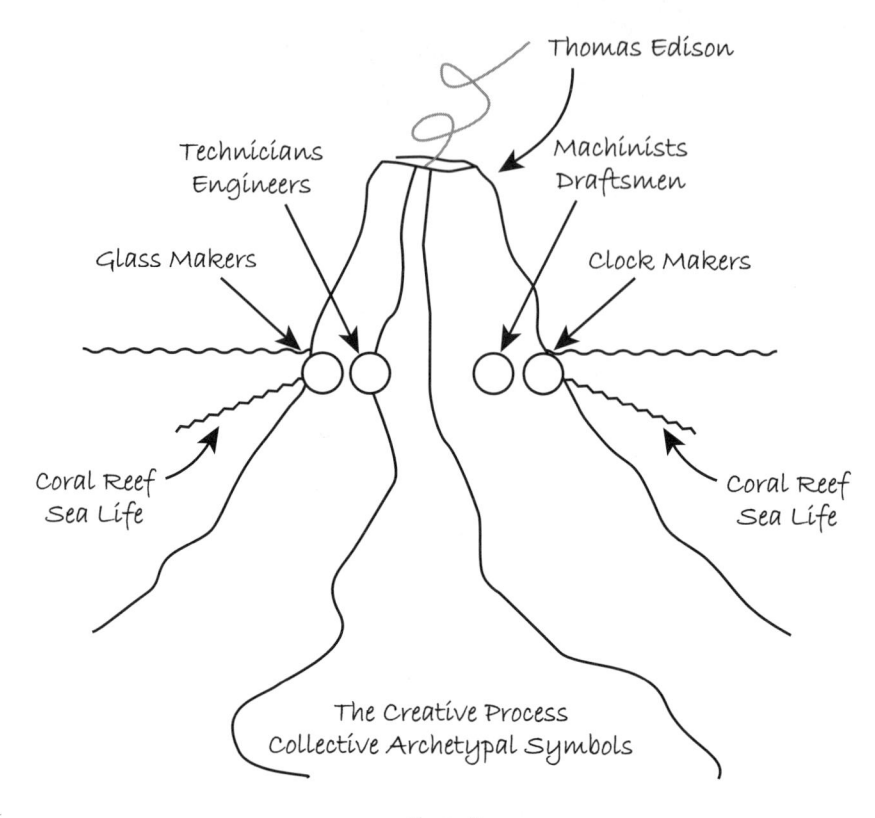

Figure 5

EDISON'S TEAM AS A VOLCANO

"Edison was a conduit down to the core of a deep underground source of the creative process. But he built a team of people around him who were creative in ways that were different from his—people who were facilitators, supporters, and enablers of the creative process. Edison would not have been nearly as successful without this team of creative people. It was the entire team that transformed multiple creative insights into the creative acts of innovation and patentable inventions. Over one hundred years ago, Edison and his team created much of the reality we live in today, and many of the differences between our Western world and life here in PNG are due to the one thousand ninety-three patents developed by this small group of people."[47]

Thomas walked to the ship's railing and pointed off the starboard side. "Do you see that mountain, and that one, and those over there?"

Thomas used his outstretched arm to trace the vast semicircle of fourteen thousand-foot peaks that line Kimbe Bay. "There are sixteen volcanoes scattered around us. Each one is a separate landmass above the water with its own channel down to the river of molten lava at the Earth's core. If you can imagine these volcanoes as multiple Edison teams working side by side, *that* is a symbolic image of a creative organization.

"Creative organizations are hotbeds of activity where people work side-by-side as multiple channels down to the symbolic core of their common humanity. These archetypal symbols are inner standards of excellence that embody the deepest foundation of all human meaning.

"In much the same way," he exclaimed, looking from one person to the next around the table, "this dive workshop is not primarily a group endeavor. Rather, you are more like nine individual wells that go down to, and connect with, a deep underground river of collective, symbolic meaning that we all share. We are individuals working side by side, but joined to the wisdom of the ages at the deepest level of our humanity. That is why it's possible to intentionally build a creative organization. All people, in all times, in all places, in all cultures share a common humanity at the level of this symbolic river of meaning—the place where dreams come from. It's at this level that many Western people feel a longing for, and kinship with, the culture and people of PNG, but they have no inkling of how to live out that connection in their everyday lives."

That's precisely what I experienced when I connected with that woman in the village, Cindy thought. *I've got to write this on a three-by-five and set it in the middle of the table so we can talk privately.*

"So given the image of the volcanoes all around us," Thomas proffered, "why can't an owner or senior manager consciously build a creative organization by assembling teams of managers and workers who facilitate, support, and enable the creative process throughout the company?"

Dan raised his hand. "Yeah, but there aren't many people in the world like Edison," he objected cynically. "That's not the kind of creative ability that I have, if I have any at all."

Thomas walked back to the head of the teaching table to confront Dan's challenge head-on. "Of course people have different levels of talent. But most of us were socialized to believe that we don't have creative ability. We've been scripted to believe this about ourselves, even though it's not true. So when I hear you say that you don't have creative ability, it tells me that you've been deceived by a lie about yourself.

Thomas held Dan in an earnest gaze. "My response to your comment about you not having creative ability echoes Stephen Covey's words, 'Argue for your weakness and it is yours.'[48] It becomes a self-fulfilling prophecy. You can't go on telling yourself and everyone else in the world how uncreative you are, Dan, then wonder why you don't experience your creative process." Dan was caught without a comeback as he marveled at how Thomas had nailed him, but not unkindly, rather with wisdom and insight.

I tell him that all the time, Cindy mused silently. *He's got so little faith in himself and his abilities.*

"You may not know this," Thomas suddenly smiled, "but Edison only attended school for three months in his entire life. His teachers claimed he was a slow learner and almost totally unteachable, so his mother home-schooled him.

"In much the same way, Einstein was not a remarkable math student, even in high school. Where would the world be today if *they* had believed the messages that the world gave them about how creative and bright they were?

"What I wonder," Thomas now sadly shook his head, "is how many more truly creative people and even geniuses like Edison and Einstein the world would produce if we facilitated, supported, and enabled the creative process in people from the earliest years of childhood. Instead, we stomp the natural creative abilities out of our kids, then whine when they're not more creative.

"Imagine," he said hopefully, "if reality is truly a product of human creativity, and if more people were encouraged to understand, nurture, and develop their innate creative abilities, we might be living in a very different, more humane world."

The profundity and far reaching consequences of Thomas's statement created a reflective mood and spirit of contemplation that permeated the group.

"Too few people have had the experience of being a part of a great team where the creative process manifested itself and something was brought into existence that changed the world and the people working on the project." The volume and intensity of Thomas's voice began to rise as his passion and conviction increased. "There's an excitement, depth, sense of fulfillment and purpose that comes from such an encounter! People never forget it. It's an intense experience of psychological wholeness that changes some of them permanently. When that experience ends, it causes an inner hole that most people try to fill with jobs, relationships, and material possessions. But it never works because that's not what the emptiness is about. They long to feel the transforming power of the creative process—nothing else will fill that void.

"If there are no questions, I'd like to move on to a more concrete explanation of how the creative process actually works." When no one raised a hand, he continued. "Figure 6 is an adaptation of a model developed in the last century by Graham Wallas that mirrors many people's experience of the creative process."[49] Thomas reached over and flipped to the next page.

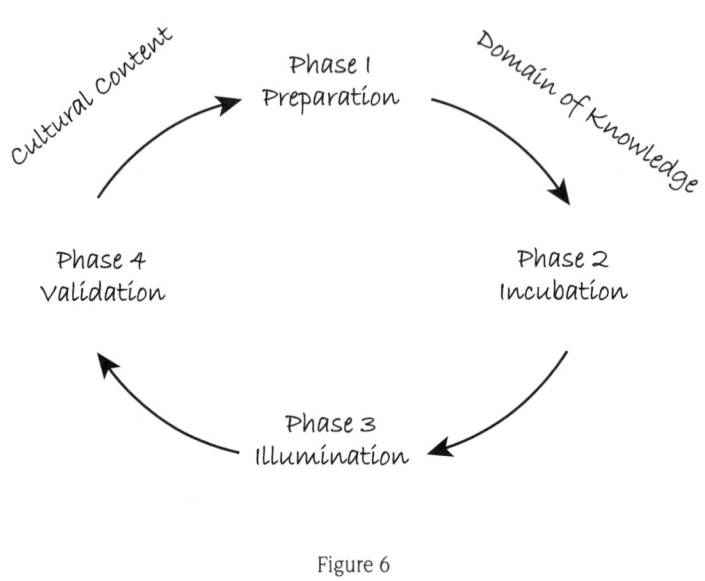

Cultural Content → **Phase 1 Preparation** → *Domain of Knowledge* → **Phase 2 Incubation** → **Phase 3 Illumination** → **Phase 4 Validation** → (cycle)

Figure 6
THE CREATIVE PROCESS

"As I mentioned at the beginning of this session, I've synthesized the three most important models of creativity into a single model. Notice how the four phases of the creative process shown in Figure 6 are constrained within the cultural context of multiple domains of knowledge. In Phase 1, Preparation, people develop expertise in a domain of knowledge, learn the tools described by De Bono and Michalko, and try to use them to solve complex problems. It is during the preparation phase that people spend extended periods of time trying to solve a problem, only to come to an immovable roadblock. When this happens, if they move into Phase 2, Incubation, and occupy themselves with other unrelated activities, or just get a good night's sleep, often times an elegant solution emerges into consciousness *intact* as the result of unconscious processes. The emergence of unconsciously developed solutions signals the appearance of Phase 3 of the creative process, Illumination."

"What you're describing sounds like a *eureka* experience when a light goes on in your head," James interjected enthusiastically.

Cindy nodded in agreement with the connection James made between the common experience and the model Thomas was teaching.

"Correct, James!" Thomas said, aiming a congratulatory fist at him. "That's exactly what happens. Sometimes, our unconscious mental processes use data, strategies, and a different perspective, and propose a solution that seems like a stroke of genius to our conscious self. Other times, we find ourselves in the uncomfortable position of having a solution or a belief emerge into consciousness that we previously rejected, or are diametrically opposed to.

"So let's go back to the last step in Figure 6." Thomas returned to the chart. "When a creative idea has been cashed out into an innovation or improvement that is publicly observable, Phase 4 requires that it be validated by the people, institutions, and knowledge domains that constitute our cultural context. The validation phase raises questions like, 'Does it add to the existing body of knowledge as a true innovation, improvement, or best practice? Does the knowledge or device actually work and solve problems?' Once an innovation or improvement passes the gauntlet of cultural validation and is used for an extended period of time, the history of its creation falls below the surface of cultural consciousness, and we can't remember a time when we lived without it. It becomes one more component of the socially constructed reality that we live in."

"Okay. I can understand how the creative process works with personal issues or in relationships." Dan sat up straight in his chair to make his point more forcefully. "In fact I've actually experienced this in my own life, despite what I said before. But the business environment is very different because of time and cost constraints. Plus, you have customers breathing down your neck.

"What happens if you have a decision to make and you give it over to the creative process and nothing happens? Do you just sit back and wait for 'the unconscious' to act while your customers are getting ready to go to the competition?" Dan asked haughtily.

"Of course you don't just wait around for 'the unconscious' to work," Thomas clarified, unruffled by Dan's mocking tone. "If a creative solution to a problem doesn't come in the time frame you need it, just do what you've always done…" Thomas made a tight fist, "*brute force it.*"

"What I'm saying is that even if you only get a creative solution ten or fifteen percent of the time, these solutions will be far superior to your normal course of action. Once you gain self-knowledge about how your creative process works and build the principles and practices that we're describing here into your organization's structures, systems, strategies, and culture, you may be able to increase the number of creative solutions to twenty percent of all your decisions.

"Now that's significant because over a long enough period of time, the number of value-producing innovations and improvements will continue to increase, and you'll find that the creative process is actually providing leadership for your entire organization."

Dan looked briefly at Cindy, then tossed out, "I think I could make what you're saying work as an employee, but as the CEO of a company I have specific fiduciary responsibilities. I can't just hand over my authority to the creative process—it's my job to run the company."

Thomas was well aware of the tension between Dan and Cindy increasing as he replied. "I hear what you're saying, Dan, but I always make the distinction between three kinds of authority—organizational, intellectual, and creative authority." Thomas flipped the page to reveal Figure 7 on the flip chart.

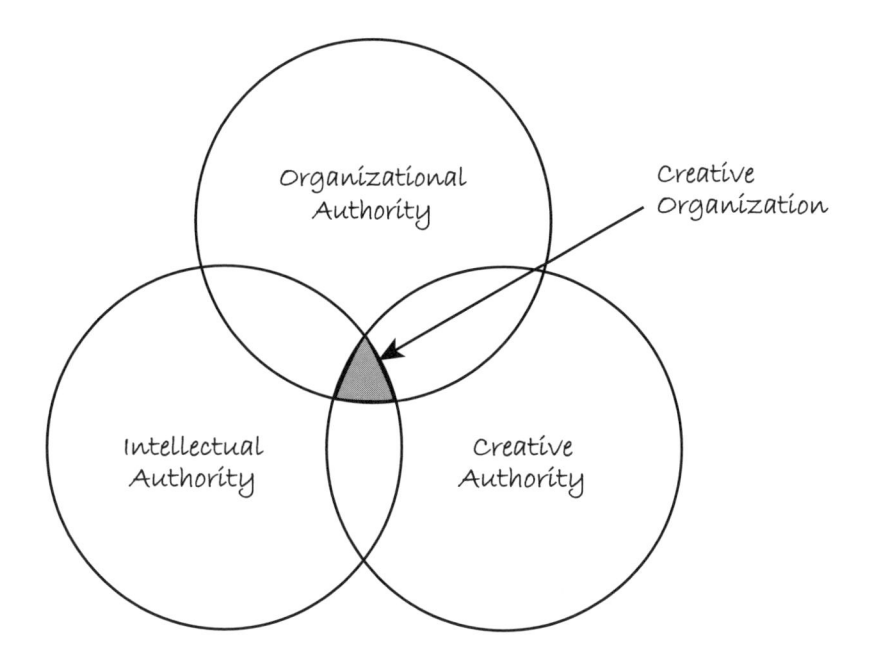

Figure 7
THE THREE KINDS OF AUTHORITY

"Organizational authority is where your name appears on the organization chart, and this is the kind of authority I hear you talking about when you tell me you're the CEO. Intellectual authority is about your level of competency and accomplishment in one or more fields of knowledge, including relevant business knowledge. I have seen people at the lowest levels of an organization demonstrate more intellectual authority than a CEO, and if that senior manager is smart, they capitalize on that employee's knowledge rather than being threatened by it and trying to ignore or suppress it." Thomas shot Dan a knowing glance. Based on personal knowledge he'd obtained as Dan's consultant, and more current information that he gleaned from reading the case studies he and Cindy turned in, Thomas understood their dynamic.

"Likewise," Thomas proceeded, taking in the rest of the group, "the person who has creative authority has learned to experience and harness the creative process as manifested in concrete examples of innovation and improvement—regardless of where they sit on the organization chart. The smart CEO knows that intellectual and creative authority are the engines that drive high performance and that momentum is easily frustrated and undermined by traditional, hierarchical views of organizational authority.

"You would hope that the top leaders of an organization have developed all three kinds of authority, but this is often not the case. Contrary to your claim that trusting the leadership of the creative process is inconsistent with a leader's authority," Thomas pointed to the center of Figure 7, "leaders in creative organizations are motivated by the *intersection* of all three kinds of authority. This earns them a deep and abiding respect from employees and managers at all levels."

That's sure not the kind of authority I use back at my parish, James thought introspectively. *Maybe I ought to examine my need to control everything—and perhaps work on developing these other two kinds of authority in myself and with others.*

"Once owners, managers, and workers personally experience the value of the creative process for themselves and for their organization, they begin to see the world differently in at least four ways." Thomas was sweating profusely as the morning sun continued to drive up the temperature even on the covered deck where the teaching table was located.

"First, ongoing experience with their own creative process gives leaders and managers deep insight into how the creative process works in their employees so they can encourage them to use creativity in their day-to-day tasks.

"Second, the creative process gives them insights into how their actions and attitudes in meetings and public settings stifle creativity and maintain the status quo.

"Third, leaders and managers begin to see how their personalities and preferences for doing work establishes and perpetuates structures, systems, strategies, and organizational culture that frustrate and oppose the creative process.

"Fourth, they begin to get a vision for how to build a creative organization."

The definition of creativity presented by Thomas troubled Nikki because she had a tendency to live in her head, planning far into the future but not connecting her plans to the day-to-day realities of life or following through to completion on projects. If true creativity required both creative ideas and creative acts, Nikki was rarely creative, although she fancied herself as such.

~~~~

A graduate of Yale's Executive MBA program, Nikki Salem was tall, with long, skinny legs, a bony torso, and a slender neck that supported a short, wiry, shagged reddish-brown spiked head of hair that pointed in every direction. The intensity of her flaming green eyes, the sly devilish smirk on her face, and her slightly slurred speech from a pierced tongue made Nikki look like a wild-woman—and she was.

Her body was restless and in constant motion—tapping her feet, chewing gum anxiously, and walking away mid-sentence in conversations. Her presence seemed scattered and distracted like the rest of her life. Nikki had a sharp, probing, and curious mind, but she acted like an instant expert on just about everything. She talked constantly and when there was no one there to listen to her, she chatted mindlessly under her breath so she had *someone* to talk to. Nikki had previously completed the RHETI and the MBTI and knew that she was an ENTP, Enneagram Type Seven who was busy, productive, playful, high-spirited, and practical.[50]

Nikki had been one of the top sales people in an international cosmetics company with a territory that covered a large part of Western Europe. She had recognized very subtle shifts and changes in Europe's creative, artistic, and fashion trends and was able to translate them into customer preferences for the products she sold. She knew how to present the most desirable image of her product lines to the right market segments, in the right countries, and masterfully outdistanced the competition. Senior management used her as a poster child for what being a marketing and salesperson was all about because she increased revenue across her territory by twenty-five percent. She was visionary.

But Nikki was burned out from being on the road one hundred fifty days a year and wanted to settle down to a more "normal" lifestyle, so she set up a meeting with John Sutton, the company president. "Look, John, I'm fried," Nikki finally admitted with a look of utter exhaustion on her face. "I know the director of the production division is moving on and I'd like you to give me a shot at that position. "I'll give it everything I've got," Nikki raised her hand as if to take an oath. "I swear I won't let you down."

"You've got an impressive track record with the company," John extolled, "but the production job will be a different kind of work. Are you sure you can handle it?"

"Of course I can," Nikki responded confidently. "I can do anything I put my mind to."

"I've been trying to bring change to that part of the company for years. They've got problems with quality, rework, and downtime in the production process. If you want the job and think you can handle it, it's yours," John said, then cautioned, "but if I were you, I'd think about it for a while."

I wonder if this is a mistake, John worried. *If she fails, I won't be able to take her back in marketing and sales because I'll already have filled that position.*

A little over six months into the position, Nikki was trying to decide if she should quit. Initially, she took her new responsibilities by storm. She was strong in the early phases of projects and had incredible skills in brainstorming, generating possibilities, and establishing overall organizational direction through strategic planning. Unlike her predecessor, she promoted a positive mood in the division and animated managers and workers alike with her enthusiasm and energy. But Nikki only performed well in the early, big picture phases of assignments. Once the job began to move toward the routine tasks of management, she lost interest and usually just moved on to another position.

After a year of implementation, the division's performance measures showed that the problems had not gone away—they may even have gotten worse. Despite these red flags, Nikki was upbeat and positive, telling the senior management team that change was coming, but in her reflective moments Nikki wanted out. As her track record showed, she got bored easily and had trouble staying focused on the details of projects that required long-term commitment and forced her to deal with the pedestrian, mundane routines of running a business operation.

The senior management team brought in a consultant to take a closer look at what was going on and this made Nikki even more uncomfortable. The assessment recommended that the company develop and implement a new performance appraisal system with the goal of increasing accountability at all organizational levels—including the senior management team.

"As you can see, the consultant's report shows that Nikki's division is one of the organizational units that needs accountability the most." John concurred as he reviewed the findings of a twenty-page report with his senior managers.

Sarah, the Chief Financial Officer, smiled slyly, "Let's make *her* responsible to fix the problem company-wide. We'll assign her to work with Barb, the HR Director, to develop a new system."

The rest of the senior managers shook their heads in unanimous agreement.

"It's brilliant," John beamed, "make it so."

Nikki didn't know that she was on thin ice with John, or that he regretted going against his gut-level instinct by giving her the job. Now he was going to force her to work herself out of the performance hole she dug for herself.

"I think we should take a traditional approach to measuring individual employees' performance," Barb said at their opening meeting.

Nikki acted like a life-long HR professional and rebutted Barb at every turn. "I think we should abolish individual performance appraisals like Deming and Kohn argue.[51] It's impossible to measure the performance of an individual employee because how well they work is simply an artifact of the effectiveness of the overall system. Trying to measure the performance of individuals lowers morale because employees can't control or change the organizational structures and systems they work in.

"Our employees need to be intrinsically motivated rather than using the carrot and stick approach that you're suggesting Barb," Nikki concluded arrogantly.

"I agree with you philosophically," Barb said, her frustration becoming noticeable, "but I challenge you to come up with a concrete approach for how to do this—that doesn't ultimately reduce to measuring the performance of individuals."

"The company should define quantitative measures for teams and business processes and use them to evaluate the staff's performance," Nikki countered, standing pat on her opinion.

"I agree that we need these measures, but the finer grained root causes of whether teams, business processes, or organizations are performing well come down to the performance of individuals," Barb insisted, for her view was based on her twenty years experience as an HR professional.

"I concede that an ideal system would synthesize the business process measurements with individual performance and intrinsic motivation," Barb continued, now even more annoyed by the smirk Nikki had on her face. "But the senior management team has tasked us to find a solution to the assessment findings. So, as stimulating as these philosophical discussions are, we have a deadline to meet!" Barb slapped her hand on the table.

Nikki's insistence on this approach is just a way of covering up for her own performance problems and those of her division, Barb thought as she tried unsuccessfully to control her anger throughout the rest of the meeting.

Underneath Nikki's bubbly, action-oriented façade was an inner life that resembled a dry, barren desert—a wasteland that her entire psychology was mobilized to defend against. This defense required her to maintain the hope that a promised land where all her desires and needs were met was on the horizon just beyond her field of vision. Her hope almost always turned out to be a mirage when she arrived at the actual experience, but this never deterred her from her strategy. Like a person on a road trip in a scorching desert who continually sees water on the blacktop up ahead, Nikki would raise her eyes to the next mirage—ever hopeful that she'd find an oasis. This was why she hated listening to the problems of her managers and staff—they reminded her of her own sadness and depression. Staying in motion and moving down the road had become a way of life for Nikki because this was how she dealt with her anxiety and pain. She just moved on to the next experience and devoured the enjoyment in life like someone who was starving.

"Hey Barb!" Nikki's voice clangored disrespectfully through the phone, "I'm not going to be able to make our next three meetings—I'm heading out of town."

Barb was stunned because the project deadline was six weeks away, and here was Nikki announcing that she was going to be on a dive trip for three of those weeks.

"You can't do this, Nikki, we have commitments to John and the other senior managers," Barb pleaded.

"Sorry, Barb," came Nikki's cold reply, "I've already booked the trip and it's non-refundable. I'll be back in time to help finish up, but till then you'll just have to carry on without me."

Little concrete progress had been made on selecting a new performance appraisal system, and Barb was frustrated to the point that she went directly to John to explain what was happening.

"She argues with me about everything, even things she knows nothing about," Barb cried in utter frustration.

John nodded, knowing Nikki's personality and style.

"Now she's off on a three-week vacation." Barb shook her head in bewilderment, then brightened slightly, "Honestly, I'm glad she's going—I'll get more work done without her!"

After a pause, Barb's facial expression darkened. "If she remains on this project, John, I promise you, it will ultimately fail."

Nikki's e-mail to John explained that she felt the dive workshop would give her new insights into how to solve the performance appraisal problem. What she didn't know when she left was that she had finally pushed John over the edge. While she was gone, he would draw up the paperwork to fire her the day she returned.

Well, how's this for irony? John mused as he signed her termination papers. *Nikki's going to a workshop to learn how to solve problems that won't be hers when she gets back.* He couldn't help but let out a laugh.

∿∿∿∿

Thomas reached across the table to fill his water glass as the rising sun and temperature had become uncomfortably warm. "It's become fashionable for business writers to articulate how desperately people want to find meaning and significance in their work. But meaning and significance can't be found in achieving external standards of excellence alone. Finding meaning and significance in work happens when employees engage their creative abilities with the day-to-day activities of their professional life. This enables them to view their daily tasks as having symbolic or even transcendent value.

"Whether an employee is flipping hamburgers, working as an airline flight attendant, or is a researcher trying to cure cancer, meaning and significance come only by experiencing the transforming power of the creative process.

"Another crucial element in learning to find meaning and significance in work is what Walter Lippmann called being *disinterested*—that is, not elevating self-interest above what's in the best interest of other people or an organization.[52] Lippmann is not talking about being detached and uninvolved from the activities of life—that's being *uninterested*," Thomas emphasized to make sure they understood the distinction.

"Rather, being disinterested means we are not motivated to secure our own needs at the expense of others. Lippmann claims that disinterestedness renders our 'passion innocent and an authoritative morality unnecessary.'[53]

"Recent events in the world of business have shown that we are in dire need of leaders who are disinterested." Thomas passed around recent news clippings of corporate executives who had been convicted of business-related crimes and sentenced to jail terms.

"In the wake of Enron, Martha Stewart, Tyco, and other scandals, most people believe that senior executives are only in business for themselves, and care nothing for employees, consumers, or shareholders.[54]

"Some business writers claim that Hollywood-style CEOs like Jack Welch and George Soros closely resemble the personality type that Freud called narcissistic.[55] But while it's easy to be outraged by these events, Diane Coutu claims that people tend to attribute this type of greed to others, not themselves.[56]

"By projecting our greed onto them, we never have to face the fact that we were also greedy when we fully embraced rising shareholder value and sky rocketing stock prices because they were in our best interest.

"The problem of greed and self-interest in the business world persists despite the fact that research shows that being disinterested pays big financial dividends. For example, Jim Collins led a study of almost fifteen hundred *Fortune 500* companies and, using stringent criteria of business excellence, he narrowed this list down to eleven companies that were truly great. When the study began, Collins gave his research team explicit instructions to downplay the role of the leader in organizations so that they didn't end up with the obvious finding that it's all about leadership.[57] But a careful analysis of the stringent criteria for business excellence eventually showed that the companies that were truly great all had what Collins called 'Level 5 leaders.'"

Thomas picked up a note card to quote Collins. "'Level 5 leaders channel their ego needs away from themselves and into the larger goal of building a great company. It's not that Level 5 leaders have no ego or self-interest. Indeed, they are incredibly ambitious—*but their ambition is first and foremost for the institution, not themselves.*'[58]

"In my parlance, 'Level 5' leaders are *disinterested*." Thomas turned his focus back to the group. "They don't call attention to themselves or their actions, but focus on the work *the company* has accomplished.

Being disinterested is one of the qualities of people who are psychologically healthy and have attained a mature character. It enables them to choose between what is good, better, and best in what Badaracco calls *defining moments*—situations where our organizational responsibilities collide with their core values.[59]

"In closing," Thomas handed out a dive slate to each attendee, "read through the summary points of the session on the dive slate." The group began to scan the list.

DIVE SLATE SESSION 1 REVIEW

Strategy 1: Find Meaning and Significance in Work
    Practice #1: Experience the Creative Process
- *Creativity is the problem-solving mechanism of the human brain*
- *Creativity is an intellectual, psychological, and cultural process*
- *The four-step creative process: preparation, incubation, illumination, and verification*
- *True creativity translates creative ideas into creative acts*
- *Volcanoes as a metaphor for the creative process*
- *Volcanoes as a metaphor for Edison's team-approach to creativity*

- *Multiple volcanoes as an image of a creative organization*
- *Allowing the creative process to provide organizational leadership*
- *Three kinds of authority: organizational, intellectual, and creative*
- *Personally experiencing the creative process gives insight into how the creative process works in ourselves, others, and organizations*

"I'd like you to clip the dive slate onto your Buoyancy Control Device (BCD) so you can reflect on the main points of Practice 1: *Experience the Creative Process* during your dive. Are there any questions?" Thomas put his hands on his hips, smiled encouragingly, and searched the faces of the group with deep inquiry.

He knew that most people needed time to formulate what they considered to be "really good questions." Plus, they were eager to get into the water where they'd find it easier to reflect on the material. Other people didn't want to pose their questions in front of the whole group. They preferred to wait and chat privately with him after the session was over. After each session Thomas liked to set aside some time for people who wanted to discuss the material covered in the session without the entire class there. That was another way he was able to get good feedback and honest dialogue about his ideas.

After about a minute of silence, Thomas gathered up his lecture materials and the three-by-five cards that people had placed in the center of the table and looked up and smiled at the group. He spotted Anita walking toward the teaching table and said, "Okay, this first dive will be a check-out dive so we can make sure of your buoyancy control and adjust the amount of weight you're wearing at a dive site where there's no current. It'll also give Anita and Janice a chance to get some sense of the level of your dive skills. Let's listen up as Anita gives us the dive brief on this site, which is called Restorf."

Anita stepped to the head of the table, clapped her hands together loudly and shouted cheerfully, "Okay—let's get started. Is everyone here?"

"Nikki's not here," Lindsey piped up. "I think she ran back to her cabin."

"Okay," Anita said, trying not to show her frustration, "we'll have to wait till she gets here." Anita motioned to one of the other crew and said, "Could you see if Nikki's in her cabin and tell her we're all waiting for her to start the dive brief?"

Anita had just finished making her request when Nikki bounded up the ladder and said unabashedly, "Sorry I'm late, guys."

Dan glared at her, clearly annoyed. Anita was also upset, but rather than lecture her on the importance of being on time, she decided to start the dive brief. "We are tied up pretty close to Restorf Island. There are two pinnacles just off the back of the boat, and you should see bump head parrot-fish, garden eels, eight-foot sea fans, manta shrimp, frog fish, and banded pipe fish. One special thing that you should watch for: groupers and sea trout are normally solitary fish, you usually see them on the reef alone. One week a year all over the world these fish group together in massive schools to spawn. We believe it happens here in PNG, but so far we've never seen it, so keep your eyes peeled and signal me if you think you see one.

"How many of you have cameras or video equipment?"

About half the group raised their hands.

"Camera and video people, you come with me, and the others please stick with Janice. Here's our procedure: once you get your gear on, just walk down the ladder to the dive platform that sits just above the water, put your fins on, then do a giant stride off the boat into the water. There's no current here, so if you get suited up and you don't want to sweat to death in this heat, get into the water and wait underneath the boat at about thirty feet and start having a look around till you see Janice or I get in the water. Then just follow us.

"Are there any questions?" Anita's face was beaming with anticipation of getting in the water and exploring the underwater splendor all around them. "Okay—the pool's open."

~~~~~

As James, Cindy, Dan, and Thomas hovered over one of two pinnacles at about twenty-five feet, the underwater world exploded with an overwhelming visual buffet of color and life. The visibility was easily one hundred feet horizontal underwater. One by one, as the group dropped below the surface of the water, Anita and Janice gave each diver the hand signal that asked them, "Are you okay?" Each diver signaled back with a thumbs-up, meaning "I'm fine."

Lindsey was still struggling with her buoyancy and how much weight to wear, but she had decided that on this trip she was going to get the buoyancy thing down once and for all. She had checked her logbook, and the last time she dove she wore fourteen pounds. But she felt this might be too much because when she let the air out of her BCD she sank like a rock, even when she was on the surface of the water. So she decided to wear only twelve pounds on her belt, and she was able to get down by pushing all the air out of her lungs long enough to sink the first five to ten feet. After that she began dropping through the water column. This was how Lindsey could tell she was weighted properly.

Once she reached about forty feet, she put a few blasts of air back into her BCD with her low-pressure inflater hose, then did some experimenting based on a tip Anita gave her. She counted to five as she inhaled a long, slow deep breath of air and felt her body begin to rise slowly through the water. Then she slowly exhaled, also counting to five, and she felt her body begin to drop through the water. She practiced the new routine over and over and had the physical experience of being buoyant at depth, as opposed to a mental image of the concept. For the first time since she'd been diving, she felt in control of her buoyancy—now she had to turn this new knowledge into a habit.

Frank was terrified, but he tried to hide it. He was breathing like a racehorse, unable to control his buoyancy. He was moving up and down in the water column, and behind the lenses of his facemask, his eyes were wide and full of fear. From a distance, Janice noticed he was having trouble so she signaled, "Are you okay?"

Frank, regardless, signaled back with a thumbs-up, "I'm okay."

They always say they're okay, even when they're not, Janice reflected.

Anita noticed that Frank was still struggling so she swam up next to him, got his attention, and emptied some of the air out of his BCD. This was what caused him to yo-yo up and down through the water column. She helped him establish control of his buoyancy, and then signaled him to calm down, to breath slowly, and relax. After a few minutes she could tell by the look in Frank's eyes that he was feeling more in control. Motioning toward the group, he and Anita swam and joined the others.

Within twenty minutes of the start of the dive, the two dive instructors already had a sense of their divers' ability. They looked at each other then at Thomas with a sense of relief. While there was a variety of dive skill levels in the group, they all appeared to have the competency needed to handle the more difficult diving they'd be doing for the rest of the trip.

The underworld exploded in a plethora of color, motion and life. The water was a warm eighty-five degrees. Pinnacles rose one hundred fifty feet from the ocean floor and were cover with sea life. Anemone carpets and soft coral waved in the gentle current as fish scampered across the reef doing exactly what Anita predicted: eating, sleeping, mating, and getting cleaned by other sea creatures. Enormous patches of staghorn coral covered the pinnacles as thousands of purple anthias, damselfish, and yellow tangs darted in and out of tiny, protective holes and passageways. Bright red whip coral, giant sea sponges, magnificent gorgonian fans, and dark orange elephant ear sponges covered almost every available inch of the reef.

Over seventy percent of the Earth's surface is covered with water, and in some places it plummets to more than thirty thousand feet deep. While Darwin's theory suggests that humans evolved over eons from creatures that formerly lived underwater, today we are clearly terrestrial creatures who live, grow and reproduce on land, immersed in an atmosphere of twenty-one percent oxygen and seventy-nine percent nitrogen. The physics of the underwater world is very different than the one we live in now. Water is eight hundred times denser than air and conducts heat away from the body twenty times faster. Objects appear twenty-five percent closer and sound travels four times as fast as it does in air. Although we have evolved into a land-based existence, scuba diving gear allows us to become like amphibians who live temporarily in a world that is in between land and sea. In both a physical and metaphorical way, for humans, breathing underwater for long periods is like going back in evolutionary time.

Cindy hung motionlessly at a depth of about sixty feet, watching the throng of underwater life. She was glad she'd come to this strange and enchanting land of life, death, beauty, and suffering. She loved diving because it was a solitary and isolated sport that was private and personal like this moment in time. Yet paradoxically it was a very social sport. Underwater you teamed up with a dive buddy or a group of divers. Then back on the ship, people shared experiences they'd had in common underwater, each from their own unique perspective. Solitude mingled with shared experiences, privacy combined with companionship, isolation juxtaposed with social interaction—diving embodied the tensions we experience in all human interactions.

The scuba refresher course that Rena and Maggie took back in Boulder built their confidence and allowed them to focus on observing the spectacular array of marine life, rather than managing their fear of being underwater. As they floated buoyantly above an enormous patch of cabbage coral on the top of the pinnacle, Maggie saw something out of the corner of her eye moving rapidly toward her—it was a banded sea snake. She took her dive knife from its sheath and banged on her tank to get Rena's attention. About five feet long, three inches in diameter, with silver and black zebra stripes, banded sea snakes are air breathers who periodically return to the surface of the water, but can remain submerged for more than an hour. They feed primarily on small reef fish, and are not known to attack divers, but their venom is ten times more poisonous than their terrestrial relatives. The two women hung there motionless as the snake turned and disappeared deep into the coral. Rena reached for her dive slate and wrote the word "WOW!" in large block letters. Maggie nodded and gave her the thumbs-up as the two women continued the dive—now more cautiously.

PNG has some of the finest and most pristine coral reefs in the world. Even renowned diving locations like the Great Barrier Reef in Australia have sustained damage. Reef life is damaged by too many divers and other man-made threats like chemical and nutrient pollution from farming, business, and industry, and sediment that runs into the ocean when land is cleared for building and industrial development. By contrast, PNG has had so little social and technological development, and so few divers, that the reef that surrounds this nation of six hundred islands is relatively untouched and probably looks much like it did one thousand years ago.

Once they were back on the boat, Thomas found Frank reading a book on marine life alone in the dining room. "Hey, Frank," he asked in a cheery, upbeat voice, "is this a good time to discuss the note you gave me on the three-by-five?"

"Sure," Frank responded enthusiastically, eager to explore the topic in more depth. "The connection you made between Edison having the creative ideas and Kruesi doing the device-building, in combination with your comment that my reaction was based on my Enneagram and MBTI type went 'click' in my head during the session. That's why I wrote in my journal: creative ideas plus the creative act equals true creativity."

Frank opened his logbook to show Thomas what he had written.

"So what was the insight that went click?" Thomas probed, trying to satisfy his own curiosity.

"Well, of course, an INTP, Enneagram Type Five who spends all of his time *up in his head* watching and analyzing the world go by would ask a question like, 'Doesn't creativity reduce to creative ideas?'" Frank sighed, deeply satisfied with the valuable insight. "I think lots of creative thoughts. My problem is that I don't cash them out into creative acts like Kruesi.

"I also struggle to express my deepest feelings through that volcanic conduit you talked about, and this only intensifies my habit of being cerebral and withdrawing into my intellectual world. I know one of my biggest challenges is to move out of my mental sanctuary and connect to everyday life with solid, concrete follow-through and action, but I'm always amazed at how much trouble I have just *doing* this."

"I couldn't have said it better myself," Thomas beamed, pleased with Frank's open and honest attitude. "Is there anything else you'd like to discuss?"

"No—I'm alright for now. I think I'll just sit here, get up in my head, and write some creative ideas in my journal."

Both men laughed heartily at Frank's wry humor. Thomas then congratulated Frank on his willingness to learn, and the good-natured way he poked fun at himself.

SESSION 2: LEARN HOW FEAR INHIBITS CREATIVITY

The ship steward just finished placing trays full of finger sandwiches, egg rolls, and warm, freshly baked cookies on the teaching table as Thomas rang the bell for the 11:00 A.M. session to begin. He stood in front of his flip chart, gazing out over the sea, and waited until everyone was seated.

"Since creativity is such a valued and sought after commodity and the creative process can be fairly well-defined, why don't organizations and society as a whole produce more truly creative individuals?" He asked rhetorically to spark their curiosity. "In this session I will suggest that while owners and managers lament the lack of creativity and innovation in their employees, those same owners and managers oppose the creative process at every turn. The root cause of this opposition is a deep and abiding sense of *fear* that mobilizes in direct response to employees exercising their creative abilities. In other words, as the creative activity in an organization increases, the level of fear and opposition to the creative process increases proportionally."

Thomas stepped away from the flip chart to reveal the already familiar Figure 3 that he had turned back to.

Figure 3

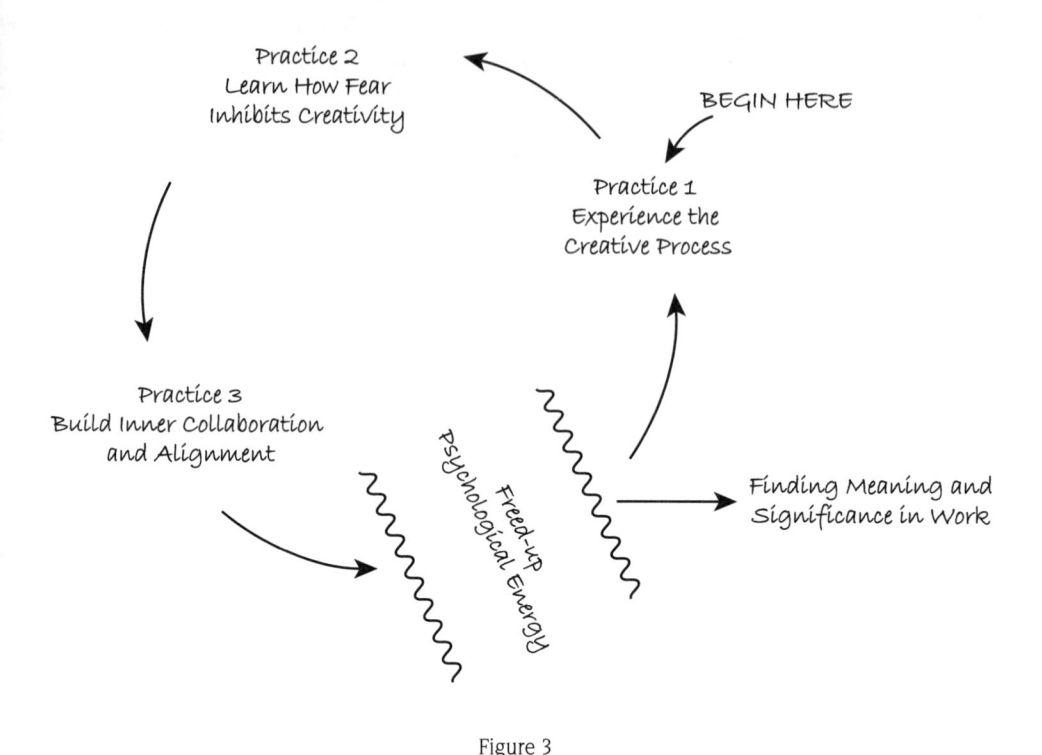

THE FIRST STRATEGY: LEARN TO FIND MEANING AND SIGNIFICANCE IN WORK

"In this session we'll discuss Practice 2—Learn How Fear Inhibits Creativity. It's fear that stifles and kills the creative process in organizations and in individuals, so we need to learn how to recognize its devastating effects.

"One of the crucial roles of leadership is to raise organizational consciousness," Thomas emphasized as he shot a quick glance at Dan. "What are organizations unconscious about? They're unconscious about their strengths, weakness, opportunities, and threats.

"Organizations are unconscious of what customers really think about their products and services, what their employees feel about how they're treated and how the company is being run. Organizations are also unconscious about how much time, energy, and money they squander on personality clashes and misalignments in organizational structures, systems, and culture. But most importantly, most organizations are unconscious about the degree to which *fear* frustrates and opposes the creative process."

Thomas grasped the chart pages and turned them till he arrived at Figure 9. "To return to the question I raised a minute ago, *why don't organizations and society as a whole produce more truly creative individuals?* Do you see the outer area of Figure 9 called Cultural Fear?"

The group nodded in unison, their eyes glued to the flip chart.

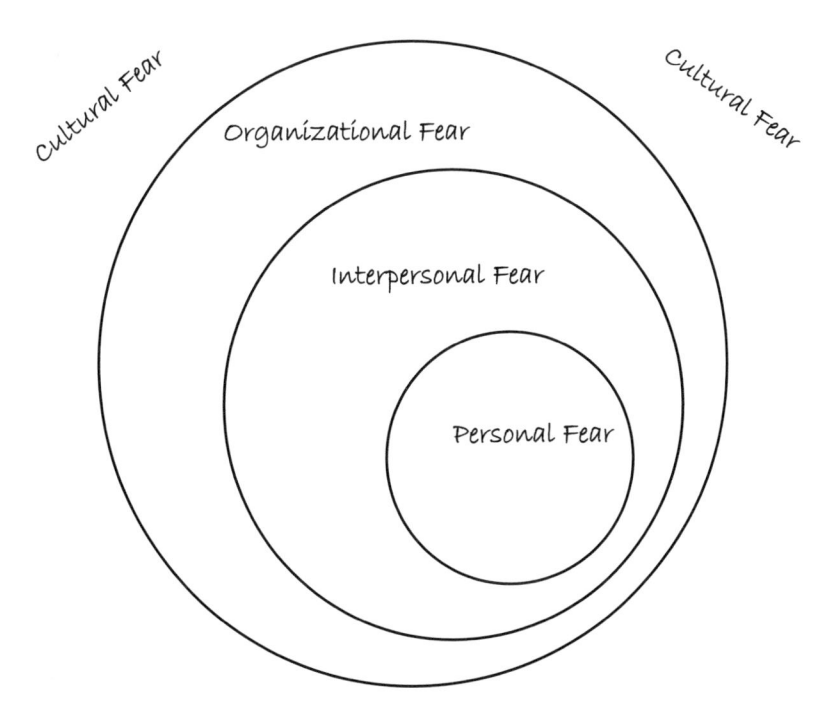

Figure 9
THE FOUR DIMENSIONS OF FEAR

"Society at large has a timeless fear of creative people like artists and scientists because, as post modernist writers claim, creative people threaten to deconstruct the values, beliefs, and social structures of all ages."[60]

Thomas glanced down at a note card to quote Rollo May, "'[Creative people] are the ones who threaten the status quo, which each society is devoted to protecting....It is out of rebellion that the creative act is born....But that is precisely what makes them feared by any coercive society. For they are the bearers of the human being's age-old capacity to be insurgent.'"[61]

Bethany and Dan squirmed in their chairs, as Thomas's deep conviction about the necessity for creative people to "break the rules" created tension around the teaching table.

"Stop and think about the most celebrated people in history. It's no accident that the saint and rebel turn out to be the same person, separated only by time. Joan of Arc was a rebel when they burned her at the stake. Martin Luther King Jr. opposed the system when he stood up for people of color and their rights. Socrates was condemned to death as a heretic because he supposedly led the youths of Athens astray by teaching about the natural world without reference to the gods. But today, these people are revered as major contributors to Western civilization—some have become saints."

"Okay—let's discuss the three dimensions of fear *within* organizations that frustrate and oppose the creative process." Thomas pointed to the outer circle on Figure 9. "The second dimension, Organizational Fear, has two interrelated components. First, all too often employees fear their organization because they've learned that exercising their creative abilities and expressing novel ideas is often opposed by managers and can actually result in retribution. Even in the absence of actual retribution, the perception that it might occur can inhibit the creative process."

Thomas picked up a copy of Edwards Deming's book, *Out of Crisis*, and said, "Listen to what fear sounds like in the workplace...

'I am afraid to put forth an idea. I'd be guilty of treason...and my next annual rating may not recommend me for a raise.'

'If I did what is best for the company, long term, I'd have to shut down production for a while for repairs and overhaul. My daily report on production would take a nose dive, and I'd be out of a job.'

'I am afraid to admit a mistake...'

'My boss believes in fear. How can he manage his people if they don't hold him in awe? Management is punitive.'

'The systems that I work in will not permit me to expand my ability.'

'I'd like to understand better the reasons for some of the company's procedures, but I don't dare ask about them.'"[62]

Thomas took a marker from his breast pocket and wrote the word FEAR on the flip chart in large block letters, then let the group absorb the profound effect of the word. "When employees are afraid of retribution, they clam up. They won't share their best ideas. They keep innovations and improvements to themselves out of passive aggression, fear of being penalized, or fear of losing their jobs. As Perlow and Williams suggest, this kind of silence can kill an organization's creativity.[63]

"Maslow echoes this sentiment, arguing that fear and anxiety are the primary emotional blocks that undermine our courage to speak up, our confidence in our professional abilities, and eventually it undermines our self-esteem."[64]

I've been dominated by fear all of my life, Bethany lamented silently. *It's my single biggest motivator and colors my actions and deepest emotions.*

"The second component of Organizational Fear is how companies fear creative employees because they disrupt the status quo. The rebellion of the creative person leads to a spirit of *insurgence* that threatens owners, managers, and workers, but it especially threatens the organization's formal and informal power structure. A creative employee will question *why* things are done the way they are, and they'll suggest new ways. In response, managers and workers get defensive and fight or repress their creative ideas. When this happens, creative employees learn to keep their mouths shut and just do what they're told. But their silence signals the death knoll for the creative process in an organization."

"We can't just throw away policies, procedures, and lines of authority," Dan snapped, his body stiffening as he spoke. "My corporate experience has taught me that staying in business *requires* well-defined business and work processes that are implemented flawlessly. Most times when people make suggestions for 'improvement,' they don't understand the big picture of company operations, or they're trying to get out of a job they don't want to do."

Wow—where did all that negative energy come from! Thomas wondered as he glanced at Cindy who was shaking her head in frustration.

"Of course there's a place for policies, procedures, and lines of authority when they facilitate organizational effectiveness, but that should always be the litmus test—polices and procedures *to what end?*"

"That's right," Lindsey seconded Thomas's response, "my company is bogged down in a bureaucratic morass of useless procedures."

"Let me offer a counter example to illustrate my point." Thomas continued, looking directly at Dan. "Most meetings, reports, forms, policies, and procedures are developed originally to solve real business problems, but companies often continue using them long after they've stopped being effective. For example, suppose your company had a sales report that required a combined effort of forty man-hours a month to prepare, but no one read it or used it, including you.

"Let's say a creative employee became an insurgent and challenged the value of the report and suggested it be abolished. The CEO of a creative organization would embrace the suggestion, implement it immediately, and reward the employee. But imagine a CEO who got defensive and rejected the suggestion like the auto immune system of the human body rejects invading bacteria. That employee would quickly get the message that their creative ideas were not welcome and that they should shut up and get back to work. The creative process is then stifled, driven underground, and lost to that organization because of the attitude and behavior of that senior manager."

"Okay," Dan nodded, reluctantly, "I see the distinction you're making."

Thomas walked to the flip chart and pointed to the center circle of Figure 9. "The third dimension, Interpersonal Fear, is embedded within the organizational culture and powerfully opposes the creative process because employees fear the effect that their creative abilities will have on interpersonal relationships. While Organizational Fear is propagated through and informally sanctioned by an organization's structure and authority, Interpersonal Fear happens in one-on-one relationships, regardless of where people appear on the organization chart. Employees are afraid to discuss their creative ideas with others, especially if they go against the other person's view of how things should be done in the workplace. People fear being shamed or mocked by co-workers when they express their creative ideas."

Rena raised her hand and waited for Thomas to acknowledge her before speaking, "Jackman and Strober's article claims that most people have a generalized fear of feedback—I know I do. They argue that this fear leads people to practice behaviors that negatively affect their performance on the job. I was actually surprised at how many of the things they listed that I do all the time—procrastination on important tasks, denial that there is any problem, brooding when the world doesn't behave the way I want, and even self-sabotage."[65]

"Good point, Rena," Thomas smiled, surprised by her candor. "Most people are deathly afraid of any kind of feedback and, unfortunately, following their creative impulse often forces them to go *against* the party line and politics at the office. So, living out the creative process in an organization that opposes it demands enormous courage. As Rollo May reminds us, the root of the word *courage* comes from the French *coeur*, which means to have heart. May argues that 'Courage makes possible all the psychological virtues. Without courage other values wither away into mere facsimiles of virtue. Without courage our *fidelity* becomes conformism.'"[66]

Bethany picked up a three-by-five card and wrote, "How do I stop being a coward, and develop the kind of courage you're talking about?" then set the card, writing side down, in the center of the teaching table.

"Expressing creative ideas and producing creative acts *requires* a person to develop both courage and insurgence with the goal of isolating, defining, and deconstructing ineffective systems and reconstructing new ones that are more effective. Contrary to those who defend the status quo, creative insurgence does not mean being an anarchist against *all* structures, systems, authority, and bodies of knowledge. It means that creative people do not view formal or informal rules of organizational culture, technological boundaries, or even the laws of physics or biology as 'sacred cows' that can't be challenged. Following in the footsteps of Copernicus they demand to know, 'who said the earth *has to be* at the center of our solar system?'"

Bethany could hardly contain her excitement "That's exactly what Perlow and Williams argue! They say that *deviance* is at the heart of the creative act because exploring uncharted paths is the only way people will discover new ways of doing things."[67]

"Exactly," Thomas said, pointing at her, then eyeing the group. "So the bottom line dilemma for leaders who want to build creative organizations is that the insurgence that ignites and fuels creativity is precisely what strikes fear in their hearts because deep down they oppose the creative process."

Thomas reached for a glass of water and cleared his parched throat. "Okay, let's move on to the fourth dimension of fear." Thomas pointed to Figure 9 on the flip chart. "I want to discuss the third dimension of fear—Personal Fear."

He turned the flip chart page to a list of nine basic fears that Don Riso and Russ Hudson had identified based on Enneagram type. "You know your Enneagram type based on your RHETI scores, so take a moment to identify the fear that goes with your type, then scan the rest." He stood back and crossed his arms as the workshop attendees read slowly through the list taking notes as they went.

TYPE ONE: *Fear of being bad, corrupt, evil, or defective*
TYPE TWO: *Fear of being unworthy of being loved*
TYPE THREE: *Fear of being worthless or without inherent value*
TYPE FOUR: *Fear of being without identity or personal significance*
TYPE FIVE: *Fear of being useless, incapable, or incompetent*
TYPE SIX: *Fear of being without support or inner guidance*
TYPE SEVEN: *Fear of being deprived or trapped in pain*
TYPE EIGHT: *Fear of being harmed or controlled by others*
TYPE NINE: *Fear of loss of connection, or fragmentation* [68]

Thomas noticed that a number of workshop participants were still writing, and said softly, "Take another minute to finish up."

When everyone was done writing, he said, "You and your employees will experience these fears based on your Enneagram type. For example, as a Type Five, the fear that Frank will deal with is of being useless, incapable, or incompetent. And James, a Type Eight, will deal with the fear of being harmed or controlled by others. These fears go deep into our psychology and they color every decision we make in life, including how we relate to the creative process. Take another moment to reflect on how the one associated with your Enneagram type frustrates and opposes your creativity."

Thomas looked at the chart to focus on the fear associated with Type Four. He then looked toward the group, some of whom were writing in their journal, while others stared out to sea, in deep reflection. "The desire to avoid or mitigate these fears helps create the repertoire of behaviors, emotions, motivations, preferences, fixations, and decision-making bias that becomes our personality type, and these characteristics seriously undermine the creative process.

"What I suggest is that when we probe to a deeper and more collective level, we are either driven by the fear of biological and psychological survival or are motivated by a sense of trust that we will survive. Let's discuss this in more detail.

"Questions about the foundation of human fear circle around the nature-nurture question. In other words, is fear innate and hard-wired into the human brain as part of our biological history, or do we acquire fears through life experiences—our psychological history?" Thomas paused to allow the group to ruminate on his question, then said, "The answer is both. Some fears are probably innate and related to the drive of our species to survive physically, while others are probably learned from our family and cultural context. While many people still heatedly debate the nature-nurture question, recent work in brain physiology has made this argument largely academic because whether fear is learned or innate, it ultimately becomes part of the human brain. As Joseph LeDoux claims, innate and learned sources of fear are simply two different conduits into the same synaptic ledgers."[69]

Thomas reached over, grabbed a stool, and made himself comfortable, knowing that what he was about to say might make the group a little uncomfortable.

"An exploration of our fears takes us to the deepest level of human motivation—the biological-psychological interface. This is where the hamburger or the salad you ate for lunch becomes the inspiration to develop a new marketing plan, redesign your living room, or any other of life's tasks. The biological-psychological interface is like two sides of a coin."

Thomas noticed a couple of people looking at him skeptically, so he thrust his hand toward the group, palm up, and continued. "On the biological side of the coin, the interface contains a genetic map that helps determine who we will become *physiologically*."

He flipped his hand to the backside. "The psychological side of the coin contains an archetypal map of symbols that helps determine who we will become *psychologically*."

Thomas pointed off the port side of the ship to another magnificent cumulus cloud formation. "As we already discussed, the outside-in and inside-out views of that cloud are very different, but neither one is the absolute true view. Now apply this principle to our discussion of the foundations of human fear. Imagine that I could cut through your skull and view your brain outside-in. Even with a microscope all I would see is a mass of neurons firing in zero and one patterns like a light switch. Now imagine that I'm inside your brain and can view your world inside-out so now I see the world psychologically through your personality. At the deepest level where your dreams come from, my inside-out view of your world would be seen through the archetypal symbols that define who you are—the ones we discussed in the last session.

"So when we view fear from the outside-in *biological* side of the interface, scientists like LeDoux and Damasio tell us that a very primitive part of our brain, the amygdala, determines whether or not a danger is present, activates the fear system, and initiates a protective, defensive response.[70] The fear of biological survival taps into the most primitive and deeply engrained of human emotions, which are part of our evolutionary history as a species. Our workplace experience is deeply connected with our fear of biological survival because this is how people 'support their families'—how they provide food, shelter, clothing, and survive in the world. In fact, Goleman argues that we bring these primitive, fear-based emotions to the workplace with us, and that professional success requires that we learn to deal with them through *primal leadership*.[71]

"When we view fear from the inside-out *psychological* side of the interface, employees are either *driven* by the emotions of the fear of psychological survival, or they are *motivated* by the trust that we will survive psychologically." Thomas clenched his fist and shook it at the group to drive home how powerfully fear can control our lives. "Fear and trust are the fundamental drivers to which all other human motivations can be reduced. Maslow's *abundance-deficiency theory* claims that psychologically healthy and fully functioning human beings are motivated out of *abundance,* which derives from trust, while neurotic people are driven out of a sense of *deficiency* or *basic need* that finds it origin in fear.[72]

"Some people experience the fear of psychological survival as consternation and anxiety about whether they can actually 'survive' the long-term pressures and demands that their jobs place on them. Others experience dread, or even panic, that their identity as human beings would be deconstructed if they lost their job.

"Leavitt argues that most people's position in an organization's hierarchy has much more significance than just a 'title.' Titles are so key to some employees' identity that when you ask them to tell you who they are in three short descriptions, most times one of them will have something to do with their position in an organization.[73] For many, being demoted, passed by, or laid off becomes a matter of psychological and biological survival."

Thomas took a marker out of his chest pocket and wrote the words WORK IDENTITY = SURVIVAL on the flip chart in large block letters, so the group could visualize and absorb the import of what he was saying.

"That's how I felt when reengineering was the 'flavor of the month' and I got laid off," Lindsey volunteered, still exhibiting the pain of the experience in her voice. "It did nothing but terrify people and devastate morale."

"Yeah, where I once worked, you never knew who was going to get laid off next!" Nikki slapped the table with her hand in anger. "I'll never forget the day my manager ordered me to confiscate my office-mate's keyboard when she got called down to HR to get laid off—they were afraid she'd destroy company data before leaving the building."

Nikki shook her head as she relived the emotional damage of her lay off situation.

She's staring at me, Dan thought looking at Cindy. *She's thinking, 'I told you so.'*

Not wanting to discuss SciTech's situation in front of the group, Dan grabbed a three-by-five and wrote, "What about the positive things reengineering accomplishes like cutting costs and allowing a struggling company to survive? All you talked about were the negatives!" Dan slammed the card down in the center of the teaching table writing side up so everyone could see it, before shooting a glare at Cindy.

James was fast tiring of Dan's insolence toward Cindy. *He really is a hard-ass,* James thought. *Maybe I should start hammering on him just to show him what it feels like!*

Thomas sensed the growing tension between Dan and James over Cindy but he wanted to deal with it privately, so he quickly said, "In closing," handing each person a dive slate, "read through the summary points of the session, then clip it to your BCD." Most of the group scanned the list, but James continued to glare at Dan in anger from behind his dark sunglasses.

DIVE SLATE SESSION 2 REVIEW

Strategy 1: Find Meaning and Significance in Work
  Practice #1: Experience the Creative Process
  Practice #2: Learn How Fear Inhibits the Creative Process
- *The role of leadership is to raise organizational consciousness about fear*
- *The four dimensions of fear (cultural, organizational, interpersonal, personal)*
- *Reengineering created the fear of biological and psychological survival*

He waited a moment for them to finish. "Are there any questions?" Thomas put his hands on his hips and scanned the faces of the group. "If not, then let's go diving."

∫∫∫∫∫

Once again Nikki was late for the dive brief. Dan and James were peeling off their three-mil wetsuits so they wouldn't die of the heat waiting for her. Anita was annoyed and had already sent a crew member to retrieve this chronic late-comer from her cabin.

Looking at the members of the group and sensing their growing frustration with Nikki's tardiness, Thomas smiled inwardly.

It's amazing how quickly annoying patterns of behavior emerge when people spend so much time together. Since Anita is in charge of the diving part of the trip, I think I'll just sit back and watch how this situation unfolds and see how she handles it.

Upon hearing Nikki coming up the stairs from the deck below, Anita began the dive brief.

"Okay!" Anita said, her voice barely concealing her irritation with Nikki. "The name of this dive is Kristy James, and I think you will find it to be an amazing hard coral dive. You'll see cluster after cluster of table coral eight feet in diameter, fields full of cabbage coral and staghorn coral. Lots of snappers, ocean trout, trevally, puffer fish, Spanish mackerel, and multiple schools of barracuda."

Anita quickly scanned the group and said, "If there are no questions—the pool's open."

One by one the divers jumped off the back of the ship and began to fall through the water column. Thomas welcomed the quiet time of reflection and the much needed break from teaching that diving afforded him. He found his mind wandering around the issue of personality type and the other material he had presented. He was amazed by the fact that two people doing the exact same dive profile would experience it very differently because of contrasting preferences in their personality type.

He looked at James with his introverted intuitive preference and thought, *I'll bet this dive will be a time for inner meditation and philosophical reflection for him.* Turning toward Nikki he thought, *I'll bet her extraverted intuitive preference is filtering what she sees to produce ideas about new projects and strategies.* Then he glanced down to the reef and noticed flashes of light, as Bethany took multiple pictures of a lion fish swimming just above the coral. *There's the extraverted sensing preference in action,* Thomas nodded. *She's trying to take digital images that correspond to the colors, motion, and behaviors of the sea life she's observing.*

Thomas knew that personality fixation sentenced people to live in different worlds and that the totality of these different perspectives on reality could never be fully known by a single individual. That's why he valued the differences between people—they helped him learn to see his world differently.

Frank remembered how terrified he was on the first dive, and based on the topic of the last session he found his mind wandering to the ways in which fear affects scuba divers. Although millions of people have been scuba-certified, many never dive again. Some realize they don't like the sport, and others have physical difficulties, like not being able to clear their ears at depth. But hundreds of thousands of the newly certified never dive again because of *fear*. Many claim they get "claustrophobic" under water, but claustrophobia is a fear of being trapped in a narrow, small, enclosed space, which is not the case when a diver has one hundred-foot visibility horizontally in all directions. Strictly speaking, these divers are probably more afraid to suffocate and drown underwater. Frank wondered why he continued to dive, despite his fear, and he vowed to ponder and reflect on these deep emotions until he found a way to move past them.

People who *do* deal with their fear of being underwater find that diving gets them out of their heads and present in their bodies. On land, breathing falls below the surface of consciousness and most people breathe on automatic pilot. But underwater, the slow, relaxed, consciously-performed in and out motion of a diver's breathing makes them conscious of their body in a powerful way. Like the relaxing effects of deep-breathing Yoga exercises, the bodily awareness of a diver's breath pattern, combined with the silence of the underwater world, is what makes diving so relaxing. Slow, steady, deep, conscious breathing is what connects diver's to their bodily existence in powerful ways—they become 'Zen' divers who are obsessed with exploring the world beneath the sea.

The two groups of divers were within sight of each other in loosely organized clusters. Dan, James, and Cindy dropped down to one hundred feet to get a closer look at three large, gray reef sharks that were lurking in the shadows out in the deep blue. Sharks have existed for three hundred million years and stopped evolving over a million years ago because they're perfectly adapted to their environment. They have remained the predators at the top of the food chain and have ruled the oceans of the world for a half million years. Sharks are large fish that require enormous amounts of food, but live in an ocean that is largely empty of prey, so they've developed incredibly sophisticated sensory detectors. Sharks can detect a single drop of blood in a volume of water that fills an Olympic-sized swimming pool. They can also detect sonic and subsonic vibrations in the water that lead them to wounded or struggling fish over half a mile away.

As James watched the gray reefs cruise effortlessly through the water, he became increasingly aware of the strange kinship he'd always felt with these primitive creatures. Both of them preferred to be left alone, and neither hesitated to defend their boundaries brutally when intruders got too close.

Once the sharks cruised out of sight, Cindy looked up toward the surface of the water and saw the blurred fuzzy outline of the morning sun shining in the sky. She was floating motionless under ten stories of liquid. Then about twenty feet up, a swarming school of fifty barracuda appeared and circled in the water column above them. James tapped his index finger on the dive computer he wore on his wrist signaling Dan and Cindy that they were accumulating too much nitrogen at that depth. The three of them began a slow ascent to join the rest of the group, who were exploring the reef at shallower depths.

Once they were back on the boat, Thomas found Cindy, James, and Dan talking about the sharks and other sea life they'd seen on the dive. He stood there listening quietly for a moment, then volunteered some of the sights he'd seen underwater. During a lull in the conversation he looked at Cindy and asked, "Do you want to take a few minutes to discuss your three-by-five card over in the dining room?"

"Sure, but let me run back to my cabin and grab my journal first," Cindy replied, glad to get out of the hot sun. "I'll see you guys later." She rose from her chair and pulled her tee shirt over her sweaty torso. "I'll meet you in the dining room in five minutes, Thomas."

∿∿∿∿

"I'll never forget it," Cindy said softly, reconstructing her experience with the village woman from the vivid details she'd written in her journal.

"You know how they say that the eyes are the windows of the soul?" Thomas nodded, deeply connected to what she was saying.

"It was like we were gazing down into each other's depths and felt our mutual pain at not finding the answers to life's ultimate questions," Cindy paused as she felt the onset of tears.

"Compared to the standard of living we have back in the States, this woman has a *horrible* life—hard labor, wide-spread disease, and devastating poverty that routinely kill members of her family and her friends. I'd have to be *crazy* to give up what I have for how she lives, yet I'm still grieving to the depths of my soul with a hunger and thirst for her simple life." Cindy moaned and began to weep, as Thomas put his hand on her shoulder, trying to comfort her.

"It makes no sense—no rational sense." She pounded her fist on the table in utter frustration with the paradox her emotions had forced upon her. "When you used that metaphor in class, it sounded like you knew what I was going through."

"Which metaphor?" Thomas probed gently.

"Well, you said our group was nine individuals working side by side like wells that went down to a deep underground river of symbolic meaning—the place where all people share a common humanity. Then you said this was why Western people longed for the PNG culture and way of life, but that they didn't know how to connect their feeling to the way they live. Somehow, the words of that metaphor touched the depth of my longing and pain, but I don't know why."

"Can I use your journal to draw a diagram?" Thomas took a pen out of his shirt pocket and drew a picture of the metaphor he'd used in the session.

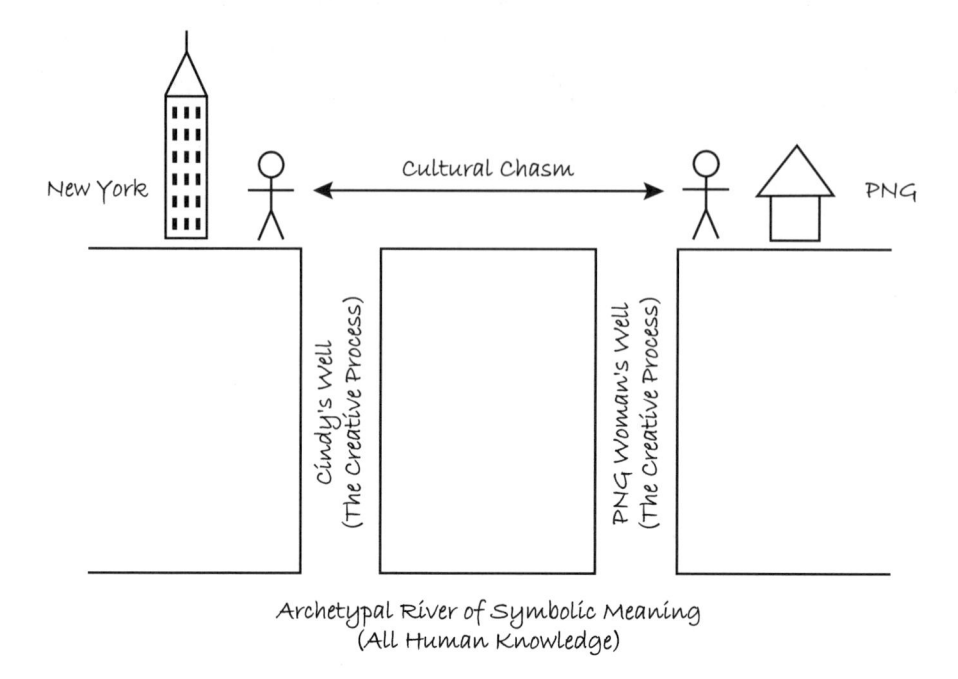

Figure 11

THE CULTURAL CHASM AND SYMBOLIC CONNECTION

"It sounds to me like your experience with the PNG woman placed you in the presence of the creative process." Thomas pointed at the distance between the two stick figures he had drawn. "The cultural chasm between you and this woman could not be wider. But your individual wells go down and connect both of you to the same archetypal river of symbolic meaning. When you experience the power of this mutual symbolic connection *juxtaposed* with the cultural chasm of your life in New York and hers in PNG, it creates the intolerable psychic tension that's haunting you. Connecting at the symbolic level produces the pain and longing you feel for her simple existence, but seeing the 'reality' of village life creates enormous frustration because, as you said, it makes no rational sense for you to *literally* live the way she does."

"But how does this relate to being in the presence of the creative process?" Cindy asked, reenergized by his explanation.

Thomas pointed to the drawing again. "Imagine that you and the woman both connect to the archetype of Human Knowledge at the level of the symbolic river—in other words, all Human Knowledge in all places and cultures throughout history. When the creative process concretizes that symbol through each of your competencies and knowledge base, *you* might design a high-speed graphics chip to show how knowledge is stored and transferred, *she* might paint a picture on the wall of a cave, but both creative acts express the same underlying symbol."

Thomas paused as Cindy wrote furiously in her journal.

"Let me bounce one more thing off of you," Cindy pleaded. "This experience with the woman is like a deep inner itch that I don't know how to scratch. I've been wondering if spending some time in PNG might provide some relief for this." Cindy filled Thomas in on the Dean's invitation to go to the University of Goroka for a year. "What do you think?" she asked anxiously, wanting him to validate a decision she'd already begun to make.

Thomas reached into his pocket, grabbed his thinking stone, and began turning it over and over in his hand. "When someone asks me my opinion about whether they should quit their job, sell their house, and move to a log cabin in the woods, or make some other radical change in life, I always ask whether this is something they need to do *literally* or *symbolically*?"

Then, pointing alternately to the cultural chasm and the symbolic river on the diagram he had drawn in her journal, he said gently, "The creative process often puts us under the kind of inner pressure you're experiencing. It does this to produce psychological growth, and we experience the prodding and probing of the creative process as an inner calling to find meaning and significance in life—in other words, to find our destiny. So the question you have to resolve is whether the creative process is calling you to literally take the Goroka job, or whether it's leading you to scratch your inner itch symbolically with creative acts like painting a graphics chip on the wall of a cave back in New York."

Cindy gazed at Thomas intently as he turned the stone over and over in his hand. "Let me warn you. I've never seen it fail. When the creative process calls a person to act out the inner pressure *symbolically*, but they *literally* quit their job and move to that cabin in the woods, they inevitably regret it—so be careful what you decide."

Cindy reached over and hugged Thomas closely, "Thanks for your insight, my friend. From now on, I'm going to keep my journal with me at all times to log any insights I get, and when you see me turning my thinking stone over in my hand, I'll be earnestly contemplating the literal-symbolic alternative you just talked about."

SESSION 3: BUILD INNER COLLABORATION AND ALIGNMENT

Most of the group was sitting around the teaching table chatting by 3:00 P.M. when Thomas rang the bell to begin the next session. When everyone was seated, he pointed to the flipchart and the already familiar Figure 3. "When we build competency in Practice 1, we gain a personal knowledge of how the creative process works, so we can recognize and support its activity in ourselves and others. Competency in Practice 2 teaches us to identify how fear inhibits the creative process in individuals and the organizations they work in."

Figure 3

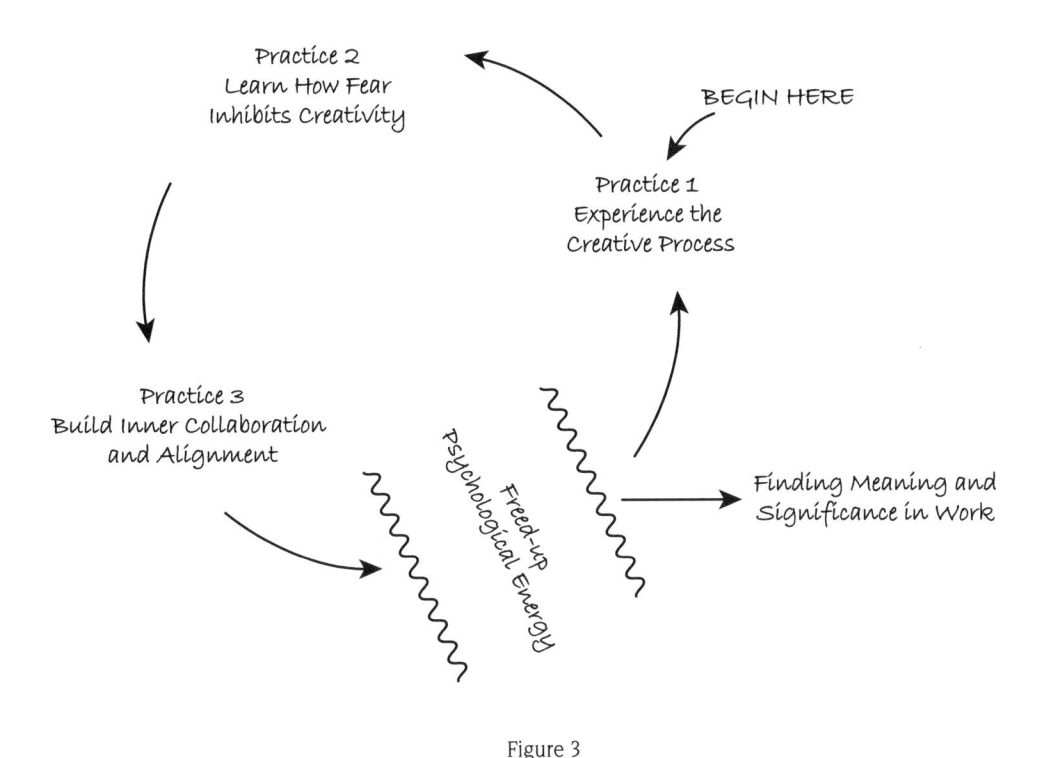

THE FIRST STRATEGY: LEARN TO FIND MEANING AND SIGNIFICANCE IN WORK

"In this session I'll discuss Practice 3: Build Inner Collaboration and Alignment. When we build competency in all three practices and learn to use them, psychological energy that was formerly squandered on conflict is redirected toward things that really matter in life. Together, the first three practices enable us to find a sense of meaning and significance in our work and this is the goal of the first powerful strategy for building creative organizations." Thomas used his index finger to trace the counter clockwise motion of the first three practices shown in Figure 3.

"We live in the three-pound universe between our ears, but it's amazing how little most of us know about ourselves. The overall human personality develops from our earliest years as we accumulate and build a pattern of character, behavioral, emotional, and intellectual traits that, in addition to our distinct physical appearance, distinguish us from all other human beings. It becomes the person we are, the 'I' who is sitting in this workshop, the one who has had all these experiences, the 'me' who I call my 'Conscious Self.'"

Thomas stepped back to the head of the teaching table to face the group directly and focus their attention on him. "Personality typologies like the Enneagram and MBTI tools identify preferences, regularities, and patterns in the way people view and interact with the world. I use the Enneagram and MBTI tools because of how reliably they describe and predict people's behavior, emotional states, and their preferences for decision-making style and problem-solving strategies.

"We develop these preferences, regularities, and patterns so early in life that they slip below the surface of consciousness, go on automatic pilot, and become what is commonly called our personality type. Chris Argyris claims that the vast majority of the knowledge that causes our behavior is tacit and largely unconscious.[74] In other words, people can skillfully perform tasks or make decisions effectively and they don't have to consciously think about what they're doing. When we ask them how they know what they know or do what they do, they can't tell us because this knowledge exists below the surface of consciousness. In much the same way, the unconscious nature of personality type frees up psychological energy that would otherwise be required to navigate through a world that demands constant decision making and problem solving.

"But the preferences, regularities, and patterns of personality type are a double edged sword. While they allow us to make decisions and solve problems unconsciously, which free us up to do more tasks in life, they also can become *too* automatic and ultimately self-defeating. For example, when a person consistently chooses a problem- solving strategy, maintains a belief about the world, or has a powerful emotional response to something even in the face of powerful evidence to the contrary, this indicates that the preferences, regularities, and patterns of personality have become fixated and calcified. Their decision-making and problem-solving strategies become biased, and they exhibit predicable errors in judgement as they respond to situations in a predictable and predefined way. As Abraham Maslow said, 'He who is good with a hammer makes everything a nail.'"

Thomas walked to the flipchart, pulled a marker out of his chest pocket and wrote the words PROBLEM and SOLUTION in large block letters then drew an arrow between them. "To the degree people's decision making and problem-solving skills are fixated, to that same degree they use prepackaged, prepared answers, responses, and strategies to deal with life. No matter what kind of problem or issue walks through the door, they tend to use the same tired responses regardless of how ineffective they have proven themselves to be. Their resistance to deviating from the automatic pilot reactions of personality fixation drives creativity and innovation away. Creative and innovative solutions are rarely considered as an option, because personality fixation frustrates and opposes the creative process."

"Equating personality fixation with Maslow's metaphor of the hammer and the nail really *drives* the point home!" Nikki chirped, motioning a downward fist toward the table as the group laughed heartily. Thomas chuckled as well. When he had the group's full attention again, he continued.

"The fact that personality fixation opposes the creative process has serious implications for building creative organizations. Most traditional definitions of leadership argue that organizational culture is created by leadership style interacting within the company and with the business environment.[75] But this definition doesn't reach far enough back into the mechanism that creates leadership style to explain what leadership actually *is*.

"My own view is that the psychological preferences, regularities, and patterns of personality type *create* leadership style, and that style in turn creates organizational culture as it interacts within the company and with the business environment.

"To the degree that a leader's personality preferences are fixated, to that same degree they will exhibit decision-making bias and make predictable errors in judgement in organizational matters. If they become defensive and filter out feedback that could enable them to see their fixations for what they are, they'll fail to become the kind of leaders and managers who exhibit mature character, sound business judgement, and disinterested 'Level 5' leadership.[76] More importantly for our topic, these leaders will fundamentally oppose the task of building creative organizations."

"Do the Enneagram and MBTI tools really allow you to predict the way leaders will lead and managers will manage with *that* degree of accuracy?" Frank asked, surprised at how strongly Thomas was making the claim.

"Good question, Frank." Thomas looked directly at Dan and said, "For example, given her MBTI and Enneagram preference scores, I'll bet Cindy's leadership style focuses on creative and innovative ideas and vision of strategic, long-term issues, but she has problems dealing with the everyday, concrete details of organizational life. She probably has a distinctly personal approach to employees that humanizes the workplace and makes managers and workers feel heard and understood, but her interest in her work and her efficiency and productivity are directly tied to her moods, both good and bad."

Dan shook his head affirmatively. "You've just articulated some of the biggest problems that I have working with her."

Then, Thomas turned to Cindy and said, "I'll bet Dan is overly focused on details, and this prevents him from seeing strategic, long-term issues. His decision-making process becomes slow in the face of uncertainty because he insists on more and more accurate and precise details before acting. Given your personality type, I predict that his fear of taking risks and making mistakes not only inhibits innovation and creativity, but it drives you crazy."

Cindy imitated Nikki's hammering motion. "Yep! You hit the nail right on the head." The entire group roared with laughter, including Dan.

So he's got a sense of humor after all, James marveled.

When the group settled down, Cindy asked, "If these characteristics are so predictable, why don't we recognize them more readily when we're actually making bad decisions and errors in judgement?"

Thomas grinned like the Cheshire Cat. "Because we all have blind spots about our personality fixations and our leadership style.[77] We know we're in the grips of a blind spot when everyone else can see our fixation, but we can't. It's like having a piece of food on your face—everyone else notices it, and you don't."

"But, if the personality preferences that create my leadership style are at least partly learned, can't they be unlearned through training and development?" Dan argued.

Thomas's eyes widened, hoping that Dan was pondering the task of changing the inappropriate behaviors and attitudes that Cindy described in her SciTech case study and the ones he'd been displaying toward her during the workshop. "Well, people like Goleman suggest that your range of emotional skills is written into your brain circuitry by your mid-twenties, and Drucker argues that people's preferences for how they perform work result from their personality and are codified years before they actually start working.[78] My own view echoes people like Jung and Maslow who argue that our personality is largely formed in the first few years of life. So, while personality fixations can be unlearned, it's extremely difficult, and behavior-based training is almost useless in the face of these deeply engrained habits."

Thomas flipped another chart page. "I'll show you what I mean. Look at Figure 12 and let's go through the steps in the flow diagram.

"Since I'm answering your question, can I use you as an example, Dan?" Thomas queried, hoping he would accept the challenge to reflect on his own behavior.

"Sure," Dan responded nervously, wary of where the exercise would lead.

"Okay, Cindy," Thomas encouraged with a soft smile, "identify an unsatisfactory performance of Dan's that disrupts the effectiveness of your organization and that you've confronted him about repeatedly."

"He pounds the table with his fist in meetings and screams when my staff disagrees with him," Cindy replied without hesitation.

"Are you okay using that as an example, Dan?" Thomas asked cautiously.

"Sure, but I don't do that *all* the time," he insisted defensively, then glared at Cindy for airing their "dirty laundry" in front of the group.

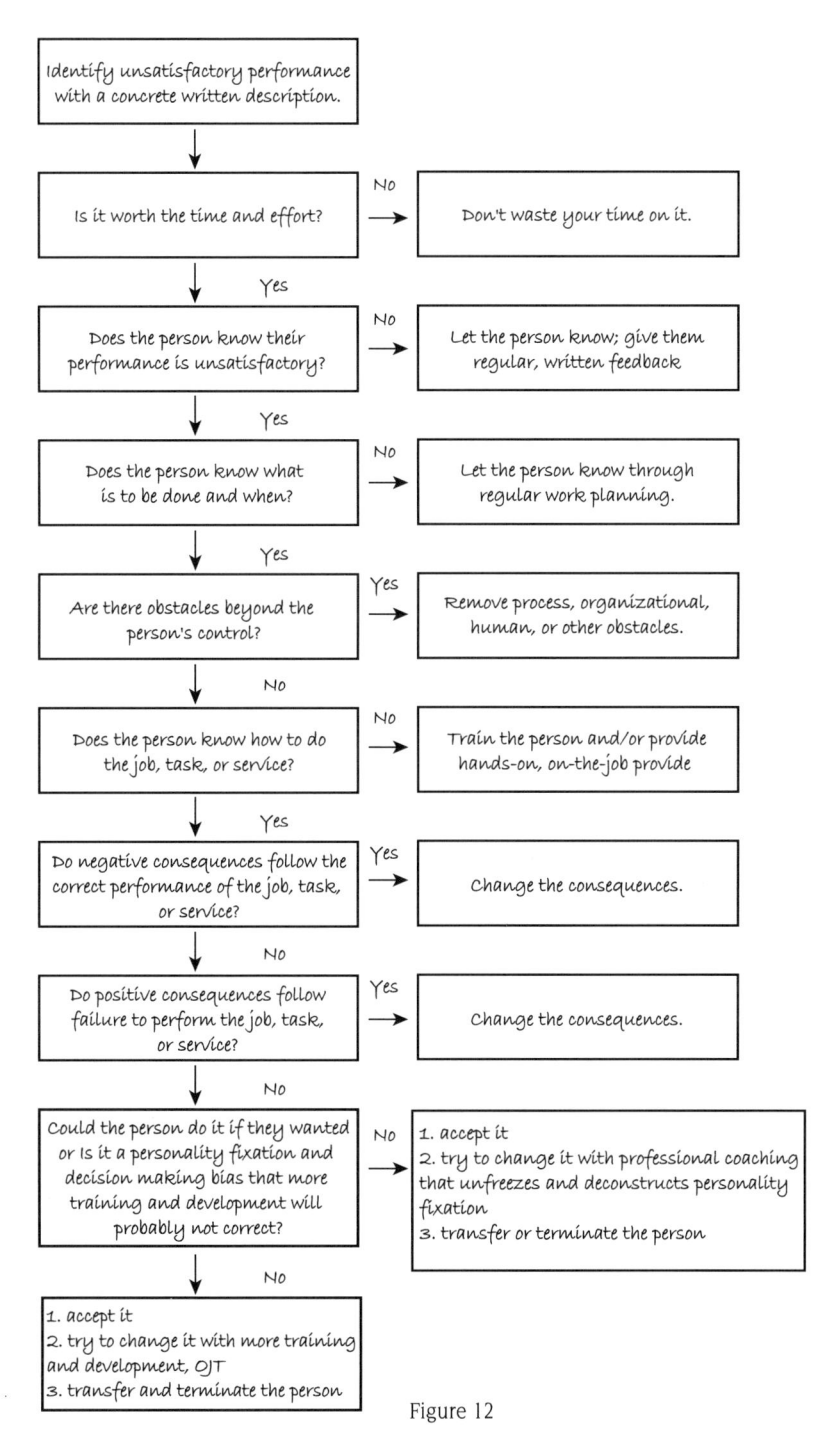

Strategy 1: Learn to Find Meaning and Significance in Work 197

```
┌─────────────────────────────────┐
│ Identify unsatisfactory         │
│ performance with a concrete     │
│ written description.            │
└────────────┬────────────────────┘
             ↓
┌─────────────────────────────────┐     No    ┌─────────────────────────────┐
│ Is it worth the time and effort?│ ────────→ │ Don't waste your time on it.│
└────────────┬────────────────────┘           └─────────────────────────────┘
             ↓ Yes
┌─────────────────────────────────┐     No    ┌─────────────────────────────┐
│ Does the person know their      │ ────────→ │ Let the person know; give   │
│ performance is unsatisfactory?  │           │ them regular, written       │
│                                 │           │ feedback                    │
└────────────┬────────────────────┘           └─────────────────────────────┘
             ↓ Yes
┌─────────────────────────────────┐     No    ┌─────────────────────────────┐
│ Does the person know what       │ ────────→ │ Let the person know through │
│ is to be done and when?         │           │ regular work planning.      │
└────────────┬────────────────────┘           └─────────────────────────────┘
             ↓ Yes
┌─────────────────────────────────┐     Yes   ┌─────────────────────────────┐
│ Are there obstacles beyond the  │ ────────→ │ Remove process,             │
│ person's control?               │           │ organizational, human, or   │
│                                 │           │ other obstacles.            │
└────────────┬────────────────────┘           └─────────────────────────────┘
             ↓ No
┌─────────────────────────────────┐     No    ┌─────────────────────────────┐
│ Does the person know how to do  │ ────────→ │ Train the person and/or     │
│ the job, task, or service?      │           │ provide hands-on,           │
│                                 │           │ on-the-job provide          │
└────────────┬────────────────────┘           └─────────────────────────────┘
             ↓ Yes
┌─────────────────────────────────┐     Yes   ┌─────────────────────────────┐
│ Do negative consequences follow │ ────────→ │ Change the consequences.    │
│ the correct performance of the  │           │                             │
│ job, task, or service?          │           │                             │
└────────────┬────────────────────┘           └─────────────────────────────┘
             ↓ No
┌─────────────────────────────────┐     Yes   ┌─────────────────────────────┐
│ Do positive consequences follow │ ────────→ │ Change the consequences.    │
│ failure to perform the job,     │           │                             │
│ task, or service?               │           │                             │
└────────────┬────────────────────┘           └─────────────────────────────┘
             ↓ No
┌─────────────────────────────────┐     No    ┌─────────────────────────────┐
│ Could the person do it if they  │ ────────→ │ 1. accept it                │
│ wanted or is it a personality   │           │ 2. try to change it with    │
│ fixation and decision making    │           │    professional coaching    │
│ bias that more training and     │           │    that unfreezes and       │
│ development will probably not   │           │    deconstructs personality │
│ correct?                        │           │    fixation                 │
│                                 │           │ 3. transfer or terminate    │
│                                 │           │    the person               │
└────────────┬────────────────────┘           └─────────────────────────────┘
             ↓ No
┌─────────────────────────────────┐
│ 1. accept it                    │
│ 2. try to change it with more   │
│    training and development, OJT│
│ 3. transfer and terminate the   │
│    person                       │
└─────────────────────────────────┘
```

Figure 12

TEASING APART TRAINING FROM PERSONALITY

"We'll start at the top," Thomas said pointing to the first and second steps of the flow diagram. "So the unsatisfactory performance is table pounding and screaming." Thomas turned to Dan. "Why don't you walk us through the rest of the steps aloud, Dan?"

"Okay," he nodded hesitantly, "I know my performance is unacceptable because Dr. Reeder constantly reminds me of it." He gave Cindy a prolonged glare. "Based on her critique of me as CEO, I know what I'm supposed to do and when. I have the power to remove all organizational obstacles and I know how to stop pounding the table. There are no negative consequences that follow my table pounding other than Cindy nagging me—which I normally ignore. I suppose a positive consequence that reinforces this negative behavior is that no one in the company can take formal HR action against me—I have to reprimand myself."

Thomas held up a hand to stop him before he got to the last box. "Let's say that Dan actually wants to stop pounding and screaming, but these good intentions are disrupted because he can't overcome the automatic pilot responses of his personality fixation." He turned the flip chart page to reveal Figure 13 and added Dan's name to the diagram.

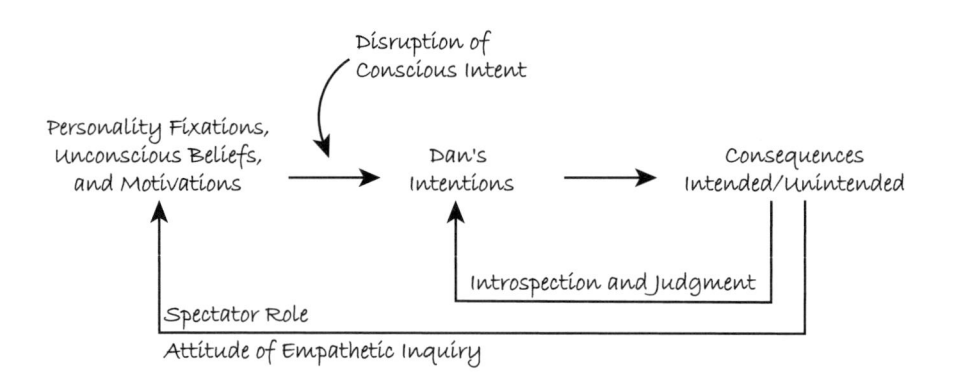

Figure 13
THE DISRUPTION OF DAN'S INTENTIONS[79]

"In other words, Dan intended to do one thing, but did the exact opposite, so his pounding and screaming were *unintended* consequences that prove that he can't just 'decide' to control or change behaviors that come from personality fixation."

Dan was squirming in his seat, embarrassed at how close to home the example was hitting.

Looks like I don't have to hammer on Dan, James smiled with satisfaction. *Thomas is doing it for me in a more constructive way than I would have.*

Then, pointing to the inner arrow in the diagram and the words 'introspection and judgement,' Thomas continued. "So the first reaction is to loop back and hammer himself about his own behavior; then Dan's new intention becomes to try *even harder* not to pound the table and scream. But as Cindy can probably verify, this new resolve is also disrupted by personality fixation. So the causal foundation of Dan's leadership style is much more about automatic pilot personality fixations than anything Dan 'intends' to do. This exercise reveals the duplicity between what leaders *say* and what they actually *do*. When there's a disconnect between what a leader says and does, as Dan's example demonstrates, you should always believe what they do, *not* what they say."

Thomas paused to make sure that the significance of his last comment registered with everyone, then turned the chart page back to Figure 12.

"Let's go back to the last decision box on the flow diagram." Thomas walked over to Dan, put his hand on his shoulder, surveyed the group, and said light-heartedly, "What do you think, Dan? Should we send you to a workshop on anger management, or some other form of charm school?"

Thomas gazed down at Dan intently and waited for a reply.

"I've already done that," Dan answered, "more than once." He was unable to conceal how deeply the critique had penetrated his usual defense mechanisms.

"That's not surprising," Thomas responded confidently. "Sending people to behavior-based training when the root cause of a performance problem is personality fixation may give the appearance of solving the problem, but it's an illusion. In most cases, it's a waste of time and money.

"Moving beyond personality fixation requires sustained effort over time to unfreeze and deconstruct the prepackaged, prepared answers, responses, and strategies that build up over the course of a lifetime. So to return to your question about 'unlearning' personality fixation, Dan, while it can be unlearned it requires a deep commitment to radical personal change, and this rarely happens in behavior-based workshops where people forget seventy percent of what they learn within forty-eight hours."

Thomas walked back to the head of the teaching table and began to use generic examples to take Dan off the hot seat. "Owners and managers faced with making the choice about throwing more training at an ongoing performance problem or investing the resources into trying to change deeply engrained behaviors, beliefs, and emotional responses that result from personality fixation should factor in the cost benefit of their decision. Can the manager accept the situation the way it is? Should they embark on the long arduous process of deconstructing and unfreezing personality fixations? Should the manager transfer or terminate the employee?"

Lindsey gestured toward the flip chart and said circumspectly, "As a former HR manager and now a senior manager, it seems like you put your people in a difficult spot when you use this approach."

"True," Thomas nodded in full agreement, "but the process shown in Figure 12 demonstrates how difficult it is to make deep change. I've seen employees whose personality fixation was conflict avoidance attend assertiveness training workshops at a cost of thousands of dollars, then fail to learn to assert themselves."

Thomas paused to let the ineffectiveness of this approach sink in. "I've seen managers whose personality fixation was aggression and pushing people's boundaries who attended high-dollar workshops to improve their 'communication' skills show no progress when they returned to the workplace. These problems were not initially caused by a lack of knowledge or training, they were due to personality fixation, and no amount of behavior-based training will ever change them. My model just confronts people with this reality, it doesn't make any decisions for them."

Frank asked quizzically, "I see the power of personality typologies like the Enneagram and MBTI tools to describe and predict behavior, so why don't more organizations use them?"

"Good question, Frank," Thomas smiled, pleased that he had raised this issue. "There are at least three reasons. First, it's difficult for some people to remember all the letters and numbers and what they mean. It's almost like learning a foreign language, so it takes a commitment of time, effort, and persistence. Second, it requires a lot of psychological energy to stay conscious of responses that are normally on automatic pilot, and much less energy to allow our fixations and decision-making bias free reign.

"The third reason organizations don't use personality typologies is because they *actually work*," Thomas said dispiritedly. "Knowing someone's personality type helps to level the corporate playing field, so the psychological warfare of office politics is much less effective when everyone knows each other's personality type."

Frank nodded, clearly satisfied with Thomas's explanation, while others noted the points in their journals.

"*In Search of Excellence* was published over twenty years ago. Even back then, Tom Peters recognized that transformational leaders had to make conscious what was unconscious in followers as well as manage the ambiguity, paradox, and irrationality so typical of organizations."[80]

Thomas put a hand to his chest. "My claim is that the irrational element of the creative process is precisely what makes it seem so unpredictable and why people fear it so much. But the process of building inner collaboration and alignment reveals the actual mechanism of the creative process. Once this is understood, creativity becomes a more *predictable resource* for individuals and organizations alike.

Thomas noted that several members of the group were wearing puzzled expressions. "Let me explain. Most people consider themselves to be a single unified entity—what I have called our Conscious Self. But if we hold to a unified sense of self, how can we explain the experience of saying we're going to do one thing, then doing the exact opposite, even though 'we' didn't want to?"

Thomas became intense as he probed the group with rapid-fire inquiry. "How can we explain the fact that we can't change our emotions because they have us, rather than us having them? How do we explain making a commitment to a person, project, or activity, only to have that commitment evaporate because something else inside of us refused to keep it?"

Thomas turned to the flip chart and drew an organization chart, then pointed to the title PRESIDENT in the top box. "Imagine you are the president of a small company. As president, you have bottom line responsibility for the company, and you can develop organizational structures and systems to control company operations. But your success depends on your employees, even though you can't directly control their emotions, commitments, or desires. To put it another way, your employees are *objective* to you, meaning they exist independently of you, and they are *real* in the sense that their performance determines whether your company fails or succeeds."

Thomas paused for several seconds and waited until everyone had focused their attention on him. He wanted to be sure each one of them fully understood the key issue he was about to introduce. "Now, do a thought experiment with me where you turn your concentration within, introspectively. Try to imagine that you're the president of the Rena Company—or the Frank Company—and that the corporate facility is your body. Now imagine that you have Inner People who occupy an Inner Company. But, like employees in an actual organization, you don't have direct control over their emotions, commitments, and desires, so *you* want to go in one direction and *they* want to go in another. You want to slow down and work fewer hours, *they* want to climb the corporate ladder. You want to stop hammering on your employees, *they* try to hammer harder than ever. You say you want to increase your sales, *they* are too introverted and shy to pick up the phone and sell."

"Is this like having different 'sides' to your personality?" Frank asked, looking a little confused, but trying his best to understand.

"Yes and no," Thomas replied hesitantly. "The Inner People are like semi-autonomous personalities that make up your overall personality, but you can't directly control them. Having this multiplicity of personalities within us is a normal, psychologically healthy phenomenon that we all experience. If we were 'abnormal,' we would move from one personality to another and be totally unaware of the shift, or the Inner People would control us to the point that we lose our grip on reality. *Consciousness* about the presence and activities of the Inner People and some ability to control their activities is the difference between being categorized as 'normal' or 'abnormal' psychologically.

"The Inner People exist in a virtual state and only become real when they take over your body, because only then can they make a physical difference in the world. You say you're going to be nice to your employees, and one of the Inner People grabs hold of the 'microphone'—your vocal chords—and hammers them verbally." Thomas grabbed his voice box between his index finger and thumb to illustrate the point.

"Sometimes you don't even realize they've taken you over till after the fact. For example, one of the Inner People takes over your facility and grabs your credit cards and goes on a shopping spree just when you swore to your spouse that you'd stop spending. Or they take over your facility and you find yourself pounding your fist on the table just after you promised not to do that anymore." Thomas glanced at Dan, hoping he would make the connection.

"When the Inner People have charge of your body, they can control the way you talk, what you do, how you feel, where you go, and how long you stay. What they do when they have control of your facility can vitally effect the course of your life. They can make or break you just like the employees in your actual company.

"Most of the Inner People are underdeveloped psychologically and socially because we've locked them away in the unconscious and haven't given them much facility time. Imagine locking a baby in a closet for the first few years of its life. When you finally let it out, it would be psychologically and socially stunted. That's the way the Inner People are, so when they finally get control of your body, it's like they've broken out of an inner prison. That's why they're so problematic and act so inappropriately!

"The Inner People develop their own preferences, regularities, and patterns for interacting with the world, and they have their own personality fixations. Because the Inner People have accumulated different knowledge and problem-solving abilities than we have, when a question is asked they reach very different conclusions than we do.

So when they grab your facility's microphone and articulate a view you are diametrically opposed to through your vocal chords, you're shocked to hear those words coming out of your mouth."

"I don't get it," Rena interjected, scratching her head in confusion. "How could the Inner People have different information than *me* when we all live in the same body and have had the same experiences?"

"Good question, Rena." Thomas beamed with delight at her inquisitiveness and how boldly she was participating. "Let's say you have lunch with your boss and his name is Joel. This experience might result in a total of one hundred different experiential elements. Your Conscious Self might select only ten based on its personality preferences and filter all the rest out because they produce anxiety and fear for you. Some portion of the other ninety experiential elements is attracted by, and becomes part of, the information of your Inner People based on *their* personality preferences and what creates anxiety and fear in them."

Thomas became more intense as he spoke, trying to drive the importance of this idea home. "Those aspects of the experience of 'having lunch with Joel' that were drawn to the Inner People become the *other side of the story* about Joel, and may contradict or be fundamentally different from the view of 'Joel' held by your Conscious Self. Maybe, something in his body language, what he says, or how he says it will come from one of Joel's Inner People who resents you because you have so many creative ideas—feelings he may be largely unaware of or would never admit.

"Whether it's a business associate who's intimidated by you, a friend who wishes she'd married your husband, or a neighbor who's jealous about how nice your house is, the other side of these stories register valuable information with the Inner People that is not part of conscious awareness. That's why the perspective of the Inner People is often contradictory to the image that your Conscious Self has about a person."

Rena sat up straight, pressed her stomach against the teaching table, and leaned forward on her elbows trying to grasp everything Thomas was saying. "Have you ever sensed that people are not what they seem, they're not to be trusted, they really don't mean what they say, or don't care about you as much as they say they do? Often this is how we experience the activity of *their* Inner People—parts of their personality that they may be largely unaware of. This is why I say we should believe what people do, not what they say. The other side of the story in relationships only comes to light by watching people's actions."

"Thomas," Rena asked quizzically, tapping her fingertips on the table. "When you say the Inner People have personality preferences that are different from the Conscious Self, are you suggesting that my Inner People have MBTI and Enneagram types that are *different* than mine?"

I can't believe the depth of her curiosity and insight, Maggie found herself thinking proudly. *I've never seen my daughter this engaged in anything before.*

Thomas's eyes lit up in appreciation of Rena's increasing contribution to the discussion. "That's precisely what I'm saying, Rena. The Inner People, what Jung called complexes, have well-defined and predictable MBTI and Enneagram type. Let's call one of your Inner People your Shadow Self and another your Inferior Self. As an ISFP Enneagram Type Nine, your Shadow Self has the personality preferences of Type Six with introverted intuition, and your Inferior Self will have the preferences of Type Three with extraverted thinking."

Thomas quickly passed around a matrix that explained the personality preferences of the Inner People for all the workshop participants.[81] Members of the group stared at the chart in silence and struggled to decipher what the numbers and letters meant.

CONSCIOUS SELF	SHADOW SELF	INFERIOR SELF
James Tuffs INTJ [N_i T_e], Type Eight	Type Five, F_i	Type Two, S_e
Rena Unitus ISFP [F_i S_e], Type Nine	Type Six, N_i	Type Three, T_e
Dan Wright ISTJ [S_i T_e], Type One	Type Four, F_i	Type Seven, N_e
Lindsey Barker ISFJ [S_i F_e], Type Two	Type Eight, T_i	Type Four, N_e
Maggie Spinner ENTJ [T_e N_i], Type Three	Type Nine, S_e	Type Six, F_i
Cindy Reeder INFP [F_i N_e], Type Four	Type Two, S_i	Type One, T_e
Frank Brighton INTP [T_i N_e], Type Five	Type Seven, S_i	Type Eight, F_e
Bethany Wringer ESTP [S_e T_i], Type Six	Type Three, F_e	Type Nine, N_i
Nikki Salem ENTP [N_e T_i], Type Seven	Type One, F_e	Type Five, S_i

"But, what if I were an ISFJ, Type Nine?" Rena blurted out, hardly able to contain her excitement.

"Of course," Thomas said looking down at the chart, "conceivably you could have any combination of Enneagram and MBTI preference scores, so if you were an ISFJ, Type Nine, the MBTI component for the Shadow and Inferior Self would change to introverted thinking and extraverted intuition.[82] People spend the first part of their life developing the preferences of the Conscious Self, while the preferences for the Shadow and Inferior Self normally don't appear until the second half of life—after age thirty-five. Some combinations of Enneagram and MBTI preferences create more psychological tension in the personality than others, and various combinations also help explain subtle differences that we observe between people of the same Enneagram type."[83]

"Can a given Enneagram type really have *any* combination of MBTI type?" Rena continued probing.

"Absolutely. I've seen Enneagram Type Eights who had INTJ, ISTJ, ESTJ, ENFP, and INFP preferences score—I don't know how you can get a broader cross-section of differences than that." Thomas shrugged his shoulders, indicating the complexity of the situation.

Several people looked confused by the discussion, so Thomas said apologetically, "I told you the letters and numbers were like a different language. Listen Rena, these are great questions but they're beyond the scope of our discussion. Take a look at the two books that you have in front of you—Myers's *Introduction to Type* and Riso's *Discovering Your Personality Type*—and let's talk about them on the break."

She reached for a three-by-five and wrote, "My mother's MBTI preference scores are exactly opposite to mine. What are the implications of this for our relationship?" Then she placed the card writing side down, in the center of the table.

"Okay." Thomas clapped his hands to get the group's attention back, "Let's get back on track. I want to talk about how the Inner People are an important part of the actual mechanism of the creative process."

Thomas grabbed a fistful of chart paper and turned back to the diagram of the creative process in Figure 6.

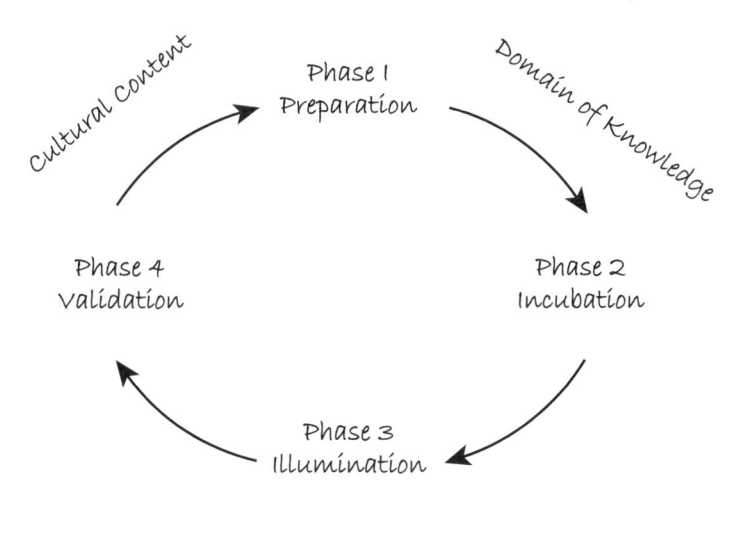

```
        Cultural Content          Phase 1              Domain of Knowledge
                                Preparation

     Phase 4                                              Phase 2
    Validation                                          Incubation

                              Phase 3
                            Illumination
```

Figure 6
THE CREATIVE PROCESS

"After spending an extended period of time trying to solve a problem in the preparation phase, if we stop thinking about it and allow the problem to incubate while we do something totally different, a solution often rises into consciousness when we least expect. What's going on here?" Thomas asked rhetorically. "I suggest that when 'we' stop thinking about the problem, we're actually handing it over to the Inner People to solve."

Rena's eyes widened at the implications of what Thomas was suggesting. "That's right—no sooner than you stick your regulator in your mouth and jump off the back of the boat, the Inner People are forming themselves into problem-solving teams. They're huddling up to figure out, 'How do we solve *this* problem?' Remember—your Inner People exist in a virtual state and only become real when they take control of your body and make a physical difference in the world; so they have a vested interest in coming up with elegant solutions to problems, then having you implement them as creative acts. They're able to craft novel insights to problems we've failed to solve because they use different problem-solving strategies and information than are available to us."

Thomas took a marker out of his chest pocket and wrote the words INNER COLLABORATION on the flip chart in large block letters, then turned toward the group. "Here's the most profound implication of what I'm saying for building creative organizations. To the degree that we build inner collaboration and alignment with the Inner People, to that same degree our creative process becomes more predictable—it becomes something we can count on, a valuable resource to us and our organization."

Thomas paused for a moment to allow people time to reflect on the concept.

"I understand what you mean by the Inner People," Frank said incredulously, "but is this a metaphor, or are you saying that I'm actually going to hear voices in my head?"

"Well, not *literal* voices," Thomas chuckled, "but some people experience it as inner mental chatter or what others call the 'monkey mind.'"

Members of the group laughed and shook their heads vigorously, having experienced exactly what Thomas was talking about.

Thomas waited for the laughter to subside, then continued. "Let's discuss some practical ways to begin building inner collaboration and alignment. First, we must develop an awareness of what William James called the *fringe of consciousness*, something most people experience all the time.

"Extend your arm as far as you can to your side so your hand is just slightly less than one hundred eighty degrees to the side of your head." Thomas demonstrated the maneuver and waited until all the attendees had their arms in the proper position. "Now move your hand back and forth in and out of your field of vision. That's called the fringe of your vision. The fringe of consciousness is similar in that ideas, insights, thoughts, emotions, motivations, and guidance on critical issues in our lives seem to pop into our heads 'out of nowhere.' But after we learn about the Inner People, we know that nowhere is really somewhere.

"One way to increase your awareness of this activity is to log the insights and ideas that pop into your head in your journal." Thomas picked up his journal and gestured toward the group with it to make the point. "Thomas Edison had hundreds of logbooks in which he recorded his ideas and inventions. When one idea after another came to him in his workshop and he went from table to table applying his insights to unrelated projects, I'll bet this was the work of his Inner People. In fact, I believe that most of his greatest inventions, the ones that have created the Western reality we live in, came from the Inner People working through the creative process I just described."

I'm just blown away by the implications of what he just said, Cindy thought, grappling with the enormity of Thomas's claim.

"How do you get to the place where you're working *with* the Inner People rather than waging war against them?" Rena asked fervently, eager to know more.

"Rena's question is crucial to understanding the creative process." Thomas thrusted a proud forefinger in her direction. "It takes us back to last session's discussion of being driven by the fear of survival or motivated by the trust that we will survive.

"Turn your eyes inward and imagine the inner life of the personality—the war between the Conscious Self and the Inner People for control of your life." Thomas's voice became sad and circumspect. "Imagine how the totalitarian rule of your Conscious Self has locked the Inner People out of consciousness, repressed their ideas and perspective on life, and denied them existence by depriving them access to your body. The Conscious Self and the Inner People have been locked in a mortal battle for psychological survival.

"The Conscious Self is *driven* to maintain control of consciousness, investing enormous amounts of psychological energy in its defenses because it fears this struggle is a matter of life and death. In a sense it is, because the Conscious Self experiences its loss of control over consciousness as a kind of psychological death.

"In the same way, the Inner People only exist in a virtual state and are *driven* to take over the facility because their reality depends on them making a physical difference in the world. For the Inner People to remain in a virtual state is to not survive, so they fight for control of the facility for the same reasons that the Conscious Self does.

"On the other hand, when the Conscious Self repetitively experiences the psychological death that happens when the Inner People take over, *and it survives*, a basic trust begins to emerge that it will continue to survive and be stronger because of the experience." Thomas's face radiated hope at the prospect of what he was saying. "The Conscious Self begins to be *motivated* by a sense of abundance where control of the facility can be shared with the Inner People. In much the same way, when the Inner People see that the Conscious Self will *voluntarily* give up control of your body to allow them to be the authors of innovations and improvements, a trust begins to emerge that they too will survive.

"The promise of the psychological survival of all elements in the personality builds an enormous *trust in self* that gives us a deep and abiding belief that the total personality is robust, balanced, and can survive the onslaughts of life. The Conscious Self and the Inner People come to the realization that no part of the personality will be killed off, banished, or sentenced to psychological isolation just to satisfy some other, more powerful, part of the psyche."

Rena waved her hand frantically and blurted out, "Thomas? That's a theoretical answer to my question. Other than writing the ideas of the Inner People in my journal, what can I actually *do* to make peace with them and build the inner collaboration you're talking about?"

"Yes." Thomas smiled patiently. "I was just getting to that.

"The only way to build true inner collaboration and alignment is with an attitude of empathic inquiry that seeks to understand life from the perspective of the Inner People. To illustrate, let's discuss Carl Rogers' idea that empathy can improve the degree of collaboration and alignment in our day-to-day relationships at home and in the workplace.

"Rogers used empathic understanding as a psychotherapeutic tool for removing the barriers to authentic interpersonal communication and as a key to developing deep and fulfilling relationships. He claimed that our tendency to judge, evaluate, to approve or disapprove of what other people say and do was the greatest barrier to interpersonal communication and relationships.[84] The antidote was to develop an empathic understanding of the other person's point of view—to see a situation, or disagreement, from the other person's perspective—to walk a mile in their shoes."

Thomas turned his gaze toward Cindy. "So if Dan and Cindy had an attitude of empathic inquiry, they'd listen to each other, try to understand the other's personal meaning; they'd learn what the situation looked like from the other's perspective. When Cindy really felt heard and understood, powerful forces of change would be released deep within her, and subsequently that would change her relationship with Dan profoundly." Cindy bit her lip and tried to stave off tears as Thomas spoke the powerful words of healing that she longed for.

But Dan's facial expression showed no emotion, as he stared off the port side of the ship.

"My experience in problematic relationships has been that when I really listen to someone, when they really feel heard by me, and respected by me for who they are, what they think, and how they feel, they become more open to understanding my point of view as well. The exchange of empathic inquiry on both parts produces the power of change within both people and transforms the relationship."

"I've experienced what you're talking about when dealing with deep, bitter, long-standing employee-supervisor disputes," Lindsey tendered. "When either person begins to listen to the other with empathic inquiry and that person feels 'heard,' the level of hostility and conflict decreases visibly, and the two people are often able to talk about solutions to their problems, and sometimes even salvage the relationship."

"Yes!" Thomas waxed exuberant, pleased with Lindsey's practical application of the concept to the workplace. "The hostile and negative energy begins to disappear when we empathically inquire into how others see the world. It's amazing how psychological energy that was formerly squandered in conflict is freed up as creativity and constructive solutions to interpersonal barriers begin to unfold in the relationship. The negative energy used to defend our mutual positions gets redirected into building the relationship."

"Now to Rena's question," Thomas said abruptly to draw her back into active dialogue. "We have to use the same kind of empathic inquiry to resolve conflicts and build inner collaboration and alignment between 'us' and the Inner People. We have to learn to see the ideas and attitudes of the Inner People *from their perspective*. Through empathic inquiry we learn how the Inner People have been repressed, locked out of consciousness, and offended by the arrogant, self-serving stranglehold that we have maintained on consciousness.

"Only when the Inner People feel heard and respected to the point where some of their personality preferences are integrated with the Conscious Self, will the battle begin to cease. Then enormous amounts of formerly squandered psychological energy are *freed up* by the creative synthesis of opposing worldviews—theirs and ours.

"One day we wake up and the inner battle is over. This kind of deep change *happens to us*. We might be standing in the shower or taking our morning walk with the dog and we realize, things are different—we're different. All we have to do is stay in dialogue with the Inner People long enough, just like we would in any other relationship at home or at the office."

Thomas walked to the flip chart and grabbed a fistful of pages. "Look back at Figure 3." He used his index finger to trace the counter-clockwise motion of the diagram.

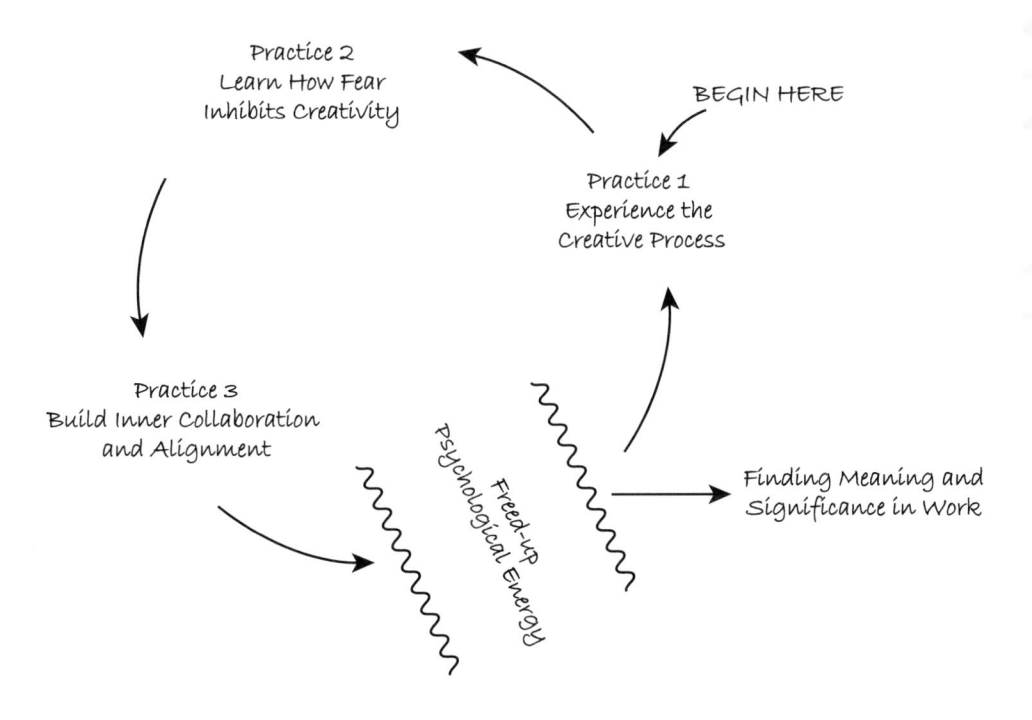

Practice 2
Learn How Fear
Inhibits Creativity

BEGIN HERE

Practice 1
Experience the
Creative Process

Practice 3
Build Inner Collaboration
and Alignment

Psychological Energy
Freed-up

Finding Meaning and
Significance in Work

Figure 3
THE FIRST STRATEGY: LEARN TO FIND MEANING AND SIGNIFICANCE IN WORK

"When you build competency in the first three practices, psychological energy that was formerly squandered on toxic relationships and defending your blind spots is freed up. This kind of deep, personal change gives us new access to our creative process. That's why most traditional self-help approaches don't work. They normally exhort us to try harder, bear down, use discipline, and think positively, which require us to muster more psychological energy that is already in short supply.

"One of the most profound timeless principles that I know, I learned from David Hanna: 'All organizations are perfectly aligned to get the results they get.'[85] We will discuss this principle tomorrow when we turn our attention to aligning organizations, but I want to mention it now. If Dan's goals are heading in this direction," Thomas pointed to the bow of the boat, "and Cindy's are going in the opposite direction," Thomas indicated the stern, "and we add up those directions, we will get an overall direction for their organization. SciTech is perfectly aligned to get the results it's getting.

"The same is true of you and your Inner Company." Thomas pointed at James, then Frank, then Lindsey, and said, "Your life is perfectly aligned to get the results you're getting. If your Conscious Self is pulling you in one direction and the Inner People are pulling you in another, your life will be aligned to produce enormous inner conflict. When you lack inner collaboration and alignment your creativity *can't* work and your creative process *won't* produce innovations and improvements because the Inner People will oppose you and what you want at every turn.

"In closing," Thomas said, handing each person a dive slate, "read through the summary points of the session, then clip it to your BCD so you'll have the material with you underwater." The group scanned the list.

DIVE SLATE SESSION 3 REVIEW

Strategy 1: Find Meaning and Significance in Work
    Practice #1: Experience the Creative Process
    Practice #2: Learn How Fear Inhibits the Creative Process
    Practice #3: Build Inner Collaboration and Alignment

- *The Enneagram and MBTI tools reliably identify our personality type*
- *Personality fixation and decision-making bias oppose the creative process*
- *Personality fixation creates leadership style, which creates organizational culture*
- *You can't change personality fixation with behavior-based training*
- *Three reasons why organizations don't use the Enneagram and MBTI tools (a new language, takes self observation, it works)*
- *The model of the Inner People (IP) as semi-autonomous, objective little personalities that you can't directly control, and take you over*
- *The IP are the mechanism of the creative process*

- *We must build inner collaboration and alignment with the IP through empathic dialogue*
- *Collaboration with the IP frees up psychological energy and creates deep inner alignment*

He waited a moment for them to finish reading. "Are there any questions?" He smiled encouragingly and paused for a moment. "If not, then let's go diving."

Bethany was the last person off the boat because she was fooling with the new camera equipment that she didn't quite know how to work. Some divers are obsessed with their underwater cameras—they spend all of their time switching lenses, estimating exposures, lubricating the o-rings on housings, and getting their strobes to work. On occasion they hold up entire groups of divers, saying, "Oh, I didn't know we were doing *that* dive profile—I have my macro lens on—I'll have to switch my lens." Some divers argue that looking through the lens and taking pictures actually improves their dive experience because it forces them to focus on the details of the underwater world. Others claim they like to take in the entire gestalt of the dive experience unencumbered by cameras that can't capture the true reality of the underwater experience.

About twenty feet down, Bethany grabbed the anchor line that led across a deep channel toward the gray image of the monolithic pinnacle on the dive site, South Emma. The reef was over one hundred feet away, just at the limit of the visibility, and the current was screaming as Bethany inched her way down the anchor line that was attached to a mooring pin on the top of the pinnacle. Once the divers reached the wall of the pinnacle, they quickly dropped down along its shear vertical wall and hid from the constant press of the current; then they made their way down to a swim–through cave that was at one hundred ten feet.

Prior to the dive, Anita had shown Maggie a new way to enjoy diving in a strong current. Maggie always had trouble dealing with this aspect of diving, and her fear of losing control underwater limited her diving experience. On the one hand, strong current pushed large volumes of plankton and other nutrients through the water, so the greatest diversity of coral and fish life was always found in strong current, especially soft coral and sharks. On the other hand, the unrelenting power of millions of gallons of water pressing against her body at a velocity of three or four knots terrified her with the thought of being carried out to sea.

Anita had lent her two pieces of equipment that she said would help her actually enjoy strong current dives. First was a pair of split fins that were designed to make extended periods of kicking easier by propelling you through the water using less energy. When Maggie first dove into the water and began kicking, the new fins were so easy to manipulate that it felt as though she had forgotten to put fins on. As she kicked and felt the current push back against her body, she was amazed at how well she was moving against it through the water. It's paradoxical how fear tells a person's mind one thing—"I can't kick against this current"—even though they're kicking their hearts out. But that belief can be corrected by sense perceptions when they see themselves moving across the bottom with their own eyes.

The second piece of equipment was a reef hook, which was a four- or five-inch long stainless steel hook with a blunted end, attached to a three-foot nylon rope, and a clasp on the other end. When Maggie and Anita had done the swim-through, they came up over the edge of the wall and began swimming over the top of the pinnacle. This was where the current was the strongest. The split fins enabled Maggie to swim against even this current until she found a nonliving piece of coral. Following Anita's example, she secured the hook and fixed the clasp to her BCD. As the rope straightened out from the current pressing against her body, Maggie floated, suspended three feet above the top of the coral where she could watch the underwater sea world swarming all around her. Two ten-foot gray reef sharks cruised by a school of a hundred barracuda that was directly in front of her, while thousands of schooling jacks and bigeye trevally swam effortlessly above and beside her.

Nothing revealed this competitive struggle of the ocean more than sharks, and Maggie loved to watch them in action. Sharks sometimes attack surfers and snorkelers because they resemble seals or sea otters, and the slapping sound of their fins on the surface of the water draws the sharks' attention. But other than the rare occasion when a scuba diver has a string of bleeding fish attached to him while spear fishing, sharks rarely attack scuba divers. They are the quintessential hunters who don't like to work any harder for their food than they have to. Even diminutive Maggie looked almost seven feet long underwater with her fins on. That's more work than all but the biggest sharks want to do for a meal.

In PNG, occasional attacks by saltwater crocodiles are much more prevalent than shark attacks. Maggie remembered seeing the picture of a twelve-foot-long croc on the wall of the breakfast room back at Walindi, but there are documented cases of crocodiles in PNG that are sixteen feet long. They grab you with their powerful jaws and take you deep underwater to their cave where you quickly drown. Then they store your body and come back periodically to snack on you.

∽∽∽∽

Once they were all back on the boat, Thomas saw Dan sitting alone at the teaching table, facing off the port side of the ship, glancing through the Enneagram and MBTI books that each attendee had received and making notes in his journal.

Dan has always been a little hardnosed, Thomas thought. *But on this trip he seems madder than a wet hornet. I wonder what's going on with him?*

"Hey, Dan," Thomas spoke softly, not wanting to startle him, "is now a good time to discuss your three-by-five, or would you rather be alone?"

"Now's fine," Dan replied, sounding discouraged. "I just didn't want to talk about the details of SciTech's problems in front of the group."

Thomas grabbed the chair next to him, sat, and braced himself for the interaction.

"So what's going on?" Thomas probed with empathy, trying to draw Dan out.

"I'm depressed, and I'm not sure if I can even articulate what's wrong," Dan said flatly. "I'm just really depressed. Like I tried to explain in my case study, I've got serious problems back at SciTech and Cindy is one of them."

"Yes, I read her case study and yours—it sounds complicated," Thomas whispered, acknowledging the weightiness of his concern. Glancing down at the card Dan had given him, he asked, "So do you want to talk about the positive aspects of reengineering, or is there something else you'd like to discuss?"

"Honestly," Dan moaned painfully, "I know there's something wrong, but I don't know what it is. You said that having a blind spot was like having a piece of food on your face—others can see it, but I can't. So given our case studies and what you see going on between Cindy and I, you tell me. What's wrong? What do we need to talk about that I don't see?"

Thomas was caught off guard by Dan's vulnerability, so he paused, gathered his thoughts, and chose his words carefully.

"Can I sketch something in your journal that might help?" Dan passed the book to Thomas without hesitation, then watched as Thomas drew an image of the Enneagram with the workshop attendees' names, then darkened the line with an arrow at both ends that connected his name and Cindy's.

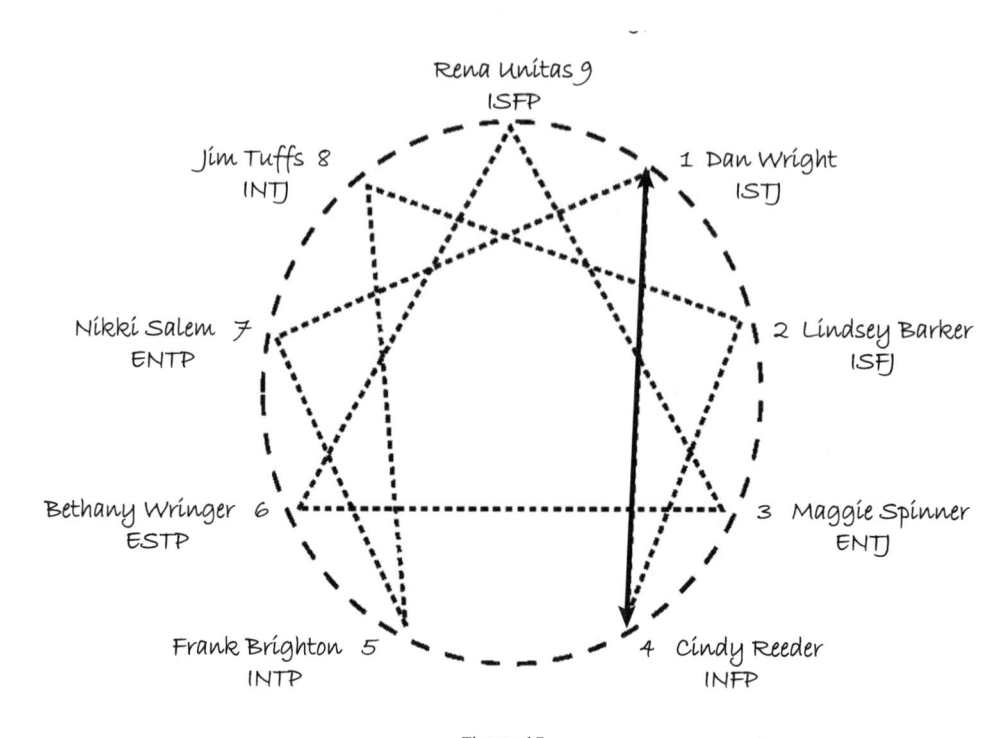

Figure 15

THE PROBLEM OF ENNEAGRAM CONNECTING POINTS

Enneagram positions:
- 9 Rena Unitas — ISFP
- 1 Dan Wright — ISTJ
- 2 Lindsey Barker — ISFJ
- 3 Maggie Spinner — ENTJ
- 4 Cindy Reeder — INFP
- 5 Frank Brighton — INTP
- 6 Bethany Wringer — ESTP
- 7 Nikki Salem — ENTP
- 8 Jim Tuffs — INTJ

"The problems you're having with Cindy are described and predicted by the connecting points on the Enneagram," he said confidently, pointing to the darkened line between Dan's name and Cindy's. Then below the figure Thomas wrote the words WE ALWAYS HATE WHAT WE SECRETLY ARE in large block letters. "I call it the 'projection principal.' Whenever we *can't stand* behaviors and attitudes in others and we're *consumed* by negative energy, most times we're projecting our own unconscious issues onto them. In other words, if you were to write a list of the things that you really hate about Cindy, that list probably describes personality characteristics that you have blind spots about. That's why I say, 'We always hate what we secretly are.'" Thomas paused and scanned Dan's facial expression to see if he was following this line of reasoning.

"Look at the personality matrix I handed out during the last session." He handed Dan a copy. "Then go back to the darkened line I drew on the diagram in your journal... What do your notice?" Thomas asked, encouraging him to probe deeply.

CONSCIOUS SELF	SHADOW SELF	INFERIOR SELF
James Tuffs INTJ [$N_i\ T_e$], Type Eight	Type Five, F_i	Type Two, S_e
Rena Unitus ISFP [$F_i\ S_e$], Type Nine	Type Six, N_i	Type Three, T_e
Dan Wright ISTJ [$S_i\ T_e$], Type One	Type Four, F_i	Type Seven, N_e
Lindsey Barker ISFJ [$S_i\ F_e$], Type Two	Type Eight, T_i	Type Four, N_e
Maggie Spinner ENTJ [$T_e\ N_i$], Type Three	Type Nine, S_e	Type Six, F_i
Cindy Reeder INFP [$F_i\ N_e$], Type Four	Type Two, S_i	Type One, T_e
Frank Brighton INTP [$T_i\ N_e$], Type Five	Type Seven, S_i	Type Eight, F_e
Bethany Wringer ESTP [$S_e\ T_i$], Type Six	Type Three, F_e	Type Nine, N_i
Nikki Salem ENTP [$N_e\ T_i$], Type Seven	Type One, F_e	Type Five, S_i

Dan looked alternately at the matrix, then back to the diagram Thomas had drawn in his journal. He finally exclaimed, "Cindy's Enneagram type is the same as my Shadow Self, and my type matches her Inferior Self."

"Exactly!" Thomas nudged Dan's shoulder. "And how did you describe your frame of mind when we first sat down? You said, 'I'm depressed.'"

Dan nodded in agreement.

"You've read the description of the Enneagram Type 4—what are they like?" Thomas slapped his palm on the table, almost demanding an answer as he locked his eyes with Dan's.

"They're moody, melancholy, and depressed!" Dan exclaimed, as if a light had gone on in his head.

"Absolutely! You've just seen one of your blind spots." Thomas smiled as Dan pondered this new self-knowledge.

"Now, if we follow the connecting point in the other direction, what does the Enneagram predict about your interaction with Cindy?" Thomas pointed to the darkened line once again.

"Underneath Cindy's creative, spontaneous, free thinking, emotionally sensitive, and aware personality is a glass half empty, perfectionist, rigid, hard-ass like me!" Dan almost shouted, as the significance of this insight flooded into his consciousness.

"Right, so when these two Inner People—your Shadow Self and her Inferior Self—get control of your mutual facilities, you both stand there wagging your fingers at each other's weaknesses and faults, but most of it is projection. You and Cindy are much more alike than either of you would care to admit."

Dan just stared at him, as the power of Thomas's words penetrated his hardened heart and began to soften it.

I hope he's smart enough to see that his other connecting point goes to Nikki's Enneagram type, Thomas thought, worried about how tense the interaction was becoming between the two of them. *Hmm...no, I won't bring it up now—I'll discuss that with him some other time.*

"Remember this phrase, Dan: 'It's personality, it's not personal.' In other words, although you get angry about Cindy's behaviors and attitudes and get offended like she's doing it to you on purpose, most times it's just personality differences along the Enneagram connecting point, so don't take it personally.

"Instead," Thomas smiled brightly while holding up three fingers, "try a little three-step exercise. First, identify exactly what it is that bothers you about her. Second, review the behaviors and attitudes predicted by the Enneagram connecting points. Finally, search for any blind spots that you might have. But remember, most times it's personality, it's not personal."

∽∽∽∽∽

PNG is only six degrees off the equator so the sun rises and sets more quickly than it does farther north on the Earth's surface. Cindy and James were sitting in hammocks on the top deck with cold, locally brewed beers called South Pacific that locals referred to as SP. Cindy was watching the deep pink, orange, and red hues of the sunset, but James could not keep his eyes off her shapely thighs.

"There's something of the eternal in the sunset tonight," Cindy said quietly from a sense of inner peace and tranquility. "What we're looking at is probably the way it's been for a million years, and the islands we see off in the distance look much like they did ten thousand years ago—they still don't have the scars of modern civilization."

Now James was alternately watching the sunset and surreptitiously glancing at Cindy's dark, well-proportioned breasts. He was trying to make some sense out of his erotic dream with the Melanesian woman and the powerful feelings it had caused in him about Cindy. The dream and the discussions he'd had with Cindy were deconstructing some of his most fundamental beliefs about God, people, and the world. For the first time in his life, James was able to see below the façade of everyday life to peoples' true humanity and not have to protect himself from what he saw.

When he went down the stairs to get them another cold SP, Cindy's intuition told her to talk to James about her observations on his behavior. He was back in a flash, handed her a beer, then sank into the hammock and watched the last light of day disappear.

After a moment of silence, Cindy said, "That was an incredible experience in the Highlands wasn't it?"

"Yeah," he quickly responded, "it blew me away. I learned a lot by listening to your questions, noticing your curiosity about the things you were interested in, and by just *watching* you."

"I know," Cindy looked him dead in the eye. "I've noticed that you've been *staring* at me," she said, consciously changing his word.

James knew that he should come clean about what was going on. "Can I tell you a dream I had while I was up in the Highlands?"

"Sure." she nodded affirmatively, then turned back toward the sunset.

As James recounted his dream in all its detail, complexity, and passion, Cindy sat up straight in her hammock and faced James directly. "And when I awoke and had finished logging it in my journal, I knew that the young Melanesian woman was you, Cindy." Gusts of salt air swirled around them in silence as James probed her. "Do you have any idea what these images might mean?"

At first, Cindy was speechless, then she regained her composure, "James, when did you have this dream?"

"The night before we left the Highlands." He took a deep drink from his bottle of SP.

She gazed at him in the diminishing twilight and whispered, "It was the very next day that you began staring at me."

James nodded—glad he had finally revealed his secret.

"Those are some deep and powerful archetypal symbols, my friend. Don't try to figure them out—just let the images roll around in your head and periodically bring them into consciousness." Then reflecting on her discussion with Thomas, she said, "James, whatever you do, don't interpret what happened in the dream literally; view the images symbolically, as if the creative process is using them as a pattern of wholeness to lead you down the path of psychological growth."

"I can't keep the image of you out of my mind," James confessed. "That's why I've been gawking at you."

"Well, now that I know what's going on," Cindy whispered in a light-hearted tone, "it won't make me feel as uncomfortable. In fact, the thought of it kind of turns me on, so you'd better watch yourself Father James!"

Cindy jumped up and gave the huge, hulk of a man a bear hug as the two of them laughed with deep satisfaction.

When the dinner bell rang at 8:00 P.M. some of the group were already sitting at the table laughing and sharing what they saw on today's dives. It was obvious they really enjoyed talking to each other and telling stories. Tonight, the table was covered with a lime-green colored tablecloth, accented with yellow colored dinner candles, as smooth Brazilian jazz played softly in the background. As the steward poured wine, the rest of the group took their seats and Anita and Janice placed freshly baked hot bread and salads on the table. Not surprisingly, Nikki was the last person to be seated because she was trying to convince Artie to join them after dinner to share some stories from his childhood days in Goroka.

Once the table had been set, Anita sat down next to Cindy.

"So how long have you been in PNG, Anita?" Cindy asked, eager to hear her experience in the country.

"About four years," she responded, then took a deep drink from her water glass. "I've spent most of my time on the ship diving, but I've been to a fair number of places throughout the country on my time off."

"Really? What are the most interesting land-based things to do here in PNG?" Cindy's curiosity was piqued given the prospect of living in Goroka for a year.

"Well, the first rule is to stay out of Port Moresby." Anita shook her head in a warning manner. "It's a filthy, crime-ridden, urban sprawl of a town that has an international reputation for being a very dangerous place. There are about two hundred seventy-five thousand people living there, but the overall layout of the city lacks any real character. You see these palatial homes owned mostly by expats hung precariously on the hillsides, then thousands and thousands of people who have come from all over the country living in poverty in squatters settlements scattered along the outskirts of town. Not that there aren't some things to do or see there, but in my opinion it's the very worst that the country has to offer."

Thomas interjected, "I agree—even when I only have to stay in that area for one night to catch a plane the next morning, I never overnight in Port Moresby. I always go to a place called Loloata Island Resort that's about twenty minutes south."

"Yep." Anita nodded in concurrence. "They've got some pretty good diving at Loloata too."

"Sounds like Mt. Hagen only bigger," Cindy replied, recalling her recent experience there on the tour bus. "Now that's a scary place!"

"Yeah, I forgot," Anita said, passing the salt and pepper to Thomas, "you've already been to the Highlands."

"Well, we were only in Mt. Hagen, but I've heard there are places that are more interesting."

"You've got to go to Tari in the Southern Highlands Province."

Anita became animated just thinking about it. "Stay at the Ambua Lodge—it's incredible—set up on a high mountain overlooking the valley. That's where the Huli wigmen are, the ones who paint their bodies from head to toe with magnificent colors and wear elaborate headdresses made out of human hair."

"Where are the other good places to dive here in PNG?" Nikki interjected, always looking for more excitement.

"Well, it depends what you're looking for," Anita replied. "There's some great diving down south of here in the Milne Bay area. It's real remote and there aren't many accommodations, but that region has more reefs and islands than any other province in PNG."

"Yeah—the reefs grow right up to the shoreline, so it makes for some fine diving," Janice agreed, having been there many times. "There are big dropoffs with lots of big stuff like hammerheads, bull sharks, manta rays, and even whale sharks."

Anita nodded to second Janice's commentary on the diving there.

"But if you *really* want some of the most pristine diving in the world, head out to the Eastern Fields, south of Port Moresby in the northern part of the Coral Sea," Janice continued. "It's a ten-hour boat ride, but the diving is incredible and the reefs are almost untouched because very few divers ever go there. You'll see dozens of schooling scalloped hammerheads, plus tiger, gray reef, and silvertip sharks—and the hard and soft coral is simply amazing. You know how we told you to set your reef hook into a nonliving part of the coral reef on one of today's dives, well in the Eastern Fields there is no nonliving part of the coral reef!"

"Is it shore-based diving or should I do a live-aboard?" Nikki asked, excited by the thought of going to such a remote and adventurous place.

"There's nothing there on land—it's totally isolated. But there's a live-aboard dive boat called the *Golden Dawn* that goes out there regularly for seven- or fourteen-day trips. That's probably the best way to see that area if you're really interested in going. They always have some cancellations, so I'll bet you could book a place on the boat when we get back—they give incredible discounts for last minute bookings."

Maybe I could change my plane reservations, stay another week, and head down there and check it out, Nikki seriously considered. *I'll bet Barb's doing just fine on that new performance appraisal system without me.*

When the steward began clearing the dishes, Thomas signaled across the table to Bethany, "Would you like to talk about your three-by-five now, or is it too late?"

"Let's talk now," she smiled, pointing to a quiet place to sit at the back of the ship.

"I have Dana's full support," Bethany insisted, reiterating what Thomas had already read in her case study, "but I lack the courage to stand up for and defend what I know is true! "What's wrong with me, Thomas?" she cried in bewilderment.

"It's not about outer validation, Bethany," Thomas replied, trying to deflect some of her self-condemnation, "you lack inner validation that you're on the right path. Even if you had ten bosses like Dana who affirmed you every step of the way, you'd still need the inner sense that you're on the right path."

"I know," Bethany admitted, staring over the rail of the ship into the night.

"Look, you started on a path you believed in with the goal of providing better social services for those in need—it's just been rougher than you'd anticipated, that's all. Remember there's nothing your staff and the other managers can do to stop you, because the same dysfunctional system that protects them will also protect you. So *stand up* against the old 'paperwork first' culture and become an *insurgent*—a rebel for the cause of your clients in the field. I can't imagine you won't prevail!" Bethany's eyes widened with excitement as Thomas pounded one of his fists into the other palm trying to galvanize her commitment to stay the course.

～～～～

Lindsey and Maggie were out on the back deck of the ship sharing from the depths of their hearts. Maggie opened up about some of the problems she'd been having with Rena.

"Your daughter is something else," Lindsey gushed with deep admiration in her voice. "Her questions are so insightful, so poignant and probing—I'd be very proud of her if I was you."

"I am...and I realize how demanding I've been about her opening that new branch down in Colorado Springs and taking over my business so Troy and I can have a baby and enjoy the good life. I need to lighten up. I love her deeply, Lindsey, but those feelings are so deep inside and it's so hard for me to express them. I can write them in my journal, but somehow saying them to her is a different story."

The words were hardly out of Maggie's mouth, when Rena rounded the corner. "I'm going to turn in," Rena yawned, almost on cue.

Maggie looked at Lindsey, then back at her daughter and said, "I think I'll join you."

Lindsey poured herself another glass of wine, content to have the back deck all to herself as she began pondering the problems she had in intimate relationships.

Day 2
DUGOUT CANOES AT THE REAR OF THE SHIP

Strategy 2:

Use Alignment to Gain Competitive Advantage

THE DAY BEGINS

They had sailed all through the night in open seas that bounced the ship from side to side like a toy as it pushed through the pounding waves. Even so, the clean fresh air and the physical rigors of diving caused most of the group to sleep better than the previous night. In the wee hours of the morning, the crew moored the ship at Father's Reef—about eighteen miles due west of Lolobau Island in the eastern sector of Kimbe Bay.

By 6:00 A.M. Monday morning the smell of brewing coffee and freshly baked breads and rolls was permeating the ship. A few members of the group were at their usual breakfast tables, chatting away with Artie, laughing at his endless stream of jokes and stories as Pachelbel played softly in the background. As breakfast time proceeded, people were scattered around the decks of the ship drinking coffee and waking up in the warm morning sun. Rena, Frank, and some of the others were up on the top deck looking at the smoke rising from the perfectly formed, fourteen thousand-foot high, cone-shaped volcano called Father's. Some geological experts claim that the conditions are right for this giant to blow, and that the resulting devastation will be far greater than the destruction caused by Mt. St. Helen's, over ten thousand miles north of PNG along the Ring of Fire. As they stared silently at the magical image of this natural wonder, the bell rang at 8:00 A.M. sharp, to begin the first session of the day.

SESSION 1: ALIGN THE ORGANIZATION TO SPEAK WITH ONE VOICE

"Good morning." Thomas smiled, then took a sip of his coffee. "As I mentioned yesterday, building creative organizations requires three strategies. Yesterday, we discussed the first one—learn to find meaning and significance in work. The practices that constitute Strategy 1 are about experiencing the creative process, learning how fear inhibits creativity, and building inner collaboration and alignment. Strategy 1 taught us that the first key to building creative organizations is to learn to think outside the box—and the box is that three-pound universe between your ears called your 'personality fixation.'

"Having challenged the biases through which you view the world in yesterday's sessions, today I want to cover the second strategy—use alignment to gain competitive advantage. You'll notice that the feel and texture of today's discussion will be very different because it focuses on organizations, but I'll try to connect today's material to what we've already covered." Thomas motioned toward the flip chart, already turned to Figure 16.

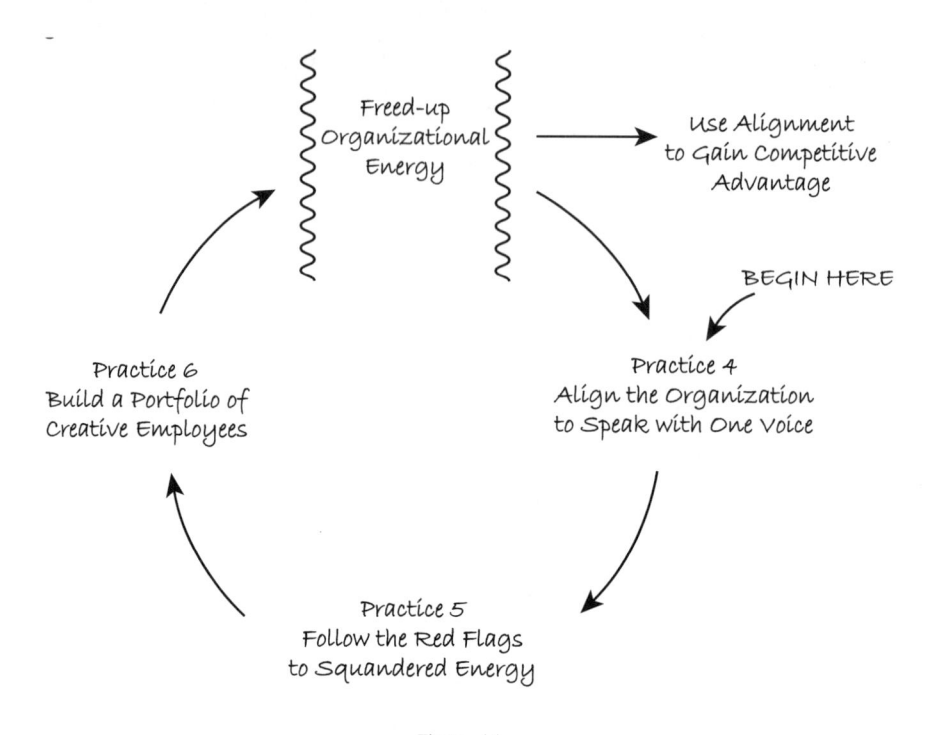

Figure 16
THE SECOND STRATEGY: USE ALIGNMENT TO GAIN COMPETITIVE ADVANTAGE

Diagram shows a clockwise cycle beginning at Practice 4 (Align the Organization to Speak with One Voice), proceeding to Practice 5 (Follow the Red Flags to Squandered Energy), then Practice 6 (Build a Portfolio of Creative Employees), leading to Freed-up Organizational Energy, which is used to Gain Competitive Advantage.

"Notice how the second strategy consists of Practices 4, 5, and 6, and gaining competency in them frees up fixated organizational energy and makes it available to fulfill the purpose and business objectives of a company, which in turn produces competitive advantage."[86] Thomas traced the clockwise rotation of the three practices with his index finger, then tore the sheet of paper from the flip chart, grabbed a roll of masking tape, and taped Figure 16 to the wall next to the flip chart for ready reference.

"I want to begin the discussion of Practice 4 by reiterating a timeless principle we discussed only briefly yesterday. 'All organizations are perfectly aligned to get the results they get.'[87] If some of the employees in your company are heading in this direction," Thomas pointed to the stern of the boat, then the bow, "and others are going the opposite way and we add up those directions, we'll get an overall direction for your organization. But these misalignments are like running this boat full throttle with the anchor dragging along the bottom, or like driving a car with one foot on the gas and the other on the brake. In fact, Peter Drucker argues that companies, like people, have values and beliefs. Serious misalignments about the values, beliefs, purpose, and direction of an organization condemns managers and employees to frustration and non-performance."[88]

The group nodded their heads in understanding.

"Misalignments between people, organizational structures, and systems squander enormous amounts of energy. Psychological and organizational energy are like two sides of the same coin that cannot be separated because business processes don't do work, people do. On one side of the coin, *psychological energy* is the most precious resource in life because it makes all of life's tasks possible. There's only so much psychological energy in the human personality, so when the number of misalignments between you and the Inner People reaches a critical mass, they oppose you at every turn."

Cindy shook her head vigorously in agreement.

"On the other side of the coin, *organizational energy* is the most precious resource that a company has because it makes all the tasks of business processes possible. There's only so much organizational energy in a company, so when the number of misalignments becomes large, this squanders enormous amounts of organizational energy that is unavailable to achieve the organization's purpose and business objectives."

"Practice 4 is a five-step process for finding misalignments within an organization and then aligning it to speak with one voice." Thomas pointed to the list on the flip chart. "I'll discuss each step in turn."

STEP 1: BUILD TIMELESS PRINCIPLES INTO A QUESTION SET

"In Step 1, we take the timeless principles we've been talking about and organize them into a model that has eight sectors and covers the most important areas of organizational development." Thomas turned the page to reveal the list.

SECTOR 1: *Creativity and Involvement*

SECTOR 2: *Personality and Leadership*

SECTOR 3: *Decision-Making Style and Adaptability*

SECTOR 4: *Strategy, Planning, and Goal Setting*

SECTOR 5: *Internal Environment*

SECTOR 6: *Business Environment*

SECTOR 7: *Communication and Squandered Energy*

SECTOR 8: *Human and Computing Resources*

"I've codified many of the timeless principles from *HBR* and books on business excellence into the set of questions. Currently, I've refined the set to just over one hundred questions, but I'm constantly looking for ways to reduce the number and retain or improve their measurement accuracy.

"I'd like you to break up into three small groups so you can review and discuss the items, then we'll come back together as a large group and share your insights. Group one will be composed of James, Rena, and Dan and will meet around the table at the back of the ship. Group two will consist of Lindsey, Maggie, and Cindy, and they'll meet in the dining room. Group three, Nikki, Bethany, and Frank, can stay right here around the teaching table. As you review the questions, discuss how you would tailor them to your organization. You'll only have twenty minutes to complete your discussion, so I'll float from table to table to answer any questions that arise and to make sure that you stay on track." Thomas handed out the list of questions and signaled the groups to move to their meeting locations and begin reviewing them.

SECTOR 1: CREATIVITY AND INVOLVEMENT

- *My suggestions for innovations and improvement are taken seriously and acted on?*
- *I am encouraged to use creativity to solve work-related problems (creativity is not viewed as "unofficial" activity)?*
- *I can propose creative solutions to problems and issues without fear of retribution from the organization?*
- *I can propose creative solutions to problems and issues without fear of being embarrassed or alienated by coworkers?*
- *I find a sense of meaning and significance in my work (it's not just a job)?*
- *Teams of people with multiple perspectives and competencies are used to stimulate more effective problem solving?*
- *This organization provides the resources for me to develop and apply my creative abilities to my work (training, development, mentoring, coaching)?*
- *I know how to use my creative abilities as a resource to solve job-related problems?*
- *People do not use organizational rules, polices, procedures, or goals to oppose innovations, improvements, and the creative process?*
- *Innovation and risk-taking are viewed as opportunities to learn and improve, even when they end in failure?*
- *People are encouraged to appropriately question "how things are done" and challenge the status quo?*

SECTOR 2: PERSONALITY AND LEADERSHIP

- *My managers listen to feedback about their blind spots and are not defensive?*
- *My managers act on the feedback they receive?*
- *My managers practice what they preach?*
- *My managers have the appropriate knowledge and experience in the organization's business areas to do their job competently?*
- *My managers reevaluate their business philosophy about how the organization should be operated using objective data?*
- *Senior managers can ignite and sustain organizational change?*
- *Senior managers have taken corrective action on issues identified in prior organizational assessments?*
- *Senior managers will adopt and act on the findings of this survey?*
- *This organization has a well-defined purpose and business objectives?*
- *This organization has a well-defined set of core values that functions as an inner organizational compass?*
- *The unwritten (informal) rules for how people get ahead in the organization are not different from the written (formal) rules?*
- *Managers at all levels in this organization are held accountable for modeling the organization's core values?*
- *On important matters like organizational purpose, core values, and business objectives, managers and employees at all levels have consensus and speak with one voice (we're all going in the same direction)?*

SECTOR 3: DECISION-MAKING STYLE AND ADAPTABILITY

- *I work as if time is my most important resource (time is money)?*
- *In this organization, decisions are made based on internal measurements and quantitative analysis of business objectives and goals?*
- *In this organization, decisions are not made based on political agendas, or self-interest?*
- *In this organization, decisions are made based on external measures of customer satisfaction and other objective feedback from the business environment?*
- *In this organization, decisions are made based on managers' and employees' knowledge and experience about internal operational factors (capacity of facilities and equipment)?*
- *In this organization, decisions are reached in a timely manner by considering alternative options and by gathering sufficient information and data?*
- *In this organization, financial criteria are not the sole factor in decisions and don't override other criteria (customer satisfaction or employee feedback)?*
- *I know who has authority to make decisions in this organization?*
- *In this organization, decisions are made without excessive bureaucracy?*
- *Bottoms-up input from the "right" people is required when making decisions?*
- *In this organization, decisions balance short-term pressures and goals with long-term business objectives and overall direction?*
- *This organization successfully completes the projects and initiatives it begins (they don't get bogged down and die a slow death, with nobody knowing why)?*

- *This organization terminates poor performing projects and initiatives based on objective evidence and data (they're not kept alive, with nobody knowing why)?*
- *The people I work with will do whatever it takes to respond to challenges and demands from customers and the business environment?*
- *Organization structure is changed or redesigned to remove bottlenecks that frustrate and undermine effectiveness and high performance?*
- *This organization brings in "fresh blood" to stimulate change, innovation, and improvement?*
- *Outdated and unnecessary tasks and procedures in the areas I work in are eliminated or redesigned?*
- *This organization helps employees work through the stress of change that happens immediately (a reorganization) and the ongoing process of coming to terms with the organizational and personal effects that change causes?*

SECTOR 4: STRATEGY, PLANNING, AND GOAL SETTING

- *This organization believes that short- and long-term interests and forces can be reconciled?*
- *This organization has a strategic plan that has clearly defined business objectives, goals, and quantitative measures of performance for the entire company?*
- *This organization's strategic plan is linked to a strategic budget?*
- *Progress on achieving strategic objectives and goals is periodically monitored and communicated to employees at all levels in the organization?*
- *My business unit has an annual operating plan that has defined goals and quantitative measures of performance?*

- *My business unit's annual operating plan is linked to our annual budget?*
- *My manager monitors our actual performance against the goals and performance measures in the business unit's annual operating plan and communicates these results to everyone in my unit?*
- *The goals and objectives in my performance appraisal are connected to the purpose, business objectives, and goals of the entire company?*
- *There is a cause and effect relationship between achieving the goals and objectives in my performance appraisal and amount of compensation I receive from the company?*
- *This company's policies and procedures facilitate achieving the organization's purpose, core values, business objectives, and strategy?*
- *Policies and procedures are applied fairly to people at all levels in the organization?*

SECTOR 5: INTERNAL ENVIRONMENT

- *Individuals are held accountable for organizational performance (not organization units)?*
- *Superior work is recognized with actual and symbolic rewards?*
- *Poor work is confronted and dealt with in a fair and constructive manner?*
- *Authority is delegated to the lowest organizational level where the work is performed?*
- *The "system" does not inhibit managers and workers from exercising authority in their sphere of responsibility?*
- *Authority and responsibility for work are not ambiguous (it's clear who is supposed to be doing what)?*

- *The organizational boundaries between business units do not inhibit getting work done?*
- *There is no confusion between business units about roles, lines of responsibility, and interfaces (business units are clear about who does what, when)?*
- *This organization factors people's personality into who gets promoted to management and leadership positions?*
- *This organization factors people's personality into work assignments and work planning?*
- *The organizational structure I work in is aligned with the business priorities and cultural values of the company?*
- *My work environment has manageable levels of stress?*
- *This organization has a systematic approach to customer satisfaction measurement and management?*
- *This organization has a systematic approach to marketing and sales?*
- *This organization has a facilities and equipment utilization plan?*
- *This organization has well-defined procedures on quality assurance and quality control (rework, downtime, customer complaints, returns, etc.)?*
- *My business unit benchmarks its performance against other organizations?*
- *My business unit monitors and tries to improve their product and service delivery record?*
- *In my business unit, business processes and work processes are documented?*
- *I have the appropriate level of Information Technology and computing support needed to perform my work and achieve my objectives and goals?*

- *This organization has a systematic approach to managing how meetings are conducted to ensure that time is used effectively?*
- *I use a formal time-management system to organize myself (Franklin-Covey, Day Runner, etc.)?*
- *I align my daily and weekly appointments and tasks with the organization's goals and measures of performance?*
- *The projects I am assigned to are well-organized, with fixed timetables, milestones, and deliverables?*

SECTOR 6: BUSINESS ENVIRONMENT

- *The expectations of boards, stockholders, and other owners are communicated within the organization?*
- *This organization understands the nature of the industry it's in (growth rate and market demands)?*
- *This organization has effectively dealt with social, political, ethical, or legal problems from the business environment?*
- *This organization has effectively dealt with pressures from federal, state, or local laws and requirements (OSHA, EPA, FDA, etc)?*
- *This organization effectively confronts their competitors' ability to undermine and frustrate their business performance?*
- *The cost of doing business (cost of capital, facilities, skilled employees, products and services, or technological trends) does not adversely affect the organization's ability to perform effectively?*
- *I clearly understand my customers' needs and requirements?*
- *I meet my customers' needs and requirements to their satisfaction?*
- *I solicit input from my customers about how I can improve my products, services?*

- *Customers believe we compare favorably to our competition in regard to price?*
- *Customers believe we compare favorably to our competition in regard to level of service?*
- *Customers believe we compare favorably to our competition in regard to quality?*
- *Customers believe we compare favorably to our competition in regard to timeliness?*

SECTOR 7: COMMUNICATION AND SQUANDERED ENERGY

- *The communication style in this organization is open and direct (we go to people directly when we have an issue with them rather than discuss it with others)?*
- *The information and message communicated through formal channels (the organization's newsletter, memos, intranet) is consistent with the information communicated through the "rumor mill" or "grapevine?"*
- *The managers and staff I work with communicate and cooperate so that key information does not get bound in organization "silos" (e.g., the left hand knows what the right one is doing)?*
- *I am informed about issues that affect my job?*
- *The people I work with do not have "hot buttons" and do not become inappropriately upset about decisions and work related issues (I don't have to walk on eggshells)?*
- *The people I work with use conflict that arises over personality differences constructively to stimulate learning and improvement?*
- *The people I work with do not allow conflict that arises over personality differences to become destructive, thus undermining and frustrating learning and improvement?*

- *The people I work with use their time and energy to do productive work, rather than squandering it on toxic interpersonal conflicts?*
- *The people I work with submit views about why objectives and goals were missed to public tests and scrutiny, rather than privately blaming coworkers or those outside the organization?*
- *The people I work with believe they have the power to effect change in the organization?*
- *The people I work with discuss their dissatisfaction about the organization publicly in constructive ways, rather than venting it privately to others in the organization?*
- *My organization achieves the objectives and goals it sets for itself (they are not disrupted by unknown organizational causes)?*
- *In discussions and meetings that I attend, everyone participates freely (they don't withdraw and not express their views until coworkers make mistakes)?*
- *This organization does not have powerful alliances and subgroups that accumulate power (budgetary resources, knowledge, space, equipment, etc.) and use them to oppose its purpose, core values, objectives, and goals?*

SECTOR 8: HUMAN AND COMPUTING RESOURCES

- *This organization has a strategic staffing plan to attract the needed employee knowledge and skill base?*
- *This organization has a succession plan that aligns with the purpose, core values, and business objectives of the company?*
- *This organization has systems for training and developing the competencies and skills of all employees?*
- *This organization has the appropriate systems for appraising the performance of employees and compensating them?*

- *The turnover/reassignment of personnel is not above average (compared to the organization's historical average)?*
- *This organization has a strategy for managing employee relations that includes environment, safety, health and wellness?*
- *This organization's Information Technology infrastructure links all the organizations functions so they can communicate effectively (financial management, business and work processes, company and business unit objectives and goals, and the data from the business environment)?*
- *My manager treats the people who report to them as if they were self-motivated and needed only to be challenged?*
- *I believe people can change deeply?*
- *I believe the individual's welfare is balanced with the welfare of the organization?*
- *The people I work with express their emotions constructively?*
- *Conflict between people or organizations is dealt with appropriately?*

Thomas moved between the three groups as they vigorously discussed which questions applied to specific problems they were experiencing—issues they'd documented in their case studies.

After about twenty minutes, he went to the first two groups and said, "Okay, I hate to break off this good interaction, but let's get back into a large group around the teaching table." Once everyone was seated, Thomas asked, "Who wants to begin the discussion?"

"I see many of the principles we've been discussing built into this question set—it's like one big dive slate review of what you've been saying," Lindsey said, still scanning the list.

"That's correct," Thomas responded. "The three powerful strategies are not pie-in-the-sky organizational theory but have concrete application to all companies."

"What about financial information?" Frank asked, clearly impressed by the otherwise thoroughness of the questions.

"I do a separate financial analysis," Thomas replied, "and I didn't include it here because most owners and managers have a myopic preoccupation with financial indicators anyway. As I already mentioned, financial information is a lagging indicator because it's historical and you can manipulate it. These questions capture the essence of the leading indicators of employees, customers, and shareholders. For our purposes, I won't go into it here, but I use Kaplan and Norton's Balanced Scorecard (BSC) approach to integrating financial and non-financial measures of performance.[89] The BSC really rounds out the picture of organizational measurement."

"I wondered what you'd actually learn from the questions in the business environment section?" Maggie commented skeptically. "You really need objective data from customers and external constituencies in order to get a complete picture of how effectively your organization interacts with the business environment. Otherwise, it's just *your* internal perception, and that's a real problem."

"Absolutely." Thomas winked, seconding her point. "I have a separate subset of questions that I use to poll customers about their interactions with the organization. Contrary to popular belief, customers often see beyond a company's boundary into the inner workings of organizational structures, systems, and culture. That's why some of the most valuable suggestions for innovations and improvements come from customers. Asking the questions you reviewed in your small groups identifies misalignments that squander psychological and organizational energy within the company, but anchoring these data to the perspective of the customer provides a much more robust and reliable snapshot of the company."

Maggie nodded in complete agreement with his analysis of the problem.

"Many of the questions didn't seem to fit a nonprofit organization," James commented, wondering if he could apply them to his parish.

"Thanks for pointing that out." Thomas gave him a thumbs up. "I've got a nonprofit version that you can tailor to fit your situation back in my cabin. I'll give it to you between sessions."

"When you're a CEO like I am, how do you answer questions like, 'My manager acts on the feedback they receive?'" Dan queried, trying to make sense of the assessment's line of questioning.

"I was just getting to that," Thomas replied, thankful that Dan was making a positive contribution. "We ask the senior managers to comment on the same issues as everyone else, but we ask the question in a slightly different way *because they're where the buck stops*! Only they have the organizational authority to create, manage, or deconstruct organizational structures, systems, and culture, so I hold them to a higher level of accountability and transparency."

Thomas glanced down at the list of questions. "So, for example, in the Personality and Leadership sector, the senior manager's questions are all worded in the first person: 'I listen to feedback about my blind spots and am not defensive. I act on feedback I receive. I practice what I preach. I can ignite and sustain organizational change.' Then we compare their answers to everyone else in the organization."

"But that puts a lot of pressure on them don't you think?" Dan replied, trying to grasp how the approach would actually work.

"It sure does," Thomas concurred. "I hold senior managers to a much more stringent standard than everyone else in a company because they have the power to make or break the system. 'To whom much is given, much is required.'" Thomas smiled. "That's why they make the big bucks."

Dan and the group laughed at the irony of his words.

"The list of questions is enormous." Cindy shook her head, overwhelmed. "In our group, the discussion of something like, 'What is our company's purpose and business objectives?' could have gone on forever. How do you narrow down this list to the *significant* misalignments that squander energy in a company like mine that has over one hundred employees?"

Others nodded, indicating that they'd had the same question.

STEP 2: ASK THE QUESTIONS TO FIND MISALIGNMENTS

"That's a perfect lead-in to Step 2." Thomas shot her an index finger, then pointed to the flip chart. "As we discussed yesterday, a person's MBTI and Enneagram type preferences are like different perspectives on the world, and this can create bias in decision making and problem solving. These differences emerge when we ask people questions like the ones in front of you and see how differently they respond. So I ask these questions of employees in a company like SciTech using a tool called the *Island of Excellence Organizational Assessment;* then I analyze the degree of variance, or misalignment, in their responses. The practice of aligning an organization to speak with one voice is crucial to becoming an Island of Excellence," Thomas said intensely. "As Jim Collins's *Built to Last* study showed, ninety-nine percent of pursuing excellence is investing the time and energy to get a company aligned."[90]

"The assessment is designed to collect information about the operation and culture of companies and how people at all organizational levels work together and interact. Because the responses to the questions are sent directly to me, not the company, the assessment is totally confidential and no one in the organization ever has access to individual responses. Strict confidentiality helps ensure that participants give the most accurate and honest responses to the questions, especially in organizations where fear inhibits the creative process. Individual responses are compiled into a summary report, so individual answers can't be identified.

"I tell those taking the assessment that I want their *personal knowledge* about three things. First, I want to know how the organizational structures and systems either work or don't work. Second, the assessment asks pointed questions about the behaviors of people that employees work *for* and work *with*. Third, I ask about the organizational environment, atmosphere, and culture of the company. If an employee has secondhand knowledge or no knowledge at all, they are instructed to answer that question, 'I don't know' or 'no response.'

"The questions are distributed within the three triads and eight sectors shown here in Figure 17." Thomas pointed to the diagram on the flip chart. "I do four levels of analysis looking for misalignments.

Organizational Assessment

CULTURAL CHANGE INDICATOR

- 1 Creativity and Involvement
- 2 Personality and Leadership
- 3 Decision-making Style and Adaptability
- 4 Strategy, Planning and Goal Setting
- 5 Internal Environment
- 6 Business Environment
- 7 Communication and Squandered Energy
- 8 Human and Computing Resources

STRATEGIC HUMAN ALIGNMENT

STRATEGIC BUSINESS ALIGNMENT

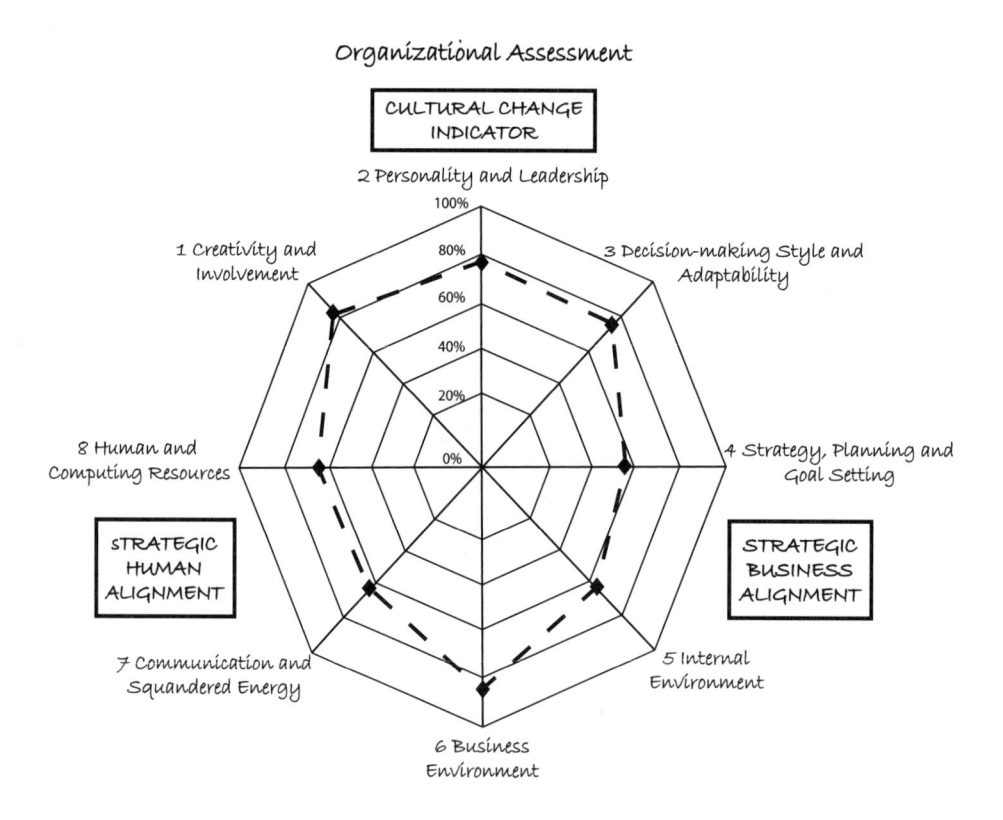

Figure 17

ISLAND OF EXCELLENCE SELF-ASSESSMENT LEVEL ONE ANALYSIS

Members of the group were studying Figure 17 carefully, so Thomas paused for a moment to let them finish. "The three triads—cultural change and strategic business and human alignment—are in distinct boxes, but notice that there are no defined boundaries between them. This is because organizations are interrelated, holistic systems composed of people and business processes, fueled by psychological and organizational energy. To reiterate—organizations are collective-cultural entities that are led, managed, and changed one person at a time."

Some members of the group nodded, while others wrote furiously in their journals.

"The answers to the questions in Sectors 1, 2, and 3 begin to define how difficult it will be to create and sustain change in the organization. Sectors 4 through 6 indicate the degree to which organizational structures and systems are aligned, while Sectors 6 through 8 help determine the degree to which human resources are aligned. The measurement scale indicates the degree of alignment between the people answering the questions and the timeless principles, so when the answers given by employees in a particular sector are aligned with this standard of excellence, the score is one hundred percent. As the score drops, the degree of misalignment between the organization and the timeless principles increases." Thomas pointed to the zero percent center point of the diagram.

"So does a perfect score and complete alignment mean that all the people in that organization are clones?" Nikki snickered, only half in jest.

"No," Thomas chuckled, along with several others, "they're not clones. In fact, each personality type has a very different set of problem-solving skills that is required to round out the overall set of competencies in that organization. When a company speaks with one voice, those different problem-solving skills are all aligned and focused on achieving the same purpose and business objectives of the organization. One voice means that people with different personality types commit to go in the same direction—they choose a common purpose and end."

Nikki and the others jotted more notes in their journal, satisfied with Thomas's answer.

"At Level Two, we begin evaluating the degree of misalignment between the people in the organization by polling different populations. In an organization that has three levels of management—senior managers, managers, and workers—and about one hundred people, it's possible to look for misalignments across the entire organization." Thomas turned the page and pointed to the three different sets of data plotted in Figure 18.

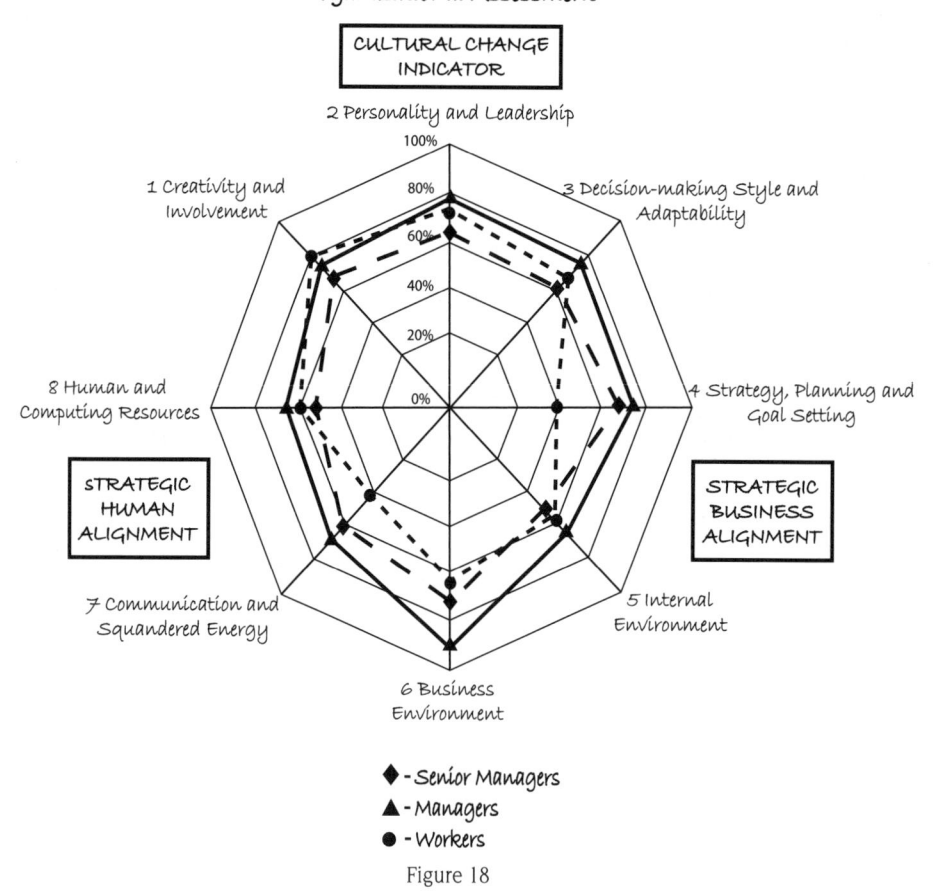

Organizational Assessment

CULTURAL CHANGE INDICATOR

1 Creativity and Involvement
2 Personality and Leadership
3 Decision-making Style and Adaptability
4 Strategy, Planning and Goal Setting
5 Internal Environment
6 Business Environment
7 Communication and Squandered Energy
8 Human and Computing Resources

STRATEGIC HUMAN ALIGNMENT

STRATEGIC BUSINESS ALIGNMENT

♦ – Senior Managers
▲ – Managers
● – Workers

Figure 18

ISLAND OF EXCELLENCE SELF-ASSESSMENT LEVEL TWO ANALYSIS

"Level Two analysis compares the overall scores of the three populations of senior managers, managers, and workers and shows the degree of misalignment with each other and with the timeless principles in the question set. Look at the profile for strategy, planning, and goal setting in Figure 18—there's almost a forty percent misalignment between workers and managers and sixty percent variance between workers and the timeless principles."

Thomas raised his voice to underscore the importance of what these data indicated. "In organizations that have more complicated organizational structures, the manager category can be divided into middle managers and front-line supervisors. Unfortunately, because most organizations do not speak with one voice, the organizational span between four levels of management is extremely large. Most senior managers have no idea what's going on two or three organizational levels below them, nor do workers know what's going on at the very top of an organization. Consequently, the assessment data in organizations that are extensively misaligned only show one thing—that they don't speak with one voice."

Thomas waited until the group finished scrutinizing the diagram, then turned the page and pointed to Figure 19. "With Level Three analysis, we can identify misalignments in the way the three populations answered individual questions, then add in data from the customer perspective on select questions."

Personality and Leadership

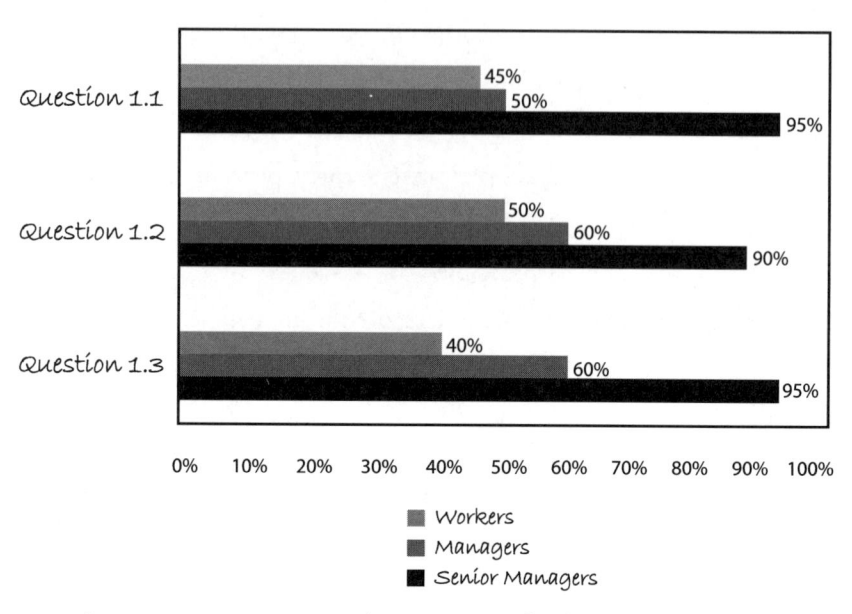

	Workers	Managers	Senior Managers
Question 1.1	45%	50%	95%
Question 1.2	50%	60%	90%
Question 1.3	40%	60%	95%

Question 1.1 - My manager listens to my feedback about his blinds spots and is not defensive?

Question 1.2 - My manager acts on the feedback he receives?

Question 1.3 - My manager practices what he preaches?

Figure 19

ISLAND OF EXCELLENCE SELF-ASSESSMENT LEVEL THREE ANALYSIS

"Take a question like, 'My manager practices what he preaches,' where senior managers answered in the first person, 'I practice what I preach.' What does it mean when there's over a forty percent misalignment on this question? How does this degree of misalignment manifest itself in the day-to-day life of this organization?"

Cindy stared at Figure 19 and pondered the implications of Thomas's question at SciTech. Meanwhile, Dan stared at Cindy, wondering how their conflict would end.

"At Level Four, I use mathematical analysis to identify the most significant misalignments between two populations at a time. Level Three analysis averages the differences between individual answers in a given population into a single number and this can hide significant and interesting misalignments."

Some members of the group looked confused by what Thomas was saying, so Frank jumped in, eager to contribute to the discussion. "It's like averaging five one hundred percents on school exams with one score of zero," Frank summarized, eyeing the group. He understood how crucial this analysis was to the overall method. "When you average all six scores into a single number, that one zero pulls your overall score down to about eighty-three percent."

"That's exactly what I mean." Thomas smiled, thankful for the clarifying example Frank had used. "The mathematical analysis narrows the data down to the most serious misalignments—about twenty issues that squander eighty percent of the organization's psychological and organizational energy."

Thomas pointed to Figure 20 on the flip chart. "This figure compares the misalignments of senior managers and managers, but we can also compare misalignments between senior managers and workers, or between managers and workers.

Cultural Change Indicator
Senior Managers and Managers

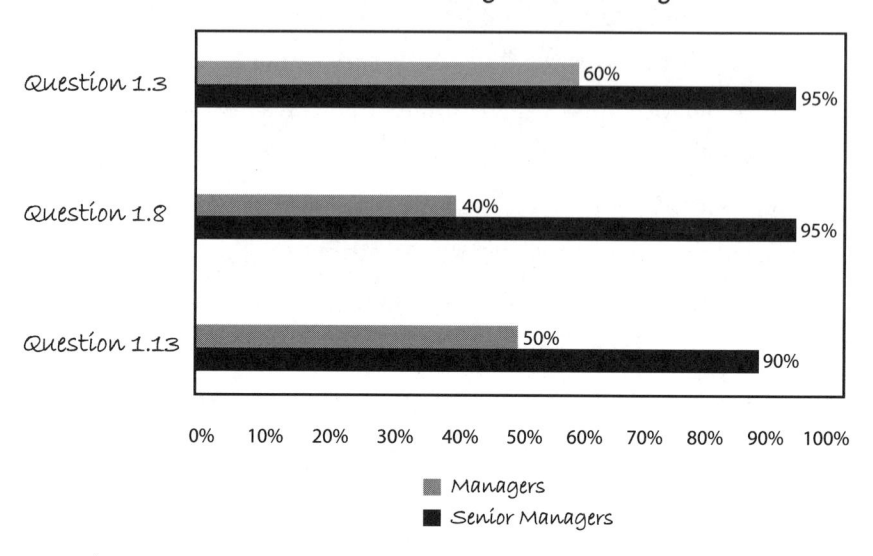

Question 1.3 — Managers: 60%, Senior Managers: 95%
Question 1.8 — Managers: 40%, Senior Managers: 95%
Question 1.13 — Managers: 50%, Senior Managers: 90%

Question 1.3 - My manager practices what he preaches?

Question 1.8 - Senior managers will adopt and act on the findings of this survey?

Question 1.13 - On important matters like organizational purpose, core values, and business objectives, managers and employees at all levels have concensus and speak with one voice (we're all going in the same direction)?

Figure 20

ISLAND OF EXCELLENCE SELF-ASSESSMENT LEVEL FOUR ANALYSIS

"At Level Four we're down to a comparison where senior managers say they're open to feedback, but managers and workers say they're not. Senior managers claim they encourage creativity, but workers say they don't. Senior managers claim that the organization is not dominated by fear and retribution, but managers claim it is, although they're afraid to admit it even on a confidential assessment. These are the kinds of issues that an organization must focus on to begin the journey to becoming an Island of Excellence."

"It must be possible for questions that appear to have significant misalignments at Level Three to not show up at Level Four?" Frank theorized, probing the assessment's methodology at a deeper level.

"That's correct." Thomas smiled, impressed with Frank's insight and knowledge of statistical matters. "That's what your example of averaging test scores spoke to. If the spread of answers within one of the three populations is very large and you average those individual answers into a single number then display it as a percentage on the bar graph, it might *look* like the misalignment is larger or smaller than it actually is. That's why we do the mathematical analysis—to screen for this type of problem."

"Can misalignments between the two bars on a given question at Level Four ultimately be reduced to differences in personality type?" Rena asked, her curiosity clearly piqued.

"Yes they can!" Thomas beamed, quite pleased with the depth of her insight and persistence in applying the material in practical ways. "When we do a fifth level of analysis and look for misalignments within a given population, some variance between the answers of a group of managers or workers can be attributed to their educational background, life experience, gender, or culture. But their level of personality fixation is an underlying bias of many of these differences. Fixation biases their beliefs and choices about which educational field to pursue, how they interpret life experiences, and how their gender develops within their cultural setting.

"To reiterate," Thomas emphasized, "organizations are collective-cultural entities that are led, managed, and changed, one person at a time. In the end, *all* differences between people are vitally constrained by, and partly reducible to, their level of personality fixation."

"Do you realize the implications of what you're saying for traditional organizational theory?" Nikki asked, reflecting on what she'd learned during her graduate education in business. "This is the first OD model I've ever seen that tries to integrate the descriptive and predictive power of personality theory with the best of organizational theory."

"That's correct," Thomas responded flatly, without qualification. He paused for a moment to punctuate the importance of Nikki's observation.

STEP 3: VALIDATE THE RESULTS

"Okay," Thomas pointed to the flip chart and continued, "let's move on. In Step 3, we try to validate the results of the assessment and determine how disruptive the misalignments are to the performance of individuals and the organization. But I want to warn you—validating misalignments is an extremely difficult task because even ones that squander enormous amounts of psychological and organizational energy do not normally show up on the bottom line."

"Why is that?" James queried, looking confused.

"There are at least five reasons. First, as I've already stated, financial information is a lagging indicator—it's historical, and you can manipulate it. By the time misalignments show up on the bottom line, things are normally so bad that the overhead costs of employee turnover, recruiting, hiring, training, and litigation *can't* be ignored.

"Second, most organizations don't have measurement systems that are sensitive enough to detect the revenues lost due to misalignments in ineffective work processes, rework, poor quality, and declining performance of employees caused by psychological stress, backbiting, and interpersonal conflict.

"Third, the *causes* of squandered organizational energy are so far removed from the *effects*, that it's difficult to link them in a cause-and-effect way, so it's nearly impossible to connect these misalignments to definable costs in traditional financial accounting systems. They go to the bottom line eventually, but do so in invisible ways that go undetected.

"Fourth, many senior managers, managers, and workers use defense mechanisms to deny or cover up the fact that there even is a problem. They fear opening Pandora's box, so poor performance, inappropriate behavior, and missed sales targets become undiscussible. Employees begin to question their own perceptions of reality as the psychological atmosphere in the organization becomes more and more confusing. The culture becomes bifurcated, so on the surface of organizational consciousness, people smile at each other in meetings and talk nicely. But just below the surface you can cut the air with a knife. Why should we be surprised by the fact that neurotically squandered energy doesn't show up on the bottom line when owners and managers refuse to measure it and pretend the problem doesn't exist? Argyris calls this skilled incompetence.[91]

"The fifth reason misalignments don't show up on the bottom line is because companies have what Frost and Robinson call 'toxic handlers.' These are key people who absorb and vessel the pain and toxicity that build in companies so these misalignments don't do more organizational damage.[92] The organizational waste that is part of the day-to-day activities of neurotic organizations gets channeled into the hearts and minds of toxic handlers, so you never see it on the bottom line until they quit, get sick, or die.

"I've played the role of a toxic handler all my life," Rena said sadly, as others in the group nodded that they'd had similar experiences.

I wonder if she's playing that role in my organization—covering for the hard-driving, competitive field general that I am with my employees? Maggie thought, suddenly concerned about the pressure she'd been putting on Rena.

"I warn you!" Thomas said sternly. "The psychological and physical toll that being a toxic handler takes on people is enormous. The *HBR* article I referenced discusses how people who are toxic handlers for too long have literally dropped dead or developed serious psychological or physical problems. What is most unconscionable is that most times they don't get one word of thanks from the people they protect—so be careful of being a toxic handler."

Cindy looked at Dan, then back at Thomas and said, "This is why a lot of owners and managers don't want to learn about the creative process: because it requires them to deal with the spring-loaded, toxic, and irrational dimensions of their organization that toxic handlers absorb. They'd have to admit to the self-serving strategy of using toxic handlers rather than really solving their problems."

"That's correct," Thomas answered, shuddering at the thought. "Their experience with neurotic conflict and squandered energy conspires against them ever getting a vision to become a creative organization because the creative process often *requires* intense, prolonged, constructive conflict. Owners, managers, and workers can't tease apart the difference between the *constructive* conflict that is essential to the creative process, and the *destructive*, neurotic conflict associated with squandered and repressed energy. This is why leaders so often 'speak with forked tongue' about their desire for creativity, innovation, and improvement. On the one hand, they lament the lack of creativity in their workers, but on the other hand they fight, stifle, and kill the creative process in those same workers in order to protect the status quo."

"But if it's so difficult and time consuming to validate the assessment results, and if the misalignments don't show up on the bottom line anyway, is it even worth stirring the pot?" Lindsey asked, concerned at how disruptive the process might be to the organization.

"Let me answer your question by asking *you* a question," Thomas countered, surprised by Lindsey's suggestion to ignore these issues. "Let's say you've got a problem with a significant other. Should you try and work that problem out, or should you ignore it out of fear of stirring the pot?"

"That depends on how bad the situation is," Lindsey replied, trying to be truthful about her own situation with men without going into the details.

"Well, that's the same answer I'd give for whether you should address misalignments in an organization. It just depends on how bad you're hurting. When the pain of dealing with misalignments becomes less than the pain of losing employees or going out of business, then leaders have no choice but to face it head-on, even if it means stirring the pot," Thomas said confidently.

Lindsey was cut to the quick by how close to home the discussion hit, but was too embarrassed to pursue it in front of the others. She nodded to show agreement with Thomas's analysis of the situation, then picked up a three-by-five and wrote, "I know my identity is tied up in my relationships with others, but why are my interactions with men so problematic that I use a cat as a stand-in for the husband I desperately want? Would you help me stop and take a hard look at this issue—even if it stirs the pot?" Then with a sense of relief and trepidation, she set the card writing side down in the center of the teaching table and rejoined the discussion.

STEP 4: SEARCH FOR ROOT CAUSES

"Okay," Thomas clapped his hands to get the group's attention, then pointed to the flip chart. "After validating that the issues identified by the assessment are problems worth pursuing, I use Step 4 to identify the root causes of the misalignments and to begin aligning the organization. Once again, I rely on Rogers's technique of empathic inquiry to help the dissenting parties understand the world from the other person's perspective. I also use empathic inquiry to explore the rationale that motivated the creation of an organizational structure, system, or cultural elements that have become ineffective, but are still used.

"I normally have senior managers lead a disinterested, empathic dialogue in an attempt to break down the barriers to communication. When done in an honest and transparent way, the interaction builds trust and drives out the fear that inhibits the creative process." Thomas paused, then said empathically, "Building this kind of shared understanding, common focus, and agreement between senior managers, managers, or workers is what I mean by alignment and speaking with one voice. When a shared understanding is finally forged, energy that was squandered only minutes earlier to defend mutual positions is redirected toward achieving the purpose and business objectives of the organization."

I wonder if I could forge that kind of shared understanding in my parish using the strategic planning process if I changed my approach? James hoped inwardly.

STEP 5: DEVELOP A CORRECTIVE ACTION PLAN

Thomas pointed to the flip chart and pushed on, "Once the organization reaches a synthesis of opposing views and speaks with one voice, I use Step 5 to map out concrete corrective action designed to create organizational change. Whether you use a method like the one shown in Figure 12 to tease apart training from personality issues, or a formal corrective planning system, the key is to assign milestones and deliverables to competent employees, then to track and measure how effective the fixes are."

"I feel like this level of analysis would stifle my creativity," Nikki objected.

"The key is freedom within boundaries," Thomas responded. "It's like football. The field has a precise size, boundary lines, and well-defined rules with imposed consequences that are rigorously enforced by multiple referees. Yet, talented players have an enormous amount of freedom within those boundaries to play the game creatively. Ever hear of Robert Herbold?"

Most of the group shook their heads no, but Frank offered, "Wasn't he the COO of Microsoft?"

"That right." Thomas was pleased at yet another example of Frank's vast knowledge. "He came to Microsoft for the purpose of setting up organizational structures and systems that balanced centralized discipline and measurement with individual innovation. In his *HBR* article, he called it, 'efficient innovation.'[93] One day, toward the end of his first quarter on the job, he and Bill Gates were talking in Gates's office when the CFO walked in and Bill asked him, 'So how'd we do?'

"The CFO started hemming and hawing and said something like, 'Well, it's difficult to say.' Gates was outraged and threatened to confiscate his laptop and extract the information over the weekend, but this would not have solved the problem. Microsoft's organizational unconsciousness was deeply rooted and systemic—operating units across the company had developed incompatible financial and operating systems, divergent practices, and multiple ways of measuring and reporting on financial and performance data, and none of these systems talked to each other. Herbold headed up a project to choose a new company-wide financial system and it was installed and operational in one year. His Microsoft experience taught him that in companies where creativity is so crucial to the organization's existence, there had to be a balance between the imposition of discipline from the top of an organization and delegating authority down through the line organization so that innovation and creativity were encouraged."[94]

"Well that kind of balance is hard to reach, and in most companies the kind of measurement you're talking about *does* stifle employees' creativity. In fact, that's my biggest fear about the new performance appraisal system I'm implementing back at the office." Nikki slapped her palm on the table, utterly frustrated by the discussion and the prospect of working with Barb when she returned to the office.

"Part of me agrees with you, Nikki, because I've seen that happen in organizations I've worked with," Thomas said in a conciliatory tone. "But other aspects of my experience have shown me that while people say that measurement 'stifles their creativity,' the truth is that this kind of structure forces employees to face problematic personality fixations and preferences for how they do work. When you look a little deeper, many complaints about stifled creativity are how employees push back on structures that challenge their decision-making bias and MBTI and Enneagram type preferences. Sometimes, it's even a way of trying to avoid accountability for their performance. Fixated ways of working that result from personality are the single biggest roadblock to the creative process in organizations.

"It's not so much that '*We've* never done it that way' as it is, '*I've* never done it that way.' Even a balanced approach to structures and systems makes these people feel uncomfortable because they have to think outside the box that resides between their ears. I'll discuss a more complete solution to this problem in the third session today, but in the short-term the only solution that I have found is to just let people whine and tell them to do it anyway!"

He's trying to egg me on and provoke me, Nikki whispered softly under her breath, her anger tempting her to challenge him in front of the entire group. Instead, she reached for a three-by-five and unloaded on him in writing: "Why are you publicly accusing me of hiding behind my creativity as a way of avoiding accountability for my performance!" Then she slapped the card down in the middle of the table face up, so others could read it.

"In closing," Thomas said, handing each person a dive slate, "read through the summary points of the session, then clip it to your BCD so you'll have the material with you underwater." The group scanned the list as Thomas picked up the cards from the center of the table and stuck both in his shirt pocket without reading them.

DIVE SLATE SESSION 4 REVIEW

Strategy 1: Find Meaning and Significance in Work
   Practice #1: Experience the Creative Process
   Practice #2: Learn How Fear Inhibits the Creative Process
   Practice #3: Build Inner Collaboration and Alignment
Strategy 2: Use Alignment to Gain Competitive Advantage
   Practice #4: Align the Organization to Speak with One Voice
      ◆ *Organizations are aligned to get the results they get*
      ◆ *Misalignments squander psychological and organizational energy*
         Step 1: Build timeless principles into a set of questions
         Step 2: Ask questions with Island of Excellence Organizational Assessment and find misalignments
         Step 3: Validate results (five reasons misalignments don't show up on the bottom line)

Step 4: Search for root causes using empathic inquiry (Rogers)
Step 5: Develop a corrective action plan with milestones and deliverables

He waited a moment for them to finish. "Are there any questions?" Thomas put his hands on his hips, smiled encouragingly, and searched the faces of the group with deep inquiry. "If not, then let's go diving."

"This site is called Father's Reef," Anita began pointing to a diagram of the location on the white board. "Father's is a hook-shaped reef-chain that we'll do as a wall dive because it drops one thousand vertical feet straight down into an abyss—so watch your depth on this one. The current is normally screaming here, but it looks like we caught it exactly at full high tide, so there'll probably be almost no current."

"Are there any questions?" Anita scanned the faces of the divers, looking for last minute issues or unresolved concerns. "Okay then—the pool's open."

Thomas was the first person off the boat. He dropped to about forty feet, began moving toward the wall, then glanced back toward the others. With visibility this good, he saw a few people still near the boat floating at about fifteen feet pointing to their ears, indicating they were having trouble equalizing the pressure as they descended. This was the first trip where the entire group dove this long without ear trouble. In order to feel the effect of *low* pressure on our body, most people have to ascend to altitudes beyond ten thousand feet above sea level. But because water is eight hundred times denser than air, you get fifty percent of the full pressure differential within the first thirty-three feet from the surface—that's two atmospheres. Once divers equalize the pressure in their ears at that depth, they feel almost no difference whether they're forty feet down or two hundred, which is why it's important for divers to watch their depth, especially on wall dives.

Within five minutes, the entire group had equalized, descended, and reached the wall. The color of the hard and soft coral was magnificent. There were twenty kinds of soft coral-like trees waving in the gentle current and Gorgonian fans that were five feet high. Colony after colony of knob, staghorn, table, and cabbage coral were teeming with the symbiotic life of a thousand species of reef fish, crabs, mantis shrimp, and octopus. The elegance, complexity, and pulsating throb of this living mural of color and motion were more than the human mind could absorb at one time.

Thomas reached for his underwater flashlight so he could explore the darkened crevices between the coral, but as he felt for it in the pocket of his BCD, the negatively buoyant light slipped out and started falling through the water column. By the time he figured out what had happened, he looked down and watched it slowly disappear into the bottomless abyss below him. He chased after it and as he descended to eighty, one hundred, one hundred twenty feet, he sensed he was being drawn downward into the deep by some inner force, a voice that whispered, *just keep going*. The flashlight continued to fall from sight, so finally at one hundred sixty feet he stopped and looked up toward the surface of the water and the others who were one hundred feet above him. Thomas was shaken to his core by the irrational import and power of the experience and vowed to record it in his journal once back on the ship. For now, he looked down one last time, then began ascending slowly to rejoin the group.

History records breath-held diving in Rhodes, Athens, Crete, Ceylon, and India as early as the third century B.C. These people dove under the surface of the water to search for food, sunken treasure, and to fight their enemies in war. By the nineteenth century, the tethered, surface-air supplied dive helmet had been developed, and this allowed humans to breathe underwater for extended periods of time.[95] By the mid-twentieth century, self-contained underwater breathing apparatus

(SCUBA) had been developed. This gave divers enormous mobility and freedom to explore the underwater world because they carried their air supply with them, on their back. Although diving equipment has changed substantially over the years, what hasn't change is that the air that most recreational divers breath from their tanks is like the air above the surface of the water, twenty-one percent oxygen and seventy-nine percent nitrogen. The oxygen is metabolized into the blood stream, but nitrogen dissolves into the fatty tissues around nerve cells and builds up in the diver's body. Surfacing with too much nitrogen left in the body is how people get decompression sickness, or what's commonly called 'the bends.'

Nitrogen has another interesting effect on people when they go too deep. While the effect varies from diver to diver, most people going to depths beyond one hundred feet experience the narcotic effects of nitrogen, colloquially known as 'getting narced.' When a diver is narced, the effect is similar to being intoxicated—like having a second or third glass of wine. It's a common scuba joke how narced divers pull their regulators out of their mouths so they can kiss the fish on the lips. On the serious side, getting narced lowers a diver's sense of danger and their respect for safety measures, consequently putting themselves or those they're diving with in jeopardy at depth.

Out of the corner of her eye, Maggie spotted an enormous creature rising straight from the ocean bottom; then she spotted a second and a third—manta rays. She went to get Rena's attention, but she had spotted them, too. These gentle giants can grow to have wingspans of up to eighteen feet. Related to the shark family a million years ago, they evolved into placid creatures who open their three foot diameter mouths and scoop up billions of microscopic plankton, their main source of sustenance. Both women were humbled in the presence of these magnificent creatures.

When he rejoined the others at shallower depth, Thomas buddied up with James and Cindy who were hanging by their reef hooks about three feet above the top edge of the reef. They were engulfed in a school of hundreds of barracuda, a wall of yellowtail kingfish, and hundreds of batfish. Cindy looked down on the reef and spotted a cuttlefish changing colors to perfectly match the visual appearance of the coral, then scuttling to safety. Thomas stared over the edge of the pinnacle and out into the blue ocean and drifted into deep reflection. This was the origin of all life, the primordial soup from which life emerged and he was immersed in it. His inner reflection was suddenly terminated when the high-pitched alarm from his dive computer signaled that he only had five hundred pounds of air left and it was time to surface. He looked around, and James and Cindy had already gone back to the ship, which only intensified his experience because he was contemplating the presence of this visual array—alone.

Thomas was the last person to reach the boat, as he hung there doing his three-minute safety stop at a depth of fifteen feet. He looked up and saw the bottoms of about ten dugout canoes pulled up to the back of the boat and local children jumping into the water and chasing his bubbles as they rose to the surface. As he climbed the ladder onto the ship he stepped out of the water into the midst of twenty or thirty women, children, and young men from the nearby island—they had paddled out to the ship to trade.

Artie was at his finest when he was trading with the locals, speaking Pidgin fluently and using the vast resources of the ship to help the people in these remote villages who had so much less than he did.

Artie explained to Cindy who was standing nearby, "We never give them money because they don't live in a cash-based economy—we always trade for goods." Cindy watched him hand a mother with two children a large bag of rice, a few packages of noodle soup, a can of cured ham, and a shirt in exchange for a small bunch of bananas and a coconut. "We always make sure they get the best end of the deal. Here, Cindy—the kids love the lollies." He gave her a handful of candy mints to hand out to the children, waiting with eager faces.

After a few more minutes he yelled out loudly in Pidgin, "If you're done trading then move away from the boat so others can come in to trade. Hey kids—don't drop the candy wrappers in the water—either leave them here on the boat or take them ashore with you."

Then suddenly, as if someone turned on a faucet in the sky, it began raining with drops so large and forceful that the sound of them pounding the water, the dugouts, and the ship was almost deafening. With the sun hidden behind enormous gray and black rain clouds, the temperature dropped almost instantly and the mothers and children sitting nearly naked in the dugouts began to shiver from the cold. They crowded in closer to the ship and each other, resolute to get their turn trading so they didn't paddle back to the island empty-handed.

Cindy walked up the stairs onto the dive deck to get out of the rain and watched Artie from a distance as she turned her thinking stone over and over in her hand. On the other side of the dive deck, Thomas peeled off his wet neoprene, rinsed it in the dunk-tank, then warmed himself with a hot shower. As he toweled off, he saw the immense sorrow in Cindy's eyes as she stared at a shivering family who had finished trading and was paddling back to the island, fighting against the unrelenting downpour.

I'm gonna walk back upstairs into the dining room, grab a fresh-baked cookie, a soda, and watch these people paddle back to the only reality they know, Cindy thought, almost overwhelmed by the pain and grief that gripped her.

Thomas finished drying off, put on a dry shirt, wandered over to Cindy's side of the boat and said quietly, "Amazing isn't it?"

Cindy smiled at him warmly, but said nothing.

"It's one thing to talk about the fact that reality is a man-made product of the creative process, but I always see the truth in that statement most powerfully when these dugout canoes pull up to the back of this ship," Thomas whispered, experiencing the cultural chasm profoundly.

"I think it was Dag Hammarskjold who said something like, 'It is more noble to give yourself selflessly to one human being than to spend a lifetime bringing salvation to the masses.'" Thomas stopped speaking and looked at Cindy dead-on.

"That's what Artie's doing, he's making a difference in these people's lives—one person at a time," Cindy replied pensively, as they both watched him finish trading with the last dugout.

"I'm a modern woman, Thomas. I couldn't literally live like them without sacrificing too much of who I am. I'm deeply ashamed of feeling this way, yet taking a purely symbolic approach back in New York doesn't feel like it will scratch my inner itch either. A year at the university in Goroka is a middle ground that allows me to use my education and background to help solve some of this country's overwhelming problems. I'll make a concrete difference in people's lives...like Artie's doing."

"You're probably right about Goroka being a middle ground." Thomas smiled warmly, pleased that a solution to her struggle was beginning to take shape.

"My itch has always been about the ultimate meaning of human life," he confessed, with melancholy eyes. "I've never known how to scratch *that*. I can't deny that improved medicine, food production, science, and technology have allowed these people to live *longer*—the average life span of an adult has gone from thirty-five years old during World War Two to about fifty-five years old now. But while they live longer, my question is whether they're living *better* and what part of their humanity they've sacrificed in the process? They long for our lives, and we long for theirs. It's a compensatory balance—there's no one right way."

For the first time, Cindy stood in the presence of Thomas's lifelong, existential dilemma. He had always shared freely and been there for her with words of insight and comfort. But his strength and courage combined with her self-absorbed focus on her own needs had blinded her to who he really was and what he needed from life. Now she stood face to face with that reality, and words escaped her, so she pulled him close and hugged him as tears of shame and self-condemnation streamed down her face. He smiled at her, moved by her compassion. Then she left him there alone and wandered up to the top deck to reflect on what she'd just experienced. Thomas gazed out at the dugouts paddling toward shore and lingered in the sweet sorrow of having been touched so deeply by Cindy. But these were emotions he had, they didn't have him, so he decided to put his dark mood aside and go find Rena.

"Hey, how was your dive?" Thomas asked in a subdued tone, having found Rena on the top deck reviewing the session material and writing in her journal.

"It was incredible, and the issue that I wrote on the three-by-five card kept floating in and out of my mind," Rena replied, eager to explore the issue.

"That's what I came to talk with you about," Thomas replied. "Can I sit?"

"I noticed on the chart you handed out that my mom and I are complete opposites on the four MBTI indices—she has ENTJ preferences and mine are ISFP. This difference has to vitally affect our communication and how we view each other."

"That's absolutely right, Rena. It's like you and your mom both speak English, but what you mean by the words is very different. Can

I draw something in your journal?" She handed it to him gladly as Thomas sketched a diagram based on their MBTI scores.

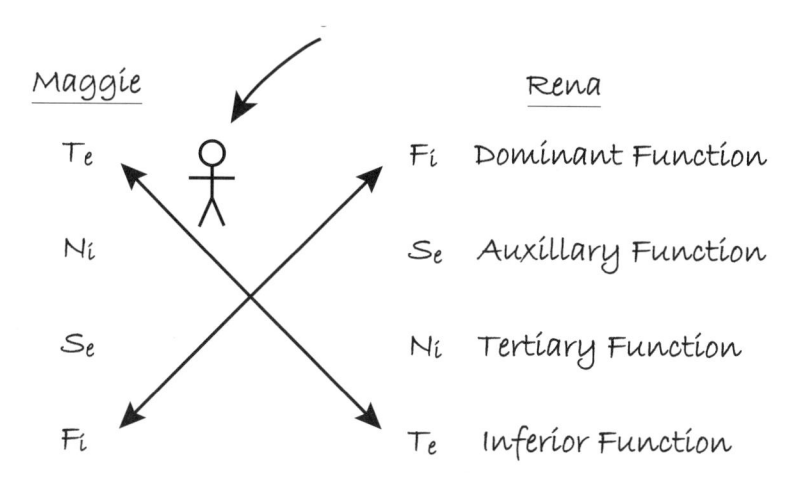

```
Maggie                    Rena

 Te        ↘  ↗    Fi   Dominant Function
              ×
 Ni        ↗    ↘  Se   Auxillary Function
              ×
 Se        ↘    ↗  Ni   Tertiary Function
              ×
 Fi        ↗    ↘  Te   Inferior Function
```

Figure 22
MBTI COMMUNICATION GRADIENTS

"What I've done in this diagram is taken the dominant, auxiliary, tertiary, and inferior functions for both of you and laid them side by side. The steeper the gradient between functions shown by the lines, the more difficult it will be for you and Maggie to communicate."

"That's exactly how it feels between Mom and I—she says 'up' and I say 'down'; I say 'good,' she says 'bad.'"

"Precisely." Thomas smiled, pleased that she was connecting the figure to her actual experiences. "Your inferior function is the same as her dominant function and vice versa, so ideally you can both grow to be more like the other. But imagine you have a big rubber band around your waist that pins you to your inferior function—extraverted thinking—Maggie's strongest preference." Thomas pointed to the arrow between Rena's inferior function and Maggie's dominant one. "When you try to communicate with her, you move out along the line shown here in the diagram, but the rubber band around your waist gets tighter and tighter, until it snaps you back to your inferior function.

"What is probably most important for you to recognize is that your path of psychological growth lies in stretching that rubber band so it gets looser and looser, thus transforming the weakest part of your personality into a strength. From what I've read in both of your case studies and the conflict you're having about you taking a leadership role in the company and her starting a family, this is something you both need to work on. Bottom line—you have to become more like her, and she has to become more like you. In many ways, you and your mom share a common path and psychological destiny, but you'll have to approach it from opposite directions." Thomas was pleased with how receptive Rena was to what he was saying.

"I'll bet we'd answer most of the questions on the assessment very differently, too!" Rena's eyes widened as she began to understand why Maggie viewed her role at the office so differently.

"That's correct, and most times people tend to take those disagreements personally, as if the other person is 'against' them and their view." Thomas reached for her journal and wrote the words, 'It's personality, it's not personal,' under the diagram.

"You're right," Rena nodded with renewed hope about her relationship with Maggie. "My problems with Mom are about personality differences; they're not personal."

Thomas glanced down at his watch, "I've got to go ring the bell for the 11:00 A.M. session. Let's discuss this some more later if you want."

Imagine that! I've got to become more like her and she's got to become more like me, Rena pondered the paradox. *That's going to cause real problems with Joel and me.*

SESSION 2: FOLLOW THE RED FLAGS TO SQUANDERED ENERGY

Thomas was standing at the head of the teaching table re-reading what Nikki had written on her three-by-five and wondering how to approach the situation when they talked later that day. He had rung the bell at precisely 11:00 A.M. and everyone was seated except for Nikki.

"Who are we waiting for, Thomas?" Dan asked cynically, as Nikki rounded the corner and took her seat.

"He's waiting for me," Nikki snapped, not caring if she provoked him.

I can't stand her! Dan hissed inwardly, his face red with anger. *That spiked hair, pierced tongue, and her total disregard for rules and other people's time—she needs to grow up!*

Thomas noticed the interaction, but chose not to deal with it now, feeling it would be unfair to the rest of the group to take up their workshop time. *I'll talk with her later when we discuss her three-by-five,* Thomas decided, then began.

"Let's say you perform the organizational assessment we discussed in the last session, follow the five steps, produce a corrective action plan, and assign the tasks to your most competent employees—the ones most committed to organizational change. The change initiative starts off with a bang; then mysteriously you begin to encounter covert resistance. Conflict between different organizations gets in the way, and disagreements arise between manager-level peers or between managers and their direct reports. Over the course of the next few months, unseen organizational vampires slowly suck the life out of the initiative through weekly budget and operational reviews; then your vision for becoming an Island of Excellence loses momentum and dies of its own weight. Ironically, the people involved all shake their heads and wonder what happened."[96]

"Practice 5," Thomas said as he indicated the flipchart, "follow the red flags to squandered energy, is a framework that helps us make sense of how change initiatives are frustrated and undermined, and suggests ways to overcome these self-defeating organizational behaviors."

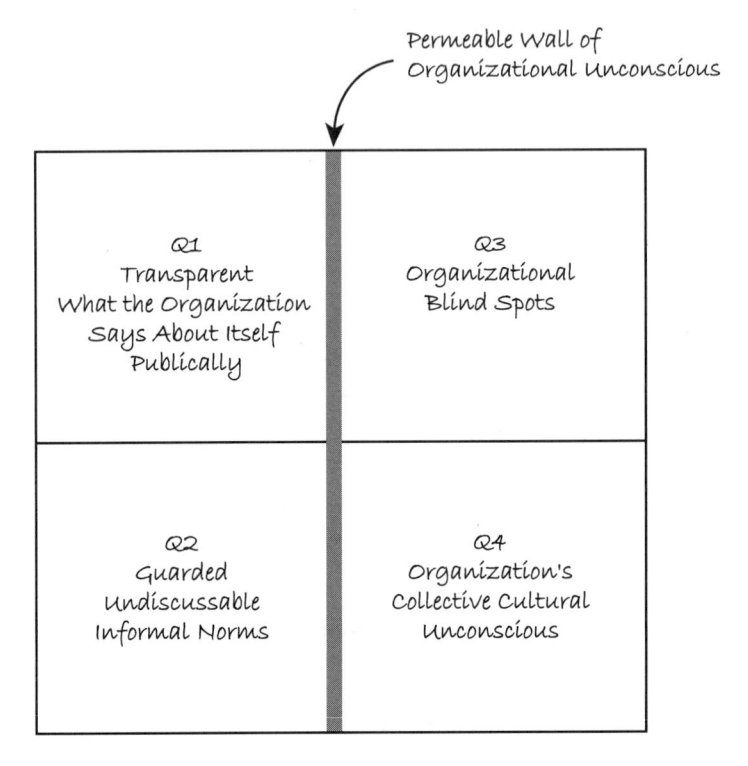

```
                    Permeable Wall of
                    Organizational Unconscious
                           ↓
┌─────────────────────┬─────────────────────┐
│                     │                     │
│         Q1          │         Q3          │
│     Transparent     │    Organizational   │
│ What the Organization│     Blind Spots    │
│  Says About Itself  │                     │
│      Publically     │                     │
│                     │                     │
├─────────────────────┼─────────────────────┤
│                     │                     │
│         Q2          │         Q4          │
│       Guarded       │   Organization's    │
│    Undiscussable    │  Collective Cultural│
│   Informal Norms    │    Unconscious      │
│                     │                     │
│                     │                     │
└─────────────────────┴─────────────────────┘
```

Figure 23

THE FOUR LEVELS OF ORGANIZATIONAL CONSCIOUSNESS

"Figure 23 describes four levels of organizational consciousness,"[97] Thomas continued, pointing to the various quadrants accordingly. "Things that appear in the Transparent quadrant, Q1, are what a company *says* about itself publicly, for example, its policies, procedures, organizational structure, and the formal rules of the game for getting promoted and moving up the corporate ladder. The Guarded quadrant, Q2, contains the informal rules of the game for how things are done, but there are strong social and cultural inhibitions against talking about them publicly, even though everyone knows what they are. As Senge says, they're undiscussible.[98] The most common cause of derailed change initiatives is when people publicly say they will support change, Q1, then covertly frustrate and undermine the creative process in Q2 because the informal rules are opposed to deviating from the status quo. In fact, Shapiro claims that one of the first steps to changing organizational culture is to understand the distinction between the Q1 formal rules of the game and the Q2 informal way things *actually* work, which rarely resembles an organization's public pronouncements.[99]

"Opposition to change initiatives also occurs because people become aware of resistance within themselves that they were honestly unaware of. They intend to support the change, but oppose it after-the-fact, because their hidden change of heart, like everything else in Q2, is undiscussible. William Bridges characterizes this delayed reaction as the difference between *change*, which is instantaneous like a reorganization, and *transition*, the psychological process people go through to come to terms with that change.[100]

"The things that are in Q3 are organizational blind spots. In other words, people outside the organization see them clearly, but those inside don't. You or I might look at Maggie's company and see multiple instances where they frustrate and oppose the creative process by stomping on suggestions for improvement in meetings. She and her managers look at these same instances and argue that it's their job to keep projects on track, so they have to force these people to get back to work."

"This sounds like the organizational equivalent of individual blind spots where a person has an issue that everyone else sees, but they can't," Cindy interjected spiritedly, connecting the concept to the material discussed earlier.

"That's correct," Thomas nodded, "and much like individuals, Q3 barriers to organizational change and the creative process are submerged below the surface of organizational consciousness, so companies are truly unaware of them. So the real question is, how does an organization become aware of what it's unaware of or refuses to speak about? When these issues are Guarded in Q2 or Blind Spots in Q3, they won't show up on an organizational assessment because people are either honestly unaware of them, or they just refuse to talk about them. So how *does* an organization stop repeating the costly mistake of starting, then unconsciously derailing, organizational change initiatives?" Thomas pointed to Figure 16 that he had taped to the wall during the previous session. "Practice 5 teaches us how to follow the red flags to squandered energy—the tell-tale signs of below-the-surface issues that frustrate and oppose change initiatives."

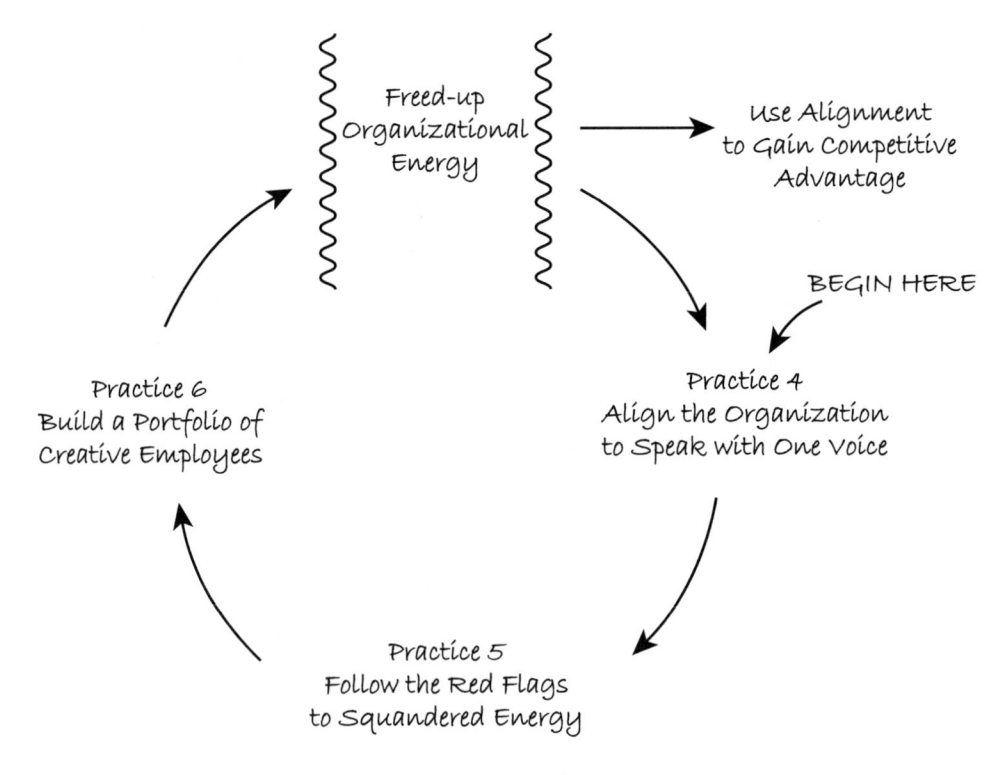

Figure 16

THE SECOND STRATEGY: USE ALIGNMENT TO GAIN COMPETITIVE ADVANTAGE

"I want to use a metaphor to explain what I mean by the red flags." Gesturing slightly over the heads of the group and out over the sea beyond them, he continued. "The vast majority of the ocean is deep blue sea, and the majority of underwater topography even around these islands is sandy bottoms—there's no coral reef. I learned this the hard way during a previous dive workshop. We'd decided to do some exploratory diving, so I said, 'Let's just dive over there and see what we find.'" Thomas pointed to a place on the other side of the bay from where the boat was moored. "There was nothing but sand.

"So how do you find coral reef in an enormous body of water when the total amount of reef in the entire world represents a tiny fraction of the ocean's area? We find it by exploring, but once we locate a good dive site, we tie a *mooring ball* that floats on the surface of the water and connect it to a concrete block on the bottom near the dive site so we can find it when we return.

"Finding coral reef in the vast ocean is not unlike finding squandered energy. Of all the experiences and issues that happen in the day-to-day activities of organizational life, where would you begin to identify the barriers that frustrate and oppose productive change and the creative process? How would you have any level of confidence that if you put your shoulder to the wheel and pushed through these issues, that this work would actually result in real organizational change?"

Thomas pointed over the side of the boat and asked, "Do you see that mooring ball over there? The red flags are like mooring balls on the surface of organizational consciousness that indicate unconscious misalignments below the surface. The red flags are powerful indicators of unseen activities and beliefs that derail change initiatives and oppose the creative process. I want to discuss four of them." He reached over and turned a page on the flip chart.

THE RED FLAGS

Disruption of organizational intentions
Excess energy
Organizational and individual defense mechanisms
The unconscious perspective

"Whenever an organization sees one of these red flags, it should stop dead in its tracks, take note, and dive in to a thorough analysis of the situation using an attitude of empathic inquiry and exploration. Let's discuss each red flag in more detail.

"The *first red flag*—disruption of organizational intention—is commonly known, but rarely understood in organizations." Thomas turned the flip chart page and pointed to Figure 24. "Given a company's business objectives, goals, and strategies, companies take input from the business environment and transform them into products and services that are sold to customers. A disruption of organizational intentions occurs when the organizational structures and systems fail to produce these intended outcomes; instead they obtain what Senge calls an *unintended* consequence.

```
                    Disruption of
                      Intentions
                          |
                          v
Cultural Fixations
Unconscious Organizational  →  Organizational  →  Consequences
      Barriers                   Intentions        Intended/Unintended
         ↑                           ↑                    |
         |               Introspection, Judgment, Fear    |
         |_____|
    Spectator Role
  Attitude of Empathetic Inquiry
```

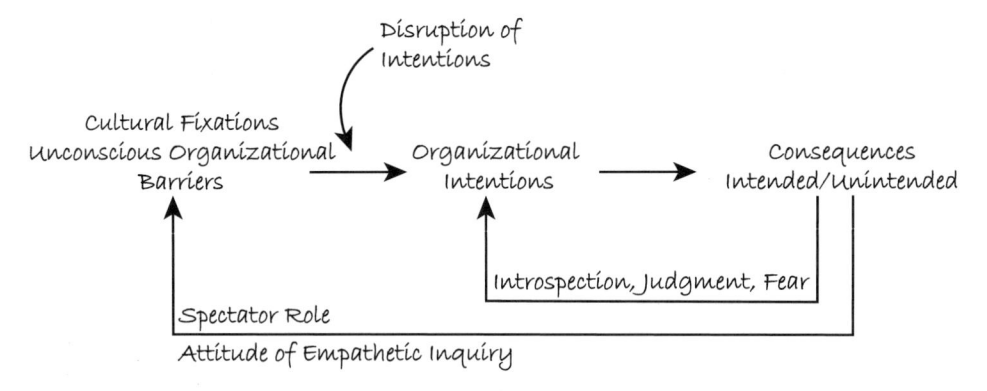

Figure 24

DISRUPTION OF ORGANIZATIONAL INTENTIONS

"So when a company commits to a change initiative or to building a creative organization and fails, this is an unintended consequence. When a project is off track and managers know it probably should be stopped, but it isn't, this is an unintended consequence. Unintended consequences manifest themselves as lost clients, rework, computing downtime, a key hire that goes sour, business objectives and goals that are not met, and policies and procedures that are not implemented uniformly across an organization. These types of situations are obvious and the list could go on and on. Whenever an organization defines business objectives, sets goals, or develops a plan and they fail to get the expected outcome because of issues that emerge from within the company, this is an unintended consequence—a disruption of organizational intentions by the blind spots associated with unconscious barriers to organizational change."

People in the group were shaking their heads in concurrence and jotting down notes in their journals, as Thomas continued.

"What I've found is that when an unintended consequence results from a misaligned organizational structure or system, if we continue to press for deeper explanations and root causes, we always come back to the decisions and actions of *individuals*. These decisions are often made based on tacit assumptions and decision-making bias of employees' personality, fear that is used to establish and maintain organizational control, and collective cultural assumptions about 'the way things are done around here.'"

"So the unintended consequences you're discussing now are like the misalignments identified in the assessment?" James asked, trying to sort out the relationship between the two concepts.

"Not really," Thomas countered, "because participants may have been unaware of the misalignments prior to the assessment—in other words, they were blind spots. But in this case, the assessment made the participants aware of the problems, they committed to corrective action, but unconscious misalignments still sabotaged the organization's conscious plans for corrective action. Do you see the distinction?" Thomas inquired.

"Yes—it's subtle but profound," James nodded.

"The *second red flag* is 'inappropriate and excess levels of energy.' For example, your emotional response to a new marketing plan, organizational change, work procedure, or customer feedback is entirely exaggerated—it *has you*, rather than you having it. When there's a red flag, the level of effect displayed is entirely out of proportion to what was said or done—like screaming at a staff member who makes an innovative suggestion in a meeting. Excess levels of psychological energy become stored around an issue like a 'hot button,' whether it's the installation of new software, getting a new office, selling a new product you don't like, or getting a marginal performance review from a supervisor you don't respect. People get consumed, taken over, grabbed by the scruff of their emotional necks about issues that to outsiders seem like no big deal."

"I've had the experience where I get gripped by some issue, then an hour later I'm wondering why I was so upset about it!" Maggie shook her head in self-reproach, aware of how deceptive her blind spots could be.

"That's exactly it, Maggie." Thomas gave her a thumbs up. "When excess energy *has you*, you'll explode because Jane got promoted by playing the informal rules of the game, and you got demoted because you played by the formal rules, or some similar reason. These toxic releases can be overt and aggressive, or covert and passive-aggressive. They can be positive, like being enamored by a new product line even though it's not selling—or negative, like conflict between the sales department and production about performance targets. When you detect excess emotional energy, this is a red flag. Stop dead in your tracks, get curious about what's happening, then dive in and explore below the surface of the issues.

"The *third red flag*—defense mechanisms—occurs at both the organizational and individual levels. Defense mechanisms purposely distort and obfuscate our knowledge about what's going on and where the causes of the problem lie—in us or in others. At the *organizational level*, Chris Argyris argues that organizational defense routines are designed to protect organizations from embarrassment or threat.[101] Defense routines can be any policy, procedure, structure, system, or action that prevents an organization from being embarrassed or threatened—and at the same time prevents employees from identifying or eliminating the causes of that embarrassment and threat.[102] For example, let's say managers in an organization say publicly that they want honest staff feedback, but employees who dare to actually give it are punished or fired. In other words, what this organization *says* is not what it actually *does*. I call this the 'Say-Do Gap of Duplicity.'"

"I've seen that over and over again," Nikki grouched. "Ask for input, then shoot the messenger."

Bethany shook her head vigorously, having had the same experience.

"Situations that threaten to expose the Say-Do Gap are defended against with enormous amounts of energy. Organizational defense mechanisms might take the form of technical arrogance, the 'not-invented-here' syndrome, an attitude that says, 'we know what the customer wants' without asking them. Or, it's an unrealistic view of how well the company performs without knowing its true operating costs. When an organization is pressed or held accountable for such duplicities, they are normally embarrassed or threatened by the prospect of having the problem exposed. Argyris claims they use four strategies to prevent the problem from being found out." Thomas turned the flip chart page, pointed to a list, and waited as the group scanned it.

ARGYRIS'S FOUR STRATEGIES OF DEFENSE ROUTINES
STRATEGY 1: *By-pass the real issue*
STRATEGY 2: *Give inconsistent messages about what was actually "meant"*
STRATEGY 3: *Cover up the situation*
STRATEGY 4: *When pressed harder, cover up the cover up*

"Give us an example," Frank asked, eager to connect what Thomas was saying to his own situation with his son-in-law Rick.

"These days the examples are legion." Thomas shrugged in dismay. "Accounting firms like Arthur Anderson, who were a symbol of fiscal integrity, couldn't endure the threat or embarrassment of clients knowing that they'd been 'cooking the books.' Owners and managers who have gone on record saying that they value employees' feedback can't publicly admit to taking retribution on those who give it. Companies that stress hard work and loyalty as the way to get ahead can't publicly own up to the fact that playing the game and managing your way up with 'bright' comments in meetings is really the way people get promoted—so these organizations *defend* themselves. They try to by-pass the real issues, give inconsistent messages when the Say-Do Gap is probed, cover up evidence of organizational duplicity, and when really pressed they cover up the initial cover up."

"Sounds like lying to me," Cindy muttered.

"It *is* a kind of lying," Thomas responded quickly. "This kind of psychological and organizational dishonestly is a complex form of self-deception—a refusal to face the truth of the situation."

"I want to quote Argyris at length here because his description of defense mechanisms is so revealing and poignant." Thomas glanced down at a note card. "'Defense routines…*require* people to communicate inconsistent messages, but act as if they are not doing so. In order for these actions to be effective, they must be covered up while being enacted. In many cases, the cover-ups must also be covered up. To do this, individuals learn to communicate inconsistent messages, act as if the messages are not inconsistent, make previous actions undiscussible, and make the undiscussibility undiscussible. Individuals on the receiving end of these actions must collude. If they recognize the cover-up, they learn to act as if they do not recognize it. They also expect the deceiver, distorter, or manipulator to not recognize the collusion.'"[103]

Thomas turned the flip chart page and said, "Read through Argyris's list of typical organizational defense mechanisms."

ARGYRIS'S DEFENSE MECHANISMS[104]

- *Blaming coworkers or those outside the organization but avoiding public tests of the validity of the blame.*
- *Distancing themselves from any personal responsibility for a situation.*
- *Arguing they are helpless to effect change in the organization.*
- *Not expressing their ideas until coworkers have made mistakes.*
- *Criticizing themselves to cloak their criticism of others (e.g., "I know we've got problems, but the marketing group is really messed up.").*
- *Expressing opposition to the use of defense mechanisms privately, but refusing to discuss them publicly in a constructive way.*
- *Communicating indirectly (e.g., venting frustration about a person or problem, but refusing to discuss it with the responsible party).*
- *Using written communications (e.g., e-mails and memos) to build an organizational reality that defends their position while deconstructing the realities built by others.*

"Help me relate the descriptions of *organizational* defense mechanisms to the defense mechanisms used by *individuals*. They seem so similar," Nikki interjected.

"I was just getting to that," Thomas replied, thankful that she was contributing to the discussion constructively. "The relationship between individual and organizational defense mechanisms is what I call the *individual-collective paradox*. Remember that organizations are collective-cultural entities that are led, managed, and changed one person at a time, so organizational actions ultimately reduce to the behaviors of individuals. My view is that individuals are ultimately responsible for organizational defense mechanisms because the organizational culture that defends against recognizing these blind spots can only maintain its power when individuals act out and embody the culture's edicts.

"Argyris emphasizes the organization's role in maintaining defense mechanisms because they occur frequently as blind spots that are independent of an individual's conscious choice—they're unconscious habits that are on automatic pilot.[105] Regardless of whether you focus on the individual or organizational side of the equation, it's a circular self-reinforcing process that begins with individual actors who create cultural norms that become reified, then those norms act like a social mirror that reflects back what's expected of employees in that cultural setting.[106]

"Does that clear up the distinction, Nikki?" Thomas probed, looking for body language that would reveal her current mood in light of the issue on her three-by-five.

"Thanks." She nodded without making eye contact.

He shrugged and turned the flip chart page. "So let's discuss two of the more common defense mechanisms used by owners, managers, and workers that are based on descriptions in the *DSM-IV*.[107]

Passive Aggression: The indirect expression of anger and aggression toward others through covert resistance, resentment, or hostility that is covered up with a façade of agreement.

Projection: Attributing one's own unacceptable emotions, impulses, or thoughts to other people."

"Can you give us a more detailed explanation of what you mean by projection?" Nikki asked, pointing to the flip chart and still not making eye contact with Thomas or the others.

"*We always hate what we secretly are,*" Thomas replied without hesitation, "because when we project, we unconsciously attribute what's going on inside of us to others. So when we get gripped by excessive levels of emotional energy about a person or issue and we list what's bothering us about *them*, that list is often a description of unconscious attitudes, beliefs, and behaviors in *us*. It never fails—we always hate what we secretly are."

Wow! That's what all that energy was about with the issue I wrote on the three-by-five, Nikki reflected as she wrote in her journal. *I need to set things straight with Thomas.*

"Thomas!" Bethany almost shouted, "I'm confused. The *DSM-IV* is what psychiatrists use to diagnose 'crazy people' isn't it? If *we* use these defense mechanisms, are you saying we all have psychological problems?"

"Well, yes and no," Thomas said hesitantly, shocked by how forcefully she'd registered her objection. "Let me give you some background on the historical development of psychology as a way of establishing a context for answering your question directly. You're articulating a tired and worn-out view of psychological problems and neurosis. Prior to Freud, society thought crazy people were a minority and we 'cured' them by chaining them to walls in mental hospitals. Despite all the bad press that Freud has gotten about his obsession with sex and phallic symbols, he taught us two important things that changed the face of psychological theory.

"First, he was one of the pioneers of developing the *talking* cure—

meaning that people could actually overcome their psychological problems simply by talking about them.[108] This is an assumption that we just take for granted today. Second, Freud challenged the view that neurotic people were in the minority. His book, *The Psychopathology of Everyday Life*, argued that neurosis was a common, widespread phenomenon that typified most people in society.[109]

"In reality, day-to-day life in some organizations is pretty neurotic because owners, managers, and workers are just a cross section of the psychologically unhealthy world we live in. Like Erich Fromm, I believe that the empirical evidence indicated by organizational and individual red flags supports the claim that our twenty-first century society as a whole is not sane.[110] My experience has taught me that we all have some psychopathology to work through, so in *that* sense everyone does have psychological problems. The only people who don't are those who have recognized their issues and used tools like the ones we're discussing in this workshop to move beyond them."

The entire group was silent as Thomas scanned their faces for comprehension, then continued. "Let's move on to the *fourth red flag*: the unconscious perspective. We experience the unconscious perspective as ideas, insights, thoughts, emotions, and motivations that appear on the fringe of consciousness. To reiterate, this is the domain of the Inner People—the mechanism of the creative process that we discussed earlier in the dive workshop.

"As a consultant, the unconscious perspective is my most valuable tool because the Inner People provide me with insights and intuitions about organizational and interpersonal issues that are not apparent. I even use work-related dreams to help solve organizational problems that have defied other solutions."

Cindy quickly picked up on this last comment. "So are you saying that organizations have an unconscious like individual people do?"

"Yes," Thomas responded without hesitation. "There have been many studies performed on the unconscious dimension of organizations from a psychoanalytic or Jungian perspective, so let's review a few of the more important ones.

"Howell Baum argues that organizations have both conscious and unconscious intentions that are often in conflict, and that the conscious goals of a company are often derailed and frustrated by unconscious motivations that act independent of the organization's intended goals.[111] This is simply another way of describing what I called the disruption of organizational intention, or unintended consequences. James Mosse claims that organizations have observable social structures and functions, and an unconscious that is analogous to the unconscious in individuals. For Mosse,'...institutions pursue unconscious tasks alongside their conscious ones, and these affect both their efficiency and the degree of stress experienced by the staff.'[112] I already described one manifestation of this as the formal and informal rules of the game in organizations.

"From a Jungian perspective, Arthur Coleman likens the unconscious of organizations to Jung's notion of the collective unconscious.[113] This is why I entitled Quadrant Four in Figure 23, 'The Organization's Collective-Cultural Unconscious.' Finally, Schaef and Fassel have shown how many of the psychologically dysfunctional and unconscious elements of addiction are fundamental to organizational culture. Let me quote what they have to say about this." Thomas picked up a note card and read, "'Often, persons who come from dysfunctional families find their organizations repeating the same patterns they learned in their families....We have begun to recognize that many of the behaviors considered 'normal' for individuals in organizations are actually a repertoire of behaviors of an active addict or a non-recovering co-dependent....Why have those who work with and study organizations been so reluctant to recognize this reality? One of the reasons, perhaps, is that the basic defense mechanism of addictions is denial.'"[114]

That's fascinating, Bethany thought, grasping the implications of what Thomas was saying and applying them to her work environment. *That explains why so many of our clients stay in jobs that 'enable' their psychological and social problems!*

"Probably the most serious problem with the unconscious dimension of organizations is the development and activity of organizational complexes.[115] When issues are driven below the surface of consciousness, they can become like magnetic foci around which alliances with other employees are formed, and these organizational complexes can accumulate and hold captive enormous amounts of psychological and organizational energy.

"Organizational complexes can form around technical, process-related, political, hardware-software, or interpersonal issues. The power of an organizational complex gets stronger as it draws more and more of the company's psychological and organizational energy to itself, like a ball of yarn gets larger as more strands are wound around it. This is a self-reinforcing process because the complex's power grows as a function of its ability to attract more and more people, budget, resources, intellectual property, political clout, power through knowledge, office space, equipment, and other forms of organizational and psychological energy to itself. Sometimes, complexes gather organizational momentum like a snowball racing down a steep hill."

"That's exactly what's going on in my organization!" Bethany interjected passionately. "A group of disgruntled employees is trying to derail the initiative to refocus the department on client satisfaction that I described in my case study. They're stirring the pot and trying to build support for their position, hoping to undermine the changes we're trying to make."

"It's a common problem." Thomas nodded to acknowledge her comment, then moved on. "Organizational complexes are the collective-cultural equivalent to the Inner People. In other words, organizational complexes exist in a virtual state and only become real when they take over a company's decision-making process and resources in overt and covert ways. Organizational complexes are almost never 'disinterested' in Lippmann's sense of the term because they optimize their own position, power, resources, and sub-optimize organizational units, other organizational complexes, or the overall company. They take control of organizations by resisting or derailing change, stirring the pot, and by undermining and covertly reversing decisions, projects, or change initiatives that threaten their existence.

"In some instances, when complexes become extremely powerful, they function like hidden mini-companies within the overall company. Owners and managers may or may not be aware of the number of complexes and their power until it's too late. Then an organizational complex can challenge the productivity or actual survival of the entire company."

"But are organizational complexes good or bad?" James asked, half frustrated, half defensive about the view Thomas was proposing.

"That's a very important question that doesn't have a black and white answer," Thomas conceded, "because it raises the issue of who actually *owns* and *controls* a company or organization. In addition, it touches on the interrelationship between organizational, intellectual, and creative authority that I discussed in the very first session. Let's say Maggie wanted to open a new branch of her company in another city, but one of her employees began forming an organizational complex designed to frustrate and undermine that plan—would that complex be good or bad?"

"She owns the company so she can do what she wants, regardless of what any employees think," James snapped, confident in his position.

"Suppose her company was a C-corporation that had many shareholders," Thomas countered, "and one division developed into a powerful organizational complex that opposed her plan for a new location—would that complex be good or bad?"

"Line management has fiduciary responsibilities to the shareholders to run the company, and people who challenge that should be fired immediately!" James barked, clearly upset by the thought of such insubordination.

"What if the organizational complex grew out of the insurgent authority of the creative process, and senior managers were actually opposing what was best for the company's owners out of self-interest? In other words, the organizational complex was taking a *disinterested* position and championing what was in the best interest of the owners and the long-term sustainability of the company." Before James could respond, Thomas pressed on, "Studies have shown that change often begins in organizations as what I'm calling a 'complex,' then moves horizontally across the organization; then eventually it's accepted by senior managers.[116] What if *that* happens? Is that complex good or bad?" Thomas crossed his arms, looked at James, and waited for a reply.

"When that happens, senior managers take the credit for the initiative and claim it was their idea all along!" Bethany bellowed, and the group roared with laughter.

"What Bethany's saying is truer than you might suspect," Thomas interjected, bringing their attention back to him. "It's almost a kind of organizational pragmatism—when the outcome works, it's good and when it doesn't, it's not.

"But regardless of whether an organizational complex turns out to be good or bad, they have a vested interest in remaining hidden because therein lies their power. They remain invisible by utilizing powerful defense mechanisms like the ones we just discussed. Because they stay below the surface of organizational consciousness, we don't see that they've taken a company over until after the fact. Only then do we learn that the organization's communication and decision-making style, its view of time and planning, its ability to adapt, and untold other organizational elements have changed. What an organization doesn't know can hurt it by frustrating the creative process, or it can help it by revealing the blind spots and cultural fixations that hinder it from becoming a creative organization. Unseen organizational complexes can make or break your company. They'll drive you toward high performance or out of business—it just depends on the complex.

"In closing," Thomas began handing each person a dive slate, "read through the summary points of the session, then clip it to your BCD." The group quickly scanned the list, anxious to get into the water.

DIVE SLATE SESSION 5 REVIEW

Strategy 1: Find Meaning and Significance in Work
  Practice #1: Experience the Creative Process
  Practice #2: Learn How Fear Inhibits the Creative Process
  Practice #3: Build Inner Collaboration and Alignment

Strategy 2: Use Alignment to Gain Competitive Advantage
   Practice #4: Align the Organization to Speak with One Voice
   Practice #5: Follow the Red Flags to Squandered Energy
- *Four levels of organizational consciousness*
- *RF #1: Disruption of organizational intention*
- *RF #2: Excess energy*
- *RF #3: Organizational and individual defense mechanisms*
- *RF #4: The unconscious perspective (organizational complexes)*

He waited a moment for them to finish. "Are there any questions on the red flags? If not, then let's go diving."

James realized that Thomas had described the methodology he was using to wrestle control of the parish away from Shawna and the core group of powerful vestry members. He was forming an organizational complex that would allow him to take the congregation over by force and probably drive them out. The two questions it raised in his mind were, Who owned the church? And was James acting out of self-interest, or disinterest? He picked up a three-by-five and wrote, "I'd like to discuss the actions and motivations of organizational complexes in more detail." Then he handed the card to Thomas as the others got ready to go diving.

It had almost gotten to be a rule where someone had to go find Nikki so the entire group was not standing there waiting for the dive brief to begin. As Janice walked up the stairs with Nikki, Anita began the dive brief, but Dan was so furious that when she finally arrived on deck and took a position next to him, he turned to her and growled, "Why are you so damn inconsiderate? We always have to wait for you!"

Dan turned to Anita and Janice for support, knowing they were equally frustrated with Nikki's tardiness. But the two of them remained silent. "Next time, I say we go diving without her!" Dan challenged the group, hoping they'd back him up.

Nikki looked at her watch and snapped back, "Why are you such a grouch? It's only seven minutes after." Then, addressing the group, she said, "We're on 'island time' aren't we?"

Anita quickly stepped between them to try and diffuse their anger. "Okay, you two—let's finish the dive brief so we can jump in the water and cool off."

"*I* don't need to cool off," Nikki sneered under her breath. Before Dan could retaliate, Anita threw up two silencing hands, aimed at both of them.

"Okay," Anita announced, asserting that she was in control, "this dive site is called Jayne's Gully. It's a dramatic dive in a deep channel that has soft coral and six-foot-high gorgonian fans growing on either side. The current is running pretty good, so keep your eye out for gray reef, white tip, and hammerhead sharks, enormous tuna, barracudas, manta and spotted eagle rays. When you drop in off the back of the boat, get up against the wall as soon as possible to get out of the current, then move up onto the top of the reef. We'll hang around the edge of the wall so those of you that like the big stuff can watch the parade cruising up and down the channel. Those who want to see the small stuff can hang out on the top of the reef and take in the coral and reef fish action. Let me warn you though, there is a small olive-colored anemone-type creature called corallimorph all over the top of the reef."

Anita drew a figure of what it looked like on the white board and continued, "If you touch them they'll sting you and give you a painful rash that you won't forget—it lasts for weeks and can leave scars. So beware of touching the reef even with gloves on.

"Okay—the pool's open."

This has gone too far. I've got to talk with her privately as soon as this dive is over, Anita thought to herself, totally frustrated with Nikki's behavior.

One by one the divers dropped off the back of the ship, drifted toward the wall, and moved up on top of the reef. There were four or five gray reef sharks cruising up and down the channel eyeing up a thick school of trevally that swam as effortlessly against the two-knot current as they did with it. Cindy spotted a zebra striped moray eel bobbing its head in and out of a crevice between two large colonies of coral, and on closer examination she saw two tiny shrimp in the creature's mouth cleaning its enormous, pointed, razor-sharp teeth. This was the paradox of the marine world, fierce competition and predation for survival between species, existing side by side with true symbiotic dependence.

Anita had not exaggerated the panoply of coral and sea life that covered the reef. There were elephant ear sponges, yellow, orange, and red feather stars, and barrel sponges that were three feet in diameter. Orange and purple anthias, damsel fish, and blue-ringed angelfish darted in and out of the long slender branches of crimson colored sea whips that waved in the current, as brightly colored anemone balls with purple and red hues alternately closed then let their poisonous tentacles wave back and forth.

Bethany set her reef hook and was floating in the current like a bird soaring through the sky. She spotted a huge red sea anemone carpet that was home to an entire family of six whitebonnet anemone fish, a species that is endemic to PNG and the Solomon Islands. She tried to get a picture of this rare sight, but her body was being thrown from side to side by the constant motion of the current. She let some of the air out of her BCD to get closer to the reef, steadied herself, and prepared to get a better shot.

As she peered through the lens of her camera, framing and focusing the exact shot she wanted, powerful elements of human creativity were unleashed within her as she contemplated the gravity of Thomas's claim, "our twenty-first century society as a whole is not sane." The reality of day-to-day life back at the agency really was neurotic. Joan and the others who opposed her were simply a cross section of the psychologically unhealthy world we live in. The central theme of the session resounded in her mind—people may publicly support change, but when it moves them out of their comfort zone and threatens them psychologically, more times than not, in the end, they'll undermine it. She had learned from her own personal experience that the only way to move beyond neurotic issues like these was to recognize them and use tools like the ones discussed in the workshop to confront them head-on.

Bethany felt the transforming power of the creative process at work deep within her, inspiring her to be *insurgent* against the status quo that robbed desperate clients of care and at the same time protected the self-interest and incompetence of workers at the agency. She decided to stay the course that she and Dana laid out to improve client satisfaction. She felt Thomas was absolutely correct when he told her that the same dysfunctional system that allowed and protected her opposition would enable her to see the task through. So what did she have to lose, especially with Dana on her side?

Bethany longed to find meaning and significance in her life—to discover her unique calling. She wanted to view her work as a manager as having symbolic meaning—something that made a difference in the lives of the staff and clients. She needed to construct new conduits through which her creative abilities could flow into her day-to-day activities and genuinely contribute to the agency's purpose, business objectives, and goals. Now she had a concrete way of doing that. Using the strategies and practices from the workshop, she was determined to become an *Island of Excellence* back at the agency.

Bethany snapped out of her inner reverie and while she had taken some incredible shots of this rare family of fish, she began to feel a stinging sensation all over her legs. She looked down. In her excitement to take the pictures she had used her legs to stabilize herself and rested them on a wide patch of corallimorph. As her pain grew, she knew she'd been stung badly—right through her three-mil wetsuit.

Everyone was back on the ship and Janice was already putting cipro medication on Bethany's stings to ease her pain. Anita had just rinsed off her wetsuit in the dunk tank and hung it up to dry.

I've got to find Nikki and speak my mind, Anita thought as she toweled off from her hot shower.

She found Nikki on the back dive deck checking out her gear. "Nikki," Anita said as calmly as she could, "I really need to talk with you for a minute."

"Sure, what's up?" Nikki casually replied as she continued tugging on the dump valves on her BCD without making eye contact.

"I haven't said anything about you being late to the dive briefs because you're a customer and I know you're on vacation, but it's really bothering the others, especially Dan." Nikki stopped and looked directly at Anita. "From now on, I'm not sending anyone to find you—that's only encouraged your tardiness. If you're not present when the dive brief begins, I won't allow you to do the dive. You'll have to snorkel."

"You can't do that!" Nikki said angrily.

"Oh yes I can!" Anita asserted without hesitation. "I'm the senior dive official on this ship, and I have the final authority to decide who dives and who doesn't, especially when it comes to safety issues like divers going into the water without an adequate brief on a dive site. I'll make sure Thomas knows what I've decided." Anita turned to walk away, then said in a softened tone, "Look, Nikki, just make sure you're on time and this problem will be over—okay?"

"Alright," Nikki muttered, annoyed and feeling like she'd been lectured to like a child.

The fact that you're so annoyed with Anita and Dan is just another instance of your defense mechanisms blaming them for your issues, the Inner People whispered in her mind. *Just like the three-by-five issue with Thomas, you've got to learn to think before you act.*

~~~~

"Hey, Lindsey," Thomas said cheerfully, "do you want to discuss your three-by-five card now?"

"Sure," she responded, but a little hesitantly. "You hit pretty close to home with that discussion, you know. Although I joke about the fact that my cat, Oscar, is a stand-in for a husband, it pains me deeply to admit this—I view it as my biggest failure in life."

Thomas said nothing, maintaining eye contact and listening with empathy.

Lindsey picked up the cue to continue and forged ahead. "Over the last two years, I've begun the process of analysis with a Jungian analyst. I've been exploring the hidden parts of my personality in the hope of gaining a more complete understanding of who I am, not just my façade of being a giving servant to everyone. We've done a lot of work with the Enneagram, and I've begun to experience deep change, but mostly in my professional relationships."

"What kind of Enneagram issues have you been working on and what have you been discovering about yourself?" Thomas probed to set the stage for the discussion.

"Well, like the matrix you handed out earlier, I've focused on the Enneagram connecting points, so since I'm a Type Two I've been exploring the aggressive, power hungry control aspects of Type Eight, my Shadow Self, and the moody, depressed, melancholy characteristics of Type Four, my Inferior Self. When I'm totally honest about my weaknesses on the job, those two Inner People keep taking me over and creating the vast majority of my work-related performance problems. Within the last year, my inner growth in work-related situations has been so pronounced that even my detractors supported Mario's decision to reorganize and make me Vice President of Operations.

"But my analyst and I have not been able to extend that success to my personal, intimate relationships, and that's why your comment struck me so deeply, and why I wrote what I did on the three-by-five. I know that it's easier to deal with problems on the job because they don't go as deep as the ones in intimate relationships do. When it comes to love, intimacy, and sex, I know I've got blind spots big enough to drive a Mac Truck through, but I honestly don't know what they are. Is there anything you see that I don't?" Lindsey sat there silently, hoping that he had some crucial insights to share.

Thomas paused to choose his words carefully. "One of the timeless principles that I've learned is that you can't leave your personality at the door when you go to the office. If you're opposed to the core values or culture of an organization, you can play the role, suck it in, and behave the way you're 'supposed' to for a while. But when the pressure is on, what you are and who you are come through—they can't be hidden permanently."

Lindsey nodded in concurrence, but it was obvious that she failed to see how his comment applied to her situation.

"My point is that there's a symmetry here," Thomas tried again. "If you were able to make deep change in your professional relationships, the same methodology ought to help to identify problems in your personal relationships."

Her eyes widened with hope as she contemplated this idea, something she honestly hadn't considered.

Thomas was encouraged. "We just talked about how the red flags can lead us to unconscious barriers that frustrate and oppose the creative process. Life is like a labyrinth—full of twists and turns that don't make sense when we're going through them—but when we step back and gain perspective, a pattern emerges. Use your journal to record red flags that happen in your intimate relationships with men. Start viewing the red flags as clustering around a *mini process* of psychological growth within the *life-long process* of discovering who you are. While incidents that happen between you and men may seem random and unrelated, over time, with perspective, you'll begin to see a hidden pattern, and figure out how to move beyond these negative interactions. More importantly, the pattern will probably reveal how having an intimate relationship with a significant other fits with your unique calling in life."

The smile that spread across Lindsey's face as she had this significant breakthrough touched Thomas deeply.

SESSION 3: BUILD A PORTFOLIO OF CREATIVE EMPLOYEES

The sun was beginning to move toward the horizon, and some of the workshop attendees had already taken their seats around the teaching table and were discussing the material from the last session as Thomas rang the 3:00 P.M. bell to start the final session of the day.

As people gathered, it was clear that Bethany was uncomfortable as the stinging sensation in her legs attacked her with a vengeance. The cipro medication Janice had given her when she first got out of the water was working too slowly for Bethany's liking on the painful raised blotches. Janice told Bethany that the stings were not poisonous, but that the rash just had to run its course. Since there was nothing more that could be done, she might as well attend the sessions and go diving with the rest of the group because the salt water would actually help the long process of healing.

"Take a look at Figure 16 again." Thomas pointed to the diagram that he taped to the wall next to the flip chart. "There are three practices that make up the second strategy."

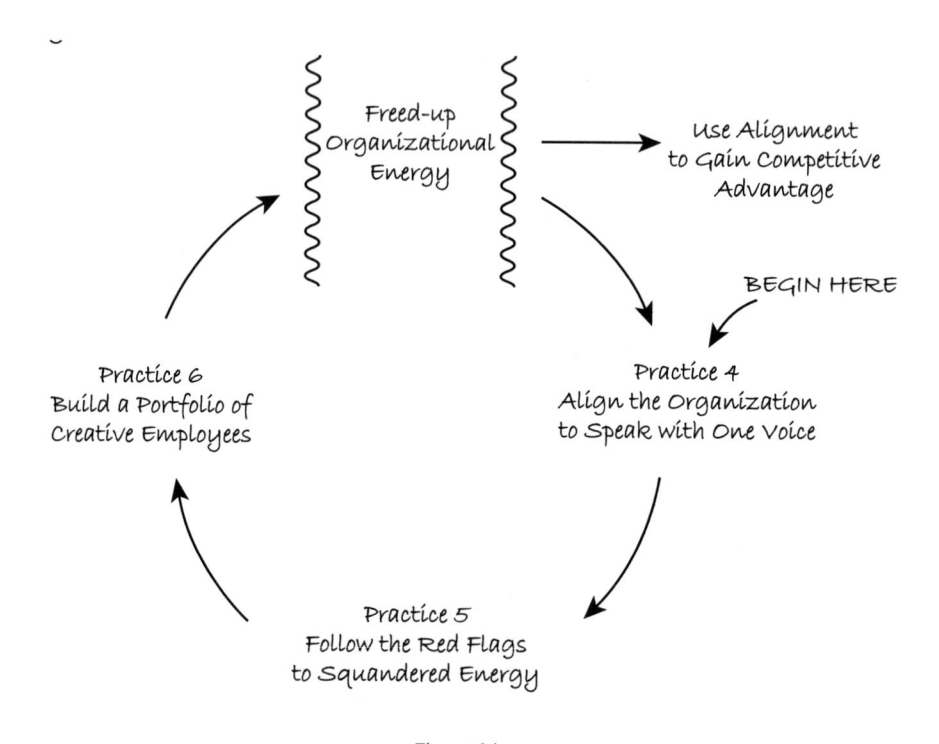

Figure 16
THE SECOND STRATEGY: USE ALIGNMENT TO GAIN COMPETITIVE ADVANTAGE

"Practice 4 taught us to align the organization to speak with one voice, and Practice 5 showed us how to follow the red flags to squandered energy that frustrated and undermined organizational change and the creative process. In this session, I'll discuss Practice 6—build a portfolio of creative employees—the kind of people who facilitate, support, and enable the creative process.

"Most people evaluate their creative abilities against the misguided notion that being creative somehow means being *artistic*. The common perception is that it's the painters, sculptures, musicians, actors, and writers who are creative, not us. Nothing could be further from the truth. Creativity is the natural problem-solving mechanism of the human brain and is innate to all people, in all cultures, in all times, in all places, unless frustrated and opposed by psychological, organizational, or cultural barriers. So building a portfolio of creative employees is not about identifying a 'profile' of what creative people look like. Rather, it is about ensuring that employees don't become barriers to a naturally occurring creative process that's operating all around them.

"There are many criteria as to why people choose to hire employees. Some people focus on a candidate's education, background, experience, and other competencies, or their ability to contribute to the organization's success. Others focus on positive personality characteristics that become evident through the interview and hiring process. There are even more criteria for choosing to retain, train, develop, and promote employees. Here, the focus is on the employee's performance, their problem-solving capabilities, their ability to manage, lead, or work with coworkers, and positive personality characteristics."

"You're not suggesting that these criteria aren't important, are you?" Lindsey asked, unsure of what he was getting at.

"Of course not—these criteria are crucial to building a high-performing work force," Thomas countered, "but creative organizations *add* one crucial criterion. They ask, 'To what degree does this employee facilitate, support, or enable the creative process in our organization?'

"Employees in organizations normally fall into a well-defined distribution that follows a 10-10-60-10-10 rule. In any given situation, twenty percent of the people in an organization will be strong supporters of creativity and twenty percent will be strongly opposed. The twenty percent groups on both ends of the distribution are normally so firmly set in their beliefs that no amount of persuasion will change their views." Thomas pointed to Figure 26 on the flip chart.

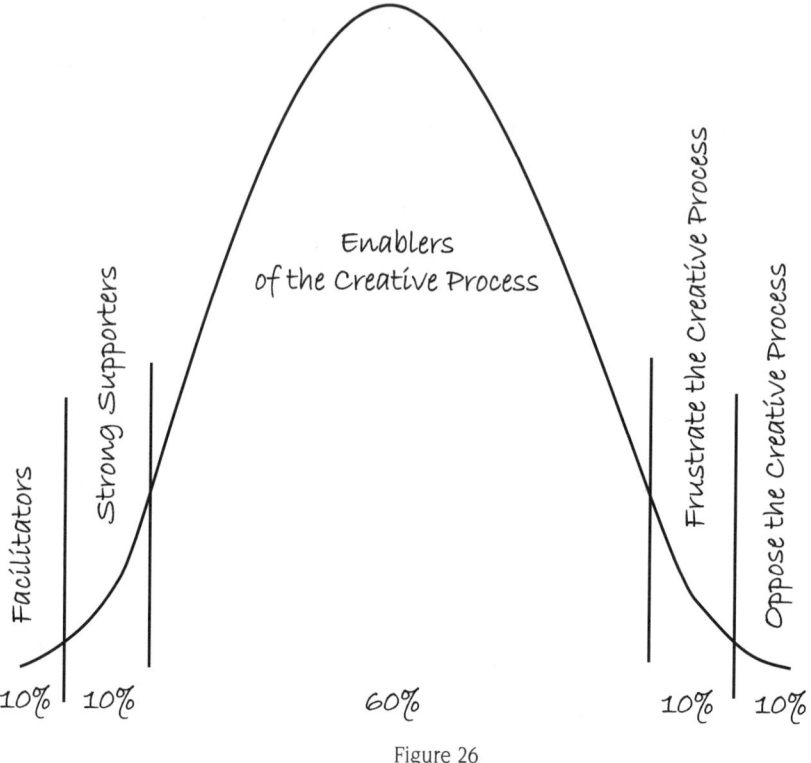

Facilitators	Strong Supporters	Enablers of the Creative Process	Frustrate the Creative Process	Oppose the Creative Process
10%	10%	60%	10%	10%

Figure 26
THE CREATIVITY DISTRIBUTION

"Figure 26 shows a normal distribution of employees in an organization. About ten percent will be what I call Facilitators of the creative process and ten percent will be Strong Supporters of creativity. On the other end of the distribution, ten percent will be employees who frustrate the creative process, and ten percent will be those who overtly or covertly oppose creativity. The remaining sixty percent are Enablers of the creative process.

"Let's review the criteria that I have up here on the flip chart," Thomas said, turning the pages, and then read aloud:

"FACILITATORS OF THE CREATIVE PROCESS ARE PEOPLE WHO:

- *See creative abilities in us that we don't see and mirror back until we see them for ourselves.*
- *Have deeply experienced their own creative process and help others see how the creative process works.*
- *Are able to identify subtle red flags that point to misalignments in organizational structures and systems that frustrate and oppose the creative process.*
- *Develop constructive approaches for exposing and deconstructing barriers to change, and for conquering the fear that drives them.*
- *Model creativity, consistently produce innovations and improvements, and find meaning and significance in their work. Whether through personal interaction, or through stories, books, or movies about their lives, they inspire and challenge others to be creative."*

"Like the stories you told us about Thomas Edison?" Rena interjected as if on cue.

"That's right." Thomas turned a page then alternatively pointed at the flip chart and turned to face the group. He continued reading:

"STRONG SUPPORTERS OF THE CREATIVE PROCESS ARE PEOPLE WHO:

- *Vitally connect the creative process to their work and view work as having symbolic meaning and even transcendence.*
- *Consistently work to expose and conquer the fear that frustrates and undermines the creative process.*
- *Have cultivated the practice of being disinterested and who act in the best interest of other people and the organization.*

- *Recognize how defense mechanisms work in themselves and their organization, and commit to find and eliminate them.*
- *Respect and maintain the balance between organizational, intellectual, and creative authority.*
- *Use their creative abilities to produce innovations and improvements in their organization.*
- *Are willing to pay some professional, social, or personal price to support innovation and improvement."*

Thomas grabbed a glass of water to wet his parched mouth, then turned the page and continued:

"ENABLERS OF THE CREATIVE PROCESS ARE PEOPLE WHO:
- *Are learning to connect their creative abilities to their work.*
- *Are striving to be authentically disinterested and act in the best interest of others and the company.*
- *Have begun to recognize how defense mechanisms are anti-learning devices that frustrate and undermine the creative process.*
- *Refuse to frustrate or oppose the creative process, and keep work life on an even keel so others can pursue creative ideas and creative acts.*
- *Perform their work competently and contribute to achieving the purpose, business objective, and goals of the organization."*

Thomas flipped another page, then began to pace the entire length of the teaching table, as his tone of voice became more intense:

"EMPLOYEES WHO FRUSTRATE THE CREATIVE PROCESS ARE PEOPLE WHO:
- *Talk about connecting their creativity to their work, but continue to view their work as being just 'a job.'*
- *Talk about being disinterested but continue to elevate self-interest above what's best for others and their organization.*
- *Are intermittent barriers to the creative process and become defensive when confronted about it. They say they'll change but they take one step forward and two steps back.*
- *Are legalists and use company policies and goals to oppose innovation and improvement—their philosophy is, 'If it ain't broke, don't fix it.'*
- *Take more psychological and organizational energy than they give.*
- *Perform with marginal competency, reduce organizational effectiveness, and squander energy so creative employees have to compensate for their poor performance and not pursue innovation and improvement."*

Thomas turned another page, walked back to the head of the teaching table. His physical presence became less intense, but his tone of voice was very serious. "The people you have to guard against at all costs are employees who actively *oppose* the creative process:

"EMPLOYEES WHO OPPOSE THE CREATIVE PROCESS ARE INDIVIDUALS WHO:
- *Hate their job and refuse to learn how to connect their creativity to their work, but they deny doing this.*
- *Refuse to be disinterested and consistently elevate their own interests above others and the organization, but they deny doing this.*

- *Are constant barriers to the creative process and use defense mechanisms to deny their actions when confronted about them.*
- *Are builders and architects of technicalities, company policies, and goals that oppose innovation and improvement, but they deny doing this.*
- *Are organizational vampires who consume psychological and organizational energy, and drain the creative life from others, but they deny doing this.*
- *Refuse to take personal responsibility for their actions and their emotional life, but deny it even in the face of objective evidence to the contrary."*

Cindy squirmed in her chair then tossed out, "Teresa Amabile has a couple of things that you should probably add to your list, like undermining employees' autonomy by continually changing their goals, interfering with their work processes, or by putting teams under severe time and resource constraints."[117]

"Yes." Thomas nodded in wholehearted agreement. "Amabile calls these 'actions that kill creativity in employees.' My criteria are not exhaustive, and you'll have to tailor them to your organization. I know of companies where creativity is killed because senior managers take forever to make a decision, or because they reward the wrong behaviors. Take my lists and customize them to your organization—you'll be horrified by how many other ways in which the creative process is stifled, killed, or driven underground.

"Building a portfolio of creative employees means that you should try to migrate employees to the left side of the distribution shown in Figure 26 if at all possible."

"How exactly do you migrate them to the left?" Cindy asked.

"Creative organizations build the message of who they are, what they want, and where they're going so deeply into their infrastructure that it's difficult or impossible for an employee *not* to get the message—unless they don't want to. When a company becomes an *Island of Excellence*, employees at all organizational levels embody the timeless principles and speak with one voice. Therefore, the pressure to conform becomes so powerful that people who don't buy-in will normally self-select out of the organization based on the criteria I just mentioned."

"How do you handle employees who don't self-select out and who continue to frustrate and oppose the creative process?" Lindsey asked, looking for a tangible solution to a problem she was facing back at the office.

Thomas turned another page and pointed to the flip chart. "I use a tool called the Six-Step Decision-Making Model, shown here in Figure 27.

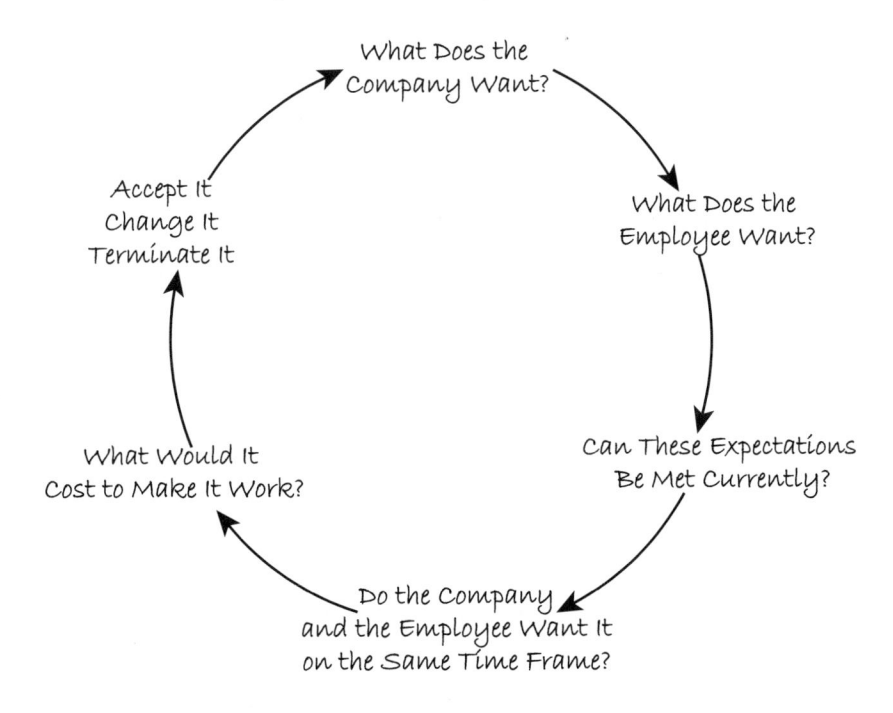

Figure 27
THE SIX-STEP DECISION-MAKING MODEL[118]

"These six questions can be used to evaluate problem employees, regardless of whether they're your direct report, a working associate, a manager, or even the owner of the company," Thomas said, flipping to the next page, and read:

"THE SIX-STEP DECISION-MAKING MODEL
- *What does the company really want from the employee?*
- *What does the employee want from the company?*
- *Can these expectations be met in the current situation?*
- *Do the company and employee want it on the same time frame?*
- *What would it cost to make it work (time, energy, money, etc.)?*
- *Can I accept the employee's performance, should I go on trying to change it, or should I terminate the employee?*

"Sometimes an organization wants very different performance and attitudes from an employee than the employee wants to give, regardless of whether they are senior, middle, first-line managers, or workers. Sometimes the company and the employee both want the same thing, but they can't make it happen in the present context. For example, an employee might have the attitude, 'I would really like to move into sales. I just don't want to do it in this company because of the position I'd have to start at.'"

Lindsey and the group nodded as Thomas reviewed other scenarios.

"Maybe the company and the employee want the same things, and they even want them within the present context, but they want them on very different time frames. For example, the company wants you to move to a new position, but they can't afford it till next fiscal year, and the employee needs to make the move now. Sometimes companies and employees want the same things in the work relationship, on the same timeframe, but one or the other may be unwilling to pay the price it would take to make the professional relationship work. Based on these questions, we always have three choices.[119]

"One: we can accept the employee the way they are. Two: we can try to change the employee. Or three: we can terminate the employee.

"Deciding to accept or change a situation means that we cycle back to the first question and ask it again—what does the company really want from the employee? Moving on may be a temporary solution where we put the problem on the *backburner*, and then try to reengage the process by returning to question one at a later time. Sometimes we just terminate the employee. The Six-Step Decision-Making Model doesn't make the decision for you, it only confronts you with your options." Thomas scanned the facial expressions of the group, looking for their reaction.

It troubles me to think what would happen if I would honestly go through those questions with Rena, Maggie thought. *I'm not sure she'd still be with the company.*

Lindsey raised her hand and asked, "The thing I was thinking about when we ran through the criteria for employees who oppose the creative process was, what do you do when the person who opposes creativity is your star performer?"

"Excellent question, Lindsey," Thomas beamed, thankful she had raised this difficult issue. "My view is that if you have a high performer who supports the creative process, you *model them*. If you have a moderate performer who supports the creative process, you *work with them*. But if you have a high performer who does not support the creative process, you have to *fire them* because they will undermine the culture of creativity and become living proof that the organization is duplicitous and does not speak with one voice."

"That's easier said than done," Lindsey countered with a furrowed brow.

"I know it is," Thomas replied evenly, "but what's your alternative? If you don't fire them, you *betray* yourself and the company's core values and this will eventually unravel the fabric you've woven as a creative organization."

Maggie was troubled by the prospect of running Rena through the six questions, so she grabbed a three-by-five and wrote, "I need to talk to you about how my daughter would stack up to those six questions." Then she set the card face down in the middle of the teaching table.

"Creative organizations consciously and continually look for the twenty percent of the employees who frustrate and oppose the creative process. If they can't move them to the left of the distribution, and if they won't self-select out of the company, they intentionally move them out the door," Thomas said intensely, pounding his fist into the palm of his other hand. "*Absolutely no one* should be allowed to work in an organization if they don't really want to be there, or if their purpose and core values are seriously misaligned with those of the company." He paused to let the import of what he had said resonate in the air.

"I want to conclude this session by going back to Figure 16 and reflecting on the Three practices that constitute the second strategy. I can't even explain how much organizational energy these three practices free up." Thomas shook his head. "Imagine if all the energy from toxic, spring-loaded, ineffective, misaligned activities were reclaimed and made available to do productive work—to fulfill the purpose and business objectives of the organization. This is real organizational power, the definition of intrinsic motivation—the corporate engine that drives competitive advantage.

"In closing," Thomas began handing each person a dive slate, "read through the summary points of the session, then clip it to your BCD so you'll have the material with you underwater." The group scanned the list.

DIVE SLATE SESSION 6 REVIEW

Strategy 1: Find Meaning and Significance in Work
    Practice #1: Experience the Creative Process
    Practice #2: Learn How Fear Inhibits the Creative Process
    Practice #3: Build Inner Collaboration and Alignment

Strategy 2: Use Alignment to Gain Competitive Advantage
    Practice #4: Align the Organization to Speak with One Voice
    Practice #5: Follow the Red Flags to Squandered Energy
    Practice #6: Build a Portfolio of Creative Employees

- *To what degree do employees facilitate, support, or enable the creative process?*
- *The creativity distribution (Facilitators, supporters, enablers, frustrators, and opposers of the creative process)*
- *The six-step decision-making model*
- *Supporting a culture of creativity is crucial*
  Model high performers who support the culture
  Work with moderate performers who support the culture
  Fire high performers who don't support the culture

He waited a moment for them to finish. "Are there any questions?" Thomas put his hands on his hips, smiled encouragingly, and searched the faces of the group with deep inquiry. "If not, then let's go diving."

For once, Nikki was on time for the dive brief. Anita was relieved and Dan felt vindicated about his outburst prior to the last dive.

After looking around to make sure everyone was there, she began. "We're going to do another dive here at Jayne's Gully, but this time we are going to dive the other side of the channel."

Anita looked directly at Bethany and said, "The same warning goes for this dive—stay off the top of the reef because it's covered with the same kind of corallimorph that Bethany unfortunately discovered on the last dive."

"Oh look!" Nikki jumped out of her seat and ran to the railing. "There's a pod of spinner dolphins!"

Most of the group moved to the railing to watch these playful animals jump two or three feet out of the water and rotate in the air like a top. James took a quick look, then began the ritual of pulling his half-dry wetsuit over his warm body—he wanted to get in the water.

"Are there any questions?" Anita shouted playfully, trying to get the group's attention back.

"Yeah—could you watch me underwater and give me some pointers about improving my bottom time? I want to be a totally relaxed 'Zen diver' like Thomas here!" Cindy patted him on the shoulder as the group roared with laughter.

Thomas flushed at the off-handed compliment on his dive skills.

"His record bottom time is one hour and fifty-four minutes with an eighty-cubic-foot aluminum tank," Dan announced. "I was there at Big Island Divers in Kona when he did it!"

"He must be part fish," Frank chortled, playing along with the fun. "I don't know anybody that gets that kind of bottom time."

"I'll keep my eye on you *and* Mr. Thomas," Anita called out, trying to focus the group's attention on her once again. "So if there aren't any more questions—the pool's open."

Lindsey was the first person off the boat and as she dropped through the water column, her right ear exploded with pain at a depth of fifteen feet. She slowed her descent, held her nose, and blew gently trying to equalize the pressure inside and outside her head. As she hung there, the pain lessened and her attention was drawn to the mooring ball floating about fifteen feet above her on the surface of the water, then alternately down to the reef forty feet below. Somehow this underwater perspective gave her new insight about the process of exploring the red-flag interactions on the surface of her intimate relationships, and the deeper structures below the surface of consciousness that inhibited them. Rather than avoid relationships with men because they were so problematic, she would have to seek out those "mooring balls," then dive in and explore the below-the-surface issues that had determined the course of so much of her life.

Anita swam up next to Cindy and held her dive slate close enough for her to read what she'd written: "Slow your breathing down! Count slowly to five as you breathe out, then count to five as you breathe in. FEEL the buoyancy of your body in the water and relax."

Cindy practiced the breath-counting maneuver as Anita observed.

"You've got it!" Anita wrote on her dive slate in large letters, then gave her the thumbs up and rejoined the group.

Cindy watched how slowly Thomas was breathing as he floated motionlessly—as if he was in a trance.

This is how it is with blind spots, the Inner People whispered on the fringe of her consciousness. *You need trusted people to watch your life, like you're watching Thomas, and give you feedback about things you can't see for yourself.*

Cindy nodded silently in agreement with the insight they proposed, then jotted a note on her dive slate as a way of honoring the growing collaboration between her and the Inner People, and to remind her to log it permanently in her journal once back on the ship.

While Nikki was still within sight of the group, Anita's well-intentioned reprimand and the growing psychological pressure from the Inner People made her want to be alone. Powerful forces of human creativity were flowing from deep within her as she gathered the courage and soberness of mind to face the blind spot she had about her anti-authoritarian conflict with personal accountability and any kind of structure and system. The workshop material convinced her that the philosophical tension between a traditional approach to measuring the performance of individuals and Kohn's notion of intrinsic motivation could be resolved by building a creative organization.

The workshop had also given Nikki insight into her restlessness about her work. John was exactly right—success in marketing didn't automatically translate into success as Director of Operations. She needed to admit how poorly she'd been performing as a manager and leader. Not only did the operations job require different skills, it forced her to work against deeply engrained personality fixations. Creating and sustaining organizational change meant planning in the early strategic phases, but it also required *staying* with the project till the transformation was complete. She had lots of creative ideas, but lacked the ability to navigate the implementation process that turned creative ideas into creative acts, so her projects died before birth. Nikki needed to move beyond these fixations, but wanted to do it privately, not on stage as the Director of Operations. From now on, personality had to be factored into every career choice she made.

The transforming power of the creative process was at work within her, motivating her to find a professional path that had symbolic meaning for her life. Based on the model Thomas had presented, she was a high-performing marketing professional who did not support the changes she was trying to make with the new performance appraisal system. That's why she'd been stiff-arming Barb—distracting her with idea after idea. When she returned, Nikki would tell John that she wanted to transfer back to the marketing department. This was a much better fit for her personality and would allow her to make a meaningful contribution to the purpose, business objectives, and goals of the company, while she faced her fixations outside of the spotlight of being a senior manager.

With everyone back on the ship, the crew pulled off the mooring ball and began the long, open sea, overnight journey west to the Witu Islands—the last area they would dive before heading back to Walindi. Thomas set about the task of finding Nikki. As he rounded the corner of the Lido deck, he saw her sitting alone in her usual spot at the teaching table, writing furiously in her journal.

Hmm...I wonder if now's a good time to talk to her? Thomas thought, anxious about how the interaction would go. *Well there's no way of knowing unless I ask.*

"Hey," Thomas said quietly not wanting to startle her, "do you want to talk about your three-by-five or is now a bad time?"

Nikki looked up at him and smiled, "Sure. Come and sit down—I'll be done in a second."

He waited silently for a moment, then she set her pen down and began, "Actually, I'm embarrassed about what I wrote on the card, and I owe you an apology. You weren't trying to egg me on and provoke me. If anything, that's what *I* was trying to do to you and the others." Nikki paused and looked directly into Thomas's eyes with deep sorrow and regret. "I know this stuff, Thomas—many of the timeless principles that you're teaching I've known for a long time. What's wrong with me that I still don't seem to get it?" Her eyes filled with tears, as she hammered herself with judgement and self-reproach.

"Don't be so hard on yourself, Nikki." Thomas smiled gently to reassure her. "These principles are really difficult to apply in everyday life. It takes more than an intellectual knowledge—you have to be able to see applications and make changes in real life. Do you remember the story, *A Christmas Carol*, by Charles Dickens?"

"Yeah," she sniffled, wiping the tears from her eyes.

"The three ghosts made Scrooge examine his attitudes and behaviors by observing the actual events of his life from a distance. What I've always found most interesting about this method of teaching was that the ghosts didn't change the details of a single historical event! Scrooge saw and heard *exactly* what actually happened. The difference was, he witnessed his attitudes and behaviors from a distance. For the first time in his life, he heard the words he spoke and saw the deeds he'd done *as others had experienced them*—and this horrified him."

"That's what you call getting into the spectator role?" Nikki asked with a growing sense of hope.

"That's right," Thomas said, putting a comforting hand on her shoulder. "You need to get into the spectator role. Learn to stand apart from yourself and observe what you do and what you say—think before you act. The road to effectively applying the timeless principles and moving beyond personality fixation begins by examining your attitudes and behaviors from a distance."

"I'll work on that, Thomas." Nikki smiled with renewed hope.

At 7:45 P.M. most of the group were milling around the deck having cocktails and waiting for dinner to begin at 8:00 P.M. Smooth Brazilian jazz played softly in the background. Once again, the teaching table had been transformed into an elegant dining space with aqua table clothes, candles, and the rest of the fine dining accoutrements they'd become accustomed to.

Once the group was seated for dinner, the steward rolled the wine cart to each place setting. He first asked them whether they preferred fresh pan-fried red pinjalo snapper that the crew caught off the boat that day while they were diving, or roasted rack of lamb. Then he offered them a variety of red, white or blush wines to complement their dinner selection. The candlelight added an ambience that transformed the deck of the ship into a fine dining experience.

It was Rena's birthday. Earlier, Maggie asked Artie to bake a cake for the special occasion. Rena was enjoying the dive workshop much more than she'd ever thought and had learned a lot about herself, her mother, and how the Spinner Group could improve its performance. But this was the farthest she'd ever been from home and Rena was missing her husband, her dog, and the Rocky Mountain feel of Colorado. Maggie sensed how homesick she was and wanted to cheer her up with a surprise celebration of the occasion.

After the main courses of dinner had been served, Artie marched out from the galley with a cake that had twenty-six candles blazing on top and started the group singing a hearty round of "Happy Birthday" to Rena.

The young woman's jaw dropped as her eyes widened and filled with tears of joy. "Did you put them up to this, Mom?" Rena shouted, pleased by how thoughtful Maggie had been.

"I knew you were homesick and I wanted to make this your special day," Maggie beamed, pleased that Rena was delighted with the impromptu ceremony.

For the first time on the trip, Artie sat down at the dinner table with the group, had a piece of birthday cake, and joined in on the discussion that Cindy, James, and Lindsey were having about what they'd seen on the reef that day.

Cindy was tired of confrontations with Dan, so she purposely sat at the other end of the dinner table to avoid having to interact with him over dinner. She was dying for more information about Goroka. A little buzzed from the wine, Cindy gave Artie a playful punch to his chest and with her deep, masculine-sounding voice and polished Harvard-style Boston accent she said, "Hey, Artie…tells us what life's like in Goroka."

Artie, in his usual jest, overreacted to the punch. The others laughed as he asked, "Do you want to hear the way it *used* to be, or the way it is now?"

Cindy, playing along, acted like she was torn between the two, then said, "How about some of both?"

"Okay," Artie pretended to roll up his nonexistent sleeves, "I'll start with something that gives you an insight into the culture in PNG. I moved here with my parents when I was four years old. My father was a teacher and my mom managed a hotel and some other businesses in the village of Kainantu, about a forty-minute drive southeast of Goroka. When my mom was first running the Kainantu Hotel, she discovered that these two guys on the grounds crew had broken into the food storehouse and had stolen a bunch of food, but they both denied it.

"She was going to call the police, but Bamu, a local who was one of Mom's most trusted supervisors, advised her differently. 'If you call the police, they'll only deny it and the police will never arrest them because then they'd have to pay compensation and be subject to payback.'

"So," Artie laughed, "following Bamu's advice, my mother called the witch doctor who came and did a ceremony with all the employees present to discover who had stolen the food. When the witch doctor finally pointed out the two men as the culprits, they got up and walked away with their heads down in shame and eventually they paid back what they had stolen. To this day in remote villages, it's the witch doctor who wields the greatest power, not the police."

Cindy hadn't noticed that Dan had slid closer in order to pick up on the discussion. She was practically bubbling over when she asked, "Artie, what's Goroka like today? What's the University of Goroka like, and what would it be like if I moved there? Would I fit in?"

Is she seriously considering moving to Goroka? Dan wondered silently. *Or is it just the wine talking?*

"Well, that's a little complicated." Artie scratched his head and made a face like he had been asked to explain quantum physics. "Let me give you some background before I answer your question. I speak fluent Pidgin and grew up spending many weekends with my friends in remote villages. They lived in circular thatched huts with a hole in the roof and a fire in the center of the dirt floor. There was a raised wooden ledge all around the perimeter of the hut about eighteen inches wide and the same distance off the ground where the humans would sit and sleep, while the pigs and dogs slept underneath on the dirt floor. My friends and I would dress up like mudmen, shoot the bow and arrow, and play in the forest all day long. So I lived in the culture from the time I was a little boy."

Dan moved still closer and was no longer eavesdropping from a distance. He listened carefully as Artie spoke, and intermittently glanced at Cindy to observe her reactions to what he was saying.

"When I grew up," Artie gestured at his enormous size and laughed, "I married a local girl named Miriam and we had a child named Eva, who is now seven years old and lives with my mom in Goroka. When I went to Cairnes for three years to attend chef's school, I took Miriam and Eva. For the first time in her life, Miriam was in the minority, and the stores, traffic, different food, indoor plumbing, and having to wear clothes most of the time freaked her out. She lasted three weeks and went home to her village. I stayed for three years and raised Eva myself and tried to help her understand the western world in relation to the culture in PNG. I still go back to visit my ex-wife's village, Talasea, although she doesn't live there anymore. I'm still part of the family, so even though we're divorced I still have to pull my weight by bringing gifts and money when I go back."

Artie stopped speaking and the sound of the sea wind closed in around the dinner table as he realized that the group was hanging on his every word.

He hesitated for another moment, then spoke in a subdued manner that was so deep, reflective, and philosophical, it seemed to contradict his normally jovial self. "So having given you some sense of how deeply I've lived in this culture, let me now try to answer your question about what it would be like for you to live in Goroka, from my perspective. I could never truly fit in even though I speak the language, know the culture, and have gotten to the point that my light skin and blue eyes are no longer an issue to my friends and most people I interact with throughout PNG."

With an even more serious, contemplative, and sorrowful expression than anyone had ever seen, Artie said, "Yet deep within, I feel like a person caught between two worlds. I don't fully belong in PNG because I'm not blood to these people like my daughter is, but the thought of living full-time in a western-style culture, back in Australia where I was born, makes my skin crawl."

The group was humbled by the open vulnerability of Artie's words because they had come so freely from his heart. "Thanks, Artie," the group said, almost in unison.

As the discussion migrated back to smaller groups of people talking, Cindy reached down and grabbed her journal from under her chair, turned to Thomas and said quietly, "He's describing the cultural chasm you drew in my journal, isn't he?" James huddled up and listened, as Cindy turned to the diagram and showed it to him.

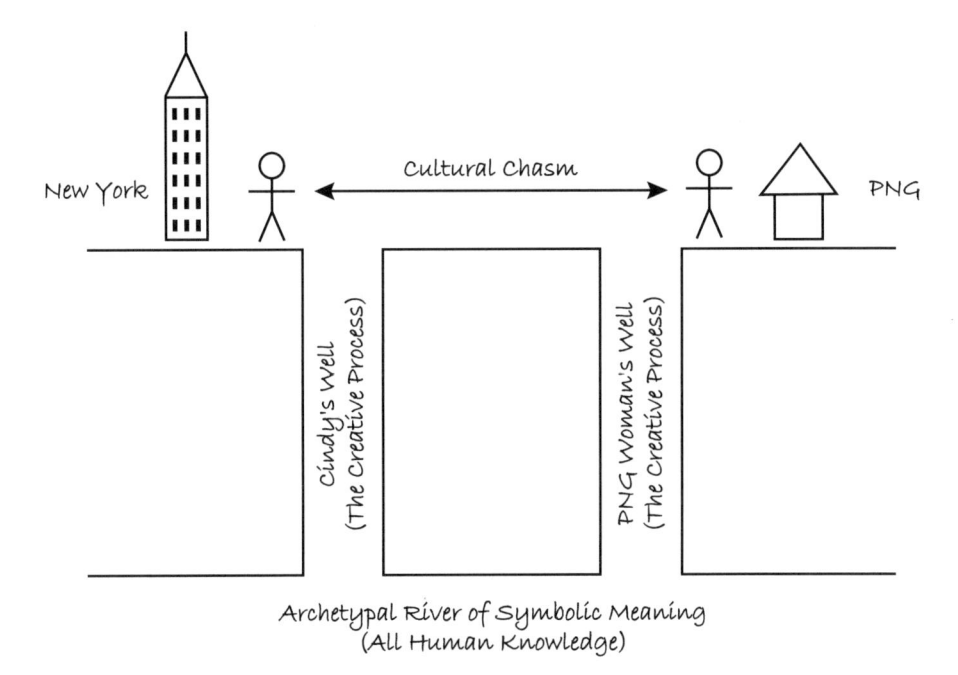

Figure 11

THE CULTURAL CHASM AND SYMBOLIC CONNECTION

"Yes. It sounds like Artie hasn't found a way to interpret his experience of being *in* the PNG culture, but not feeling *part* of it. He needs to allow the creative process to work through him and forge his own personal myth about living here."

"What do you mean by a personal myth?" James asked, as Cindy nodded, eager to hear Thomas's answer.

"Well, the preferences, patterns, and regularities of our personality systematize the constant streams of sensations, emotions, and ideas entering our consciousness from the outer and inner worlds and make them coherent and intelligible. This is how our personal self develops and ultimately how we remain sane. As Rollo May suggests, personal myths are things we discover about ourselves—patterns of wholeness that can create deep personal change."

Thomas pointed to the diagram in Cindy's journal. "Let's use Cindy as an example. Her personal myth will be a self-interpretation that she discovers about herself—something that *links* her personal self shown here as a stick figure, her collective self indicated by the Archetypal River of Symbolic Meaning, and her biological self—the fact that she's a human animal.[120]

"One way to discover our personal myth is by concretizing the personal, collective, and biological dimensions of our life into creative acts. The creative process often reveals our individual answer to the collective existential questions of life. What I'm suggesting, Cindy, is that Artie hasn't thought all this through, so he's still suffering from the same kind of sorrow, grief, and alienation that you experienced with the village woman—even though he's been here his whole life."

"So, the experience I had with the village woman is common?" Cindy ventured after a moment of silence.

"Absolutely," Thomas concurred. "In the States where there's little or no cultural chasm, it's what makes people buy new houses and quit their jobs looking for fulfillment. It's why middle-aged men divorce their wives of twenty years, buy red sports cars, new wardrobes, and hook up with women half their age."

"The old mid-life crisis!" James bellowed as he slapped his palm on the table and the three of them laughed heartily.

"I think I'm going to head up to the top deck and take some time to reflect on all this," Cindy said, as the laughter died down.

"Hey, James—is it too late to talk about your three-by-five?"

Thomas asked, not wanting to put the discussion off any longer.

"Sure—let's sit right here," he replied, watching Cindy gather up her journal and head off.

"Why don't you give me a better understanding about what your question actually is," Thomas said as he poured James and himself another glass of wine.

"Well," James rubbed his two-day growth of beard stubble with his hand, "in the case study I handed in, I tried to explain how I'm using strategic planning in my parish to drive change and fill the gap of leadership that exists. Part of this involves wrestling control of the parish away from a core group of powerful vestry members who have run it for generations. Based on your discussion about organizational complexes, I realized that I'm consciously forming a complex that will enable me to take over the congregation by force. I have the Bishop's approval to do this, but your comments during the session raised the interesting question of who actually 'owns' the church and whether I was being disinterested, or acting out of self-interest and personality fixation."

Thomas was taken back by the directness and brutal honesty of James's inquiry. He took a long, deep breath to frame his response. "I tried to be clear in the session that organizational complexes can be good, positive forces of change, especially when intellectual and creative authority are allowed to challenge the status quo of organizational authority. The juxtaposition of the three kinds of authority is one of the signatures of a creative organization. In terms of organizational authority, I'll bet the Bishop and the Diocese of Colorado actually own the building you meet in, but that's a different question than asking who owns the 'church' as a group of people."

"That's correct," James agreed, fully engaged in the discussion. "The building and property belong to the diocese, but the Church as the community of faith, belongs to God. Our authority as Episcopalians derives from three sources: scripture, tradition, and reason. Whenever there's conflict in the church, it's normally traceable to differences of emphasis or interpretation in one or more of these three."

"So I'm guessing that the conflict between you and this core of powerful parish members turns on differences between your interpretations of scripture, tradition, or reason?" Thomas said, hoping to draw out James's deeper motivations.

"Well, yes—in some broad sense. But as we've discussed here in the workshop, many misalignments about how scripture, tradition, or reason are interpreted are probably reducible to differences in personality fixation." A light went on in James's head that was so bright Thomas saw its radiance in his facial expression. "I guess I just answered my own question, didn't I?" James said sheephishly.

"Maybe you did. Look, James—carefully examine what you're doing and why you're doing it. Look for the red flags as signs of dysfunctional personality fixation. Remember that the church, like any other organization, is a collective-cultural entity that is led, managed, and changed one person at a time. Most of all, always be open and transparent about what you do and why you're doing it.

"You're an Anglican, right?"

James nodded, surprised by the question.

"When Thomas Becket, Archbishop of Canterbury, was tempted by others to commit suicide and pretend he'd been martyred, he mouthed these immortal words, 'The last temptation is the greatest treason: To do the right thing for the wrong reason.'[121] That would be my final advice to you about using strategic planning as the foci of an organizational complex to take over the leadership of your parish. Make sure you're doing the right thing for the right reason." Thomas and James were silent as the power of this timeless principle penetrated both of their hearts.

∫∫∫∫∫

Everyone was in bed except Cindy who was still up on the top deck of the ship drinking in the magnificent stars, breathing in the clean air, and getting some reflective time away from Dan and the others. The eternal and transcendent light from brightly clustered galaxies and constellations ignited the flames of the creative process within her, and she knew that the decision about going to Goroka had already been made.

You've given Dan enough years from your life, the Inner People whispered. *It's time to follow your calling, to discover your personal myth—to find your destiny.*

She was tired of fighting with Dan about everything from strategic planning to him undermining her authority with the board and her direct reports. The workshop revealed that their differences about long-term versus short-term focus, valuing cost reduction at the price of relationships, and her refusal to hammer on people when they didn't perform were all about personality. Given how fixated Dan was about his business views, Cindy had little or no hope that things would change. Since she couldn't accept the way things were, she had no alternative but to move on.

Cindy felt a growing excitement about what was happening in her life. She missed teaching and academia, but hated the frenetic publish-or-perish pace of the Cambridge universities. At Harvard, she was a small duck in a big pond, but in Goroka, she could make a significant contribution to the life of an entire nation. Cindy liked the fact that the core values of the university were built around the creative process, and although she'd be far away from the cutting edge of science and technology, Goroka would be an exciting place to be intellectually. She would construct new pathways through which her creativity could flow and make genuine contributions to the university's purpose, business objectives, and goals.

As she contemplated the journey that brought her and Dan to PNG, powerful elements of creativity were released that gave her the equanimity and courage she needed to take this bold step. Dan was perfectly capable of running the company without her. In fact, of late, with the way he questioned almost every decision she made, she wondered how relevant her presence was anyway. After listening to Artie speak at dinner tonight, she decided to press Dan for a one-year leave of absence and move to Goroka.

I'll call the Dean when I get back to Walindi and tell him I accept his offer, she thought. *If Dan won't give me the year off, I'll quit and go anyway.*

Day 3
LIFE IN THE WITU ISLANDS

Strategy 3:

Allow a Culture of

Creativity to Emerge

THE DAY BEGINS

The fourteen-hour ocean voyage to the Witu Islands was difficult even in calm seas, but the three to four foot swells that rolled across the Bismarck Sea that night made the trip even more challenging as the ship was tossed and turned like a toy. But by Tuesday, the group was physically tired from the rigors of diving three tanks a day, and psychologically fatigued from rolling the teaching session material over and over in their minds, so most of them slept like babies.

James bolted from sleep and was propelled into a quasi-conscious state by a powerful dream. Sitting erect in his bed, time seemed to stand still as he pieced together enough information from his five senses to figure out where he was—that he was in a bed, in his cabin, on the dive ship *Origin*. The motion of the boat and the visual field he saw as he looked through the porthole confirmed what was happening. He laid his head back down on the skimpy pillow that was moist from his sweat. The image of a dream where he was diving in deep blue water flooded into his mind. As he laid there almost paralyzed by the fear of being carried out to sea and drowning, images of the young Melanesian woman crowded back into his consciousness, and then were displaced by the image of him diving in deep water. He pushed the knob that back-lit the face of his wristwatch and saw that it was only 5:00 A.M.

I need to talk to Cindy—now! he commanded himself.

He threw on his shorts and a tank top, pulled his thinking stone out of his pants pocket, walked to the other end of the hall, and knocked at her cabin door as quietly as he could so he didn't wake the others.

∿∿∿∿

"Okay, tell me as much as you can about the dream," Cindy said as the two of them sat dipping their tea bags in the dimly lit dining room.

James began speaking softly, hastily. "The only thing I remember is a single image of me on a blue water dive with thousands of feet below me, swimming against a really strong current. Like most blue water dives, I was disoriented and couldn't really tell which way was up or down or whatever. I was kicking as hard as I could with my fins, but I was terrified that this was one of those down and out currents that you read about where the force of the water takes you down five hundred feet, then out to sea. Then, with my eyes glued to my dive computer, I heard an inner voice warning me, 'Watch your depth!' as if there was anything I could do at that point."

"What else?" Cindy asked, leaning forward to draw him out and encourage him to continue.

"As I lay there, the dream I had in the Highlands popped back into my mind," James wrung his hands together on the table, embarrassed that he was still dealing with that issue.

"Do you have any idea why the two dreams might be linked together in your mind?" Cindy asked, searching James's facial expression for emotions or insights.

James locked eyes with hers, turned his thinking stone over and over in his hand, and said boldly, "Well, there are some things that have been floating around in my mind since I've been awake. The reading I've done on interpreting dreams has taught me that I need to stay as close as I can to the meaning of the symbols and images. As far as the Highlands dream, I know *intellectually* that it's a metaphor about some lost religious, spiritual, and creative side to me, but as you can tell by the way I have been staring at you, it's resulted in being sexually obsessed." Shifting position, he moved his hands under the table and in the process accidentally brushed Cindy's thigh as she swallowed hard. "Now I see that the power of my sexual passion has been drawing me down into the deep waters of my unconscious emotions and threatening to carry me away, and I've done nothing about it—I haven't been watching my depth."

James looked down at the table in shame. "Sexuality is something I've struggled with my entire life—especially sex in the workplace. I know that's the reason I got bounced out of my law firm, and I'm starting to have a problem like that with an important person in my parish. When I'm honest with myself, I know there's a pattern here."

Cindy said nothing, but encouraged James to continue with a slight nod and unflinching eye contact.

"When I first told you about my dream, you said not to take the images *literally*, but to view them *symbolically* as a psychological pattern of wholeness—something the creative process was trying to express through me."

"That's right," Cindy nodded as she sipped her tea, eager to hear more.

"Do you know that the Hebrew language uses the same word to describe a deep knowledge of God and sexual intercourse?" James said with passion. "Yes, the Old Testament says, 'And the man went to her and he knew her,' where the word translated 'to know' is the Hebrew word *yada*. That's because the act of intercourse gives you a deep and personal knowledge of the other person that can be had in no other way. On the flip side of the word's meaning, that's how deeply and intimately God wants us to know him—he wants us to have a relationship where we *yada* him."

James was shocked to find himself uttering words that drew on his seminary training almost as if one of his Inner People had taken over his vocal chords and spoken through him from a source of deep inner wisdom.

"I now see that the *yada* of you and I in the Highlands dream is to be understood symbolically as a metaphor that will lead me to a new, fertile, creative, inner religious and spiritual life. I understand what a serious mistake it would be to act out this symbolic pattern of wholeness with you *literally*. The images in my dream also tell me that if I stay the course to completion, the creative path will bring a deep and divine kind of sorrow and pain, but that the outcome will be healing, wholeness, and a deep sense of inner peace and holy silence."

The profundity of the moment was suddenly shattered as the dining room lights flicked on and Artie shouted, "G'day mates! It's 5:45 A.M. You boys and girls been up all night?"

"No, just since five o'clock," Cindy chuckled.

Artie made his way to the kitchen to begin his daily chores. Cindy gave James a hug as he grabbed a cup of coffee and headed for the privacy of the upper deck to be alone. In this early morning solitude, James felt the transforming power of the creative process working deep within him and motivating him to come to terms with his lust. What he found most interesting was that as he articulated his insights about the dream to Cindy, the psychological and sexual energy that obsessed him was *gone*! Understanding the dream images and his sexual obsession as a symbolic pattern of wholeness dissipated the fixated energy and released him from the bondage to his lust without conscious effort on his part.

How could he take the deep and profound words that he'd just spoken to Cindy and construct a new self-understanding? What would he say to Shawna when he got home? How might it change his relationship with his wife and his children? Should he leave his lifelong trail of broken relationships alone, or go back and make restitution for the wrong done to countless women? What would his insights mean for his spiritual life? Would his insights change what he did as a priest and how he did it?

Powerful elements of human creativity were unleashed as James experienced forgiveness, innocence, and the courage to change his approach toward change in the parish. Thomas had hit the nail on the head—James was doing the right thing for the wrong reason, motivated by self-interest. His stealth approach to manipulating the situation behind the scenes and ignoring input from others was clearly a fixation of his personality type. In retrospect, he wondered why the Bishop had gone along with his strategy—what was *his* motivation for using James's approach throughout the diocese?

James vowed to use the same kind of empathy he displayed with Shawna the night before the retreat in everything he did. He would discover new ways in which his creative abilities could be used to train his parish members to perform the simple tasks of breaking bread, visiting the sick, proclaiming the word, and administering the sacraments—things that constituted the church's purpose, objectives, and goals.

Around 6:00 A.M. James felt the ship stop moving as the crew out on the bow began looking down through the water and struggling to find the mooring ball in the first rays of the morning sun. The shoreline was steep and punctuated with small mountain peaks that were densely covered with a carpet of multicolored, deep shades of green. Scanning the shoreline, James saw periodic breaks in the rain forest and heavy jungle and thin columns of smoke rising toward the sky indicating a number of small villages clustered along the shoreline. They had arrived in the Witu Islands.

By 6:45 A.M. the sun was bright against the deep emerald blue sky, and massive and beautifully formed clouds filled the horizon as Pachelbel played softly in the dining room and the smell of freshly baked rolls, eggs, and bacon filled the ship. Because Cindy was so interested in the PNG culture, Artie and the ship's captain had already radioed to shore and arranged for one of the leaders from the village to come out to the ship to talk with her and the others before and during breakfast.

Patrick Mann paddled out to the ship in a traditional dugout canoe. As he boarded, Artie showed him upstairs to the Lido deck where Cindy, Thomas, and some of the others were seated around the teaching table eating breakfast. Patrick was thin and muscular, about five foot two inches tall with ebony skin, dark penetrating eyes, bushy black hair, and teeth that were stained bright red from years of chewing beetle-nut.

As Artie made the introductions, the steward brought their guest some coffee and warm rolls, then Patrick looked directly at Cindy and asked, "What would you like to know about PNG?"

"Tell us a little about yourself first," Cindy said warmly, trying to draw him out.

"Well," Patrick sat up straight in his chair and puffed out his chest, "I am the Vice President of the local village council and was a financial advisor for the PNG government in Port Moresby for twelve years before returning home and getting into local politics. I'm from the pig clan and my wife is from the rope clan, so our five children are half pig and half rope."

"How did the clans get their names?" Cindy asked bright-eyed. "Did your ancestors actually raise pigs, and did the people from your wife's clan make rope?"

"I don't know." Patrick scratched his head. "For as far back as I can go into our tribal history, my family had pigs like every other clan, but never sold them, nor did my wife's family make and sell rope. These clans come from our ancient ancestors—there are five of them: pig, rope, monkey, breadfruit, and crocodile. I don't know how the names came to be. That's just the way it's been since the beginning of time."

"Tell them about the Cargo Cult," Artie interjected with excitement. "*There's* something they'd be interested in, coming from the States."[122]

Several members of the group set their coffee cups down and leaned forward, eager to hear what Patrick had to say. "Since the beginning of time, our tribal religion has told us that the spirits of our dead ancestors live in the spirit world all around us. When we take care of our ancestors and the gods and give them honor, they take care of us. We use traditional magic and the power of the gods and our ancestors to produce a good harvest of yams, taro, or fish—or to pray for good weather, or to heal our children when they get the fever."

Pointing to the sky, Patrick spoke in a solemn, hushed tone of respect. "It is believed that whenever someone is sick or has trouble in their village or family, it's because the spirits of our ancestors are angry, so they punish us by taking away our health and our prosperity.

"So PNG people have always *equated* morality with prosperity. Having wealth and possessions are the result of being good to our ancestors—good to the gods. When white people first came to our island in the nineteenth century, the amount of their wealth and prosperity told our forefathers that they must be morally superior to us. During the Second World War, we began to see black American soldiers who also had access to this wealth and prosperity, so we knew this prosperity wasn't only given to white people."

Patrick pointed off the starboard side of the boat. "That is the island of Bali. It was there that some spiritual men rose up among the people and taught that people in the west also practiced magic to *redirect* manufactured goods like machines, tools, ships, and other cargo that were originally sent to us from the ancestors in the spirit world. They also taught that our ancestors have found out what was being done and developed ways to send the cargo *direct* to us here in PNG. They said that we had to adopt the secular and religious ways of western people, so many of us built docks and airstrips to receive the cargo when it finally arrived. Only then would the goods be returned to their rightful owners— us. These and other ways have come to be called the Cargo Cult."

Patrick took a sip of his coffee as all eyes were glued on him. "Some people in PNG believe portions of these teachings to this very day," Artie interjected. "What I find most interesting about the Cargo Cult is the extent to which local people have gone to explain the vast inequities between places like Australia and life here in PNG. It also gets at the question you asked about fitting into life in Goroka, Cindy. If you believed the teachings of the Cargo Cult, *that* might bridge some of the cultural gap between your technological, scientific world and life here in PNG."

We create personal myths to make sense of the cultural chasm, and they create religious myths that do the same thing, Cindy smiled, pondering how alike all human beings are.

SESSION 1: THE EMERGENCE OF ORGANIZATIONAL CULTURE

The entire group was seated around the teaching table listening to Patrick and Artie, and it was already 8:15 A.M. when Thomas said, "I think we're going to have to get started."

After getting a nod of approval from the ship's captain, Thomas said, "Patrick, this is fascinating and it's a great lead-in to our first session today on organizational culture. Can you hang around on the ship in case people have more questions later on?"

"Of course," he replied, more than willing to participate.

Thomas stood, walked to the flip chart, and began speaking as Patrick and Artie strolled to the kitchen. "Today I want to discuss the third strategy, which is to continue implementing Strategies 1 and 2 and allow a culture of creativity to emerge. Organizational culture cannot be created *directly* any more than deep personal change can. Rather, culture emerges as the *indirect* product of thoroughly and consistently implementing the first two strategies and allowing the natural process of human creativity to manifest itself in an organization. The interaction of all three strategies is shown in Figure 29," Thomas turned the page on the flip chart.

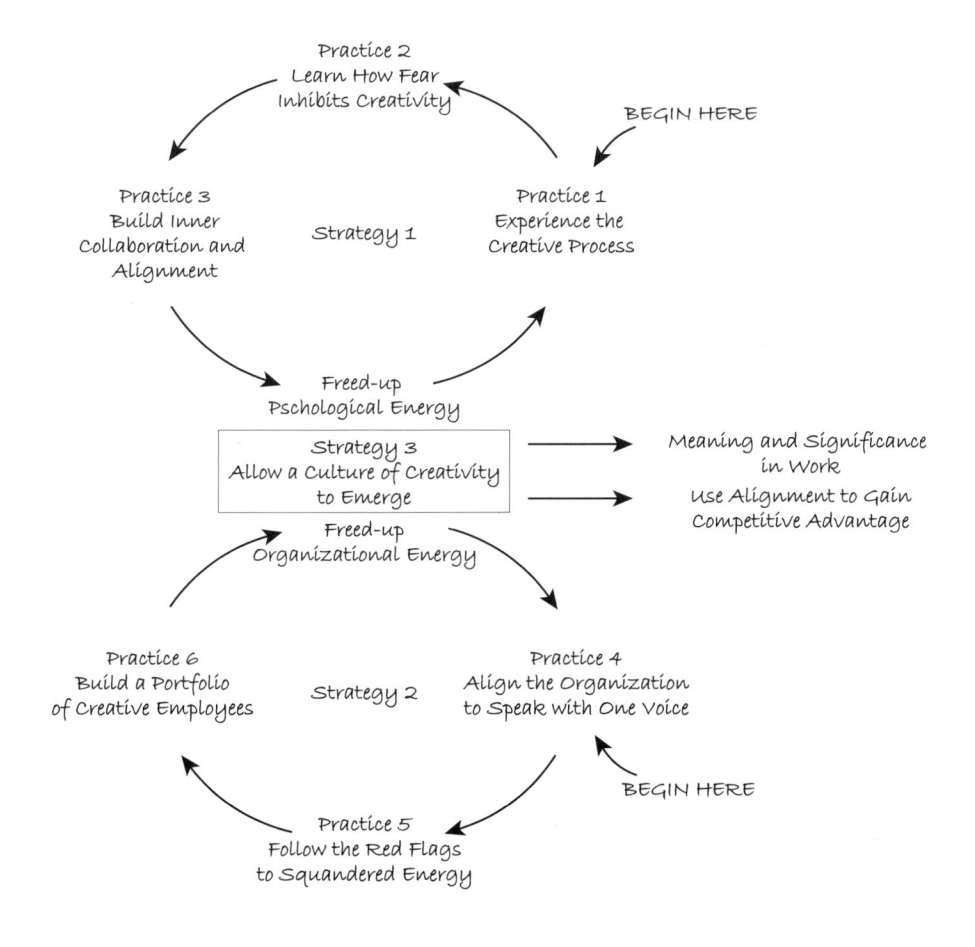

Figure 29
THE THIRD STRATEGY: ALLOW A CULTURE OF CREATIVITY TO EMERGE

"The figure shows how the first two strategies work together synergistically to indirectly produce a culture that facilitates, supports, and enables the creative process. The first strategy focuses on individual employees finding meaning and significance in their work. They do this by building competency in three practices: experiencing the creative process, learning how fear inhibits their creativity, and by building collaboration and alignment with the Inner People. The combination of these three practices working together frees up enormous amounts of formerly squandered psychological energy—energy that can be redirected toward doing the things that matter in life and finding meaning and significance in work." Thomas used his index finger to trace the counterclockwise motion of the three practices in the diagram.

"The second strategy is focused on companies using deep and complete alignment of employees, structures, and systems to gain competitive advantage. This requires that we build competency in Practices 4 through 6—we align the organization to speak with one voice, follow the red flags to squandered energy, and build a portfolio of creative employees. When Practices 4 through 6 work together synergistically, they free up enormous amounts of squandered organizational energy and create competitive advantage through creativity, innovation, and improvement.

"Look carefully at the central box in Figure 29." Thomas pulled a marker out of his shirt pocket and gestured toward the flip chart. "Notice how the third strategy emerges from the synergistic interaction of the first two along the interface of psychological and organizational energy."

"So the third strategy is to do nothing but sit around and wait for a culture of creativity to emerge?" Cindy asked, tongue-in-cheek.

"Not exactly," Thomas smiled, playing along with her humor. "As

I've already mentioned, creativity is the natural problem-solving mechanism of the human brain and occurs naturally in all people, in all times, in all cultures, unless frustrated and opposed by psychological, organizational, or cultural obstructions. So creativity is happening all around us, and the point of the third strategy is to *allow* this natural process to happen and not stifle or oppose it.

"One day we come to work and find that the organization's culture has changed. New cultural elements that foster the creative process come as easily as the ones that formerly frustrated and opposed it. A culture of creativity makes formerly fixated psychological and organizational energy available and channels it toward fulfilling the organization's purpose and business objectives. This freed up energy becomes a powerful engine to drive a company's performance to higher and higher levels."

"But when you say that the culture changes and a culture of creativity emerges, what exactly are you talking about? What *is* organizational culture?" Dan beseached.

"Good question, Dan," Thomas beamed, thankful that he was finally contributing positively. "I want to spend the rest of this session addressing this very question, starting with a fundamental definition of what organizational culture *is* and how it develops.

"As I mentioned the very first day, reality is a product of human creativity—reality is man-made. But it's easy to forget that we are its *creators* and *builders* because we *reify* it and defend it as if it were objective truth. We find ourselves saying, 'That's just the way the world is'—even though it's not. A large part of human culture is created and sustained through organizations. Whether we're talking about families, tribes, professional associations, social clubs, churches, or *Fortune 500* companies, organizations are a product of human creativity—they are man-made 'things' that don't exist naturally in our world. So the process of deconstructing, changing, and reshaping your organization's culture must also be a product of human creativity—something that can be learned."

"Can you give us a practical example of how this works?" Rena asked. The group was nodding as if she'd articulated a question they were all thinking.

"Sure! I'll use the development of culture in my own family as an example of how the process works." Thomas smiled, eager to share his personal experience.

"Since the first year we were married, I noticed that my wife, Grace, cut off both ends of the Easter ham before she put it into the oven.[123] One year my curiosity got the best of me and I said to her, 'Grace, I've never asked before, but why do you cut off both ends of the ham?'" He indicated the blunted ends with both hands. "She casually responded, 'I don't know. That's what my mother always did, and that's what she taught me to do.'

"Since her behavior seemed to have no rationale, I made a suggestion: 'Well, why don't you make this the last year you do it—it wastes so much meat.'

"'Well, why don't you mind your own business,' she barked, 'and let me prepare Easter dinner the way I always have!'

"I couldn't figure out where all that push back and energy came from. She flat-out refused to even entertain my suggestion."

Several members of the group were laughing, as Thomas asked, "What do we call this kind of excess energy?"

"A red flag!" the group bellowed almost in unison.

"That right." Thomas let out a laugh. "So I got even more curious and called my mother-in-law.

"'Mom,' I said cautiously through the telephone, 'when you make Easter dinner, do you cut off both ends of the ham?'

"Without hesitation she said, 'Absolutely, that's the way we've always done it in our family!'

"So I asked, 'But *why* have you always done this in your family?'

"'Well, I don't know,' she replied, sounding curious herself. 'That's just the way my mother taught me to do it. You should call her.'

"So I did." He laughed again. "And you know what she said?" Thomas switched to a little old lady's voice. "'Well, Thomas, I used to have an oven that was so small, that the only way to fit the ham in was to cut off both ends.'" Thomas used both hands to show how small the oven was, as the entire group roared with laughter. "It's true—it's really true," he said, guffawing along with them.

After regaining his composure, Thomas went on, "Three generations ago, when Grace's grandmother discovered that the Easter ham wouldn't fit in her oven, cutting off both ends was a logical solution to a practical problem. Year after year as Grandma continued to cut off both ends, this practical solution became a habit, went on automatic pilot, and slipped below the surface of consciousness." He pulled a marker out of his shirt pocket and wrote the words CULTURE = AUTOMATIC PILOT on the flip chart in large block letters.

"Today, even though Grandma owns a larger oven, she still cuts off both ends. This tradition became a shared cultural practice for how Easter dinner should be cooked in her family—taken for granted—the way it was. My wife saw this activity, but never questioned it, and when she started cooking Easter dinner, she not only cooked a ham, she cut off both ends without asking why. Four generations later, Grace is passing this tradition on to our children who've never seen an Easter ham without both ends cut off nor do they think to even question it."

"This was the point of my question to Patrick this morning about the origin of the five clans on this island," Cindy said with the passion of insight. "He had no idea how the clans got their names, that was just the way it had been since the beginning of time."

"That's exactly what I was thinking when you asked the question," Thomas shot her an index finger. "Culture is culture whether it's Patrick's clan, the rituals of the Cargo Cult, holiday traditions about Christmas trees and Easter bunnies, or the culture in your organization. Culture is created and changed in much the same way regardless of where it's found."

"Probably the best critique of the various views of organizational culture is Kotter and Heskett's work. They boil many of the theories in the literature down to three major models, then describe the strengths and weaknesses of each. Not surprisingly, their three models are called Theory One, Two, and Three. I want to review each of them briefly.

Thomas turned to the flip chart and wrote the words THEORY ONE in large red letters. "Theory One argues that companies should develop 'strong cultures.' A strong culture aligns purpose, core-values, and goals down through the organization; creates high levels of motivation in employees; and develops structures and controls that are not bureaucratic and don't stifle the creative process.[124] But while companies with strong cultures have a robust sense of internal stability, an overly *introverted* focus can cause the company to become out of touch with changing trends in the business environment."

He wrote the words THEORY TWO in large blue letters on the flip chart, then faced the group. "Theory Two claims that the strength of an organization's culture is not as important as whether it 'maps' to and tracks what's going on in the business environment. Companies who adopt Theory Two build a culture that is contextually and strategically responsive to changes in markets, competitors, customer preferences, and other forces and pressures in the business environment.¹²⁵ But, while Theory Two cultures reflect the business environment at a given point in time, a company with an overly *extraverted* focus may lack the internal cultural strength and stability to keep up with change over time."

Thomas turned to the flip chart and wrote the words THEORY THREE in large black letters, then circled this option with the red and blue markers. "Theory Three *combines* the introverted and extraverted cultures I just described and holds them in a dynamic tension. In other words, these companies have a culture that allows them to internally adapt *and* respond to a constantly changing business environment. Rigorous studies have shown that this is the most effective approach to long-term, sustainable performance, especially when companies focus on all three organizational constituencies: customers, employees, and shareholders."¹²⁶ He paused for a minute, scanned the facial expressions of the group for questions, then concluded, "I use Theory Three when I work with organizations."

It's the same rubber-banding principle of growth that needs to happen between me and Mom, Rena thought, as the connection between organizational culture and personality fixation became clearer. *An introverted or extraverted focus in an individual or an organization's culture only becomes a problem when it's done in excess—when it's fixated. Hmm...I'll bet the other indices of the MBTI predict cultural attributes that go beyond these three theories.* Rena logged this insight in her journal.

"Let's go back to the example that I used on the first day about Cindy's one-person shoe company and connect it to a model of how organizational culture emerges. Cindy's original vision for building a company happened within an Historical Context." Thomas pointed to Step 1 on the flip chart.

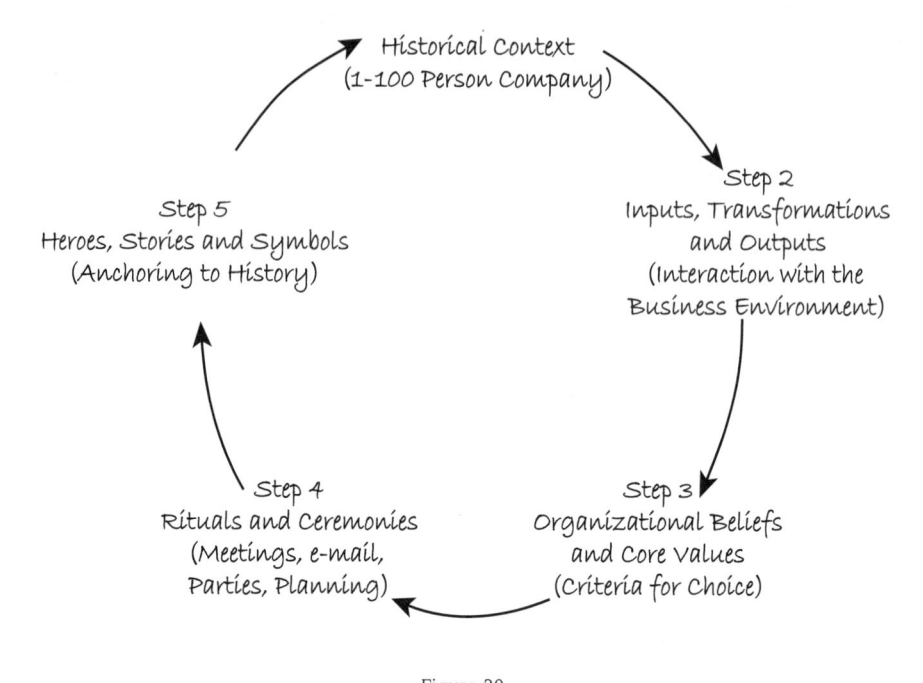

```
                    Historical Context
                   (1-100 Person Company)

    Step 5                                    Step 2
Heroes, Stories and Symbols           Inputs, Transformations
  (Anchoring to History)                    and Outputs
                                         (Interaction with the
                                          Business Environment)

       Step 4                               Step 3
  Rituals and Ceremonies           Organizational Beliefs
   (Meetings, e-mail,                 and Core Values
    Parties, Planning)               (Criteria for Choice)
```

Figure 30

THE EMERGENCE OF ORGANIZATIONAL CULTURE

"The Historical Context included how much start-up revenue she had, what her core competencies were, how big her fabrication facility was, the number of hours she was willing to work, as well as what was happening with customers, competitors, and the overall business environment at that time."

Thomas pointed to Figure 30 and continued. "In Step 2, Cindy performed every company function—she designed, fabricated, and sold the shoes she made. In other words, she took the *inputs* of raw materials like leather and shoe designs, and used her knowledge and shoe-making skills to *transform* them into *output*—products customers would buy. Sometimes she planned and documented these processes, and other times she designed, fabricated, and sold shoes by trial and error. She succeeded in some endeavors and failed at others."

Thomas pointed to Step 3 on the flip chart. "The sum of her

interactions with the business world concretized into a set of beliefs and core values about how business ought to be done—they became criteria of choice for how to 'make it' in the shoe industry."[127]

"After a couple of years in business, the regularity and pulse of Monday morning meetings with vendors, answering e-mail orders from her Web site, and entering financial information become like rituals that she did without thinking about them—they were on automatic pilot." Thomas pulled a marker out of his shirt pocket and pointed to Step 4 on the flip chart. "Over time, treating herself to a dinner around Christmas time as a reward for working hard all year long, and a weekend away in January to plan next year's strategy became like ceremonies that punctuated her organizational calendar year after year."

"So she developed traditions and ways of doing business that spanned her personal and business life," Maggie commented.

"That correct," Thomas replied. "They were woven into the fabric and tapestry of her reality."

Thomas pointed to Step 5 on the flip chart. "As time progressed, she remembered reading articles in *HBR* that taught her timeless principles that enabled her to face and overcome difficult business challenges. She adopted OD methods taught by business heroes like Jim Collins and viewed success stories like Jack Welsh of GE and Ben and Jerry's Ice Cream as having symbolic meaning about how to make her business sustainable. Over time, these exemplars, heroes, and symbols begin to anchor Cindy's one-person company to broader and deeper dimensions of history and her cultural context in a transcendent way.

"As Cindy moves through cycle after cycle of interacting with the business environment, concretizing beliefs and core values into structures and systems, codifying rituals and ceremonies, and anchoring these to the broader culture and history, her traditions, habits, and ways of doing business become increasingly *solidified*. Her company becomes real—a 'thing.' It's an interrelated network of business processes, bank accounts, equipment, Web sites, customer and supplier relationships, and traditions. Eventually the activities in the five steps may even become *reified*, but they do not become organizational culture.

"By definition, a one-person company can't have a culture. It only has Cindy's personality and how effectively she works with and communicates to customers, suppliers, and other business associates. It's her personality preferences that determine how the company thinks about and organizes its work, but again, *her* personality is the only driver of organizational performance because Cindy does every single task in a one-person company."

Thomas pointed back to Figure 30. "Then her business grows to ten employees and Cindy becomes a *manager* and a *leader* of other people, so in Step 2 she probably won't spend much time making and selling shoes. Instead, she'll be training her employees to do those tasks, and she'll focus on managing and leading the company. When employees deviate from their training, Cindy reinforces the lessons and mentors them until they 'get it right'—and getting it right means doing it Cindy's way. Even if she uses the first two strategies and allows a culture of creativity to emerge, innovations and improvements proposed by workers will probably have to be approved by her. When her preferences for how work is done are adopted by employees and are *successful* in generating revenue and solving internal and external business problems, her personality preferences begin to create organizational culture here in Step 3. Her personality preferences get *externalized* and *codified* into organizational structures and systems—the way things are done in Cindy's company.

"Kotter and Schein argue that all that is needed to create organizational culture is for employees to work together for a significant period of time and be more or less successful at what they do.[128] Over time, the solutions and ways of working that the group develops slip below the surface of organizational consciousness and go on automatic pilot, like the once practical solution of cutting off both ends of the ham."

"I see what Cindy's rituals and ceremonies are like, but what do these activities look like for an entire organization?" Rena asked.

"In a company with as few as ten employees, *organizational rituals* begin to develop," Thomas answered, pointing to Step 4 on the flip chart. "Rituals are repetitive daily, weekly, or monthly activities like the Monday morning status meetings, weekly or monthly reports, regular memos and e-mails, daily social activities around the coffee pot or at the water cooler, and informal group meetings in the lunch room. Employees who work in the company develop *individual rituals* around repetitive activities. For example, the daily commute, where you buy breakfast, reading your e-mail when you get to the office, returning phone calls, your time management system, a laptop-palm combination or yellow stickies, and how you interact and communicate with coworkers and superiors. The synthesis of organizational and individual rituals becomes a large part of a company's cultural reality—what it's like to 'work' there."

Thomas paused as people wrote in their journals, then pointed to Step 4 again. "Organizational ceremonies are company-sponsored special events that individual employees participate in—celebrations like the annual Christmas party, staff retreats, staff awards, or the company picnic. They become public expressions and ceremonial reminders of the history, beliefs, and core values of the organization.[129] Activities like the annual strategic planning meeting, quarterly strategy, budget, operational reviews, and the annual performance appraisal process become ceremonies and traditions that embody and transmit organizational culture."

"So now, rather than Cindy taking herself out to dinner as a reward for her hard work, she has to take the whole company out," Frank laughed at the thought of mushrooming overhead costs.

"You got it." Thomas smiled.

"Some of those ceremonies, like performance appraisals, involve pain, weeping, and gnashing of teeth," Bethany blurted, and laughter pealed throughout the group.

"Yeah—ceremonial suffering and annual blood-letting at review time," Thomas groaned and laughed along with the group.

"In Step 5, people identify organizational heroes, stories, and symbols that embody and teach the culture. Heroic stories about how past or present employees have succeeded or failed to solve internal company problems, or conquered challenges posed by competitors, teach new employees powerful lessons about how problems should or should not be handled. These stories also recount and explain important decisions and crucial turning points in the company's history. They become the rationale that allows new employees to make sense of, and identify with, the purpose, core values, corporate identity, and culture of the organization they've joined.[130] Then the cycle shown here in the diagram begins again."

"Now I see why you say culture is created indirectly," Frank commented, beaming with this new insight into the concept of culture. "Owners, managers, and workers go through day-to-day life doing these things, and one day they wake up and that's just the way it's done."

"That's a crucial point Frank," Thomas acknowledged solemnly. "If we use the first two strategies to build a firm foundation, then allow a culture of creativity to emerge, it will. But this requires planning and organizational intent. We consciously build a culture by getting into the spectator role and examining beliefs and core values in Step 3, using rituals and ceremonies to purposely embed the culture we want in Step 4. Then we anchor this consciously designed culture to history with purposely chosen heroic stories and symbols in Step 5.

"So following Covey's thinking in *The 7 Habits*, you can either take a *reactive* approach to culture and let it happen to you, or a *proactive* approach and control your own corporate destiny." Frank nodded, pleased he'd made yet another connection with the material Thomas was teaching.

"You got it!" Thomas beamed as he gave Frank a thumbs up.

"It reminds me of the emergence of personality type," Rena chimed in. "You wake up one day and realize that you *have* a personality the same way you discover that you *have* an organizational culture."

"Absolutely." Thomas nodded. "Most people believe that a person's leadership style and how they interact with the business environment is what creates organizational culture. But my own experience in working with people has taught me that focusing on leadership style doesn't reach far enough back into the root causes to describe the mechanism that creates organizational culture. It's really human personality that creates leadership style, which in turn creates organizational culture."

"That's Schein's argument," Cindy realized aloud. "He says that in new companies, leaders create organizational culture, then forget that it's their creation. Once the culture's reified, it acts like a social mirror that creates and selects leaders, so only managers who embody *that* culture ever get promoted."[131]

"Right." Thomas shook his head in hearty agreement. "*That* an owners' and managers' personality creates and affects organizational culture is pretty clear. *How much* it influences groups of people and how those influences play out in the development of organizational culture is fertile ground for future research. The question is, how reliably can we describe and predict the causal effects of a leader or manager's personality on employees, and how well can we *predict* and empirically verify the kinds of performance problems the organization will encounter as a result of these fixations and decision-making biases?

"Here's what I find most interesting. When we know an owner or manager's Enneagram and MBTI type, more times than not we can reliably predict what their decision-making biases are and link them to negative effects on organizational performance. Even when an owner or manager denies this, if we follow the red flags of excess energy, unintended consequences, defense mechanisms, and the unconscious perspective, we frequently find they have blind spots about their work performance in these very areas.

"If they keep denying that they behave according to personality, just put a video camera on them and watch their behavior. Eighty percent of the time they'll behave according to their type," Thomas said boldly, confident about the factuality of his point.

"I think you've been demonstrating the predictive power of personality throughout the entire workshop, using our fixations as a way of diagnosing and correcting the performance problems we've shared in class and in our case studies." James shook his head admiringly.

"Thanks, James...." Thomas blushed, taken back by the rare compliment.

"Okay," Thomas recovered, "let's move on. Organizational culture is socially transmitted through conscious and unconscious training and modeling at all levels in companies. Like cutting off both ends of the ham, we follow cultural norms without any understanding or explanation of where these behaviors and attitudes originated. People don't have the psychological and organizational energy to continually resist the subtle but profound dictates of culture even if they wanted to, so they slowly give in, and the cultural norms begin to mold how they work, make decisions, communicate, and interact with coworkers, managers, and the 'system.' This is another example of how culture *happens to us*—it's created *indirectly*. It avoids detection as a causal mechanism for organizational performance problems because it stays just below the surface of organizational consciousness. Culture doesn't show up on organizational assessments because people are honestly unaware of what they're doing and why they're doing it."

"But if organizational culture is so unconscious, how *does* it get modeled and passed on from person to person?" Rena threw up her hands in confusion.

"Let me discuss the three most important ways in which this happens," Thomas said, holding up a calming hand. "First, most of what we communicate to others is embodied in unconscious behaviors. Stephen Covey argues that up to fifty percent of all communication is non-verbal body language. Not surprisingly, that's why our children learn much more from what we *do* than anything we *say*.[132]

"Second, Richard Dawkins suggests that cultural transmission is analogous to the way genes are propagated. *Genes* are the replicators of biological life, but Dawkins discovered things called *memes* as the replicators of cultural life.[133] Memes are powerful ideas and concepts that are 'infectious' in the sense that a meme can take over and monopolize a large segment of a person's belief system."

"I'm a little confused," Rena confessed. "Does he give practical examples of what memes are?"

"Yes," Thomas assured. "Have you ever had the words to a song play over and over in your mind and you couldn't get it to stop?"

Every member of the group nodded vigorously.

"That's a meme. Memes are ideas or concepts that capture your imagination and literally take it over. Dawkins lists examples like catchy ideas in the lyrics of music, TV commercials that stick in your head, advertisements, and interesting things we read. Memes can be embodied in the philosophical views articulated by philosophers and poets, in styles of dress that we long to adopt, architecture we incorporate into our homes and office buildings, or the power of technology, religion, and other elements of culture.

"In fact, the idea of memes as the transmitting mechanism of culture *is itself* a powerful meme. Just like genes are transmitted from body to body by sperms and eggs, memes are transmitted from one person's brain to another and become beliefs that determine how they see the world." Thomas picked up a note card and quoted Dawkins: "'When you plant a fertile meme in my mind you literally parasitize my brain, turning it into a vehicle for the meme's propagation in the same way that a virus may parasitize the genetic mechanism of a host cell.'[134]

"Think about it." Thomas paused reflectively. "The genetic contribution you make to your children, Rena, halves with each generation. After about three or four generations, most of your genetic contribution will disappear back into the collective gene pool. Memes have much more staying power. I'll bet there isn't one definable gene left in the world from Alexander the Great, but by spreading the memes of Greek culture as he conquered the world, Alexander's presence still exists today in the form of the Corinthian columns on buildings in many of the world's modern cities. In much the same way, organizational culture is transmitted from person to person within companies through memes."

Focus on developing and propagating memes, Rena, the Inner People whispered in her mind. *That's the best way to make a creative difference in life—to make your presence matter.*

"A third way that culture is transmitted unconsciously comes from research on the brain." Thomas pointed to the side of his head for emphasis. "Goleman argues that the part of the human brain that produces and senses deep emotions is an open-loop system, meaning our emotional connections to other people help to establish the moods and emotional responses of entire groups of people. So emotions and the characteristics of personality type displayed by top managers in an organization spread down through the line organization."

Thomas picked up another note card and began to quote Goleman. "'Moods that start at the top tend to move the fastest because everyone watches the boss. They take their emotional cues from him. Even when the boss isn't highly visible...his attitude affects the moods of his direct reports, and a domino effect ripples throughout the company.'"[135]

Thomas pretended he was holding the neck of a guitar in one hand and striking a tuning fork with the other. "It's like hitting a tuning fork for the musical pitch 440-A near a guitar—the A string on the guitar will begin to resonate at that frequency. In much the same way, when an owner or manager's mood and personality resonate employees' feelings on an emotional frequency over significant periods of time, robust patterns of organizational culture emerge. Does that answer your question, Rena?"

Rena nodded, satisfied with the thoroughness of his three-part explanation.

"How can I understand the relationship between personality and organizational culture in a company like mine that has a thousand employees?" Lindsey asked, unsure of how she could apply the material to her specialized work environment.

"In larger and more complex organizations," Thomas said turning his attention to her, "the characteristics of personality still manifest themselves as organizational culture, but it's more difficult to identify unambiguously. The most systematic approach to linking organizational culture to personality that I know of is William Bridges's development of the Organizational Character Index.[136] It's based on Carl Jung's pairs of opposing tendencies—the same ones that the MBTI tool is based on—and can be used to type an entire organization. In terms of the Enneagram, Michael Goldberg tries to link organizational culture to

Enneagram type based on his experience as a consultant working with organizations, but he doesn't identify the actual mechanism that creates organizational culture like we've discussed here."[137]

"How do you build a robust Theory Three culture that avoids the pitfalls of reifying it?" Cindy asked intensely. "It's so easy to drift into that unconscious state of reification."

"Great question, Cindy." Thomas clapped both hands together. "The key is have a *firm commitment* to a Theory Three culture that is *disinterested* and that still allows owners, managers, and workers to be creative, improve, and innovate. When employees *reify* culture, they oppose the creative process and defend the status quo as if it were objective truth. When people are seduced by the intoxicating effects of reification, they lose their disinterested perspective. The bottom line is that we must continually be on our guard and always remind ourselves that we are the *creators* and *builders* of our culture. If that culture becomes misaligned with internal forces and pressures or the business environment, we have to deconstruct it—regardless of how long and painful this process is.

"In closing," Thomas began passing out the dive slates, "read through the summary points of the session, then clip it to your BCD so you'll have the material with you underwater." The group scanned the list.

DIVE SLATE SESSION 7 REVIEW

Strategy 1: Find Meaning and Significance in Work
    Practice #1: Experience the Creative Process
    Practice #2: Learn How Fear Inhibits the Creative Process
    Practice #3: Build Inner Collaboration and Alignment
Strategy 2: Use Alignment to Gain Competitive Advantage
    Practice #4: Align the Organization to Speak with One Voice
    Practice #5: Follow the Red Flags to Squandered Energy
    Practice #6: Build a Portfolio of Creative Employees
Strategy 3: Allow a Culture of Creativity to Emerge
    Session #1: The Emergence of Organizational Culture

- *Organizational culture cannot be created directly, but emerges indirectly as the synergistic product of implementing the first two strategies*
- *Culture is culture whether it's the Easter ham, Cargo Cult, or your organization*
- *Kotter and Heskett's 3 theories of culture: (introverted, extraverted, and combined cultures)*

- *Culture emerges by successfully working together over time*
- *The five-step process for developing of organizational culture*
- *Organizations are collective-cultural entities that are led, managed, and changed, one person at a time*
- *Personality is like a magnet in the cultural force field (social mirror creates leaders)*
- *Organizational culture is personality externalized into organizational structures and systems then reified*
- *Culture is socially transmitted by conscious and unconscious (body language, memes, brain as an open loop system)*
- *Avoid reification with firm commitment that's disinterested*

He waited a moment for them to finish. "Are there any questions?" Thomas paused for a moment. "If not, then let's go diving. Anita and Janice will give the dive brief in a few minutes."

"This site is called Barney's Reef, and it should be a nice, easy dive," Anita said excitedly. "There's almost no current, and I'll bet the visibility is over one hundred feet. The back of the ship is tied up to the mooring ball, so let's get in the water, stay along the coral drop-off, then head back to the boat in about sixty minutes. Are there any questions? Okay, the pool's open."

Dan pulled his wetsuit out of the rinsing tank—he had forgotten to hang it up to dry after the last dive. There was nothing he hated more than tugging cold, wet neoprene over his warm body. Minutes later he was alone once again in a world that was so unlike the one he lived in above the water. The overall perspective of the reef was a magnificent image of color, elegance, and teeming life. Dan settled in at a depth of about fifty feet and moved closer to the pinnacle wall. The complexity of life on the reef staggered his imagination. He hovered above an enormous colony of cabbage coral as untold numbers of fish swam in and out of this place that had become their home. They chased each other, then floated above the coral—then chased each other again.

The social structure of the group while underwater went from individual teams of "buddies" to more of a group dive where people dove with whomever they wanted, watched out for each other, but didn't trespass into other people's dive spaces. That's the thing about diving—even when you're with a group of ten people, you still have the solitude of your own psychological space once you're under the water.

There were hundreds of thousands of fish in schools scattered around the reef. Bethany saw an octopus scurry behind a patch of soft coral that was deep purple and hot magenta and was surround by six-foot-high gorgonian fans. Frank saw at least three different kinds of anthias—some were half gold and half purple, others were pink and orange with a bright red fin, still others were deep purple. Then a thick cluster of blue-fin trevally started hunting on the reef and entire schools of small fish moved instantly to escape these predators' movements.

Frank was powerfully moved by species of hard and soft coral that were too numerous to count. The visual orgy of reef fish and the choreographic drama of Darwinian survival was almost overwhelming. As he watched this spectacle, Frank felt the power of the creative process at work within him—motivating him to make major changes in his life.

He needed to honestly face the fact that he'd been bored as an accountant for years, yet he kept working at his business out of his sense of duty and obligation to his family. Frank desperately needed more intellectual stimulation and the time he'd been spending at Fermilab was exerting an increasingly powerful influence on him.

Put your business up for sale—you'll have plenty of money to support your family, the Inner People whispered. *Let Mary Beth run things until you finalize the sale, then let the new owner take care of your Rick problem while you're off getting your Ph.D. in experimental particle physics.*

Frank had always been enthralled by the fundamental elegance of the universe—everything ultimately reduced to six quarks, six leptons, and four forces. Formerly, he'd thought about being a theoretical physicist, but the workshop had shown him that he needed to work on creative acts—the kind that would be expected of an experimental physicist. As part of his doctoral program, he would have to design and physically build portions of an elaborate detector system that would be used to perform the experiment. The data gathered and the results he would analyze for his thesis would be measurements of physical processes that made a difference in the world, creative acts that went beyond the Cartesian world of theoretical concepts he felt so comfortable in.

As he hung at a depth of fifteen feet to do his three-minute safety stop, Frank felt a deep sense of resolution and wondered who he might talk to at Fermilab to get the process going. Then he heard the sound of splashing water but didn't know where it was coming from. A shadow appeared from overhead, and he looked up and saw an arm reaching down into the water from a ten foot long dugout canoe that was directly above his air bubbles. Then a face with wide, brown eyes appeared under the water and a child waved at him with excitement.

~~~~

Once they were back on the boat, Thomas looked for Maggie to discuss her three-by-five. He found her on the back of the dive deck logging her depth, time and nitrogen levels, as well as the underwater marine life she'd seen.

"Hey, Maggie," Thomas said cheerfully, glad he'd found her so easily, "is now a good time to talk about your three-by-five?"

"Sure—I was just finishing up," she replied, eager to discuss the problem with him.

"You know from what I wrote in my case study, and from watching our interaction, that Rena and I have had some tension between us. When you went through those six questions during the session, I was deeply troubled by how the answers would come out if Rena and I were to go through them together. The fact that we're a small business and *I am* the company and she's my daughter makes the situation even more difficult." Maggie looked desperate to find some ray of hope.

"Why don't we just go through the six of them now and get a sense of how the conversation might go between you and her?" Thomas asked, seeing how painful the thought of doing it with Rena was for her.

"Okay," Maggie relaxed, but only slightly. "Number one, 'What does the company really want from the employee?' I want her to gain competency in business development so she can open a branch office in Colorado Springs and eventually take over the company. I've been pushing her in that direction since she came onboard."

Thomas was silent as Maggie charged on to the second question. "'What does the employee want from the company?' She says she wants a nine-to-five job so she can work to live—not 'live to work' like she claims I do. Her husband, Joel, is an ultra-fundamentalist Christian who tells her that she's got to submit to what he says, 'As unto the Lord!' He's a major cause of the problems between her and me," she snapped. "We can't even go through the rest of the questions—we hit a brick wall after the first two." She stopped abruptly, exasperated by the apparent impasse.

"For a person her age, your daughter has profound insight into psychological matters," Thomas offered, trying to give Maggie some perspective.

"I know—I've never seen this side of her before," Maggie concurred.

Thomas said softly, "Given her Enneagram and MBTI preferences and her clear abilities in introspective matters, *are you sure* putting her in business development is the best use of her competencies and talents?"

Maggie stared at him silently as the rhetorical poignancy of his question sank in and dominated her mind. Before she could respond, Thomas said gently, "Look, Maggie, you have to factor personality type into work planning and the assignments you give people. To assign a person to a job that puts them in constant conflict with their personality fixations is to set them up to fail. Quite frankly, that's a problem with your leadership, not Rena's performance. If I were you, I'd find a position in your company that utilizes the strengths she's demonstrated here in the workshop, and get her out of business development as soon as possible."

Maggie was dumbstruck as the truth of what Thomas said gave her new insight into herself and other people.

"If you insist on keeping her in her current position," Thomas placed his hand on Maggie's shoulder in friendship, "you have three choices with regard to her performance. You can accept it, go on trying to change it, or fire her. You think about it."

SESSION 2: COUNTING THE COST

The ship steward just finished placing trays full of finger sandwiches, egg rolls, and warm, freshly baked cookies on the teaching table as Thomas rang the bell for the 11:00 A.M. session to begin.

When everyone had found their seat, Thomas clasped his hands together. "The bottom line of this final session is that becoming a creative organization is difficult—you should count the cost before embarking on this journey. The depth and breadth of cultural change needed to become an *Island of Excellence* is not to be taken lightly because it requires an enormous up-front investment of psychological and organizational energy. This type of deep cultural change disrupts the status quo and challenges an organization's belief structure and way of doing business, so organizations have to really want change badly in order to endure the chaos that the process creates.

"Schein argues that the intensity of disruption of cultural change is the organizational equivalent of psychotherapy for individuals.[138] I liken it to the task of deconstructing our personality fixations, which amounts to changing who we've been for most of our lives. Deep organizational change means creating and sustaining that kind of change for hundreds of people. It requires employees to change part of their professional identities and the way they've done their jobs for years."

"That sounds like a daunting task," James said solemnly, pondering the implications of Thomas's words.

"It is," Thomas said very seriously, "so if you really want to succeed, don't underestimate what it will take to stay the course. I can tell you from personal experience that enormous levels of fear and powerful defense mechanisms become mobilized to resist even the constructive conflict that is required to become a creative organization. In the case of cultural change, Schein dismisses the popular notion that learning is fun because the profound deconstruction of culture is coercive and produces anxiety and fear that is not unlike brainwashing.[139]

"As I mentioned previously, leaders who want to build creative organizations face a dilemma. The creative insurgence required to challenge a company's cultural norms and ignite and fuel the creative process is precisely what creates fear in the hearts of those who guard the status quo. This is why most cultural change initiatives fail." Thomas paused to allow the power of his words to settle into their minds. "Owners and managers wade into the deep waters of the change process, get in over their heads, then decide they don't want change *that* bad! Obtaining sustainable cultural change requires a company to tolerate the uncertainty that deconstructing culture causes long enough, until new cultural norms emerge to replace old ones.

"Kotter and Heskett liken the resistance to cultural change to a mattress or sofa with inner springs.[140] When you sit on a sofa, the force of your body weight changes the sofa's shape, but the springs are designed to return to their original position once the force is removed. In much the same way, leaders use the force of their authority to change the 'shape' of organizational culture, but like a sofa, it resists. When employees *say* they will support change but *do* things to undermine and frustrate it, leaders and managers must increase the amount of force proportionally, and this becomes increasingly difficult to sustain over long periods of time. When leaders diminish, remove, or inconsistently apply organizational force, the culture migrates back to its original shape just like a sofa.

"In fact," Thomas asserted, "Schein argues that most companies don't have the required organizational knowledge and resolve to see the process of cultural transformation through, so I'm admonishing you to *count the cost* before you embark on this journey."[141]

"That sounds like most of the change initiatives I've seen," Bethany scoffed. "Employees passively resist the changes and eventually the initiative loses steam and dies."

"That's often how it happens," Thomas concurred, "and each time employees succeed in derailing an initiative the culture becomes more robust and more difficult to change. It's better not to undertake a process of cultural transformation than to begin, fail, and fatigue your organization with just one more OD 'flavor of the month.'

"The metaphor of pushing on a sofa is the equivalent of changing the organizational structures and systems within which people work, trying to indoctrinate them into new ways of working and problem solving, then monitoring and enforcing the changes. We discussed this in the session on aligning the organization to speak with one voice. But moving beyond this and actually changing the culture requires employees to internalize and adopt these changes as their own. Schein argues that this happens slowly, over time, when people find the *new* ways of working more effective than the *old* ones and can rationally relate one to another. If employees can't make psychological sense out of the change, it will not be sustainable."

"My experience has been that when you try to change even one business process, like the financial accounting system, people find ways to circumvent the new process and still do things the old way," James exhorted.

"Unfortunately, James is right." Thomas shook his head affirmatively. "That's why new software packages that change the way work is done are such powerful tools for organizational change. Leaders and managers don't have to apply increasing levels of pressure to enforce the change. Instead, the new software won't allow employees to work in old, ineffective ways, so they are forced to adopt the change."

"But I've seen situations where people have spent days, weeks, or months using peripheral software packages to make the new system look and work like the old one," James countered.

"Yes," Thomas admitted, "I call those shadow systems and work-arounds. When an employee downloads financial data from a new accounting system into a spreadsheet in order to make it look like the old process, they create a shadow system. This becomes a serious problem when vast amounts of data are decentralized and reside in multiple places. Any system or informal way of doing business that has a parallel existence to formally sanctioned business and work processes becomes a shadow system and a work-around. These misalignments squander enormous amounts of psychological and organizational energy. Luckily, Practice 5 shows us how to follow the red flags that identify them, and Practice 6 challenges us to either get these people and their systems aligned or move them out the door.

"Cultural transformation is so difficult because it involves a multitude of intangibles that are fundamental to organizational life. We already discussed the slow social process by which organizational culture is *formed* using the example of the growth of Cindy's one-person company to an organization with many employees. Identifying these cultural elements, *deconstructing* them, then *reconstructing* an organization on new foundations is a complicated and formidable task." Thomas grabbed a fistful of flip chart paper and turned back to Figure 30.

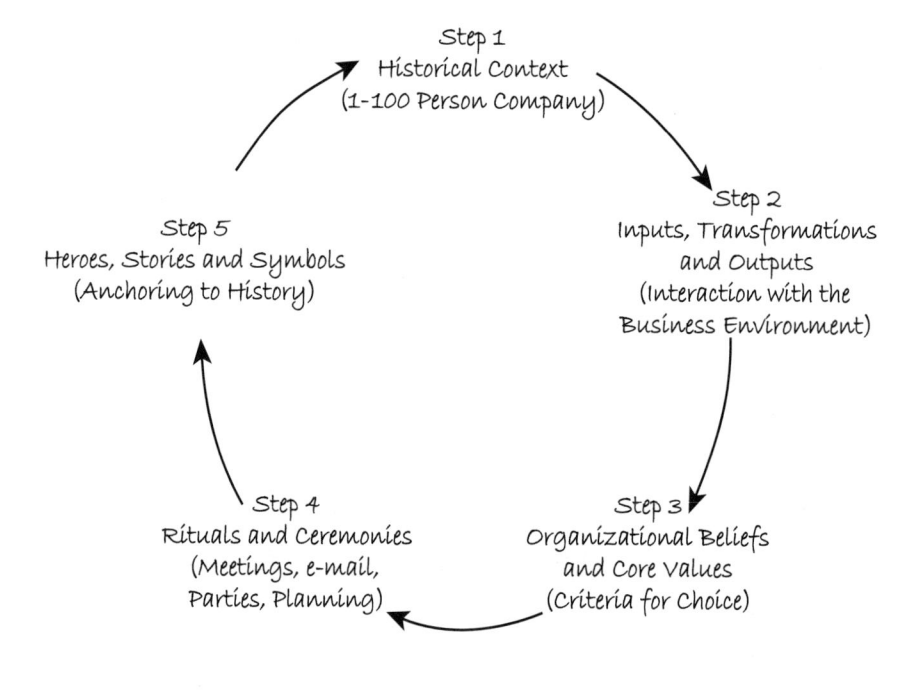

Step 1
Historical Context
(1-100 Person Company)

Step 2
Inputs, Transformations and Outputs
(Interaction with the Business Environment)

Step 3
Organizational Beliefs and Core Values
(Criteria for Choice)

Step 4
Rituals and Ceremonies
(Meetings, e-mail, Parties, Planning)

Step 5
Heroes, Stories and Symbols
(Anchoring to History)

Figure 30

THE EMERGENCE OF ORGANIZATIONAL CULTURE

"As Cindy and her employees went through the five-step process shown here in the diagram, year after year their culture slowly solidified, then slipped below the surface of organizational consciousness, becoming tacit, unquestioned assumptions—like cutting off both ends of the ham." Thomas turned the flip chart page, then turned to face the group. "So transforming these cultural elements requires that we follow the steps shown here on the flip chart." Thomas read the steps aloud:

"FIVE-STEP CULTURAL CHANGE PROCESS
1. *Initiate cultural transformation with the Three Powerful Strategies*
2. *Identify cultural elements and raise them back into consciousness with a disinterested attitude of empathic inquiry*
3. *Deconstruct cultural elements in light of the current business situation*
4. *Reconstruct and implement new, more appropriate cultural elements*
5. *Sustain the transformation using the Three Powerful Strategies*"

"That reminds me of Kurt Lewin's model of unfreezing culture, then allowing it to re-solidify," Frank exclaimed.

"That's correct," Thomas agreed, "or as Schein argues, cultural change is not just about learning something new, it's more about unlearning what we already know—things that function as unconscious psychological or organizational barriers to change.[142]

"So in the same way the culture in Cindy's company was constructed slowly by repetitive cycles of the five steps, transformation requires that these elements be deconstructed then rebuilt on new foundations."

"I'm amazed by an insight I just had," Cindy shouted, as she began to rotate her thinking stone over and over in her hand. "Can I share it with you guys?"

"Sure," the group cried out in unison.

"Okay," Cindy enthused, having received the group's stamp of approval. "Let's say as Vice President of the local village council, Patrick realized that villagers were squandering time and energy that could be used to grow food on building Cargo Cult related air strips and docks. In other words, he realized that this part of his village's culture was ineffective at dealing with the realities of the external world he learned about as a financial consultant in Port Moresby—so he decided to change the culture. He would have to use the same process that I would use to change SciTech's culture: initiate, identify, deconstruct, reconstruct, then sustain."

"That's correct." Thomas clapped his hands together and smiled, pleased with how deeply Cindy was connecting to the material.

"Wow! Your example solidified an insight I was just having." Rena gestured toward Cindy with her hand, as the group encouraged her to share what she was thinking. "Would you please turn back to Figure 30, Thomas," she asked impatiently, then waited as he flipped back to the proper page.

Step 1
Historical Context
(1-100 Person Company)

Step 2
Inputs, Transformations and Outputs
(Interaction with the Business Environment)

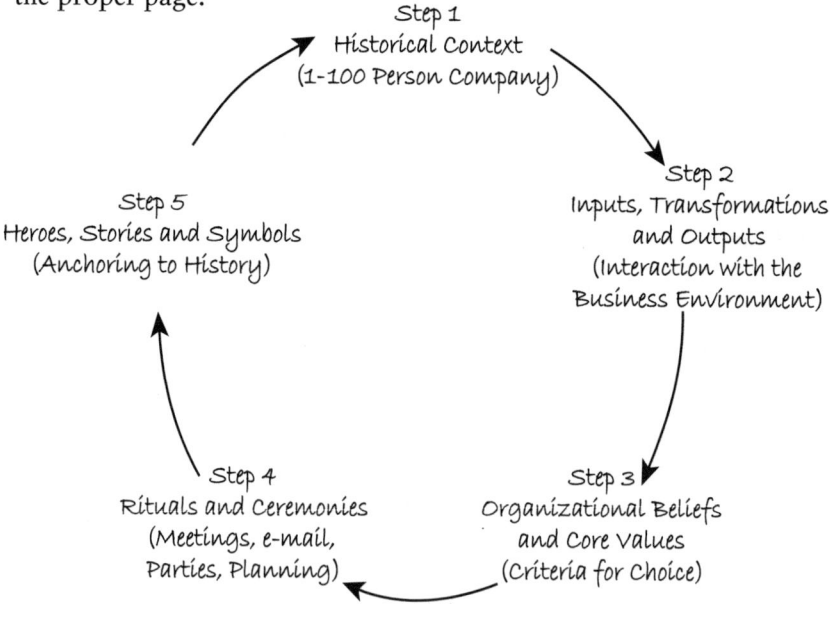

Step 3
Organizational Beliefs and Core Values
(Criteria for Choice)

Step 4
Rituals and Ceremonies
(Meetings, e-mail, Parties, Planning)

Step 5
Heroes, Stories and Symbols
(Anchoring to History)

Figure 30
THE EMERGENCE OF ORGANIZATIONAL CULTURE

"Well, if we think about the five steps on a personal level, especially Step 2 as inputs, transformations, and outputs in *my* life, then the process of creating personal identity and the process of creating culture are almost identical."

Thomas stroked his chin and shook his head slowly and deliberately, clearly impressed with the connection Rena had just made. Maggie and the rest of the group were wide-eyed and stunned by how elegantly she had tied these complex models together.

You can use this same process to build the culture of your new family when you and Troy have a baby, the Inner People whispered to Maggie.

"So what's the difference between a culture of creativity and any other organizational culture?" Frank asked, unusually confused.

"Great question!" Thomas winked. "The elements of a culture of creativity are collective and generic because they are based on the timeless principles of OD and creativity as an intellectual, psychological, and social-cultural process. Consequently, a culture of creativity is not the *specific* organizational culture that emerges through the Five-Step Process. When the strategies of finding meaning and significance in work, using alignment to gain competitive advantage, and allowing a culture of creativity to emerge are *instantiated* within the historical context of a specific organization, they take on the characteristics of a company's unique culture. Probably the best way to see the distinction in action is to codify the five areas of an organization's culture into a document. The codified elements of a culture can be used to guide decision making at all organizational levels and to initiate new employees into the company.

"Does that answer your question, Frank?" He looked up, nodded, then scribbled a note in his journal.

"Given your admonition to 'count the cost,' how do you know

whether or not you should embark on a cultural transformation?" Dan asked. He was trying to establish a framework within which he and Cindy could explore her desire to begin the process at SciTech.

"That's a pivotal question," Thomas replied.

"Using Schein's metaphor of 'offshore oil drilling,' I believe that an organization must be on a burning platform—seriously threatened by financial, political, technological, legal, moral, or internal problems—before they even think about embarking on a process of cultural transformation.[143] In fact, when owners or senior managers approach me about helping them through the process, I always ask them, 'How bad are you hurting?' If they're not under serious pressure, I normally advise them against beginning a cultural change initiative."

"Are you suggesting that only companies who are in serious trouble should consider transforming their culture?" Maggie asked skeptically. "What about successful companies that want to become great companies like the Jim Collins study you discussed on the first day?"

"Good point, Maggie, I was just getting to that," Thomas said. "There are two kinds of burning platforms: reactive and proactive. When a company is on a burning platform that is *reactive*, things have normally gotten so bad that they have no choice but to change or go out of business. In these instances, powerful negative forces, either from employees and the internal environment or competition and other factors from the business environment, challenge the company's survival as a viable entity.

"Burning platforms that are *proactive* are consciously set ablaze by visionary leaders who know that while they're not hurting *now*, they will be if the organization continues on its present course. Or a visionary leader knows that the culture that made them a high-performing, one hundred million dollar company, will not enable them to go to two hundred million dollars, so they design and implement a cultural change initiative; then they set the platform ablaze. In other words, visionary leaders detect destructive forces and pressures from the business environment while they are still a long way off.

"Let me use a metaphor to describe what I mean. Last September, I was in Washington DC when the weather service began broadcasting warnings that a hurricane was heading toward the area, but these reports were three days prior to the storm's predicted arrival. It was a bright sunny Tuesday morning, and I was supposed to fly out on Thursday—the day the hurricane was scheduled to hit. Despite how nice the weather was, I got on my cell phone and changed my flight to Wednesday night. As I flew out of the airport, the weather was clear and warm, but the next day the TV broadcast showed images of one hundred twenty-mile-per-hour winds pounding the East Coast."

Thomas waited for his example to sink in, then continued, "Only a fool wouldn't take action when a company is being pounded by competitors, dissatisfied customers, and decreasing revenues. But seeing an organizational storm coming while it's still a long distance away requires visionary leadership.

"Let me use another metaphor to make my point. From atoms to viruses, many of the most important things in life are invisible to the five human senses and require measurement tools to make them known. In the same way, many of the organizational diseases that kill companies are invisible and must be *made visible* using measurement systems that produce quantitative data that visionary leaders use to drive organizational change. As Kotter and Heskett's studies show, visionary leaders who succeeded at making deep change actually *created* measurement systems that tracked non-financial data like product and service quality, customer satisfaction, and trends in competitor organizations.[144] Then they used these data to demonstrate that change was really needed. Long before the storm hits, visionary leaders use these measurements and data to create an atmosphere of perceived but authentic crisis. In other words, they use financial and non-financial data to set the platform on fire before business problems arrive.

That's exactly what Cindy's been trying to do for the last two years, Dan finally realized. *Now that business has gotten worse because I didn't listen to her, I'm trying to pin the blame on her.* Dan was suddenly squirming in his chair, realizing the enormous mistake he'd made with Cindy.

"Visionary leaders can also set the platform on fire by being creatively insurgent toward the 'sacred cows' and reified cultural elements that grind productive companies to a bureaucratic halt. They challenge the status quo by asking rudimentary questions that deconstruct the tacit assumptions and beliefs that organizational culture is based on. They ask probing questions like, 'What is our purpose? How do we make decisions? Do we satisfy our customers' requirements better than our competition? Why do we work the way we do? What are the consequences of working this way? Why can't we do things more effectively?'"

That's the same type of questions Dana and I have been asking back at the agency, Bethany thought, *and look how much we've shaken things up.*

"How long does it take to make the kind of deep cultural change you're talking about?" Cindy asked, suspecting that Dan wasn't hurting bad enough to begin the transformation process.

"The short answer is that it takes as long as it takes," Thomas said glibly. "The long answer is…it takes as long as it takes."

The group erupted in laughter as Thomas smiled, then moved on.

"Some studies show that a change initiative requires a few years and that the momentum is lost at least once because many employees would prefer that the change does not happen.[145] In many of these cases, visionary leaders had to intervene personally to get the process back on track. In other words, they had to proactively rekindle the fire on the organizational platform and publicly reaffirm their commitment to stay the course.

"My own experience is that in a mature organization where the culture is well solidified and substantial human and financial resources are *dedicated specifically* to the process, it takes at least eighteen months to two years per level of organizational management changed.[146] In other words, if a company's organizational structure has three levels—senior, middle, and front-line managers—deep change will take about eight years of constant work. In the case of major cultural transformations, like Procter & Gamble's conversion to a new manufacturing system, the process took over fifteen years."[147]

There's no way Dan will ever support my efforts to change SciTech's culture, Cindy thought. *Maybe I should just stay at the University of Goroka once I commit.*

"I want to return to one of Nikki's questions from the first day," Thomas said, gesturing toward her. "She asked, 'Suppose you're in a business unit where the top manager won't support the creative process—what do you do then?' A department, division, or group can commit to become a creative organization within a company that doesn't support the creative process. They will have to *force* cultural change by consciously becoming an organizational complex. If that business unit succeeds in becoming a creative organization despite the opposition, they will become an *Island of Excellence* in a sea of mediocrity."

"The more difficult situation that many people face is when *no one but them* wants to build a creative organization." Thomas's voice took on a deeply serious tone. "In the final analysis, you are ultimately in charge of your own destiny. Regardless of what anyone else does, you can still decide to become an *Island of Excellence*, even if this means going it alone."

Thomas sidestepped to the head of the teaching table to get a clear view of the entire group. "I want to close the dive workshop with some final thoughts on where the creative process leads if you follow it faithfully. I was once on a dive trip on the Great Barrier Reef, and one of the crew, who knew a lot about marine life, liked to say, 'The more you know, the more you see.' I never forgot that. It's easy to get overwhelmed by the sheer number of types of coral and fish here in Papua New Guinea. But if you take the time to learn about the different types of sea life, that increased knowledge pays big dividends. Then when you dive a site like Krack-a-Fat multiple times and begin to tease apart the difference between the hundreds of kinds of hard and soft coral, and identify rare fish and mollusks that can be seen nowhere else in the world, the dive seems different every time. The more you know, the more you see.

"The same principle holds with becoming an *Island of Excellence*—the more you know, the more you see. Knowing and seeing is a continuous process of growth that spirals organizations to higher and higher levels of effectiveness."

Thomas turned the page on his flip chart and pointed to the next diagram. "Figure 32 shows the four phases of individual and organizational growth of consciousness, originally proposed by William Howell."[148]

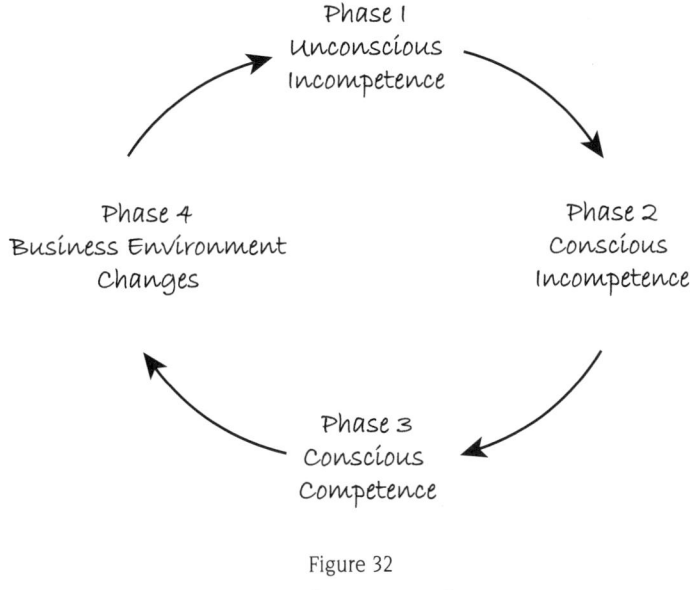

Figure 32
A Cycle of Continuous Growth

Phase 1: Unconscious Incompetence
Phase 2: Conscious Incompetence
Phase 3: Conscious Competence
Phase 4: Business Environment Changes

"Whether it's a problem between a customer and a worker, a manager and a direct report, or developing your instincts about the business environment, most of us begin in the first phase of *unconscious incompetence*. In other words, the organization has a problem, but owners, managers, and workers are largely unaware of it. In the second phase of *conscious incompetence*, the organization is confronted with empirical evidence that identifies the problem, so there's no way to deny that change is needed—employees become fully aware of their incompetence.

"If the organization uses tools like the ones we're discussing here, they move into the final phase of *conscious competence*. This is where the organization reaches its stride of effectiveness and high performance. Eventually, that competency becomes a habit, falls below the level of organizational consciousness, and becomes the tacit knowledge of organizational culture. Then, the business environment changes. New pressures emerge from customers, suppliers, and competitors that the organization is not aware of, and the organization unknowingly finds itself back in the phase of *unconscious incompetence*—but at a much higher level of organizational and personal performance. This process leads to endless cycles of innovation, improvement, and business excellence.

Thomas handed each person a dive slate. "In closing, are there any comments or questions about anything we've covered during the dive workshop?" Thomas put his hands on his hips and smiled.

DIVE SLATE SESSION 8 REVIEW

Strategy 1: Find Meaning and Significance in Work
    Practice #1: Experience the Creative Process
    Practice #2: Learn How Fear Inhibits the Creative Process
    Practice #3: Build Inner Collaboration and Alignment
Strategy 2: Use Alignment to Gain Competitive Advantage
    Practice #4: Align the Organization to Speak with One Voice
    Practice #5: Follow the Red Flags to Squandered Energy
    Practice #6: Build a Portfolio of Creative Employees
Strategy 3: Allow a Culture of Creativity to Emerge
    Session #1: The Emergence of Organizational Culture

Session #2: Becoming an Island of Excellence™
- *The difficulty of becoming an Island of Excellence (collective equivalent of therapy)*
- *Deconstructing organizational culture is like deconstructing personality fixation*
- *Cultural change is like applying pressure to a sofa*
- *Cultural change can happen over time (Schein's view)*
- *Shadow systems to preserve old culture (software)*
- *Reactive versus proactive leadership (how bad are you hurting?)*
- *Kotter and Heskett—create measurement systems to drive change*
- *It takes as long as it takes (2 years per level)*
- *Using the three powerful strategies increases the probability of cultural change, but does not ensure that it will happen*
- *A business unit can become an Island of Excellence (changes starts in the middle and move horizontally across the organization and then up through the line organization*
- *The more you know, the more you see (cycles of continuous growth)*

He waited another moment for them to finish reviewing the dive slate.

"I just want to say how much your teaching and passion about the material have meant to me," Lindsey gushed, and the group broke into a thunderous round of applause, except for Dan, who was lost in thought.

Thomas threw up his hands in acknowledgement, then took a slight bow. "Thank you, and since I know you're all anxious to get into the water, *for the very last time*, let's go diving."

Most of the group dispersed and began getting their equipment ready for the dive, but Dan sat motionless in his chair, looking deeply troubled. Thomas walked over, put his hand on his shoulder and asked,

"Dan—are you alright?"

"She's been right all along," Dan lamented, finally seeing the light. "Cindy's been trying to tell me how to turn the company around for the last year, and I've fought her every step of the way—she's truly a visionary leader." Dan was utterly distraught, as Thomas pulled up a chair and tried to comfort him, knowing that Cindy had already decided to go to Goroka.

"Dan," Thomas said compassionately, "let me ask you some questions that I just want you to think about, not answer. When have you ever been late or missed deadlines? Even when problems come up, don't you always handle them? Certainly, Cindy's MBTI and Enneagram type give her a longer range perspective than you, but why are you so hard on yourself?"

"If you only knew…" Dan moaned. Tears were beginning to well. "As hard as I appear to be on her and others, I'm ruthlessly hard on myself. I'm tired of beating up on myself. I'm my own worst enemy, my biggest critic, I carry out my own condemnation, judgment, and sentencing, but I don't know how to stop—I'm so consumed by self-loathing." Dan's hands went to his face, and his shoulders started to heave as he fought back the sobs. Thomas put his hand on Dan's shoulder to console him.

"Listen to me, Dan," Thomas said. "I want you to try to understand what I'm about to say, alright?"

Dan nodded, wiping errant tears from his face with the back of his hand.

"You're the victim of fundamentalism," Thomas said as gently as he could. "Unfortunately, the word fundamentalism has become associated with right wing conservatism, but they don't have a monopoly on it. My view is that fundamentalism is a *rigidity of mind* about an issue or worldview whether it's on the right or the left. The world is full of left wing, table-pounding liberals who are every bit as fundamentalist in *their* way of thinking as the right wing counterparts they point their fingers at in judgment. Fundamentalism is about personality fixation, reifying our personal beliefs and values, defending them as objective truth, and refusing to entertain others' views about reality. So don't focus narrowly on how you dismissed Cindy's long-term vision for the company, take on the big picture task of freeing yourself from your fundamentalist mindset."

Dan was playing back in his mind how, throughout the trip, he had been picking on Cindy like a little boy picking at a scab—he just couldn't let her alone. The conflict was apparent to others, especially James, and Cindy increasingly withdrew from interactions with him. Something about the notion of fundamentalism clicked in Dan's mind like a key turning a deadbolt lock. Dan felt the transforming power of the creative process at work within him, inspiring him to face this dysfunctional part of his personality, to move beyond it, and to begin the process of becoming an *Island of Excellence* back at SciTech and in the rest of his life.

Powerful elements of creativity were unleashed as Dan began to find the courage to follow Cindy's advice about long-term strategic planning, abandoning the BPR effort, and not laying anyone off. He decided that together they would use the timeless principles they learned at the dive workshop to pursue a long-term solution to SciTech's technological, human resource, and cultural problems—just as Cindy had suggested all along. But authentic organizational change would have to begin with him.

The creative process was calling Dan to stop hammering on himself and others so hard. He realized he had actually *manufactured* pressure and anxiety, projected it onto others, then deceived himself into thinking he was being driven by outer demands. His fear that he needed to push himself relentlessly to counter a hidden propensity to be lazy was simply out of touch with the reality of his long-term performance. The creative dimensions of his personality were inviting him to operate at a more natural pace where he worked diligently on a problem, then allowed the Inner People and the creative process to take over. Experiencing the natural rhythm of his own creative process would help Dan to encourage his employees to work in similar ways and find meaning and significance in their work. It would also allow him to enjoy life and find that inner place of peace and serenity that he wanted so desperately.

"You need to go talk to Cindy," Thomas advised, as he observed the welcome change occurring in Dan.

"I know—I'll talk to her after this dive," Dan replied, feeling a sense of hope for the first time in years.

"Come on," Thomas smiled, as he nudged Dan, "after all the stink you made about Nikki, you don't want to be late for the dive brief."

The two men laughed quietly, both appreciating the value of their relationship.

When Dan and Thomas arrived late, Anita raised an eyebrow, then winked in jest. She could tell they were tardy for good reason. She then turned to the others and began the dive brief. "The name of this dive site is Krack-a-Fat, and I'll let Artie tell you what that means in Australian if you're interested." The crew laughed and Artie blushed.

"There are thousands and thousands of schooling fish on this dive," Artie whispered to Cindy and James, "and the guy who named the site said he always was, well…excited by the time he got back to the surface."

Anita frowned playfully as she saw Artie describing the play on words to James and Cindy, then shook her head and continued, "We're going to do two dives here, and when you get into the water, you'll know exactly why. We're tied up to a mooring on the pinnacle of the dive site, and it looks like the current is moving at a pretty fast clip. So I'm going to have everyone hop off the back of the boat, swim against the current till you get to the mooring line attached to the bow, then move hand-over-hand down the line to the top of the pinnacle. Once you get there, move on top of the reef and kick as hard as you can till you reach the front edge of the pinnacle. Don't get discouraged about how fast the current is moving—just keep kicking! Once you fight your way to the front of the reef, find a non-living piece of the coral, set your reef hook, then relax and enjoy the fish action.

"Are there any questions?" Anita projected her voice strongly. "Okay, the pool's open."

Frank jumped in the water with a fully deflated BCD, began to drop down through the water column, and immediately felt the force of the current pressing against his body. He swam to the mooring line and began to descend, but had trouble descending with one hand on the line and his camera in the other. He decided to forgo Anita's advice and just swim to the top of the pinnacle holding his camera gear as streamlined as possible to minimize the drag from the current. With his camera flat against his chest, Frank put his head down and kicked as hard as he could. After a few minutes he looked up at the boat about forty feet above him then out at people who had already reached the top of the pinnacle. He was making some progress, so he put his head down and kept kicking—harder.

His breathing rate continued to increase, and after a few more minutes he looked up to get his bearings. He had not gone much farther, but he was now about eighty feet below the boat with a long distance to go to reach the top of the pinnacle. As he kicked furiously, his depth gauge told him he was now one hundred feet below the boat and no farther along, so he began to panic. Fifteen minutes into the dive, he abandoned his plan to reach the pinnacle and started kicking vertically, up, back toward the surface of the water as the current took him farther and farther out to sea, and the boat slowly disappeared from sight.

Noting his nitrogen levels, Frank didn't want to surface too quickly, but every second that passed took him farther from the safety of the boat. As is so often the case, currents run slower at depth, so as he ascended—eighty feet, sixty, forty—the movement of the water increased to over three knots. He tried to remain calm. *Breathe, relax, think,* he told himself, but the prospect of being lost at sea in this strange land so far from home now had Frank in a complete panic.

When he finally surfaced and inflated his BCD, Frank was a quarter mile from the boat. He inflated his bright orange, four-foot-high safety sausage, then depressed the button on his pressurized dive alert, which let out a deafening, high-pitched whistle blast, hoping to signal the ship. He could see the tiny figures of crew members on the deck, but no one heard him, nor did they see the safety sausage. Frank drifted farther and farther out to sea. Finally, he stuck his safety sausage under his arm, shoved his index finger into his left ear to mute the sound, then held the activation button down to produce a longer and more desperate blast. Then he waved his brightly colored safety sausage frantically in the air. One of the crew heard the faint sound of the dive alert, turned in Frank's direction, and acknowledged his position by waving his arms. Within seconds, two crew members were racing toward him in a twenty-foot-long skiff.

When Maggie reached the front edge of the pinnacle, there were schools of barracuda, jacks, and trevally swimming around her—thousands upon thousands of fish. A solitary tuna about four feet long was cruising around in the blue amidst white tip, hammerhead, and gray reef sharks. Every square inch of the top of the pinnacle was covered with a rainbow of hard and soft coral—many more species than she could identify. Her eyes were riveted to the underwater show on the reef.

Maggie cared deeply about coming across well and looking good, but she knew that diving was the great equalizer that stripped away many of her façades. On previous dive trips, she could project the image of being a seasoned, world-traveled diver with the latest, high-end equipment. She always talked a good game about where she'd been and the diving she'd done, but once she got into the water, the façade was over. The duplicity of her big surface talk was always juxtaposed with the reality of a diver who lacked the key skills of buoyancy, relaxed breathing, and the confidence to deal with strong currents. Underwater this could not be hidden—it's there for all to see.

But this trip had been different. The new split fins she wore, her reef hook, and the pointers that Anita had given her about handling current really improved her dive skills. The gap of duplicity between what she said about her dive abilities on the ship, and what she was now able to do in the water had narrowed substantially, and for the first time since she'd been diving, Maggie *was* what she'd always claimed to be. This was true integrity—narrowing the gap between what she said and what she did. It was a lesson that Maggie knew she needed to apply in other areas of her life as well.

As she clung to the rope that was attached to her reef hook, the current moved her well-shaped body through the water like the wind pressing against a kite. Thomas's discussion about continuous growth became a meme that captivated her mind. Somehow she knew that she was moving into another phase of her life. From this day forward, Maggie would pursue *inner* standards of excellence, regardless of what was dictated by the world around her. The transforming power of her creativity was inspiring and motivating her to become an *Island of Excellence*—a person who was inner-directed and committed to veracity, not deceptive image.

The creative process was calling Maggie to concretize her commitment to inner standards of excellence and integrity into a creative act by keeping her promise to Troy and having a baby. She needed to learn to view the totality of her life—professional and family—as having symbolic meaning and new dimensionality. By bringing another child into the world, Maggie and Troy would make a lasting contribution and difference in life—just like she had done with Rena.

Maggie felt empowered with the disinterested attitude and courage she needed to chart a new path for the Spinner Group. As president, Maggie would maintain forty percent ownership of the company, make Shane the COO, and allow him to buy up to twenty-five percent of the remaining shares. She would sign the final thirty-five percent of the company's stock over to Rena with the understanding that she alone would own it, not her husband, Joel, and that she would pay for it over time. Following Thomas's advice, Maggie would create a Director of R&D position and offer it to Rena. Her primary responsibilities would be to explore the psychology of marketing and identify ways to use the Enneagram and MBTI typologies to serve their clients' needs, and appeal to the deep motivations of customers in market niches. Once pregnant, Maggie would back away from the day-to-day operation of the organization and let Shane run the company without fear for Rena's security.

∿∿∿∿

During the two-hour surface interval between the second and third dives, Dan decided to find Cindy and apologize to her for being so critical and intolerant throughout the trip. He began his search on the top deck—her favorite spot. Sure enough, she was there sunning herself and reading.

"Hi," he said in as pleasant a voice as he could muster.

Cindy looked up and said, "Hey," then continued reading.

"Can I sit for a minute?" Dan gestured to the empty deck chair a few feet away. "I've got something I need to talk to you about."

"Sure—pull up a chair," she replied nervously as she closed her book and set it down on her deck chair. "I've been wanting to talk to you about something too." She sat up and faced him as he pulled the chair up close and sat down.

Take a deep breath and relax, Cindy, she told herself. *You've got to follow your calling—you've given Dan enough of your life.*

Dan hesitated a moment, swallowed hard, and tried to get control of his emotions—he felt shame for having treated one of his only friends so thoughtlessly. "Cindy...you've known me for a long time and you probably understand me better than anyone, maybe with the exception of my wife."

Dan's lip quivered as he continued speaking. "I'm sorry I've been so hard-nosed and intolerant with you on this trip. The poor performance of the company this last quarter has put me under too much pressure, and what we've been learning here at the workshop has made me realize that what's happened at SciTech is not your fault, and I should have listened to you all along."

Dan reached out and touched Cindy's hand. "Look—let's forget about BPR and laying people off, and when we get back we'll sit down and map out a plan for cultural change based on what we've learned here—what do you say?"

Cindy was so deeply moved by Dan's sincerity, tears began to flow from her eyes. She lowered her head into her hands and wept quietly, finally releasing the emotional pressure their ongoing conflict had placed her under. This silent and vulnerable display of emotions only increased the intensity of Dan's self-condemnation and judgment over his behavior. After an interminable time of emotional catharsis, Cindy regained her composure and spoke.

"Look, Dan, I've had my part in making things tough on you, too, and for that I am truly sorry. But I'm tired, old friend," she wiped the remaining tears from her eyes. "I'm tired of swimming upstream, fighting an inner pressure that just doesn't want to be president of SciTech—and never has. I told you how I felt about being a manager when you hired me as your first employee, and quite frankly I feel more strongly opposed to it today. I took over for you as president because you said you needed some time to figure out what you wanted out of life, and despite my reservations, I gave you two years—out of friendship."

Dan knew she was speaking the truth with love.

Cindy moved her chair still closer to Dan, looked intently into his eyes, shook her head from side to side, and said, "I need a break, Dan." She let the gravity of her words ring out into the air, then repeated, "I desperately need a break. I know you're probably going to think I'm leaving you midstream when the chips are down, but I need a one-year leave of absence. I've decided to call the Dean and take him up on his offer to help start that electronics and computer science program at the University of Goroka."

Dan's eyes widened and his jaw dropped as fear turned to panic then cascaded into anger that he knew he'd better not express. Finally it turned into deep sorrow and regret. He closed his eyes, shook his head, and said softy, "Cindy, what am I going to do without you and your incredible ideas and energy?"

"You'll be just fine." Cindy smiled. "You always are. I'll work with you and the management team to develop an interim plan to fill as many of the holes as I can with existing people. You have some really bright folks on our staff, but you need to get to know them and give them a chance. You learned as much as I did here at the workshop, let's take it all home and start planning and implementing before I leave."

"I really don't want you to go, Cindy," Dan whispered gently, "but I don't blame you for wanting to follow your passion, and I certainly won't do anything to stop you." Dan reached out and hugged Cindy tightly. Before they could exchange another word, Anita rang the bell for the 3:00 P.M. dive briefing.

"Saved by the bell." Cindy let out a nervous laugh.

"We'll talk about it later," Dan grinned through mixed emotions.

It feels odd that we're not gathering around the wooden teaching table, Cindy thought as she walked onto the dive deck and grabbed her wetsuit.

As the group assembled, they were all looking forward to this final dive together. "Okay, we're going to do Krack-a-Fat again." Anita rubbed her hands together in eager anticipation of getting in the water. "It looks like the current is running much slower than on the first dive, but essentially we'll do the same profile. Those of you with cameras should find it much easier to get to the pinnacle. Are there any questions? Okay, the pool's open."

Lindsey's ears were still giving her trouble so she descended slowly and hung at about fifteen feet holding her nose and blowing gently to equalize the pressure inside and outside her head. As she gazed alternately at the mooring ball on the water's surface then down to the reef below, she felt the transforming power of the creative process being channeled through the metaphor of exploring the red-flag interactions in her intimate relationships and the below-surface issues that inhibited them. This was her path to becoming an *Island of Excellence.*

She was past the major hurdle of the ISO 9000 certification, and the workshop helped her see how shortsighted she'd been about the program's long-term benefit to the company. When she returned to the office, she'd just go with the flow like Mario had been suggesting all along, back off her professional life, and focus more energy on relationships.

She realized that her life was perfectly aligned to get the results she was getting, so rather than avoid intimacy with men, she would begin dating and work through whatever problems arose with her analyst.

The creative forces within were giving her the courage and humility to become an *inner diver*—to face her problems using the tools she learned in the workshop and the conscious intent of moving beyond them.

I still love my cat, Oscar, she thought, *but I'd really like to get married.*

THE JOURNEY BACK TO THE REAL WORLD

By 4:30 P.M.. everyone was back on board *Origin* sharing stories about the fish and coral they saw, and rinsing the salt water off their dive gear in two large rinse tanks, then hanging them up to dry in preparation for the long sea-journey back to Walindi. The ship was filled with activity as people gathered masks, fins, and other pieces of equipment from their area and returned the weight belts they'd borrowed from the ship. One by one each member of the group scattered to their cabin to put on dry clothes. Some people found a comfortable chair on one of the ship's decks and relaxed with that novel they hadn't quite finished, while others took a catnap before dinner. At about 5:15 P.M., the crew was done preparing the boat for the overnight journey, so they pulled off the mooring ball and the ship headed south.

By 7:30 P.M., some of the group had gathered on the Lido deck for a before-dinner drink and to talk about their dive experiences. Brazilian jazz music played softly in the background.

Anita poked her head out of the dining room and said, "Hey, do you guys want to see the group video I've been shooting all week?"

There was a resounding "Sure!" from almost everyone.

Rena started to follow the others, but in a quiet, calm voice that was not typical of her mom, Maggie said, "Hey, Sweetheart—can I talk with you for a minute?"

"Sure, Mom," Rena said cautiously, caught unaware. Maggie led her daughter to the back of the Lido deck where they sat on the cushioned seats that lined the ship's back railing.

"Rena, there are two things I'd like to say." Maggie smiled, trying to reassure her that there was nothing wrong.

Maggie moved closer to her daughter, put her arm around her and said, "First of all, I want you to know how proud I am of you for the fine woman you've become. I've always felt that way, but I tend to keep those feelings buried deep down inside, or hidden in my journal where they don't do anyone any good—not even me. I know I've been hard on you most of your life, driving, pushing, always demanding that you do good, better, or be the best. I'm going to work on that, and I'm going to try harder to appreciate the fine person you are rather than always trying to get you to become someone or something else."

Then Maggie looked directly into Rena's eyes, took both of her hands in hers, and said, "Second, I've decided that I'm going to try to get pregnant when I get back home. It's not only a promise I made to Troy, but the workshop has helped me understand that it's something I need to do to round out my life and grow personally. I know I've always argued that your view of trying to enjoy the simple things in life—like family—are unimportant compared to succeeding and making something of yourself by corporate standards. But I've come to see the validity in your view of the world. I promise that I won't push you anymore about doing business development and going to Colorado Springs. We need to create a place for you in the company that you're more comfortable with—one that uses the innate talents and gifts that you've demonstrated here at the workshop. I've got some ideas for how we might do that, but let's not discuss them now. What I'm really thinking is, if our values and lifestyles are closer together, maybe we can become closer too."

"I'm happy for you, Mom!" The young woman hugged Maggie

with tears of joy streaming down her face.

Maggie's eyes were tearing up now, too, as she whispered, "Remember, this is our secret—I don't want others to know before Troy does."

"Okay, Mom—I promise!" Rena hugged her tighter than she ever had before.

As the 8:00 P.M. bell rang to call people to the table, Maggie wiped the tears from her face and said, "Come on—let's go get a drink and celebrate!"

Dinner did not deviate from the ritual of a fine linen table cloth, china, silverware, sparking crystal, and the soft light from the candles. People laughed and became animated as they either relived an experience they had diving or poked fun at some mannerism that Thomas had when he taught—and Thomas laughed right along with them. Dan, James, and Cindy were talking about Cindy's move to Goroka and what the path forward ought to be for SciTech in her absence, including the possibility of getting Dan's daughter Carol to help out. Given his new understanding about his sexual desires, James was more than glad that Dan had talked him into coming to the dive workshop because he now felt he could nip the precarious situation with Shawna in the bud.

Rena was enjoying the last night together with the group, but the talk she'd just had with Maggie had caused her to withdraw and reflect, so she was viewing this dinner scene from some inner distant place. Now that Maggie had finally given her the kind of affirmation she'd needed and promised to stop pushing her to do tasks she wasn't suited for, Rena wasn't really sure what she wanted. The depth and honesty of the things that Maggie had shared with her ignited the transforming power of the creative process and inspired her to become the very best—an *Island of Excellence*.

Rena's mind had been powerfully captivated by the notion that creating and disseminating memes was a more powerful way to make a lasting contribution to life and leave a legacy than having children. One way to do this would be for her to take a more active role in running the company, using the unique talents and skills that she possessed, and to put off children rearing till a little later in her life. Despite the pressure that her husband Joel was putting on her to settle down into a conventional lifestyle, Rena needed to find other ways to demonstrate that her presence mattered in the world.

As she sat in the glow of candles on the dinner table, powerful forces of human creativity were giving her the courage to stand up to her husband's demands to have a family now, and instead to take up the challenge of developing the healthy characteristics that Maggie possessed. Ironically, Rena would soon find out, the path of taking over a leadership role at the Spinner Group was also the road that would lead her toward psychological growth and help her discover her true identity as a person. Her challenge was to find a way to do this on her own terms, in her own way, utilizing her strong points. Since Maggie had decided to get pregnant and turn her attention toward the domesticated side of life, her mom would need her now more than ever. Rena decided that she would be equal to the task.

Wednesday morning, when they disembarked at the Walindi Plantation Resort, almost all of the group had already planned to stay another day to relax and see some of the sites in PNG that were *above* the water before they began the long trip home. As they checked back in at the front desk, the group had a teary-eyed goodbye with James and Thomas who were both heading to the airport to catch a mid-morning flight back to Port Moresby.

James had to get back to his parish. Thomas needed some time alone to clear his head after the long and arduous task of teaching the dive workshop, so he was headed to the Loloata Island Resort—a private island just twenty minutes south of the Port Moresby International Airport. In the local Motu language, Loloata means "one hill," and that's precisely what it is—a one hundred-foot-wide, half-mile-long slice of land that rises about twelve stories vertically out of the ocean.

Thomas arrived on the island just as lunch was being served, so the young men who picked him up and drove the boat took his luggage to his private villa, and he sat down to a magnificent buffet of freshly prepared meats, fruits, vegetables, and breads.

After lunch, Thomas decided to take a walk along the top ridge of the island. He climbed the two hundred tightly winding stone steps that spiraled up to a nicely manicured grass path that led from one end of the island to the other. He walked slowly and deliberately, taking in the magnificent view of Bootless Bay, the Coral Sea, and the mainland of PNG. All he heard was the sound of the wind and the pounding surf on the shoreline over one hundred feet below. When he reached the lookout point at the other end of the island and peered over the edge, the cliff dropped twelve stories vertically down to the shoreline of the Coral Sea.

Thomas stood silently staring over the surface of the ocean, and once again he felt the calling of a voice from the deep, drawing him downward, imploring him to descend, this time into his inner depths—*just keep going*. As he continued plummeting to greater and greater inner depths, the images of a tragedy, long past, resurfaced in his consciousness. Twenty years earlier when he was first certified to dive in Kona on the Big Island of Hawaii, he was with a group of four divers and a dive instructor named Sarah. It was an easy dive, sixty-foot depth, at a site called Hoover's, just off the shoreline where the Kona airport was located. Sarah was about fifty feet away on the ocean bottom with her head looking down into the coral trying to focus her camera on a rare fish.

One of the other divers looked like he was struggling with his buoyancy, so Thomas watched him, uncertain if he should intervene. Then the diver seemed to relax. Relieved, Thomas turned and started kicking toward Sarah. A moment later he heard someone banging furiously on an air tank with a dive knife. When he turned he realized that the diver who'd been struggling was no longer breathing. Sarah was able to quickly get the incapacitated diver to the surface, and into the boat. She immediately began giving him CPR, but he was dead from a massive heart attack before he ever reached the surface. Thomas was traumatized by the incident. He wasn't the dead man's dive buddy, nor was he leading the group like Sarah, but somehow he'd always felt responsible for not realizing what was happening while the man was struggling and still alive.

His memory of the lifeless eyes of this dead diver laying on the deck of the boat and the introspective power of the discussion he'd had with Cindy about the ultimate meaning of human existence *merged*, as myriad questions pounded in his mind like a twenty-pound sledgehammer. Where do we come from? How should we live? Where did that diver go when he died? Are we really just "stuff"—protons, neutrons, and electrons combined into molecules and cells that disappear from day-to-day life, or is there an eternal, spiritual dimension to humans? What is the ultimate meaning and significance of life? If there's wisdom and knowledge that transcends our physical existence and the quantitative and measurable edicts of science, how do we discover these things? Given the fact that reality and personal truth are a matter of perspective, is there *ultimate* truth? How can we know it? If we claim to know it, how do we know we're not deceived? And the questions continued relentlessly...

While Thomas had advised Cindy to allow the creative process to answer her troubling questions and to synthesize the personal, collective, and biological dimensions of her life into a personal myth, he'd not done this himself about his own questions.

Those who cannot do, teach! the Inner People reprimanded him silently with a parody on Woody Allen's words. *To whom much is given, much is required*, they went on, now using a biblical admonishment.

The transforming power of the creative process was confronting Thomas with his own duplicity, an inherent danger every teacher faces—not applying their pedagogy to themselves, not walking the talk.

The sweet smell of salt air, the whirling wind, and the pounding of the ocean on the shore below brought him back to the surface of consciousness with renewed commitment to be true to himself, as well as others, and to the wisdom he espoused. He would renew his commitment to integrity—to identifying and narrowing the gap between what he said and what he did. Having become a teacher, he would hold himself to a higher standard than others. From this day forward, he would follow the path of the questions posed from within, regardless of where it led. It was time for Thomas Rose to discover his own personal myth.

Epilogue (One Year Later)

LINDSEY

Mario had been right about the increased revenue and profitability that ISO 9000 certification would bring to the company, so Lindsey was able to back off her obsessive seventy-hour weeks, watch over the edifice of paper that the program created, and focus her time and energy on her personal life. She began attending the local synagogue she was raised in and joined various professional organizations in the hope of meeting quality men. She had some limited success at dating and with the help of her analyst, Lindsey was working through the interpersonal issues that manifested themselves as red flags.

MAGGIE

Maggie was six months pregnant and tests revealed that she and Troy would have a little girl that they'd decided to name Destiny. Shane was COO and twenty-five percent owner in the Spinner Group, and Rena had agreed to purchase an additional thirty-five percent over time and accept the new position as Director of Research and Development. With Shane as COO, Maggie backed away from her day-to-day involvement in the company and resumed her graduate studies in world religions at

CU Boulder, where her primary emphasis was on the mystical Sufi sect of Islam.

CINDY

Cindy had been living at the Lutheran Guest House in downtown Goroka for about ten months, working at the University, and making a difference in the lives of her students and the villages they came from. Artie became a good friend, and Cindy spent lots of time visiting with his mom and daughter, Eva, who lived in a village just outside Goroka. Cindy felt connected to, and was eager to learn about, the culture and ancient religions of PNG. She was debating whether or not to accept an offer to spend a second year at the university and fully establish the new computer science and electronics program. She was torn between her desire to make a difference in PNG and her commitment to Dan to return to SciTech after a year.

THOMAS

Thomas was on a spiritual journey that began by revisiting the religious skepticism that plagued him during his graduate studies in the philosophy of science at Berkeley. To his surprise, his major professor had quit teaching, gone into the Christian ministry, and invited Thomas to visit him in his new life. Their discussions created a deep longing within Thomas to visit Israel and to see for himself what others claimed was the basis of their faith and the truth.

FRANK

Frank had sold his accounting firm for just under a million dollars and was deeply involved in a Ph.D. program in experimental particle physics at the Enrico Fermi Institute at the University of Chicago. He would write his thesis on an experiment that would be conducted at Fermilab.

Within six months, the new owner had fired Frank's son-in-law, Rick, and Frank intervened and used his influence and business connections to find him a job in Honolulu.

BETHANY

Upon her return, Bethany had convinced Dana to conduct the Island of Excellence Organizational Assessment and use the timeless principles she'd learned in the workshop to implement the customer focus initiative throughout the agency. Now as Dana's Deputy—second in charge of the entire agency—Bethany was trying to learn how to better manage her stress. She and Matt were more hopeful about getting pregnant, despite having endured a painful series of miscarriages.

NIKKI

Nikki was terminated the day she returned to work and refused to grovel to John about moving back into her former position in the marketing department. The six months she was unemployed were stressful, and she found solace in yoga, meditation, and her growing belief in New Age Spirituality. She finally found a job working for a competitor company, where she used her network of relationships to win back her best customers. Once her strategy became clear to John, he asked her to come back, but she refused even though it would have meant more money. She realized that the success she had attained under John's leadership *required* a frenetic pace and lifestyle that negatively reinforced personality fixations she was now committed to changing.

JAMES

When James returned, he molded his relationship with Shawna into one that had appropriate boundaries, and changed his approach to strategic planning—guided by Thomas's admonition to do the right thing for the right reason. The Diocese appointed him to head the highly visible committee that would make recommendations for deconstructing the culture of the Episcopal Church as a way of returning to the primitive faith of the early Christians. With the retirement of Bishop Sands, the search committee approached James about becoming the next bishop. This would force him to publicly declare his position on controversial issues that previously he'd been able to avoid, but he felt powerfully called to pursue this leadership role.

RENA

Rena's husband, Joel, forbid her to buy part ownership in the Spinner Group and get more involved in her professional life, but she followed the calling of the creative process anyway. He continually threatened to leave her if she didn't obey him, and although torn by her evangelical Christian values, one day she called his bluff and told him to move out. Within weeks, he had filed for a divorce. Rena accepted Maggie's offer to become the Director of R&D and began a graduate program in organizational psychology at CU Bolder. She planned to write her dissertation on using the principles of personality to determine customer motivation and buying preferences. She was happy to be single and free to pursue her calling, and Shane had been showing more and more interest in spending time with her outside the office.

DAN

Cindy returned to SciTech for six weeks prior to leaving for PNG. She was able to help Dan develop a new management team out of people who formerly found it difficult to work with him. Together, they were able to implement a transition plan that took both a short- and long-term focus to turning the company around. In her absence, Dan hired Thomas to conduct the Island of Excellence Organizational Assessment and to raise the entire organization's consciousness about how personality fixation can undermine and frustrate the creative process and produce a culture of fear. In full recognition that he had to model change personally in order for it to be successful, Dan and his new management team were using the Three Powerful Strategies to begin the exciting, life-changing process of cultural transformation and becoming an Island of Excellence.

A BRIEF SUMMARY OF THE CHARACTERS' PERSONALITY TYPES

This section is written for readers who have some knowledge of the Enneagram, the Myers-Briggs Type Indicator (MBTI), or both and want to understand how they have been woven into the tapestry of the characters in the *Island of Excellence* story. Readers who want a technical explanation of the theoretical synthesis of the Enneagram, the MBTI tool, and depth Jungian psychology should continue reading into the next session.

The nine characters in *Island of Excellence* are based on the nine personality types of the Enneagram, the sixteen personality types of the MBTI, and my actual experiences with people who have these personality preferences. The Enneagram and MBTI tools not only describe and predict how we behave, they also describe many of the deeper motivations and cognitive preferences that underlie and produce our behavior. The reader can use the descriptions below as a quick reference when reading *Island of Excellence*, and obtain more detailed descriptions about the Enneagram and the complete listing of all sixteen MBTI types from the sources mentioned below and in my endnotes.

Perhaps the most accessible treatment of the Enneagram is the work of Don Richard Riso and Russ Hudson, more specifically, in *The Wisdom of the Enneagram* and *Personality Types*. Two excellent works on the MBTI tool are Isabel Briggs Myers' books *Gifts Differing* and *Introduction to Type*. For a discussion of the process by which the dominant, auxiliary, tertiary, and inferior functions unfold over the course of a lifetime, see C. G. Jung, *Psychological Types*, John Beebe, *Integrity in Depth*, and Anne Singer Harris, *Living with Paradox: An Introduction to Jungian Psychology*.[149]

Figure 34 shows how the nine characters are distributed around the diagram of the Enneagram. A matrix of how the Enneagram and MBTI preferences unfold for each of the characters can be found on page 207.

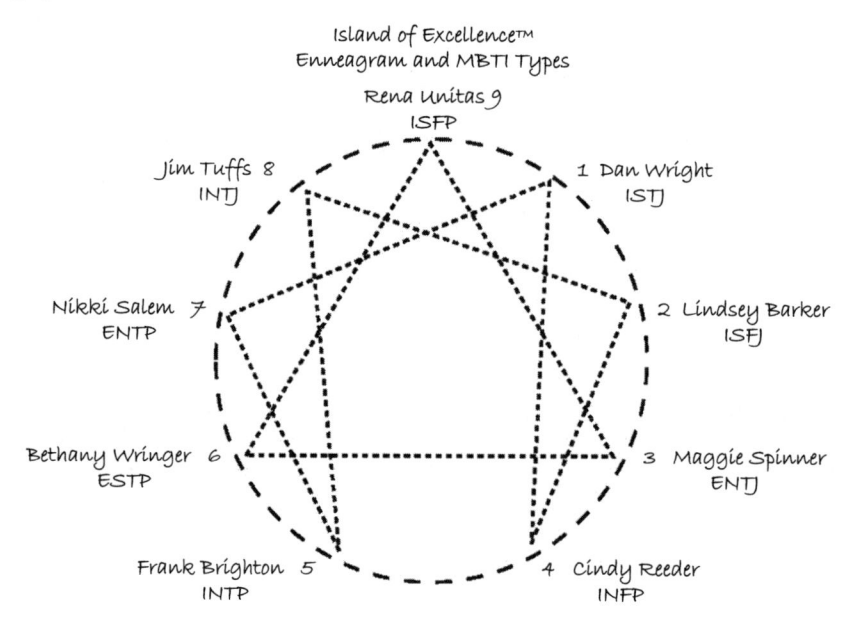

Island of Excellence™
Enneagram and MBTI Types

- Rena Unitas 9 — ISFP
- Jim Tuffs 8 — INTJ
- 1 Dan Wright — ISTJ
- Nikki Salem 7 — ENTP
- 2 Lindsey Barker — ISFJ
- Bethany Wringer 6 — ESTP
- 3 Maggie Spinner — ENTJ
- Frank Brighton 5 — INTP
- 4 Cindy Reeder — INFP

Figure 34
ISLAND OF EXCELLENCE ENNEAGRAM AND MBTI TYPES

The descriptions below describe the process of psychological growth and individuation as happening in the first and second half of life. There is no hard and fast rule for when the second half of life begins, but Jung argues that it starts at about age thirty-five. The lifelong challenge of psychological growth and individuation for all the *Island of Excellence* characters is to assimilate the compensatory, contradictory, and largely unconscious aspects of personality described below into consciousness, with the goal of establishing harmony and psychological balance in their lives.

DAN WRIGHT (ISTJ, TYPE ONE)

In the first half of their life, Type Ones like Dan Wright are principled, orderly, self-controlled, perfectionistic, and self-righteous. "They are teachers, crusaders, and advocates for change: always striving to improve things, but afraid to make a mistake."[150] During this same time period, Dan's dominant and auxiliary functions, interacting with life experiences, create his ISTJ preference. Introverted sensing (dominant) allows him to recall the concrete realities of past experience and use them as a lens through which to slowly and methodically evaluate present situations and future possibilities. Extraverted thinking (auxiliary) uses external criteria and objective analysis to arrive at logical, defendable decisions that are bounded by established rules, regulations, and principles.[151]

During life's second half, people with Dan's personality profile will be confronted by Inner People with Enneagram characteristics of Types Four and Seven (Shadow and Inferior Self), and the MBTI tertiary and inferior functions (introverted feeling and extraverted intuition), and challenged to integrate these characteristics into their lives.

LINDSEY BARKER (ISFJ, TYPE TWO)

In the first half of their life, Type Twos like Lindsey Barker are caring, interpersonal, empathic, sincere, and warm-hearted. "They are friendly, generous, and self-sacrificing, but can also be sentimental, flattering, and people-pleasing."[152] During this same time period, Lindsey's dominant and auxiliary functions, interacting with life experiences, create the ISFJ preference. Introverted sensing (dominant) allows her to recall the concrete realities of past experience and use them as a lens through which to slowly and methodically evaluate present situations and future possibilities. Extraverted feeling (auxiliary) evaluates external situations or internal ideas based on values that are cultural acceptable and strives to maintain positive, caring, and harmonious relationships by reading the feelings of other people and caring for them.[153]

During life's second half, people with Lindsey's personality profile will be increasingly confronted by Inner People with Enneagram characteristics of Types Eight and Four (Shadow and Inferior Self) and the MBTI tertiary and inferior functions (introverted thinking and extraverted intuition), and challenged to integrate these characteristics into their lives.

MAGGIE SPINNER (ENTJ, TYPE THREE)

In the first half of their life, Type Threes like Maggie Spinner are adaptable, success-oriented, self assured, attractive, and charming. They are "Ambitious, competent, and energetic, they can also be status-conscious and highly driven for advancement."[154] During this same time period, Maggie's dominant and auxiliary functions, interacting with life experiences, create the ENTJ preference. Extraverted thinking (dominant) uses external criteria and objective analysis to arrive at logical, defendable decisions that are bounded by established rules, regulations, and principles. Like a sixth sense, introverted intuition (auxiliary) uses flashes of insight from the unconscious archetypal meaning behind everyday life, to read between the lines of human interactions, to be insurgent against the status quo, and to search for life's deeper meaning.[155]

During life's second half, people with Maggie's personality profile will be increasingly confronted by Inner People with Enneagram characteristics of Types Nine and Six (Shadow and Inferior Self) and the MBTI tertiary and inferior functions (extraverted sensing and introverted feeling), and challenged to integrate these characteristics into their lives.

CINDY REEDER (INFP, TYPE FOUR)

During the first half of their life, Type Fours like Cindy Reeder are introspective, romantic, self-aware, sensitive, and reserved. "They are emotionally honest, creative, and personal, but can also be moody and self-conscious."[156] During this same time period, Cindy's dominant and auxiliary functions, interacting with life experiences, create the INFP preference. Introverted feeling (dominant) is a subjective decision-making process where an internal system of values and beliefs is used as the basis of decisions about the external world with the goal of creating internal harmony and allowing others to have their own values and beliefs. Extraverted intuition (auxiliary) scans the external world looking for abstract patterns, connections and innovative ways of doing things and generates possibilities for how the world could be by thinking "outside the box."[157]

During life's second half, people with Cindy's personality profile will be increasingly confronted by Inner People with Enneagram characteristics of Types Two and One (Shadow and Inferior Self) and the MBTI tertiary and inferior functions (introverted sensing and extraverted thinking), and challenged to integrate these characteristics into their lives.

THOMAS ROSE (INFJ, TYPE FOUR)

During the first half of their life, Type Fours like Thomas Rose are introspective, romantic, self-aware, sensitive, and reserved. "They are emotionally honest, creative, and personal, but can also be moody and self-conscious."[158] During this same time period, Thomas's dominant and auxiliary functions, interacting with life experiences, create the INFJ preference. Like a sixth sense, introverted intuition (dominant) uses flashes of insight from the unconscious archetypal meaning behind everyday life, to read between the lines of human interactions, to be insurgent against the status quo, and to search for life's deeper meaning. Extraverted feeling (auxiliary) evaluates external situations or internal ideas based on values that are cultural acceptable and strives to maintain positive, caring, and harmonious relationships by reading the feelings of other people and caring for them.[159]

During life's second half, people with Thomas's personality profile will be increasingly confronted by Inner People with Enneagram characteristics of Types Two and One (Shadow and Inferior Self) and the MBTI tertiary and inferior functions (introverted thinking and extraverted sensing), and challenged to integrate these characteristics into their lives.

FRANK BRIGHTON (INTP, TYPE FIVE)

In the first half of their life, Type Fives like Frank Brighton are perceptive, intellectually alert, insightful, and curious. "They are able to concentrate and focus on developing complex ideas and skills.... They can also become preoccupied with their thoughts and imaginary constructs."[160] During this same time period, Frank's dominant and auxiliary functions, interacting with life experiences, create the INTP preference. Introverted thinking (dominant) uses an internal process of logical analysis to precisely categorize ideas and concepts then uses them to debate and question the external world and as the basis of decision-making and finding the "truth" of situations. Extraverted intuition (auxiliary) scans the external world looking for abstract patterns, connections and innovative ways of doing things and generates possibilities for how the world could be by thinking "outside the box."[161]

During life's second half, people with Frank's personality profile will be increasingly confronted by Inner People with Enneagram characteristics of Types Seven and Eight (Shadow and Inferior Self), and the MBTI tertiary and inferior functions (introverted sensing and extraverted feeling), and challenged to integrate these characteristics into their lives.

BETHANY WRINGER (ESTP, TYPE SIX)

In the first half of their life, Type Sixes like Bethany Wringer are committed, security oriented, reliable, hard working, responsible and trustworthy. They are "Excellent 'troubleshooters,' they foresee problems and foster cooperation, but can also become defensive, evasive, and anxious—running on stress while complaining about it."[162] During this same time period, Bethany's dominant and auxiliary functions, interacting with life experiences, create the ESTP preference. Extraverted sensing (dominant) vividly experiences the concrete, tangible details of the physical world through the five senses and tries to connect theoretical explanations of people, events, and objects to the material reality of the present moment. Introverted thinking (auxiliary) uses an internal process of logical analysis to precisely categorize ideas and concepts then uses them to debate and question the external world and as the basis of decision-making and finding the "truth" of situations.[163]

During life's second half, people with Bethany's personality profile will be increasingly confronted by Inner People with Enneagram characteristics of Types Three and Nine (Shadow and Inferior Self) and the MBTI tertiary and inferior functions (extraverted feeling and introverted intuition), and challenged to integrate these characteristics into their lives.

NIKKI SALEM (ENTP, TYPE SEVEN)

In the first half of their life, Type Sevens like Nikki Salem are busy, productive, playful, high-spirited, and practical. "They can also misapply their many talents, becoming over-extended, scattered, and undisciplined."[164] During this same time period, Nikki's dominant and auxiliary functions, interacting with life experiences, create the ENTP preference. Extraverted intuition (dominant) scans the external world looking for abstract patterns, connections and innovative ways of doing things and generates possibilities for how the world could be by thinking "outside the box." Introverted thinking (auxiliary) uses an internal process of logical analysis to precisely categorize ideas and concepts then uses them to debate and question the external world and as the basis of decision-making and finding the "truth" of situations.[165]

During life's second half, people with Nikki's personality profile will be increasingly confronted by Inner People with Enneagram characteristics of Types One and Five (Shadow and Inferior Self) and the MBTI tertiary and inferior functions (extraverted feeling and introverted sensing), and challenged to integrate these characteristics into their lives.

JAMES TUFFS (INTJ, TYPE EIGHT)

In the first half of their life, Type Eights like James Tuffs are people who are powerful, aggressive, self-confident, strong and assertive. They are, "Protective, resourceful, straight-talking, and decisive, but can also be ego-centric and domineering."[166] During this same time period, James's dominant and auxiliary functions, interacting with life experiences, create the INTJ preference. Like a sixth sense, introverted intuition (dominant) uses flashes of insight from the unconscious archetypal meaning behind everyday life, to read between the lines of human interactions, to be insurgent against the status quo, and to search for life's deeper meaning. Extraverted thinking (auxiliary) uses external criteria and objective analysis to arrive at logical, defendable decisions that are bounded by established rules, regulations, and principles.[167]

During life's second half, people with James's personality profile will be increasingly confronted by Inner People with Enneagram characteristics of Types Five and Two (Shadow and Inferior Self), and the MBTI tertiary and inferior functions (introverted feeling and extraverted sensing), and challenged to integrate these characteristics into their lives.

RENA UNITUS (ISFP, TYPE NINE)

In the first half of their life, Type Nines like Rena Unitus are easy-going, self-effacing, accepting, trusting, and stable. "They are usually creative, optimistic, and supportive, but can also be too willing to go along with others to keep the peace."[168] During this same time period, Rena's dominant and auxiliary functions, interacting with life experiences, create the ISFP preference. Introverted feeling (dominant) is a subjective decision-making process where an internal system of values and beliefs is used as the basis of decisions about the external world with the goal of creating internal harmony and allowing others to have their own values and beliefs. Extraverted sensing (auxiliary) vividly experiences the concrete, tangible details of the physical world through the five senses and tries to connect theoretical explanations of people, events, and objects to the material reality of the present moment.[169]

During life's second half, people with Rena's personality profile will be increasingly confronted by Inner People with Enneagram characteristics of Types Six and Three (Shadow and Inferior Self) and the MBTI tertiary and inferior functions (introverted intuition and extraverted thinking), and challenged to integrate these characteristics into their lives.

SYNTHESIZING THE ENNEAGRAM, MBTI TOOL, AND POST-JUNGIAN PSYCHOLOGY

This section is written for readers who have considerable background knowledge in the Enneagram, MBTI, Jungian psychology (or all three) and who want a brief explanation of the theoretical and empirical synthesis of these three bodies of knowledge as found in the story and teaching sessions of *Island of Excellence.*

As I've mentioned elsewhere, for a number of years, prior to writing my first book, *Diving In,* my understanding of the Enneagram and of depth Jungian psychology ran on two separate tracks.[170] I found myself teaching and using them side by side with no elegant way to integrate the Enneagram's *empirical* power to describe and predict motives and behavior, with the *theoretical* power of a model of personality I had developed that echoed Jung's work, but was not strictly speaking Jungian. The synthesis of my post-Jungian view and the Enneagram are described in *Diving In,* and I will only recount enough of what I published there to explain how the MBTI preferences relate to this previous work.

In *Diving In,* I adopted the view that the *structure* and *dynamics* of the human personality as proposed by Jung were essentially correct. More specifically, personality was not just the fixations of Ego like so many Enneagram writers suggest, rather the human personality is composed of the three distinct levels of psychic structure articulated by Jung:

- consciousness,
- the personal unconscious, and
- the collective unconscious.[171]

I defined consciousness as a psychological space in the human brain within which we are inwardly aware of, and present to, whatever resides there. Like the RAM memory of a computer into which we load programs, consciousness has no mental contents of its own. Whatever appears in that space, we are aware of *right now*.

The personal unconscious consists of the enormous memory storage locations in the human brain. When you are able to recall your mother's name, the title of your favorite song, or the name of your second grade teacher, this information is retrieved from memory locations in the personal unconscious. Until these bits of knowledge are summoned into the space of consciousness, they exist, but we are not aware of them.

The third level of psychic structure is the collective unconscious—the biological-psychological interface that is like two sides of a coin and is where the hamburger or salad you ate for lunch becomes the inspiration to develop a new marketing plan, redesign your living room, or accomplish any other of life's tasks. On the biological side of the coin, the interface contains the genetic map that helps determine who we will become *physiologically*. The psychological side of the coin, called the collective unconscious, contains the *archetypal map* that helps determine who we will become *psychologically*. At birth, a person's archetypal map already defines many fundamental aspects of his or her personality, including *collective* cognitive and motivational preferences that eventually manifest themselves *personally* as their Enneagram and MBTI type preferences. The specific concrete nature of our personality develops over time based on our life experiences and the family and cultural environment in which we grow up. While discussions about the degree to which these personality characteristics are innate or learned are interesting, the view I express in *Island of Excellence* echoes LeDoux's—innate or learned characteristics are simply two different conduits into the same synaptic registers of the brain. If a personality characteristic does not reside in our brain, then it doesn't exist.

As *collective* archetypal preferences unfold from the moment of birth, energetic experiences from interactions with the world begin to cluster around their central core. Like individual strands that are wound and build up into a ball of yarn, this cluster of experiences becomes what Jung calls a *complex* and what I call one of the *Inner People*. When collective preferences like extraverted sensing or introverted intuition *adhere* in one of the Inner People based on actual life experience, they become *personalized,* and this signals the emergence of individuality. Increasingly, the cognitive and motivational preferences of the Enneagram and MBTI begin to filter out experiences that create fear, anxiety, confusion, or are contradictory or paradoxical.

As a complex accumulates more and more preferentially selected experiences, it gains psychological energy and acts like a magnetic field that draws still more experiences to itself in a self-reinforcing way. While the Conscious Self, what Jung calls the Ego, has a fundamental relationship with the archetype responsible for organizing and integrating the entire personality (the Self), Jung argues that the Ego (Conscious Self) is just one of many complexes in the psyche.[172] By the age of two or three years old, the Conscious Self and its MBTI and Enneagram preferences dominate the space of consciousness to the degree that the child has *identified* with this complex as being who they are. Thus, the cognitive and motivational preferences of the Conscious Self become what Jung calls the *center of consciousness* for that person.

An important implication of this model of the structure and dynamics of the human personality is that the totality of the human psyche, including the Conscious Self, is composed only of Inner People (complexes) and archetypes. Whether conscious or unconscious, cognitive preferences, motivations, emotions, experiences, attitudes, and personality characteristics like the Enneagram and MBTI do not float freely in the psyche but *cohere* in the Conscious Self, Inner People, or archetypes.

Throughout the first half of one's life, the cognitive and motivational preferences of Enneagram type and the dominant and auxiliary functions rule consciousness with an iron fist as a necessary way of establishing the person's identity. Because the cognitive and motivational preferences of the Inner People (complexes) are so contradictory and paradoxical to the personal identity of the Conscious Self, they are repressed out of consciousness and constantly battle to take control of the person's life as described in this book and in *Diving In*.[173]

But during the second half of one's life, the process of psychological growth and individuation *requires* us to intentionally integrate the contradictory and paradoxical personality characteristics of the Inner People (complexes) into our Conscious Self. In other words, the path of growth requires that we make a space for them in our lives and voluntarily give them control of our bodies—the very thing the Conscious Self fought against for half a lifetime.

As mentioned above, in the second half of life, people with the personality profile of Type One, ISTJ will work to integrate Enneagram Types Four and Seven, along with the tertiary and inferior functions of introverted feeling and extraverted intuition.[174] If the Type One happens to have ESTJ preference scores, then they will work to integrate Enneagram Types Four and Seven, along with the tertiary and inferior functions of extraverted intuition and introverted feeling. My own work with people has shown that almost any combination of Enneagram and MBTI type is possible. For example, I have personally worked with Enneagram Type Eights with preference scores of ISTJ, INTJ, ESTJ, INFP, and ENFP. My own view is that the combination of Enneagram and MBTI characteristics provides a more compelling explanation of the differences between people of the same Enneagram type than appealing to instinctual variants.

Marie-Louise von Franz characterizes consciousness as having four doors through which the dominant, auxiliary, tertiary, and inferior functions demand entrance into consciousness.[175] She argues that three of the four doors into consciousness can be closed by integrating the dominant, auxiliary, and tertiary functions into consciousness, but the fourth door of the inferior function can never be closed. Throughout life, the inferior function remains the weak spot in the armor and defense mechanisms of the Conscious Self, through which any unconscious and inferior psychic element can enter consciousness. Using my metaphor, it is the Inner People and archetypes who knock and enter through these doors.

In *Diving In* I metaphorically likened the Conscious Self, or Ego, to a boat or ship that is man-made and must be constantly fixed up and repaired, or else it will sink into the watery depths of the unconscious. I likened the life-long experience of individuation and discovering who we are to a volcanic island that rises above the surface waters of consciousness—an inner *Island of Excellence* that emerges from the depths of the sea of the unconsciousness and becomes a natural magnet of life.[176] I'd like to link the *Diving In* model to what I've said here in *Island of Excellence* and clarify the process and outcome of this psychological phenomenon.

The Conscious Self spends at least half of a person's lifetime trying to keep the Inner People (complexes) out of consciousness, but the process of finally assimilating them teaches us an amazing lesson. As Jung points out, we discover that the Unconscious Self (the Self) wants to *collaborate* for the mutual benefit of the entire personality and is finally allowed to carry out its role of organizing, harmonizing, and unifying all the complexes in the human personality.[177] The Unconscious Self is allowed to *counteract* the natural tendency toward entropy within the personality and increasingly mediates between the Conscious Self and the Inner People who have been determined to hoard as much psychological energy and body time as possible. The end result is that the Unconscious Self draws the Conscious Self, Inner People (complexes), and the other archetypes to itself so as to unite the entire human personality. In Practice 3 of *Island of Excellence*, I refer to this as developing inner collaboration and alignment.

The collaboration between all the complexes results in a major shift in the overall control of the human personality. We move from being dominated by the personality and motivational preferences of the Conscious Self in the *center of consciousness*, to a new *virtual center*—a point midway between the conscious and unconscious that Jung calls the *center of the personality,* and in *Diving In* I call the Emergent Self.[178]

The Emergent Self is a *psychological* phenomenon; it is *not* a *metaphysical* notion like Being or Essence espoused by many Enneagram teachers.[179] Living from the center of the personality and experiencing inner collaboration and alignment allows the Emergent Self to come into existence for the very first time. It "emerges" in the sense that the wholeness and integration of the personality is greater than the sum of the warring parts. This becomes a deep, hidden place of safety and guidance from which we discover our calling in life—our destiny.

I want to close this section by commenting on what I view as the most important path forward in exploring the synthesis of these three bodies of knowledge. It's unfortunate, but many people who use the MBTI pay little or no attention to the Enneagram, and those who are committed to the Enneagram have little knowledge of the deeper elements of the MBTI. Pat Wyman's book, *Three Keys to Self-Understanding*, is a welcome exception to this trend. I hope the model presented here and the fleshing out of that model in the story and teaching sessions of *Island of Excellence* will encourage readers not to view the Enneagram and MBTI as *two separate systems* or isolated *silos*. Rather, if the collective characteristics of both are viewed as archetypes of human knowledge and motivation that must be cashed out in individuals in order to become personal—that is, to become personality—many of the barriers that currently exist could be overcome.

ENDNOTES

1   Walter Truett Anderson, *Reality Isn't What It Use to Be* (San Francisco: Harper San Francisco, 1990), p. IX.

2   Antonio Damasio, *The Feeling of What Happens: Body and Emotion in the Making of Consciousness* (New York: A Harvest Book, Harcourt Inc. 1999), pp. 111-112.

3   W.K.C. Guthrie, *A History of Greek Philosophy, Volume IV, Plato: The Man and His Dialogues Earlier Period* (New York: Cambridge University Press, 1986), p. 511ff.

4   Robert E. Quinn, *Deep Change: Discovering the Leader Within* (San Francisco, CA: Jossey-Bass, 1996), p. 121.

5   Some of the better sources on Papua New Guinea include Chris Harkness, *New Guinea: The Wahgi Impact: Life in the Highlands of the Territory of Papua and New Guinea* (Coorparoo, AS: Robert Brown & Associates Ltd., 1994); Albert Maori Kiki, *Kiki: Ten Thousand Years in a Lifetime* (Melbourne, AS: Longman, Pacific Paperbacks, 1968); Michael French Smith, *Village on the Edge: Changing Times in Papua New Guinea* (Honolulu, HI: University of Hawaii Press, 2002); Peter Lawrence, *Road Belong Cargo*

(Manchester, UK: Manchester University Press, 1964); Bo Flood, Beret E. Strong, William Flood, *Pacific Island Legends: Tales from Micronesia, Melanesia, Polynesia, and Australia* (Honolulu, HI: The Bess Press, 1999), pp. 89-114; Annette B. Weiner, *The Trobrianders of Papua New Guinea* (Belmont, CA: Thomson Wadsworth, 1988); Sir Paulias Matane, *Management Problems in PNG: Some Solutions* (New Delhi, India: USBS Publisher's Distributors, Ltd, 2000); Sir Paulias Matane, *Further Management Problems in PNG: Their Solutions* (New Delhi, India: USBS Publisher's Distributors, Ltd, 2000); and Samantha Gillison, *The Undiscovered Country* (New York: An Owl Book, 1998).

6   For a description of the Enneagram, see Don Richard Riso and Russ Hudson, *The Wisdom of the Enneagram* (New York: Bantam Books, 1999), and Don Richard Riso with Russ Hudson, *Personality Types* (New York: Houghton Mifflin Company, 1996). For a description of the MBTI assessment tool, see Isabel Briggs Myers with Peter Briggs, *Gifts Differing* (Palo Alto, CA: Davies Black Publishing, 1980), and Isabel Briggs Myers, *Introduction to Type*, 6th ed. (Palo Alto, CA: Consulting Psychologists Press, 1998). For a description of Jungian psychology, see Carl G. Jung, *The Collected Works of C.G. Jung* (Princeton, NJ: Princeton University Press, 1990).

7   An online version of the RHETI, or hard copies, can be obtained from the Enneagram Institute's Web site, www.enneagraminstitute.com. A self-scoring version of the MBTI can be obtained from Consulting Psychologists Press at www.cpp-db.com.

8   The character of Dan Wright is based on my actual experiences with people who are Enneagram Type Ones and have ISTJ preference scores on the MBTI (see page 399 for a brief summary).

Dan's character is also based on detailed descriptions of the Enneagram types in Riso, *Personality Types*, pp. 376-409; Riso and Hudson, *The Wisdom of the Enneagram*, pp. 97-124; Sandra Maitri, *The Spiritual Dimension of the Enneagram* (New York: Jeremy P. Tarcher—Putnam, 2000), pp. 110-132; and descriptions of the MBTI types in June Singer, *Boundaries of the Soul: The Practice of Jung's Psychology* (New York: Anchor Books, 1994), p. 319ff.; Marie-Louise von Franz and James Hillman, *Jung's Typology* (Irving, TX: Spring Publications, 1979), p. 27ff.; Myers, *Gifts Differing*; p. 102ff.; and Myers, *Introduction to Type*, p. 14.

9   The character of James Tuffs is based on my actual experiences with people who are Enneagram Type Eights and have INTJ preference scores on the MBTI (see page 404 for a brief summary). It is also based on detailed descriptions of the Enneagram types in Riso, *Personality Types*, pp. 297-337; Riso and Hudson, *The Wisdom of the Enneagram*, pp. 287-313; Maitri, *The Spiritual Dimension of the Enneagram*, pp. 179-200; and the MBTI types in Singer, *Boundaries of the Soul*, p. 319ff.; von Franz and Hillman, *Jung's Typology*, p. 33ff.; Myers, *Gifts Differing*, p. 109ff.; and Myers, *Introduction to Type*, p. 18.

10 The character of Maggie Spinner is based on my actual experiences with people who are Enneagram Type Threes and have ENTJ preference scores on the MBTI (see page 400 for a brief summary). It is also based on detailed descriptions of the Enneagram types in Riso and Hudson, *Personality Types*, pp. 95-133; Riso and Hudson, *The Wisdom of the Enneagram*, pp. 151-177; Maitri, *The Spiritual Dimension of the Enneagram*, pp. 88-109; and the MBTI types in Singer, *Boundaries of the Soul*, p. 319ff.; von Franz and Hillman, *Jung's Typology*, p. 38ff.; Myers, *Gifts Differing*, pp. 85ff.; and Myers, *Introduction to Type*, p. 25.

11   The character of Rena Unitus is based on my actual experiences with people who are Enneagram Type Nines and have ISFP preference scores on the MBTI (see page 405 for a brief summary). It is also based on detailed descriptions of the Enneagram types in Riso and Hudson, *Personality Types*, pp. 338-375; Riso and Hudson, *The Wisdom of the Enneagram*, pp. 312-340; Maitri, *The Spiritual Dimension of the Enneagram*, pp. 42-65; and the MBTI types in Singer, *Boundaries of the Soul*, p.319 ff; von Franz and Hillman, *Jung's Typology*, p. 48ff.; Myers, *Gifts Differing*, p. 95ff., and Myers, *Introduction to Type*, p. 26.

12   The character of Cindy Reeder is based on my actual experiences with people who are Enneagram Type Fours and have INFP preference scores on the MBTI (see page 401 for a brief summary). It is also based on detailed descriptions of the Enneagram types in Riso and Hudson, *Personality Types*, pp. 134-172; Riso and Hudson, *The Wisdom of the Enneagram*, pp. 178-205; Maitri, *The Spiritual Dimension of the Enneagram*, pp. 131-154; and the MBTI types in Singer, *Boundaries of the Soul*, p. 319ff.; von Franz and Hillman, *Jung's Typology*, p. 48ff.; Myers, *Gifts Differing*, p. 95ff. and Myers, *Introduction to Type*, p. 27.

13   The character of Frank Brighton is based on my actual experiences with people who are Enneagram Type Fives and have INTP preference scores on the MBTI (see page 402 for a brief summary). It is also based on detailed descriptions of the Enneagram types in Riso and Hudson, *Personality Types*, pp. 173-215; Riso and Hudson, *The Wisdom of the Enneagram*, pp. 206-232; Maitri, *The Spiritual Dimension of the Enneagram*, pp. 201-222; and the MBTI types in Singer, *Boundaries of the Soul*, p. 319ff; von Franz and Hillman, *Jung's Typology*, p. 41ff.; Myers, *Gifts Differing*, p. 88ff., and Myers, *Introduction to Type*, p. 23.

14 The character of Bethany Wringer is based on my actual experiences with people who are Enneagram Type Sixes and have ESTP preference scores on the MBTI (see page 403 for a brief summary). It is also based on detailed descriptions of the Enneagram types in Riso and Hudson, *Personality Types*, pp. 216-258; Riso and Hudson, *The Wisdom of the Enneagram*, pp. 233-259; Maitri, *The Spiritual Dimension of the Enneagram*, pp. 66-87; and the MBTI types in Singer, *Boundaries of the Soul*, p. 319ff. von Franz and Hillman, *Jung's Typology*, p. 22ff.; Myers, *Gifts Differing*, p. 99ff. and Myers, *Introduction to Type*, p. 16.

15 The character of Lindsey Barker is based on my actual experiences with people who are Enneagram Type Twos and have ISFJ preference scores on the MBTI (see page 399 for a brief summary). It is also based on detailed descriptions of the Enneagram types in Riso and Hudson, *Personality Types*, pp. 59-94; Riso and Hudson, *The Wisdom of the Enneagram*, pp. 125-150; Maitri, *The Spiritual Dimension of the Enneagram*, pp. 155-178; and the MBTI types in Singer, *Boundaries of the Soul*, p. 319ff.; von Franz and Hillman, *Jung's Typology*, p. 27ff.; Myers, *Gifts Differing*, p. 102ff., and Myers, *Introduction to Type*, p. 15.

16 See J. M. Juran, *A History of Managing for Quality* (Milwaukee, WI: American Society for Quality Control, 1995).

17 John H. Brown, *How to Run Your Business So You Can Leave It In Style*, 2nd ed. (Denver, CO: Business Enterprise Press, 1997).

18 Eileen C. Shapiro, *Fad Surfing in the Boardroom: Reclaiming the Courage to Manage in the Age of Instant Answers* (New York: Addison-Wesley Publishing Company, 1995), p. xiii.

19 Nitin Nohria, William Joyce, and Bruce Roberson, "What Really Works" in the *Harvard Business Review*, July 2003, Volume 81, Number 7, pp. 43-50.

20 James C. Collins and Jerry I. Porras, *Built to Last: Successful Habits of Visionary Companies* (New York: Harper Business, 1994), p. 17ff.

21 Jim Collins, *Good to Great: Why Some Companies Make the Leap and Others Don't* (New York: Harper Business, 2001); John P. Kotter and James L. Heskett, *Corporate Culture and Performance* (New York: The Free Press, 1992); Peter F. Drucker, *Innovation and Entrepreneurship* (New York: Harper Business, 1985); Edgar H. Schein, *Organizational Culture and Leadership*, 2nd edition (San Fransico, CA: Jossey-Bass Publishers, 1992); Daniel Goleman, *Emotional Intelligence: Why it Can Matter More than IQ* (New York: Bantan Books, 1994); Robert S. Kaplan and David Norton, *The Balanced Scorecard: Translating Strategy into Action* (Boston, MA: The Harvard Business School Press, 1996); Chris Argyris, *Knowledge for Action: A Guide to Overcoming Barriers to Organizational Change* (San Francisco, CA: Jossey-Bass Publishers, 1993); Stephen R. Covey, *The 7 Habits of Highly Effective People* (New York: Simon & Schuster, 1989); and Peter M. Senge, *The Fifth Discipline: The Art & Practice of the Learning Organization* (New York: Currency-Doubleday, 1990).

22 Joan Magretta, "The Power of Virtual Integration: An Interview with Dell Computer's Michael Dell" in the *Harvard Business Review*, March-April, 1998, Volume 76, Number 2, pp. 73-84.

23 Michael Hammer and James Champy, *Reengineering the Corporation: A Manifesto for Business Revolution* (New York: Harper Business, 1993), pp. 29.

24 See Kotter and Heskett, *Corporate Culture and Performance*, p. 98, where they reference the source of this information as John P. Kotter, *A Force for Change: How Leadership Differs from Management*, p. 6. Also see, John P. Kotter, "What Leaders Really Do" in the *Harvard Business Review*, December 2001, Volume 79, Number 11, p. 86.

25 Alden M. Hayashi, "When to Trust Your Gut" in the *Harvard Business Review*, February 2001, Volume 79, Number 2, p. 61.

26 Morten T. Hansen, Nitin Nohria, and Thomas Tierney, "What's Your Strategy for Managing Knowledge?" in the *Harvard Business Review*, March-April 1999, Volume 77, Number 2, p 107ff.

27 John Kao, *Jamming: The Art and Discipline of Business Creativity* (New York: Harper Business, 1996), p. 4.

28 Drucker, *Innovation and Entrepreneurship*, p. 30ff.

29 Alan G. Robinson and Sam Stern, *Corporate Creativity: How Innovation and Improvement Actually Happen*, (San Francisco: Berrett-Koehler Publishers, Inc. 1997), pp. 1, and 6-9.

30 Rosabeth Moss Kanter, John Kao, and Fred Wiersema, eds., *Innovation: Breakthrough Ideas at 3M, DuPont, GE, Pfizer, and Rubbermaid* (New York: Harper Business, 1997), p. 6.

31 Diane L. Coutu, "The Anxiety of Learning" in the *Harvard Business Review*, March 2002, Volume 80, Number 3, p. 105.

32 Steven E. Prokesch, "Unleashing the Power of Learning: An Interview with British Petroleum's John Browne" in the *Harvard Business Review*, September-October 1997, Volume 75, Number 5, p. 148.

33 Tom Peters, *Crazy Times Call for Crazy Organizations* (New York: Vintage Books, 1994), p. 12.

34 Suzy Wetlaufer, "What's wrong with Creativity at CoolBurst?" in the *Harvard Business Review*, September-October 1997, Volume 75, Number 5, p. 40.

35 James C. Collins and William C. Lazier, *Beyond Entrepreneurship: Turning Your Business Into an Enduring Great Company* (New York: Prentice Hall, 1992), p. 135.

36 Edward De Bono, *Six Thinking Hats*, revised and updated, (New York: Little, Brown, and Company, 1999).

37 Michael Michalko, *Cracking Creativity: The Secrets of Creative Genius* (Berkeley, CA: Ten Speed Press, 2001), pp. 8-13.

38 See Rollo May, *The Courage to Create* (New York: W.W Norton & Company Inc., 1975); Graham Wallas, *The Art of Thought* (London: Jonathan Cape, 1926); Anthony Storr, *The Dynamics of Creation* (New York: Ballantine Books, 1993); and Arthur Koestler, *The Act of Creation* (London: Arkana Penguin Books, 1964).

39 Mihaly Csikszentmihalyi, *Creativity: Flow and the Psychology of Discovery and Invention*, (New York: Harper Perennial, 1996).

40 May, *The Courage to Create*, p. 40.

41 Jeffrey Pfeffer and Robert I. Sutton, "The Smart-Talk Trap" in the *Harvard Business Review*, May-June 1999, Volume 77, Number 3, p. 135-136.

42 Arnold M. Ludwig, *The Price of Greatness: Resolving the Creativity and Madness Controversy* (New York: The Guilford Press, 1995).

43 Tom Kelly, *The Art of Innovation* (New York: A Currency Book, 2001), p. 70.

44 Marfe Ferguson Delano, *Inventing the Future: A Photobiography of Thomas Alva Edison* (Washington, DC: National Geographic Society, 2002), pp. 26 and 32.

45 Margaret Cousins, *The Story of Thomas Alva Edison* (New York: Randon House, 1993), p. 91ff.

46 Paul Israel, *Edison: A Life of Invention* (New York: John Wiley & Sons, Inc. 1998), p. 119 ff., and Michalko, *Cracking Creativity*, p. 129.

47 Delano, *Inventing the Future*, p. 56.

48 Covey, *The 7 Habits of Highly Effective People*, p. 17ff.

49 Wallas, *The Art of Thought*, p. 20

50 The character of Nikki Salem is based on my actual experiences with people who are Enneagram Type Sevens and have ENTP preference scores on the MBTI (see page 404 for a brief summary). It is also based on detailed descriptions of the Enneagram types in Riso and Hudson, *Personality Types*, pp. 259-296; Riso and Hudson, *The Wisdom of the Enneagram*, pp. 260-286; Maitri, *The Spiritual Dimension of the Enneagram*, pp. 223-244; and the MBTI types in Singer, *Boundaries of the Soul*, p. 319ff; von Franz and Hillman, *Jung's Typology*, p. 30ff.; Myers, *Gifts Differing*, p. 105ff., and Myers, *Introduction to Type*, p. 20.

51 W. Edwards Deming, *Out of Crisis* (Cambridge, MA: MIT Center for Advanced Engineering Study, 1986), and Alfie Kohn, *Punished by Rewards: The Trouble with Gold Stars, Incentive Plans, A's, Praise, and other Bribes* (New York: Houghton Mifflin Company, 1993).

52 Walter Lippmann, *A Preface to Morals* (New York: Macmillan Company, 1933), p. 206.

53 Lippman, *A Preface to Morals*, p. 209.

54 Charles Handy, "What's a Business For?" in the *Harvard Business Review*, December 2002, Volume 80, Number 12, p. 50.

55 Michael Maccoby, "Narcissistic Leaders: The Incredible Pros, the Inevitable Cons" in the *Harvard Business Review*, January-February 2000, Volume 78, Number 1, p. 70.

56 Diane L. Coutu, "I Was Greedy Too" in the *Harvard Business Review*, February 2003, Volume 81, Number 2, p. 38.

57 Jim Collins, "Level 5 Leadership: The Triumph of Humility and Fierce Resolve" in the *Harvard Business Review*, January 2001, Volume 79, Number 1, p. 70.

58 Collins, *Good to Great*, p. 21.

59 Joseph L. Badaracco, "The Discipline of Building Character" in the *Harvard Business Review*, March-April 1998, Volume 76, Number 2, pp. 115-124.

60 Anderson, *Reality Isn't What It Used to Be*, p. ix and ff.

61 May, *The Courage to Create*, p. 19 and 24.

62 Deming, *Out of Crisis*, pp. 60-61.

63 Leslie Perlow and Stephanie Williams, "Is Silence Killing Your Company" in the *Harvard Business Review*, May 2003, Volume 81, Number 5, p. 53.

64 Abraham H. Maslow, *Maslow on Management* (New York: John Wiley & Sons, 1998), p. 226.

65 Jay M. Jackman and Myra H. Strober, "Fear of Feedback" in the *Harvard Business Review*, April 2003, Volume 81, Number 3, p. 102.

66 May, *The Courage to Create*, p 3-4.

67 Perlow and Williams, "Is Silence Killing Your Company" in *HBR*, May 2003, p. 58.

68 This list of basic fears is taken from Riso and Hudson, *The Wisdom of the Enneagram*, p. 32, and used with permission.

69 Joseph LeDoux, *Synaptic Self: How Our Brains Become Who We Are* (New York: Viking, 2002), pp. 5-9.

70 Joseph LeDoux, *The Emotional Brain: The Mysterious Underpinnings of Emotional Life* (New York: A Touchstone Book, 1998), p. 298ff., and Damasio, *The Feeling of What Happens*, p. 279ff.

71 Goleman, Boyatzis, and McKee, *Primal Leadership*, p. 22ff.

72 Abraham Maslow, *Toward a Psychology of Being*, 3rd ed. (New York: John Wiley & Sons, 1999), p 27ff.

73 Harold J. Leavitt, "Why Hierarchies Thrive" in the *Harvard Business Review*, March 2003, Volume 81, Number 3, p. 101.

74 Chris Argyris, Robert Putnam, and Diana McLain Smith, *Action Science: Concepts, Methods, and Skills for Research and Intervention* (San Francisco, CA: Jossey-Bass Publishers, 1985), p. 49ff. For the roots of tacit knowing see, Michael Polanyi, *The Tacit Dimension* Gloucester, (MA: Peter Smith, 1983).

75 By "traditional" definitions of leadership I mean writers such as, Stephen R. Covey, *Principle-Centered Leadership* (New York: Summit Books, 1991) and John P. Kotter, *Leading Change* (Boston, MA: Harvard Business School Press, 1996).

76 Paul J. Brouwer, "The Power to See Ourselves" in the *Harvard Business Review*, November-December 1964, Number 64602.

77 For a thorough discussion of the role of blind spots in organizations, see Joseph Luft, *Group Processes: An Introduction to Group Dynamics*, 3rd ed. (Mountain View, CA: 1984), p. 57ff.

78 See Daniel Goleman, Richard Boyatzis, and Annie McKee, "Primal Leadership: The Hidden Driver of Great Performance" in the *Harvard Business Review*, December 2001, Volume 79, Number 11, p. 47, and Peter F. Drucker, "Managing Oneself" in the *Harvard Business Review*, March-April 1999, Volume 77, Number 2, p. 67.

79 Figure 13 is an adaptation of the work shown in Argyris, Putnam, Smith, *Action Science*, pp. 84-88.

80 Thomas J. Peters and Robert H. Waterman, Jr., *In Search of Excellence: Lessons from America's Best Run Companies* (New York: Warner Books, 1982), p. 83, and pp. 89ff.

81 For a more complete understanding of the Enneagram components of the Shadow and Inferior Selves, see Bodnarczuk, *Diving In*, p. 138ff. The MBTI components in the chart are taken from Myers, *Introduction to Type*, p. 14ff.

82 In Jungian parlance, the MBTI component for the Shadow and Inferior Self are called the tertiary and inferior functions. For a description for all 16 MBTI types see, Myers, *Introduction to Type*, p. 14 ff.

83 Pat Wyman was probably the first person to systematically look at the interaction between different combinations of Enneagram and MBTI type. See Pat Wyman, *Three Keys to Self Understanding: An Innovative and Effective Combination of the Myers-Briggs Type Indicator Assessment Tool, the Enneagram, and Inner-Child Healing*, (Gainesville, FL: CAPT, 2001).

84 Carl R. Rogers, "Barriers and Gateways to Communication," in the *Harvard Business Review*, July-August 1952, Number 52408.

85 David P. Hanna, *Designing Organizations for High Performance* (New York: Addison-Wesley Publishing Company, 1988), p. 36.

86   For a discussion of the relationship between creativity and competitive advantage see John J. Kao, *Entrepreneurship, Creativity, and Organization: Text, Cases, and Readings*, (Englewood Cliffs, NJ: Prentice Hall, 1989), p. 20 ff.

87   Hanna, *Designing Organizations for High Performance*, p. 36.

88   Drucker, "Managing Oneself" in *HBR* March-April 1999, pp. 69-70.

89   Kaplan and Norton, *The Balanced Scorecard*, p. 10 ff.

90   Collins and Porras, *Built to Last*, p. 67.

91   Senge, *The Fifth Discipline*, p. 25, and Chris Argyris, *Reasoning, Learning, and Action: Individual and Organizational*, (San Francisco: Jossey-Bass Publishers, 1982), p. 228 ff.

92   Peter Frost and Sandra Robinson, "The Toxic Handler: Organizational Hero and Casualty" in the *Harvard Business Review*, July-August, 1999, Volume 77, Number 4, p. 100-101.

93   Robert J. Herbold, "Inside Microsoft: Balancing Creativity and Discipline" in the *Harvard Business Review*, January, 2002, Volume 80, Number 1, p. 75.

94   Herbold, "Inside Microsoft: Balancing Creativity and Discipline" in *HBR*, January, 2002, p. 79.

95   Baruch Nevo and Stephen Breitstein, Psychological and Behavioral Aspects of Diving, (Flagstaff, AZ: Best Publishing Company, 1999), p. xiii.

96   For an interesting explanation of this problem, see Ram Charan, "Conquering a Culture of Indecision" in the *Harvard Business Review*, April 2001, Volume 79, Number 4, p. 76.

97   This is a modified version of the Johari Window, see in Luft, *Group Processes*, p. 57 ff.

98 Senge, *The Fifth Discipline*, p. 195 ff.
99 Shapiro, *Fad Surfing in the Board Room*, p. 53 ff.
100 William Bridges, *Managing Transitions: Making the Most of Change*, (New York: Addison-Wesley Publishing Company, 1991), pp. 3.
101 Chris Argyris, *Overcoming Organizational Defenses: Facilitating Organizational Learning*, (Needham, MA: Allyn & Bacon, 1990), p xiii.
102 Argyris, *Knowledge for Action*, p 15.
103 Argyris, *Knowledge for Action*, p. 20.
104 The first six items on the list are modified versions of the defense routines found in Argyris, *Knowledge for Action*, p. 45, and Argyris, *Action Science*, p. 292 ff.
105 Argyris, *Knowledge for Action*, p. 20.
106 Argyris, *Knowledge for Action*, p 52
107 These two examples are a modified version of what appears in the American Psychiatric Association, *Diagnostic and Statistical Manual of Mental Disorders (DSM-IV-TR)*, fourth ed. Washington, DC, 2000, pp. 811-812.
108 Calvin S. Hall, *A Primer of Freudian Psychology*, (New York: A Mentor Book, 1982), p. 14 ff.
109 Sigmund Freud, *The Psychopathology of Everyday Life*, translated and edited by James Strachey, (New York: W.W.Norton & Company, 1965).
110 Erich Fromm, *The Sane Society*, (Greenwich, CT: A Fawcett Premier Book, 1967), p. 15.

111 Howell S. Baum, *The Invisible Bureaucracy: The Unconscious in Organizational Problem Solving*, (New York: Oxford University Press, 1987), pp. 3-4.

112 James Mosse, "The Institutional Roots of Consulting to Institutions" in Anton Obholzer and Vega Zagier Roberst eds. *The Unconscious at Work; Individual and Oragnizational Stress in the Human Services*, (New York: Routledge, 1994), p. 1 ff.

113 Arthur D. Coleman, *Up from Scapegoating: Awakening Consciousness in Groups*, (Wilmette, IL: Chiron Publications, 1995), p. xvi.

114 Anne Wilson Schaef and Diane Fassel, *The Addictive Organization: Why We Overwork, Cover Up, Pick Up the Pieces, Please the Boss & Perpetrate Sick Organizations*, (San Francisco: Harper San Francisco, 1990), pp. 1 and 4.

115 For a detailed Jungian treatment of complexes in organizations see, Georgia Lepper, "The Complex in Human Affairs" in Murray Stein and John Hollwitz eds. *Psyche at Work: Workplace Applications of Jungian Analytical Psychology*, (Wilmette, IL: Chiron Publications, 1995).

116 Coutu, "The Anxiety of Learning" in *HBR* March 2002, p. 105.

117 Teresa M. Amabile, "How to Kill Creativity" in the *Harvard Business Review*, September–October, 1998, Volume 76, Number 5, p. 86.

118 This is an adaptation of the model found in, Bodnarczuk, *Diving In*, p. 219.

119 This is a modified version of the questions found in F.C. Hawkins, *Marooned: An Inquiry into Government Business and Ethics*, (New York: Writers Club Press, 2002), p. 127 ff.

120 Rollo May, *The Cry for Myth*, (New York: A Delta Book, 1991), p. 20 ff.

121 T.S. Eliot, *Murder in the Cathedral*, (New York: A Harvest Book—Harcourt, Inc, 1963), p. 44.

122 For a detailed discussion of the Cargo Cult see, Lawrence, *Road Belong Cargo*, p. 1 ff.

123 I first heard this story from Father Rex Chambers in a sermon at St. John's Episcopal Church in Breckenridge, Colorado.

124 Kotter and Heskett, *Corporate Culture and Performance*, p. 15.

125 Kotter and Heskett, *Corporate Culture and Performance*, p. 28.

126 Kotter and Heskett, *Corporate Culture and Performance*, p. 50.

127 This point is made powerfully in the seven stages described in Lawrence M. Miller, *Barbarians to Bureaucrats: Corporate Life Cycle Strategies*, (New York: Fawcett Columbine, 1989), p. 2.

128 Kotter and Heskett, *Corporate Culture and Performance*, p. 6; Schein, *Organizational Culture and Leadership*, p. 2 ff.; and Edgar H. Schein, *The Corporate Culture Survival Guide: Sense and Nonsense About Cultural Change*, (San Francisco, CA: Jossey-Bass, 1999), p. 13.

129 For more examples see Terrence E. Deal and Allan A. Kennedy, *The New Corporate Cultures*, (Cambridge, MA: Perseus Publishing, 1999), p. 6, and Terrence E. Deal and Allan A. Kennedy *Corporate Cultures*, (Cambridge, MA: Perseus Publishing, 1982), p. 2ff.

130 See Deal and Kennedy, *The New Corporate Cultures*, p. 7 ff.

131 Schein, *The Corporate Culture Survival Guide*, p 143.

132 Covey, *The 7 Habits of Highly Effective People*, p. 235 ff.

133 Richard Dawkins, *The Selfish Gene*, (New York: Oxford University Press, 1978), p. 203 ff.

134 Dawkins, *The Selfish Gene*, p. 206-207.

135 Goleman, Boyatzis, and McKee, "Primal Leadership: The Hidden Driver of Great Performance" in *HBR*, December 2001, pp. 46-47.

136 William Bridges, *The Character of Organizations: Using Personality Type in Organizational Development*, (Palo-Alto, CA: Davies-Black Publishing, 2000).

137 Michael J. Goldberg, *The 9 Ways of Working*, (New York: Marlowe & Company, 1999).

138 Schein, *The Corporate Culture Survival Guide*, p. 102.

139 Diane L. Coutu, "The Anxiety of Learning" in *HBR*, March 2002, p. 100.

140 Kotter and Heskett, *Corporate Culture and Performance*, p. 79.

141 Schein, *The Corporate Culture Survival Guide*, p 186.

142 Schein, *The Corporate Culture Survival Guide*, p 116 ff.

143 This is Schein's list of the threats needed to motivate an organization to change, see Schein, *The Corporate Culture Survival Guide*, pp. 117-118.

144 Kotter and Heskett, *Corporate Culture and Performance*, p. 99.

145 Kotter and Heskett, *Corporate Culture and Performance*, p. 101.

146 Carol Lavin Bernick, "When Your Culture Needs a Makeover" in the *Harvard Business Review*, June 2001, Volume 79, Number 6, p. 54.

147 Schein, *The Corporate Culture Survival Guide*, p. 132

148 William S. Howell, *The Empathic Communicator*, (Prospect Heights, IL: Waveland Press, Inc. 1982), pp. 29-33.

149 Carl G. Jung, "Psychological Types," Volume 6 in *The Collected Works of C.G. Jung*, (Princeton, NJ: Princeton University Press, 1990), John Beebe, *Integrity in Depth*, (New York: Fromm International Publishing Corporation, 1995) and Anne Singer Harris, *Living with Paradox: An Introduction to Jungian Psychology*, (New York: Brooks/Cole Publishing Company, 1996).

150 This is the Type One description on the RHETI. For a detailed description of the Enneagram Type One see, Riso, *Personality Types*, pp. 376-409; Riso and Hudson, *The Wisdom of the Enneagram*, pp. 97-124; and Maitri, *The Spiritual Dimension of the Enneagram*, pp. 110-132.

151 The descriptions of the dominant and auxiliary functions for the Island of Excellence characters are based on unpublished material provided by Margaret Hartzler, Robert McAlpine and Leona Haas. For more information on their approach to the eight functions see: www.8functions.com. For a detailed description of the ISTJ preference scores see Singer, *Boundaries of the Soul*, p. 319 ff; Von Franz and Hillman, *Jung's Typology*, p. 27 ff.; Myers, *Gifts Differing*; p. 102 ff.; and Myers, *Introduction to Type*, p. 14.

152 This is the Type Two description on the RHETI. For a detailed description of the Enneagram Type Two see Riso and Hudson, *Personality Types*, pp. 59-94; Riso and Hudson, *The Wisdom of the Enneagram*, pp. 125-150; and Maitri, *The Spiritual Dimension of the Enneagram*, pp. 155-178.

153 For a detailed description of the ISFJ preference scores see Singer, *Boundaries of the Soul*, p. 319 ff; von Franz and Hillman, *Jung's Typology*, p. 27 ff.; Myers, *Gifts Differing*, p. 102 ff., and Myers, *Introduction to Type*, p. 15.

154 This is the Type Three description on the RHETI. For a detailed description of the Enneagram Type Three see, Riso and Hudson, *Personality Types*, pp. 95-133; Riso and Hudson, *The Wisdom of the Enneagram*, pp. 151-177; and Maitri, *The Spiritual Dimension of the Enneagram*, pp. 88-109.

155 For a detailed description of the ENTJ preference score see, Singer, *Boundaries of the Soul*, p. 319 ff; von Franz and Hillman, *Jung's Typology*, p. 38 ff.; Myers, *Gifts Differing, p.* 85 ff., and Myers, *Introduction to Type*, p. 25.

156 This is the Type Four on the RHETI. For a detailed description of the Enneagram Type Four see Riso and Hudson, *Personality Types*, pp. 134-172; Riso and Hudson, *The Wisdom of the Enneagram*, pp. 178-205; and Maitri, *The Spiritual Dimension of the Enneagram*, pp. 131-154.

157 For a detailed description of the INFP preference score see Singer, *Boundaries of the Soul*, p. 319 ff; von Franz and Hillman, *Jung's Typology*, p. 48 ff.; Myers, *Gifts Differing*, p. 95 ff., and Myers, *Introduction to Type*, p. 27.

158 This is the Type Four on the RHETI. For a detailed description of the Enneagram Type Four see Riso and Hudson, *Personality Types*, pp. 134-172; Riso and Hudson, *The Wisdom of the Enneagram*, pp. 178-205; and Maitri, *The Spiritual Dimension of the Enneagram*, pp. 131-154.

159 For a detailed description of the INFJ preference score see Singer, *Boundaries of the Soul*, p. 319 ff; von Franz and Hillman, *Jung's Typology*, p. 33 ff.; Myers, *Gifts Differing*, p. 109 ff., and Myers, *Introduction to Type*, p. 19.

160 This is the Type Five description on the RHETI. For a more detailed description of the Enneagram Type Five see, Riso and Hudson, *Personality Types*, pp. 173-215; Riso and Hudson, *The Wisdom of the Enneagram*, pp. 206-232; and Maitri, *The Spiritual Dimension of the Enneagram*, pp. 201-222.

161 For a detailed description of the INTP preference scores see Singer, *Boundaries of the Soul*, p. 319 ff; von Franz and Hillman, *Jung's Typology*, p. 41 ff.; Myers, *Gifts Differing*, p. 88 ff., and Myers, *Introduction to Type*, p. 23.

162 This is the Type Six description on the RHETI. For a detailed description of the Enneagram Type Six see, Riso and Hudson, *Personality Types*, pp. 216-258; Riso and Hudson, *The Wisdom of the Enneagram*, pp. 233-259; and Maitri, *The Spiritual Dimension of the Enneagram*, pp. 66-87.

163 For a detailed description of the ESTP preference scores see, Singer, *Boundaries of the Soul*, p. 319 ff; von Franz and Hillman, *Jung's Typology*, p. 22 ff.; Myers, *Gifts Differing*, p. 99 ff. and Myers, *Introduction to Type*, p. 16.

164 This is the Type Seven description on the RHETI. For a detailed description of the Enneagram Type Seven see, Riso and Hudson, *Personality Types*, pp. 259-296; Riso and Hudson, *The Wisdom of the Enneagram*, pp. 260-286; and Maitri, *The Spiritual Dimension of the Enneagram*, pp. 223-244.

165 For a detailed description of the ENTP preference scores see, Singer, *Boundaries of the Soul*, p. 319 ff; von Franz and Hillman, *Jung's Typology*, p. 30 ff.; Myers, *Gifts Differing*, p. 105 ff., and Myers, *Introduction to Type*, p. 20.

166 This is the Type Eight description on the RHETI. For a detailed description of the Enneagram Type Eight see, Riso, *Personality Types*, pp. 297-337; Riso and Hudson, *The Wisdom of the Enneagram*, pp. 287-313; and Maitri, *The Spiritual Dimension of the Enneagram*, pp. 179-200.

167 For a detailed description of the INTJ preference scores see Singer, *Boundaries of the Soul*, p. 319 ff; von Franz and Hillman, *Jung's Typology*, p. 33 ff.; Myers, *Gifts Differing*; p. 109 ff.; and Myers, *Introduction to Type*, p. 18.

168 This is the Type Nine description on the RHETI. For a detailed description of the Enneagram Type Nine see, Riso and Hudson, *Personality Types*, pp. 338-375; Riso and Hudson, *The Wisdom of the Enneagram*, pp. 312-340; and Maitri, *The Spiritual Dimension of the Enneagram*, pp. 42-65.

169 For a detailed descriptions of the ISFP preference scores see, Singer, *Boundaries of the Soul*, p. 319 ff; von Franz and Hillman, *Jung's Typology*, p. 48 ff.; Myers, *Gifts Differing*, p. 95 ff., and Myers, *Introduction to Type*, p. 26.

170 Bodnarczuk, *Diving In*, p. 2 ff.

171 Bodnarczuk, *Diving In*, p. 101 ff.

172 Carl Jung, Collected Works Volume 18, paragraph 19, p. 11.

173 Bodnarczuk, *Diving In*, pp. 126-133 and 139-142.

174 For a discussion of Enneagram connecting point and the Triangle of Duplicity see, Bodnarczuk, *Diving In*, p. 191 ff.

175 Von Franz, *Jung's Typology*, p. 54 ff.

176 Bodnarczuk, *Diving In*, p. 244 ff.

177 C.G. Jung, Psychological Types, CW, Volume 6, paragraph 204, pp. 126.

178 C.G. Jung, Two Essays on Analytical Psychology, CW, Volume 7, paragraph 365, p. 221 ff. and Bodnarczuk, *Diving In*, pp. 244-252.

179 For a more detailed discussion of my views on this topic see, Mark Bodnarczuk, "Knowing the Depths of Your Personality" in the *Enneagram Monthly*, March 2003, Issue 93, p. 1 ff.

MARK BODNARCZUK is president of the Breckenridge Consulting Group Inc. and adjunct faculty member at Colorado Mountain College. Mark has a BA from Mid-America Nazarene University in religious studies, an MA from Wheaton College in theological studies, and an MA from the University of Chicago in the philosophy of science.

Mark is a personal and executive coach, consultant, teacher, and facilitator with more than twenty years of experience working with companies in the area of high-tech, basic and applied research, pharmaceuticals, health care, retail as well as government and non-profit organizations.

He has published widely in the fields of organizational and leadership development and is the author of, *Diving In: Discovering Who You Are In the Second Half of Life*. He has trained over twelve hundred people in Stephen R. Covey's, *The 7 Habits of Highly Effective People*, and Franklin Covey's, *What Matters Most* time management, and is an instructor for the Enneagram and the Myers-Briggs Personality Type Indicator assessment tools.

Mark is a member of the International Coach Federation, the Association for Psychological Type, and the International Enneagram Association. He was trained in the Enneagram by Don Richard Riso and Russ Hudson and received his MBTI assessment tool training from Margaret Hartzler.

ISLAND OF EXCELLENCE™ ORGANIZATIONAL ASSESSMENT

- *Discovering the power of the creative process*
- *Igniting innovation and improvement*
- *Achieving competitive advantage*

For information about conducting an Island of Excellence™ Organizational Assessment in your company or organization, please contact:

Breckenridge Consulting Group Inc.

P.O. Box 5050

Breckenridge, CO 80424

1-800-303-2554

www.breckconsulting.com

or

www.islandofexcellence.com

In addition, Mark Bodnarczuk and the Breckenridge Consulting Group staff provide consulting services and workshops in the areas of:

- *Organizational Development*
- *Professional Development*
- *Small Business Development*